Ethics and Business

A Global Introduction

Bart Wernaart, LL.M., Ph.D.

First edition

Noordhoff Uitgevers Groningen/Utrecht

T0389451

Cover design: Michiel Uilen
Cover illustration: Yuri Arcurs – Getty Images
Photographs: Corbis

If you have any comments or queries about this or any other publication, please contact Noordhoff Uitgevers BV, Afdeling Hoger Onderwijs, Antwoordnummer 13, 9700 VB Groningen, The Netherlands. Website: www.mijnnoordhoff.nl.

With regard to some of the texts and/or illustration materials, despite painstaking efforts to this end, the publishers did not succeed in tracing all possible copyright holders. Should you be of the opinion that any copyright is applicable to texts and/or illustration materials in this publication, please contact the publisher.

The utmost care has been devoted to the creation of this publication. The author(s), editorial office and publisher accept no responsibility for any information included that is nonetheless incomplete or incorrect. They are always ready to make corrections to any of the data included.

0 / 18

ISBN 978-1-032-04624-2 (hbk)
ISBN 978-90-01-86518-4 (pbk)
ISBN 978-1-003-19395-1 (ebk)
NUR 737

Foreword

Ethics in the context of international business is a widely debated topic, and frequently dominates the headlines. The responsibility of companies is often addressed. Not surprisingly, mostly in cases in which this responsibility is not taken, as expected by the various stakeholders. Ethics in business is not a new topic and has been intensely discussed ever since the emergence of the so-called limited companies.

However, attention for this subject seems to have intensified for various reasons, as a result of several social trends. As we will see in Chapter 5, privatization, technological and digital innovation, changes in moral perception, economic and financial crises and globalization are important factors that stir a more recent debate on how companies should behave in our societies.

As a result of this renewed attention, many books have been written from many perspectives covering the academic discipline of ethics applied in national and international business context. We could perhaps say that the market for such books is already saturated. The literature list at the end of each chapter speaks for itself. I still, however, felt the urge to write this book, for various reasons.

As a teacher of applied sciences, I noticed that there was not really a fitting book on ethics that would truly cover all I want to teach in my lectures. There are wonderful books that discuss normative ethics in the context of the individual, focusing on ethical decision-making. There are outstanding books introducing triple bottom line thinking or circular economy concepts in the context of implementing ethics in a company. Last, there are great books discussing our global economy, geo-political relations and cultural diversity. There are, however, hardly any books that discuss and connect all three levels, while this seems to me a necessity to fully understand ethics in any economic profession.

Furthermore, I noticed amongst my students that they grew weary from the moral tone of most books on ethics. Many are written from either a European or an Anglo-Saxon perspective and communicate Western arrogance, while this does not do justice to other regions of the world, such as Asian, African, Latin American and Middle Eastern countries.

In this book I try to practice what I preach in my lectures. Ethics should imply an open debate on norms and values, using a sound methodology to get there. Ethics should cross borders: not only the borders of a country, but also the borders of someone's moral imagination. Ethics should not only be about harmony but also about conflict (and how to deal with that). Ethics should be realistic and well substantiated by academic research. Ethics should be used to understand the complexity of the world, and the challenges companies struggle with on various levels. That is why I wrote this book; with great enthusiasm I must say.

Please accept that each time when I use 'he' it might as well be a 'she'. However, the book would become less readable if I would use both.

Although writing is a lonely business, I was never truly alone. I owe a great deal to some individuals who played an important role in the creation of this book, both on a professional and a personal level.

First of all, as with each book that I write, I would like to thank my students. In each lecture, they make me understand a little more about this world by asking the right questions, challenging each other's viewpoints, or simply say brilliant things. They keep my knives sharp, and I truly enjoy their intellect and talents. Without them, there would simply be no book.

In addition, I would like to thank Therese van Oosterhout (Fontys University of Applied Sciences, Eindhoven), and Ingrid de Vries (Hogeschool Zuyd, Vlissingen) for ghost reading my draft chapters and provide valuable feedback.

At Noordhoff I would like to thank Bettina Glazenborg (my publisher), Trijnnet Oomkens (my editor) and Aernout Pilot (legal publisher) for their support, enthusiasm and confidence in my writing skills.

I would like to thank my parents and brothers, for their ongoing love and support, as well as my family in law, who all together were of great help in getting our little family up and running.

Thank you, Vik, for showing me what we are, and your untamable enthusiasm in life.

To conclude, I would like to thank my wife, Sylvia. She is the best possible sparring partner in the field of education, didactics and social studies. Our 'kitchen table talks' with a good glass of wine always lead to innovative ideas in education, which I thankfully use every day. On a more personal note, she is my partner-in-crime in many fields, including the raising of two beautiful children, music, academics and much more. During the writing process of this book, she gave birth to our beautiful daughter Bo, sister of our beautiful son Vik.

Therefore I would like to dedicate this book to our daughter. Your open attitude towards the world around you is a blessing, and will open many doors. While the world may seem a dark place once in a while, remember that it is your own morality that is the only true compass in dealing with whatever happens in life. I have no doubt that you will become a woman with the best possible compass that sterns from who you are, because that what you are, is one of the most beautiful things I have ever seen.

Bart Wernaart
Valkenswaard, summer 2018

Content

Introduction

This book is composed of three parts in which ethics is discussed at different levels. In part one we discuss ethics at the level of the individual. In part two we discuss ethic and business. In the third part, ethics is discussed in the context of a globalized world.

In each chapter, we discuss the ethical complications of each topic from various – and preferably opposing – perspectives. Each perspective is methodologically and academically substantiated. Each chapter ends with an extensive literature list in which the original sources are listed for further reading. Furthermore, at the end of each chapter, a summary is written in which the most important definitions and viewpoints are highlighted.

On the website **www.ethicsandbusiness.noordhoff.nl** you may find practice questions that can be used in preparation of an exam, an assessment or essay writing. There are three types of questions: open questions in which the student is invited to apply what he has learned, essay questions in which the student is invited to reflect on what he has learned, and multiple choice questions in which the student is invited to reproduce what he has learned.

A book is almost per definition not up to date. After its publication, the world will inevitably change. To fill this 'time gap' we will regularly publish blog posts and videos in which we comment on current developments that relate to this book. More info can be found at **www.drwernaart.com**, or on his socials. For teachers, presentations for each chapter as well as a teacher's manual are available to support lectures based on this book.

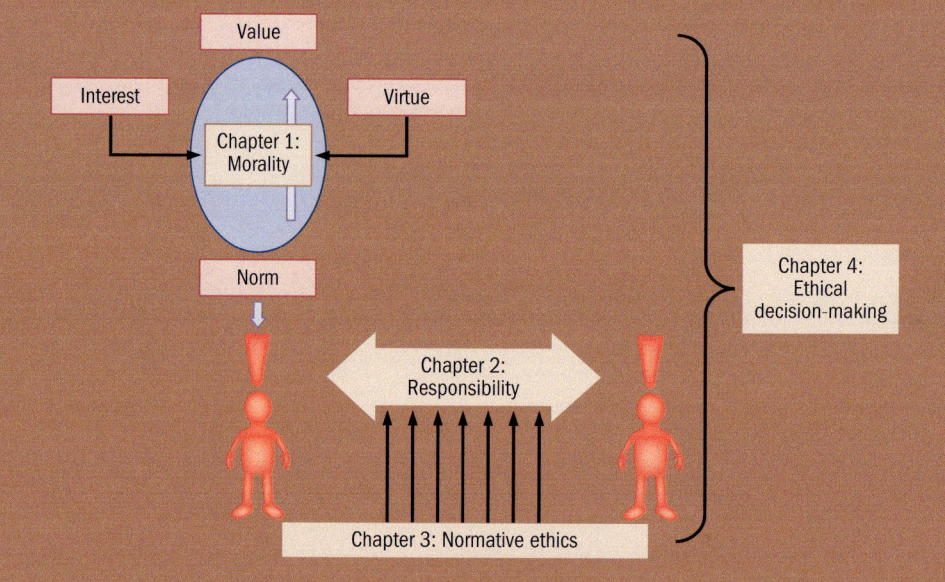

PART 1
Ethics and the individual

In the first part of this book we will examine the relationship between ethics and the individual.

To this end, we will discuss what ethics really is in chapter one, and observe that morality is at the core of this discipline. While each individual has his own morality, it may collide with someone else's sense of morality. In case of such conflicting morality, the matter of responsibility is addressed. In the second chapter we discuss what factors may affect the way an individual can and wants to take a certain responsibility in a given situation. In ethics, there are various opinions on when and how people should take on a certain responsibility in their daily lives. This is called normative ethics, which we will explore in chapter three. Finally, in the last chapter of this part, we will introduce an ethical decision model, in which the most important elements of the first three chapters are embedded. This model can be used to structurally approach an ethical dilemma.

12

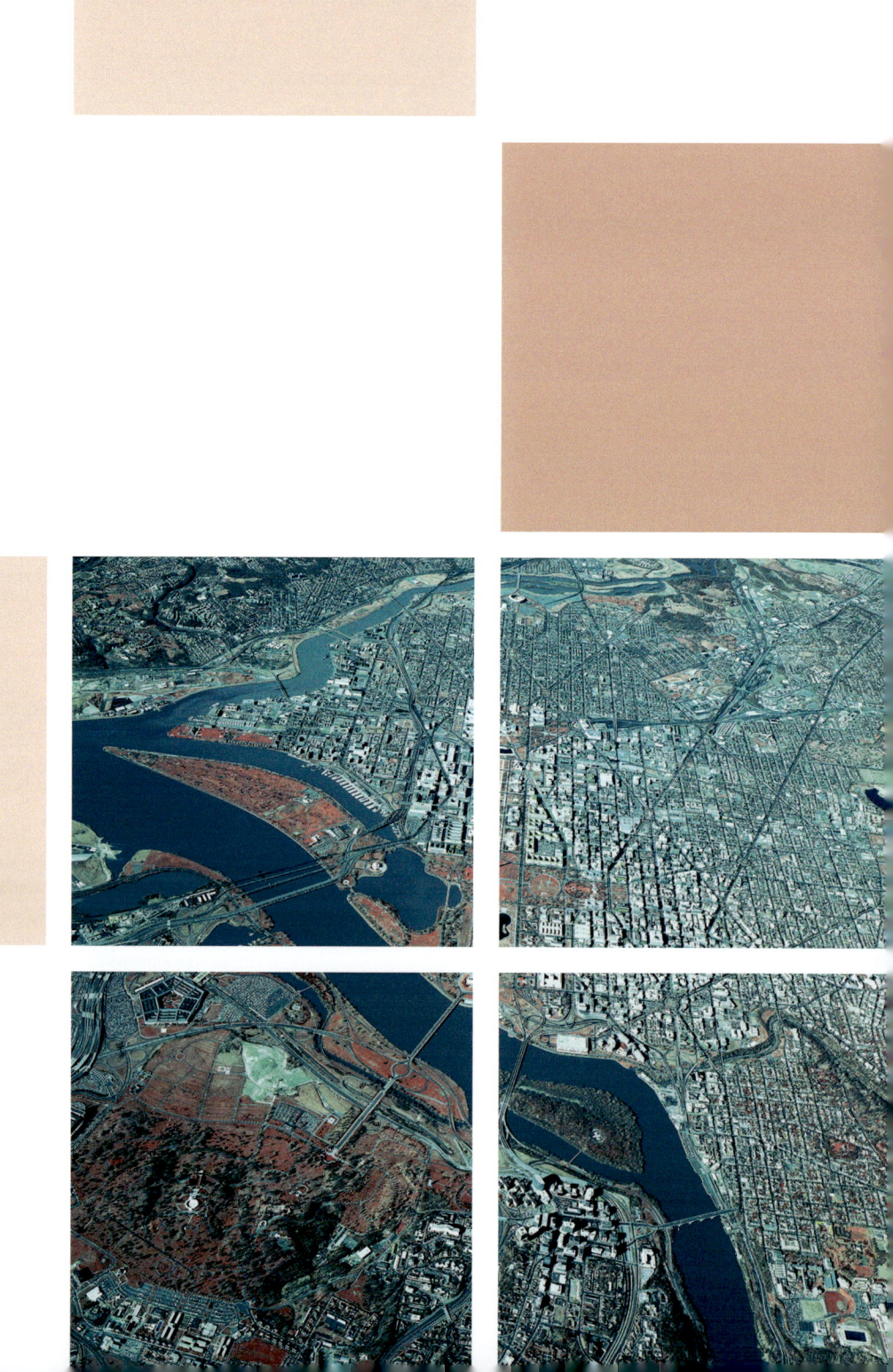

1

What is ethics?

Ethics is a word that is used by many in different meanings and contexts, but at the same time a difficult concept to easily grasp. In economic professions, ethical behaviour has been an important theme for decades. But what do words like ethics and ethical behaviour really mean? In this chapter we try to provide a clear answer to this question. We do this by first briefly introducing the challenges we might come across when we talk about ethical behaviour. Then, we will explore ethics as an academic discipline: that is to structurally analyse and evaluate morality. We will continue by discussing the meaning of morality itself, and what is needed to act in a moral way. Then, we will discuss a method by which we can analyse and evaluate morality on a structural level. Finally we will discuss academic disciplines that are closely related to ethics, but not similar.

1.1 Ethical behaviour?

We open this section with an example in which we face an ethical dilemma.

Leadership? It's in your DNA!

BrainCompass is a Dutch platform, located in Rotterdam. Together with a scientific board, they developed a method to assess employees in the field of leadership competencies. It is the view of this platform that talent is not only a combination of someone's mind-set and environmental factors (in other words: how someone is raised/nurtured). BrainCompass argues that we also need to go back to our basics in order to get a full view of someone's potential (how we are born). This can be found in our DNA. Therefore, individuals are assessed by an online development assessment and a DNA test. The first is the more 'traditional' way of assessing people regarding their professional competencies. The last method is rather revolutionary: the DNA test will tell you how your biological systems work, based on five hormonal features. For instance, someone with a naturally high level of dopamine will generally respond quicker to things that happen in his environment, and be more sensitive to such stimuli. As a result, someone with a high hormonal level of dopamine will be more qualified for a job in the sphere of sales management (Hakker, 2016).

The example 'Leadership? It's in your DNA!' can lead to discussions and is food for thought. The fact that someone's body is used to assess that person regarding his professional competencies may lead to different and conflicting opinions and is therefore a controversial topic. Some might consider this a serious violation of someone's physical integrity and privacy, while others may see this as just another method to assess someone on a voluntary basis.

This case can raise various questions that relate to ethics in various grades of complexity. For example, a journalist once called me to pose the following question regarding this case:

• 'Is it ethically right to use DNA research as an assessment tool?'

However, formulating a question like this is perhaps too easy: it will lead to an unrealistic simplification by suggesting the answer could be either 'yes' or 'no'. If I understood that journalist correctly, he expected me to give the answer 'no', since physical integrity is considered by many people to be more important than assessing people for professional purposes. Using someone's DNA for such reasons makes people feel uncomfortable. I strongly felt that the reason why he called me is that he wanted to substantiate this feeling by arguments from the ethics discipline. However, I did not give him such arguments.

Instead, I kindly told him that ethics as a discipline does not necessarily agree on something or rejects certain things. Ethics explores morality on a structural level, as we will see in the next section. It helps us to reflect on what we consider as morally right or wrong, but does not necessarily prescribe what is right or wrong. There is not a single correct answer, as we might find in a discipline such as statistics. Instead, the answer is usually very personal.

The added value of studying ethics is that it helps us structure our moral reasoning, and it gives us the opportunity to try and understand different ethical viewpoints regarding a certain ethical dilemma. This helps us better understand the world around us, and may give us a more sophisticated opinion on complex issues, such as the ethics in technological innovation. DNA research used in assessing people could be an example of this.

Since the quality of the answer is as good as the quality of the question, it all starts with asking the right question first. When you truly want a reflective and useful answer in ethics, just make sure the question you ask is specific enough to go in-depth, and open enough to allow various viewpoints reach the surface.

Therefore, in the context of our DNA case a much more relevant question would be:
- 'Under what conditions is it morally acceptable to use DNA research in the assessment of individuals regarding professional competencies?'

Or, alternatively:
- 'How far may a company go in requesting (potential) employees to undergo an assessment in which analysing their DNA is part of the procedure?'

Both questions are not simply answered with a 'yes' or a 'no'. Although we might have to reflect on formulating an answer for a while, asking a question like this will definitely lead to more in-depth answers that are more useful and do more justice to what is actually at stake.

If you really want to know: I answered the journalist that there are at least two ways of looking at this. The first is that physical integrity is a very important value that cannot be set aside too easily. There are less drastic ways to assess people than to ask them to make their bodies available for scientific research. While (potential) employees might participate on a voluntary basis regarding such assessments, it remains to be seen if an employee can truly say 'no' to such a method when his next career opportunity depends on it. The second way of looking at the issue is result-driven: in the end, alternative test methods in which we do not use someone's DNA sample will probably lead to similar conclusions. However, they are much more costly, time consuming and intense for the (potential) employee. Using a DNA sample, as long as privacy is guaranteed, is a cheaper, less time-consuming and less intense way of figuring out whether someone matches a certain job profile. In essence, everyone – including the owner of the DNA – is better off in the end. As we will see in chapter 3, this is the classic difference between deontological and consequentialist ethics. To his credit, the journalist in his article included both of my answers, concluding that there are more viewpoints from an ethics perspective, greatly depending on how such DNA samples are specifically processed.

1.2 Ethics as an academic discipline

When we consider the case 'Leadership? It's in your DNA!', we see that it is important to carefully consider what is the right thing to do. And this is exactly what ethics is about. In academic literature, there are numerous definitions on ethics which vary in length, sophistication and content. In this book, we will use the following definition, which includes most generally accepted elements of these definitions:

Ethics

> Ethics is an academic discipline that structurally analyses and evaluates morality.

This definition can be subdivided into four elements that need some further explanation: morality, structure, analysis and evaluation.
First, in ethics we try to answer the question of what is right and wrong. Someone's general perception of 'rightness' is also labelled as someone's **Morality** 'morality'. Any person, organization, country or other organized groups of people have their own idea of what is right or wrong and have developed their own morality. As we will see in the next section, morality is the combination of norms and values someone (or a group) seeks to realize.
Second, ethics as an academic discipline adds a thorough and well-**Structure** considered structure in finding this answer to the question of what is right and wrong. Most debates in ethics – especially the one that touches highly sensitive matters – will not excel in a structured conversation. Just look at any heated discussion between politicians during an electoral race. Ethics as a discipline may offer structure to such a discussion, and in taking subsequent decisions in an ethical dilemma. This structure is sought in two academic approaches: analysis and evaluation.

Analysis

In the case of analysis the researcher has a neutral attitude, and mainly tries to structurally map various ethical viewpoints on a certain matter. As you will see in section 1.4, we will use a comparative method for this called 'functionalism'. This can be a useful activity when someone tries to reach consensus in taking a certain ethical decision, and wants to find out the common ground of the involved parties, or where the difficulties can be expected. It is also a good exercise in preparation of taking your own moral decisions; you want to make sure you have considered the case from all possible viewpoints and as a result take the best decision you can possibly come up with.

Evaluation

This last activity is the structural evaluation, in which you eventually move from a neutral towards a more subjective perspective. When we evaluate, we do have an opinion about these ethical viewpoints, and carefully conclude what you consider to be the moral thing to do in a particular situation. There is no right or wrong here, since evaluating is a very personal activity, and really depends on the morality of the researcher. However, when the evaluation is preceded by a structural analysis, you will probably be better equipped to explain to others (and yourself) why you took that decision, or have a certain opinion about something.

In other words: we analyse to acquire knowledge and evaluate to take an informed decision regarding an ethical dilemma.

1.3   Morality

So, in ethics we structurally analyse and evaluate morality. At this point, we need to further specify the meaning of the word 'morality'.

| Morality is someone's perception in what is right.   **Morality**

We can consider morality on many levels, starting with the individual. However, also in organized groups we may distinguish a shared sense of what is right and what is wrong. Think of a company, a Non-Governmental Organization (NGO), a religious group, a neighbourhood, a country, or even a group of countries.

When a company upholds a moral view that is shared (or should be shared) by its employees, we usually refer to company morale. For instance, from the code of conduct of Shell we can learn that the company has some expectations of its employees with regard to ethics: *'The objectives of the Shell Group are to engage efficiently, responsibly and profitably in oil, gas, chemicals and other selected businesses and to participate in the search for and development of other sources of energy to meet evolving customer needs and the world's growing demand for energy. Our shared core values of honesty, integrity and respect for people underpin all the work we do and are the foundation of our Business Principles.'* (Shell, 2014).   **Company morale**

From this selection of Shell's company morale, you can deduce further work rules that need to be taken into account by all its employees when acting on behalf of the company. These work rules contain specific standards (norms) that aim to realize underlying principles (values).
For instance, one of the norms of the company morale of Shell is to search for other sources of energy next to the traditional ones. Obvious underlying values here are customer satisfaction and sustainability.
Furthermore, to be able to comply with this company morale you also need to show certain characteristics (virtues) and have access to certain tangible items (interests) that make this possible.
In the case of Shell, it intends to show virtues such as honesty, integrity and respect. Next to that, it needs access to raw materials that can be processed to gain energy, or alternative energy sources – its interests – to carry out its business.

1.3.1   Norms

The perception of what is right or wrong (morality) will depend on someone's norms and values. In our everyday language, these two words are usually not separately used, but rather as a single phrase (norms and values) to refer to morality as such. However, it truly adds value to explore the distinct meaning of each word in more detail. In short, the causal link between a norm and a value can be defined as:

| A norm is a rule that contributes to the realization of a value.   **Norm**

For example, a widely used norm is the rule 'ladies go first'. When a true gentleman is in the company of a woman, and they both need to walk through a doorway, he should make sure that she goes first. Most probably, the underlying value he tries to realize by doing so is the value 'respect'. What we can learn from this is that we can recognize a norm through someone's behaviour, while a value – what someone tries to achieve by this behaviour – is less visible, but might be deduced from that behaviour.

The choice to comply with certain norms may be rather individualistic. After all, each human being will put an emphasis on a unique combination of norms that will greatly determine the way he lives. For instance, each student will probably have his own routine of waking up, getting dressed and having breakfast. This routine is a combination of permanent habits that altogether contribute to realize the value 'efficiency'. Such behaviour is very personal, and differs per person. Therefore, we address such norms as **Individual norms** individual norms.

Sometimes norms are shared by groups of people however, and within these groups you are expected to comply with these norms. We refer to them as **Collective norms** collective norms. If you choose to deviate from such a norm, the group might consider your behaviour to be unethical.
For instance, a group of students might agree on communicating through WhatsApp, and respond within one hour to messages that relate to their group work. These norms contribute to realize the value 'quality (of work)', or 'cooperation'. If one of the group members fails to comply with these norms, the other members will probably consider his behaviour as 'bad'.

As we have seen above, the sense of what is right and wrong can be shared by people on many levels. The same goes for sharing norms to comply with. These groups can be small and informal, such as a household, a family or a group of friends. Such groups can also be larger, more formal and institutionalized, such as a company, a professional branch, a university, a country, or even a group of countries. For instance, we could say that there is a difference in the perception of ethics between European and Eastern-Asian countries (Donleavy et al, 2008). Where European ethics is greatly influenced by the 19th century enlightenment, Eastern Asia is more of a Confucian state of mind. This – very roughly – leads to the fact that Europeans think more individualistic than East Asians, who think more from a collectivist perspective. This difference in ethics can – amongst others – be recognized by differences in behaviour. For example, intellectual property, where the individual can claim and protect creative work and exploit this economically, is obviously a more important phenomenon in Europe compared to East Asia.

In some cases we might even consider that certain norms have a universal scope with which almost each human being agrees. Such standards are **Universal norms** universal norms. A generally shared standard of a universal scope will be: 'when an old person or a pregnant woman enters the bus and there are no more seats available, you offer her your seat'. This norm will probably not lead to any discussion or disagreement, wherever you may be on this planet. The underlying value then is most likely 'respect' or 'health' (or both). There are more of such universal norms, which can for instance be found in documents such as the Universal Declaration of Human Rights. We see in Article 3 of this declaration that *'everyone has the right to life, liberty and security of person'*. From this we could deduce the norm that 'no one should kill'. In itself a norm that seems to be rather clear and undebatable. However, does this also mean that we should abolish the death penalty for very serious crimes such as homicide? Apparently, in different regions of the world the answer to this question is also different. It is not always easy to uniformly explain universal norms, and a certain caution towards assuming that 'this will work everywhere' is recommendable.

Collective norms could be culturally determined, or have a religious background.
An example of the latter is the norm 'during a certain period you should not eat and drink during the day'. It is remarkable that this norm appears in almost each religion in some shape of form. The general underlying idea is that usually fasting will make you to come closer to God or yourself. This might lead to the realization of values such as 'reflection', 'purification', 'penance', 'forgiveness' or 'reconciliation'.

Sometimes, norms are written standards that can be enforced by an authoritative institution. For instance, norms may be considered obligatory when they are codified as legislation. Such a law may prescribe that the speed limit on the highway is 120 kilometres per hour. When you break that rule and drive much faster you might get caught and fined by a police officer. The offender may agree or disagree with that rule, but will have to comply in the end (or pay endless fines). The norm 'your speed limit on a highway is 120 kilometres per hour' obviously was adopted to contribute to the value 'safety'. When we consider such written norms there is an overlap with the academic discipline of law, as we will explore further in section 1.6.1. While writing down norms leads to predictability, and therefore all people can learn the 'rules of the game' before they participate in society, the mere fact that something is written down does not necessarily make it a stronger rule. In some countries, written law is simply not effectively enforced, or the unwritten rules of society play a more dominant role than a Penal Code. However, the idea of legislation is that the adopted rules (whether written or unwritten) can be enforced, even though some people may disagree with them.

Written norms

Also outside the discipline of law we might have the tendency to write down norms we find important so that people know they should comply with them beforehand. Think about a code of conduct in a company, the rules of behaviour in a theme park, or the rules of a board game. In all cases, these rules have some authority, and even though an involved individual may not agree with them, he is expected to comply with these rules.

It is important to note here that we should always be reflective on the relation between a norm and a value. After all, we can recognize a norm through someone's behaviour, but will not always see the underlying intention expressed in this behaviour. As we may see in the example 'holding hands, love or just friends?', the same norm may lead to totally different – even contradicting – values. Next to that, mindlessly acting in compliance with norms without verifying whether it still leads to the desired value is rather pointless. The reasoning 'a norm is a norm, and therefore we stick to it' is circular reasoning. If teachers use it, please do tell them. To illustrate this, let's go back to the 'ladies first' example. Of course this will be a good idea in most situations. However, when you're climbing stairs in summertime, and the lady in question wears a very short skirt, you might want to go first instead. And when you find yourself in the midst of a horrific school shooting, happen to be a male hiding with a female, seeking a way to flee, the remark 'ladies first' will probably lead to your value 'safety'. After all, if she survives fleeing in a certain direction, it might be safer to run in that same direction as well. This can hardly be considered an expression of 'respect', however.

1

Walking hand in hand: love, or just friends?

Consider a situation where two individuals of the same sex walk hand in hand. When this is seen in Northern European and American countries, this is usually explained as an expression of being in a sexual relationship. But in some Islamic, Asian and African countries this is an expression of a non-sexual form of friendship. In a number of African countries it is even a sign that two people are having a good but private conversation and they do not wish to be disturbed. So, the same norm leads to the realization of very different values. In the first case, walking hand in hand is an expression of the value 'love', while in the second case the value 'friendship' is emphasized. In the third case, walking hand in hand expresses the value of 'privacy'.

1.3.2 Values

Value

> A value is the ultimate goal we seek to achieve by acting in compliance with a norm.

A value is always described as an abstract concept, using a noun, not using a verb. Think of terms such as: love, respect, dignity, safety, welfare, wealth, health, friendship, reflection, anger, hatred, retaliation, equality, fun, lust, freedom, privacy and prosperity. In contrast: a norm is formulated as something you do, therefore using a verb.

In the previous section, we already explained that it makes sense to reflect on the relation between a norm and a value. Next to that, it is important to analyse in what way different values might lead to opposing behaviour.

Banning Muslims: protection or discrimination?

One of his top priorities since Donald Trump was elected president of the USA in 2017, was to sign decrees that would temporarily ban people from a selection of countries. These countries included Iran, Libya, Somalia, Sudan, Syria and Yemen. This ban was widely criticized by people who considered this ban a 'Muslim ban' since the targeted countries were countries with predominantly a Muslim population. The decrees were brought before some courts, which led to the rejection of a decree in January 2017, and partly rejection of decrees that would replace the rejected version (Rosenberg, 2017).

On the one hand, the Trump administration argued that such a ban was an urgent necessity to guarantee and maintain public safety, especially in preventing a terrorist attack. Trump argued that 'America is a proud nation of immigrants, and we will continue to show compassion to those fleeing oppression. But we will do so while protecting our own citizens and border. (…) This is not a Muslim ban, as the media is falsely reporting. (…) My first priority will always be to protect and serve our country, but as President I will find ways to help all those who are suffering' (Weber, 2017).

On the other hand, most courts considered this ban unnecessary discriminatory, and it would disproportionally harm certain groups. Examples are exchange students who would come from one of the listed countries, or foreign families who were now incomplete due to the fact that one of them was abroad at the time of signing the decree. According to some courts, the

Government did not sufficiently explain the causal link between the ban and public safety. To illustrate: a U.S. Courts of Appeals held that 'the Government has pointed to no evidence that any alien from any of the countries named in the Order has perpetrated a terrorist attack in the United States.' (United States Courts of Appeals for the Ninth Circuit, 7 February 2017).

However, ultimately, the Supreme Court of the United States allowed a third version of the Muslim ban to take effect in December 2017.

In the example 'Banning Muslims: protection or discrimination?' you can see that the values pursued by Trump are in sharp contrast with those who reject his decrees (see figure 1.1). Trump's norm to temporarily ban travellers from a selection of countries with a Muslim background is supposed to contribute to the realization of public safety. This is in contrast with the opinions of his opponents, who claim that this ban is immoral, and instead want to reject it in order to realize the values 'equality' and 'unity'. Also, they question Trump's assumption that such a ban will indeed contribute to public safety in the first place.

In this example it is not easy to reconcile the values of both parties. After all, the realization of one value (safety) causes harm to those who seek to realize the other values (equality and unity). Since this topic has proven to be a delicate issue, it is not always easy to assess which value may prevail, while sacrificing the other. This is after all part of an ethical dilemma, and will be evaluated differently by various people.

FIGURE 1.1 The relationship between norms and values regarding Trump's Muslim ban

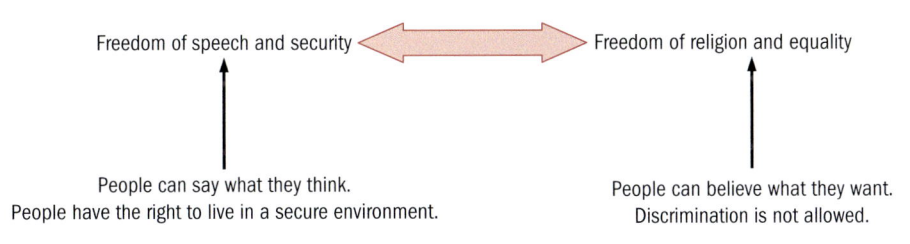

The question now is: how do you determine which value should prevail over the other in this case? This is part of an ethical dilemma and will be judged differently by different people. Can we say in general that some values are more important than others? Perhaps: in his famous works, the sociologist Milton Rokeach (1973, 1979) makes a distinction between terminal and instrumental values. Terminal values are ultimate goals people strive for. These are the essential things in life we cannot live without. Instrumental values are values that help us realize these terminal values, but are no end goal in itself. As you can see in the example 'the terminal and instrumental values of Rokeach', he classifies ambition as an instrumental value. When people act in the fulfilment of this value, it may in the end lead to wisdom or pleasure. After all, ambitious people will probably study hard at school, or earn good money which they can use for

Terminal values

Instrumental values

1

living a pleasant life. However, people may differ in which terminal values they emphasize in their behaviour. As we have seen in the example of the Muslim ban, both national security and equality are considered to be terminal values. Apparently Trump emphasizes the first in his decrees, where his opponents prefer the latter.

Please note however that the Rokeach method is not uncontested. We could criticize his selection method of the values. Mostly, because there seems to be evidence that people have a different understanding of the named values, which makes it difficult to universally claim they are terminal or instrumental (Keith & Iain, 1993).

The terminal and instrumental values of Rokeach

The terminal values are true friendship, mature love, self-respect, happiness, inner harmony, equality, freedom, pleasure, social recognition, wisdom, salvation, family security, national security, a sense of accomplishment, a world of beauty, a world at peace, a comfortable life, an exciting life.

The instrumental values are: cheerfulness, ambition, love, cleanliness, courage, politeness, honesty, imagination, independence, intellect, broad-mindedness, logic, obedience, helpfulness, responsibility and forgiveness.

1.3.3   Virtues

Usually, it will not be easy to comply with a norm in the pursuit of a value when you do not possess certain characteristics.

Virtue

> A virtue is a certain characteristic that is required to successfully comply with a norm.

A person who wants to be on time for an appointment in realizing the value politeness should be a punctual person. So, we need to have some sort of punctuality in our character – a virtue – if we want to successfully comply with the norm 'being on time for an appointment'. Because this is about someone's character, we usually refer to a virtue using an adjective or an adverb. For instance: 'he is a selfish man', or 'she is a very precise girl'.

In certain jobs, some characteristics are helpful or even required. As we can see in the example 'Luis Suárez: football with a bite': we expect a professional football player not to be an aggressive person.

The exact required characteristics may however be influenced by someone's cultural background, as we can see in the example 'charismatic leadership in Canada and Iran': in this case, the conclusion is that there are many similarities in virtues that are expected in a charismatic leader in Canada compared to Iran, but the cultural background also causes some differences.

Luis Suárez: football with a bite

With great disapproval, the world responded to the behaviour of Luis Suárez (Uruguay) during the World Cup of 2014. During a match against Italy, he bit his opponent Giorgio Chiellini in his shoulder. Unfortunately, it was not the first time in his career that Suárez lost self-control during exciting moments and put his teeth in a member of the other team. We expect a professional football player, especially at the level of the World Cup, to behave. Not only the international press, but also the FIFA made it quite clear that they would have expected mister Suárez to be a calm and restrained man, instead of a heated and aggressive brute. Unfortunately, it seems that Suárez did not possess nor master the required characteristics. As a punishment, the FIFA decided to suspend him for nine international matches, slap a fine on him, and he was banned from any football related activities for four months (FIFA press release, 24 June 2014). The fact that millions of people around the world watched the match played a dominant role in that decision, since especially in that case, Suárez was supposed to act as a role model.

It seems however that Suárez did not learn much from this experience, since he appealed from this decision at least twice, mostly in vain (FIFA press release, 14 August 2014).

Charismatic leadership in Canada and Iran

In a comparison between Canadian and Iranian managers (Javidan & Carle, 2004), researchers concluded that there were remarkable similarities between the characteristics that were expected in charismatic leadership, such as being an eloquent and tenacious leader. However, there were also differences. For instance, a Canadian executive is usually praised for being slightly rebellious and questioning the established order, where this is not so much appreciated in the case of Iran. This could be explained by some differences in cultural features: where in Canada there is a relatively low power distance, in Iran this power distance is quite high. As a result, questioning the established order might be considered a good attitude in Canada, and a 'moral sin' in Iran, where leadership is usually more authoritative.

In psychological and educational sciences we see an interesting discussion about the origin of someone's characteristics: the nature vs. nurture debate. In other words, are you born with certain characteristics (nature), or did you develop them as a result of being raised and education (nurture)? Usually it is considered that it is a combination of both, but that your upbringing and education have a demonstrable prominent role to play in the development of a person's characteristics (Stiles, 2011). In our opening case 'Leadership? It's in your DNA!' we saw that the company Braincompass also assumes that who we are is a combination of nurture and nature.

Nature vs. nurture

1.3.4   Interest

In order to comply with a norm for realizing a value, we do not only need characteristics to succeed. In addition you may require certain tangible and intangible things to help you.

> Our interest is the combination of tangible and intangible things we use to comply with a norm.

Interest

The norm 'eat healthy food everyday' contributes to the realization of the value 'health'. However, if you do not have access to healthy food, it is going to be complicated. You may live in a region where there is no food supply due to a failed harvest as a result of extreme drought, a corrupt regime or a civil war. Then you have no physical access to the necessary food in order to lead a healthy life. You may also find yourself in a situation where there is healthy food all around you, but you do not have the financial means to purchase that food. The conclusion in this example – which unfortunately is a reality for many – is that healthy foodstuff or financial means form the interest that is required to comply with the norm 'eat healthy food everyday'.

The pursuit of interest becomes problematic when:
1 it stands in the way of someone else's interest
2 the interest is scarce and people compete for it
3 it stands in the way of the realization of other values you find important

An example of the first could be the organization of a large dance festival. Some of the central values of this festival are probably pleasure, happiness and an exciting life. Norms could be: 'dance all night long', 'meet new people' or 'get slightly drunk'. The interest in this case is notably an incredibly large music system so the DJ can 'drop his beats' loudly. However, this interest may happen to stand in the way of the interest of those who live near the festival area, and try to catch some sleep (which is the norm), in order to realize the value 'a comfortable life' or 'health'. They will probably not be able to realize all this due to the loud sound system next door. Their interest is 'a quiet environment', which is at odds with the big sound system.

A second problem emerges when more people compete for gaining certain material or immaterial possessions while there is not enough to satisfy all of them. In essence, our economy is based on the assumption that there is a scarcity of products, and that the demand for such products determines the price people have to pay for this. This also means that per definition, there will always be people who cannot afford these products, and need to look for alternatives.
A geo-political example in which a conflict of interest leads to tensions is the territorial dispute in the South Chinese Sea. Neighbouring countries such as China, Vietnam, the Philippines, Malaysia, Brunei and Taiwan claim some of the territories in that sea, where others disagree with that claim. This 'no man's sea' is much desired for the huge amount of resources, such as fish and oil.

Finally, a problem may occur when some of your interest for the sake of realizing a certain value stands in the way of realizing another value. It will probably be a typical student dilemma: when you are having a good time on a Thursday night in a student bar, while you are supposed to attend college Friday morning. The student is celebrating life by drinking a fair amount of alcoholic beverages, in order to realize the values 'happiness' and 'pleasure'. These beverages are at that moment in time of interest for the student. No doubt however, that the next morning this interest stands in the way of realizing the value 'wisdom', for it will probably stand in the way of attending the class, or participate in a fruitful manner.

To conclude, and for a complete picture, the relation between morality, norms, values, virtue and interest is portrayed in figure 1.2.

FIGURE 1.2 The relationship between morality, norms, values, virtue and interest

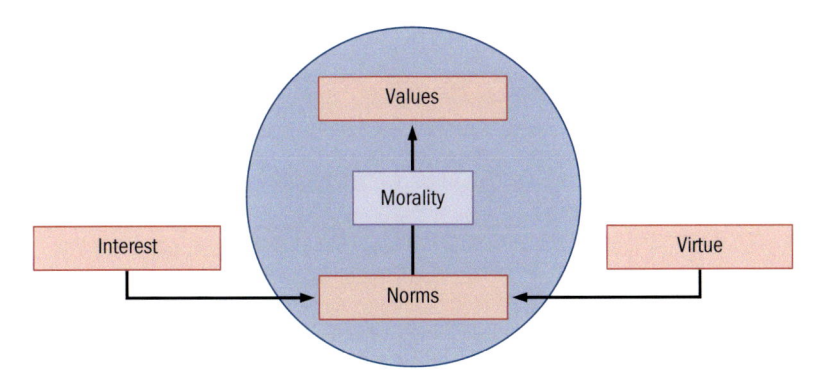

1.4 The structural analysis

In ethics, we structurally analyse morality. In many books, this analysis is composed of a structural overview of different approaches in ethics and how we should act based on those approaches. That's about it. What is often missing however is a sound methodological approach in structuralizing various viewpoints in ethics. The method used in this book allows us to compare different viewpoints based on functional equivalence. We call this comparative methodology the functional method, or functionalism.

> Functionalism is the comparison of different solutions to the same problem on the basis of functional equivalence.

Functionalism

That is quite a mouthful, so we have some explaining to do.

Homosexuality: it should be banned!

During one of my ethics classes, an unexpected fierce debate about homosexuality emerged. I was discussing various forms of discrimination, including discrimination of particular minorities, such as immigrants, disabled people and discrimination based on sexual preference. I learned that a group amongst my students opposed the idea of same sex relationships, and even voiced the opinion that it would be fine to beat up someone who publicly expresses such a relation. For me, this was not easy to listen to, since in my personal environment, homosexuality is widely accepted, and some of my best friends are in a same-sex relationship. I was especially shocked by the aggression in the debate by both those who were hostile towards same-sex relationships and those who opposed them.

For me, it was a challenge not to become emotionally involved in the discussion and lose my neutrality. It is one of my goals as an ethics lecturer to stimulate students to voice their own opinion, also when this is not 'mainstream', unpopular or extreme. It is my sincere conviction that addressing such opinions and openly discuss them leads to more good than imposing my own moral views on my students. This time however I was struggling with maintaining this neutral attitude and I had to withhold myself from starting to preach that your sexual orientation should never be a reason for different treatment.

A functional method

On the spot, I decided to try a method I fine-tuned when I was writing my PhD-dissertation: a functional method in which all solutions to a social issue are treated based on equivalence rather than judged and as a result accepted or rejected.

First, I explained to my students that apparently there are opposing views of same-sex relationships, and these views are in such contrast that it probably will be impossible to reconcile those viewpoints. However, that in itself is not a problem: those views can co-exist in a debate on ethics, and there is no need that one group convinces the other. What we do need however is a way to try and understand one another, using a functional method.

From the perspective of ethics as an academic discipline it is important to carefully formulate a social issue. This is not that difficult in this case, and probably boils down to something like 'to what extent do you think a same sex relationship is morally right or wrong?' As we have seen, my students responded differently to this question. However – different as they are – the opinions of my students respond to the same social issue, which makes them in their function comparable. In other words: the viewpoints of my students are functionally equivalent.

Towards a fruitful debate

By formulating the opposing viewpoints as functional equivalent responses to a similar social issue, the fierce tone of the students turned into a more constructive attitude. After all, when you analyse ethical viewpoints in a functional equation, there is no need in proclaiming that you would like to beat up someone who is in a same-sex relationship. Instead, my students focused on reasoning, and deduced their moral views to norms and values, instead of using overly aggressive or hostile language. Even I could participate in this, because there was no need for me to remain neutral anymore: the functional method did that for me, since all viewpoints are considered functionally equivalent.

To illustrate: those students who were offended by same sex relationships assumed that such a relation is not natural, and as such should not be accepted in our society. This contributes to the value salvation. They also argued that it was not in line with their religious mind-set or tradition that homosexuality should be allowed to exist. This norm leads to the value piety and heritage. Those who would disagree held that same sex relationships are as good as any, and should be treated equally. They clearly preferred to strive for values such as equality, respect and freedom.

This stripped down analysis of the situation is not really rocket science, but in my lecture it did make the difference. It turned a heated, aggressive debate in a more fruitful conversation. It led to mutual understanding, while both parties gently agreed to disagree regarding its content.

Functionalism is a comparative method (Wernaart, 2013). As we can learn from the case 'Homosexuality: it should be banned!', comparing several moral viewpoints leads to more understanding of a social issue compared to separately discussing a moral view on its own. First of all, because you simply know more than you did before, and also listened to arguments you would probably not have heard if you would stay inside your bubble in which your own moral view is reaffirmed over and over again. Second, because it leads to more understanding of those who think differently. You do not have to convince the other, but instead try to understand the other. It does not stand in the way of having your own opinion, but it does give you the opportunity to learn from someone else, and perhaps fine-tune (or instead reaffirm) your own moral views. This attitude is very useful in many professions, especially in international business, where you will encounter many people with different backgrounds and views on delicate matters.

Functionalism can be done through several steps. In short, you first formulate a moral question. Then you explore the various viewpoints towards this question on the basis of functional equivalence. Lastly, you try to clarify these viewpoints by narrowing them down to their underlying values.

A moral questions is the central point of the comparison. In academics we call this an Archimedean point, that is the point with which we compare. This can be a very specific problem but also a complex global issue. As we have seen in the opening case 'leadership? It's in your DNA!', it is of vital importance to formulate a well-considered moral question. Two rules of thumb are that your moral question is open enough so it cannot be answered with a simple 'yes' or 'no'. Another rule of thumb is that the question should not be biased, in such a way that there is little room for alternative answers than the desired answer. So, in the case of 'homosexuality, it should be banned!' we should not formulate the moral question like this:
- Is a same sex relationship ethical?
- What can possibly be reasons to justify different treatment of same sex relationships?

Moral questions

Instead, the following questions could lead to a more fruitful comparison:
- To what extent do you think a same sex relationship is morally right or wrong?
- How should religious values relate to the idea of same-sex relationships?

Next, you carefully map how people could answer this moral question, from various ethical viewpoints. You can collect these answers on a small scale, for instance in a classroom. You can also academically collect these answers in studying the works of various philosophers, academics, or perhaps even politicians who represent a certain group in society. You can also try to collect the answers in comparing different cultures or regions in the world, and how they generally look at the moral issue.

Ethical viewpoints

The answer to the moral question will usually come down to a norm. All the answers are functionally equivalent and therefore comparable. Examples of norms that represent an ethical viewpoint are:
1 a same-sex relationship is not natural, and as such should not be accepted in our society
2 a same-sex relationship violates traditional and religious ways of living, and therefore is unethical
3 we are all equal, and same-sex relationships are as good as any other relationship, and should therefore not be treated differently
4 a sexual relationship is a private issue, and others should not judge this nor try to forbid the nature of this relationship.

Finally, you try to explain the selected norms by narrowing them down to values. You could, for example deduce the following values from the above mentioned norms:
1 salvation
2 piety and heritage
3 equality, respect and freedom
4 privacy and freedom

Values

In figure 1.3 you may find a schematic overview of this functionalist method. As we will see in chapter 4, elements of this functionalist method are integrated in the ethical decision model.

FIGURE 1.3 The functionalist method in ethics

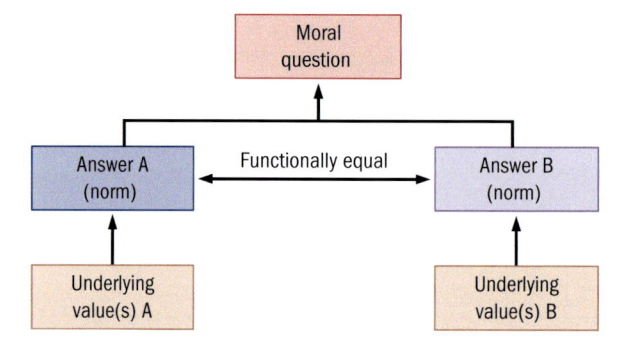

1.5 The structural evaluation

Where we structurally analyse to try to understand and explain various ethical viewpoints, the idea of a structural evaluation is to come to a well-informed decision as to which viewpoint is the best, and should be followed. In essence, where we choose to remain neutral in our analysis, we actually take a position in our evaluation.

Discrimination or a reasonable choice?

Fatima holds the position of HRM consultant in a medium-sized enterprise. Currently, she is advising one of the team leaders in hiring a new employee for the sales department. At the end of the job application procedure, there are only two suitable candidates left: Jimmy (30) and Chin (27). Both make a very good impression on the team leader and appear to have similar competencies and the same educational background. What a coincidence it is that they happen to be in the same stage of their personal life as well. During the job interviews, both Jimmy and Chin proudly told that they just got married. Because the team leader has no preference for any of them, and considers them equally fit for the job, he asks Fatima for advice.

Fatima is facing a dilemma. On the one hand, the answer to the team leader's question seems quite simple: if Chin is planning to have babies, there is a considerable chance she will try to have them within a couple of years. Jimmy is a male, while he might become a dad, he will most certainly not be on a paternity leave as long as Chin's possible maternity leave might take. For the company, a maternity leave means a lot of paperwork, looking for a temporary worker to do Chin's work while she's absent, and it will bring some extra costs. If the team leader wants to play it safe he should simply choose Jimmy, and not Chin.

On the other hand, Fatima considers that the last thing she wants is to judge people based on their gender, instead of their potential. She does not want to discriminate women. Next to the fact that it is no secret that women are hopelessly underrepresented in this branch, it would potentially damage the image of the company if such decision-making would end up in the press. Now, what should Fatima advise the team leader?

In the case 'Discrimination or a reasonable choice?' we could propose various ways of dealing with the matter. One option could be that Fatima advises to hire Chin, since she is convinced that no matter what, women should not suffer any form of discrimination. Another option would be to advise to hire Jimmy. After all, he will cause the least risk for the company in terms of maternity/paternity leave. A third option would be to advise hiring Chin with a slightly similar reasoning: it is the best for the company. First, because you will avoid suffering image damage, and second, because a diverse workforce is proven to yield better results than a homogenous. Since women are underrepresented in this field, the team leader might as well hire Chin. Fatima could put these three options in a comparative overview and check which norms and values she finds most important.

Which option Fatima will choose is her own choice, depending on her personal norms and values. Or perhaps the norms and values of the company may play a role of importance in her final decision. Whatever she chooses, by structurally analysing the various options (norms) and the underlying values, it will most likely be easier to make a well-considered assessment. If for instance Fatima wants to emphasize the value 'equality', she might advise the first option and hire Chin. If she would prefer the value 'welfare', she might go for the second option and hire Jimmy. If she rather stresses the value 'safety' and 'sustainability', she might go for option number three and hire Chin.

1.6 Ethics and related disciplines

The structural analysis and evaluation of morality relates to other academic disciplines as well. As a matter of fact, ethics is very often applied in other disciplines to guarantee that this discipline is practiced in the right way, and not used for wrong purposes. However, it remains important to distinguish ethics from those disciplines, to avoid confusion in our intentions, and make sure we are actually having the same conversation when we discuss something in a related discipline. Therefore, it is important to establish that there is a difference between an academic perspective, and a viewpoint within that perspective.

> An academic perspective is an approach towards a certain situation exclusively from the perspective of that discipline.

Academic perspective

Below, we will further explore the relation between ethics on the one hand, and law, theology, psychology, theology and economics on the other. These are all academic disciplines that may approach a situation from a different perspective. Within such a perspective, we can argue about things and have a different viewpoint, or – if you like – opinion on a certain matter.

> A viewpoint is a particular opinion within an academic discipline.

Viewpoint

Ashley Madison: it only takes a moment

Ashley Madison is a successful international dating site, specialized in discreet love affairs. Its members can rest assured that they meet people with the same goal, and their privacy is guaranteed so their partner will never find out. As it appears, the company satisfies a certain need amongst its customers by filling an untapped niche in the market: *'when Ashley Madison started in 2001, there weren't many places adults could go for discreet dating. Meeting someone at work or through friends is too risky when discretion is your number one concern. Many turned to traditional online dating websites, but found it difficult to connect with people looking for a similar type of arrangement. And so Ashley Madison was created as the first website that was open and honest about what you could find there: like-minded people looking for married dating'*. The company promotes their services on their website, in recommending people who want to cheat on their partner to '...*feel the butterflies, experience the desire, and know what it is not to just live but to really come alive? Ashley Madison is the place to start your journey, to find your moment'*. After all, *'it only takes a moment'* (www.ashleymadison.com).

What the heck?
In 2015, Ashley Madison dominated the headlines due to a massive data breach: hackers were able to reveal the names of 36 million users of the website. The motivation of the hackers was that they considered the website dishonest. One of the services of the company was the so-called 'full-delete-service'. For a fee, your account would be fully deleted and none of your personal data would be stored after your account was removed. A lie, according to the hackers, and a smart way to make money (Mansfield-Devine, 2015).

Fake woman and suicide
This has led to a large number of divorces, and it was even suggested that some of the revealed users committed suicide as a result (Baraniuk, 2016). Furthermore, it turned out that the website used fake female accounts (the so-called 'fembots') to keep the overrepresented men occupied while they were under the impression to flirt with real women. In the end, Ashley Madison paid a fine of 1.6 million U.S. dollar for failing to protect the privacy of its customers, and faced several lawsuits (Kuchler, 2016). Not surprisingly, these took a while.

Take for instance the case 'Ashley Madison, it only takes a moment'. We can consider what happened in this case from various academic disciplines. We could have a discussion about whether the privacy protection was adequate according to the law, or whether or not it is legal to use fembots as fake accounts to keep men occupied. We could furthermore wonder if Ashley Madison can be held responsible for suicide, and face charges for murder. In a court room, the lawyer of Ashley Madison will probably have a different viewpoint on these legal aspects compared to the public prosecutor, and defend this viewpoint accordingly until a judge imposes his viewpoint on the disputing lawyers.

We can also consider this case from the perspective of the economic discipline. We could ask ourselves the question to what extent there is a consumer's need for an online environment in which people can 'safely' cheat on their partner. Considering the initial success of the website, the company took full advantage of the untapped niche in the online dating market. At some point in time, the responsible employees probably had a debate about the economic potential to offer a full-delete-service. During this debate, various viewpoints on the economic potential of such a service were balanced. In the end, the decision was made to offer the additional service, fulfilling the consumer's desire to having a sense of privacy, and keeping a grip on their personal data.

From an ethics perspective we could ask the question to what extent it is morally right to make money in facilitating people to cheat on their partner. There will be various viewpoints concerning this topic. Some might say that cheating is a wrong thing to do, and therefore the company is exploiting something that is morally offensive. Others might say that cheating happens anyway, so it would be ethical to reduce the sadness and hurt that might result from 'clumsy' cheating. Therefore a professional website specialized in this matter may reduce the harm that can be done. Another viewpoint might be that cheating is a personal matter, and the company is not responsible for the things people share with one another through their website. As a result, the company is morally neutral.

It makes sense to separate the disciplines in a debate. When I ask my students to consider the Ashley Madison case and raise the question to what extent they believe it morally right to make money in facilitating cheating, they sometimes give me answers from a different discipline. Some answer that the behaviour of the company is not forbidden by law, which leads to the conclusion that it is not unethical. Or some may emphasize the fact that there is a consumer's need, and the company merely fulfils this need, and as a result the behaviour cannot possibly be unethical.
However, the fact that something is not forbidden, or may be profitable, says very little about the question whether something is ethical. You might circumvent the issue, and confuse a viewpoint from the law or economic discipline with a moral justification. Please note that this does not change the fact that it is always a good idea to consider things from various disciplines, as long as you do not mix up the viewpoints within a discipline with viewpoints from another discipline.

In figure 1.4 we see a schematic overview of the relation between an academic discipline and a viewpoint.

FIGURE 1.4 The relation between an academic perspective and a viewpoint

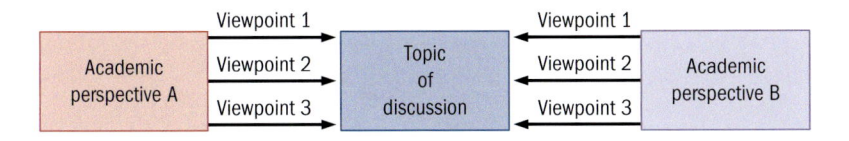

1.6.1 Ethics and law
As we have seen in the previous section, law is different from ethics.

| In law we ask ourselves the question whether something is legal. **Law**

Of course, there is an overlap between ethics and law. Sometimes, law is a codified expression of morality. This sense of morality is then formalized, and can be imposed on the citizens within the jurisdiction of that law. This can be done at different levels. At international level, morality is codified in international legal norms, such as a treaty or international customary law. For instance, Article 11 of the International Covenant on Economic, Social and Cultural Rights stipulates that everyone has a right to an adequate standard of living. Also on a national level, countries adopt legislation that can be considered as an expression of morality. For instance, Article 102 of the Malaysian Penal Code reads *'the right of private defence of the body commences as soon as a reasonable apprehension of danger to the body arises from an attempt or threat to commit the offence, though the offence may not have been committed; and it continues as long as such apprehension of danger to the body continues.'* In other words: you have the right to defend yourself when someone seeks to harm you. Even at individual level, legislation may play a role. Think of a permit granted by the city to your university to organize a music festival at the beginning of the academic year. Apparently, the town considers it a good idea to open the year with some fun. In all these examples we can read some kind of morality: it is the right thing to make sure that everyone has an adequate living standard, protect yourself if someone inflicts harm on you, and open the academic year with some music. In that sense, there is an overlap between ethics and law: in ethics we ask ourselves what is right and wrong, where in law we codify what we think should be right or wrong.

Consequences

There are of course also differences between ethics and law. The first is that the consequences of unethical behaviour are different from the consequences of violating a law. Law can be enforced, so violating a legal norm can lead to punishment such as a fine or a prison sentence. In some countries even the death penalty applies, and violating a law could lead to the loss of your own life. When violating a norm in ethics, the consequences are not the same. While probably most people consider adultery as something that is wrong, this is not forbidden in most countries. So, cheating on your partner will not lead to a prison sentence. However, those who are related to the cheater will most likely think poorly of him, and perhaps act accordingly by excluding him, or end their friendship. The main difference between the consequences of violating a legal and an ethical norm therefore is that in case of the first, the consequences are institutionalized and enforceable, where in case of the latter, the consequences are informal and not enforceable.

A second difference between ethics and law is that law is not always an expression of morality. Where we could argue that law is an expression of morality when law is intended to deliver justice, this simply is not always the goal of adopting legislation. In legal philosophy, it is generally accepted that next to justice, law should achieve two other goals as well: opportuneness and legal certainty (Habermas, 1992).

Justice

So, justice as a goal in law indeed relates to the question what should be considered as right in a given society. In general, we consider it a wrong thing to kill someone, and this act is mostly forbidden by law. That is quite clearly an expression of morality. However, a law should also be opportune.

Opportuneness

This means that a law should be practical. Lawyers can hypothetically try to make legislation that theoretically delivers most justice, but this is so complex that it cannot be executed by a legal professional. Unfortunately, this law will then not be opportune. Next to that, law is sometimes simply used to practically organize something in society, without an explicit moral charge. Think about the choice to ride a car on the left or right side of the road. In each country, traffic laws will dictate which side of the road must be used in that society. However, the choice in itself says little about morality. It is just a practical decision to choose one side, and enforce that choice.

A last function in law is to guarantee legal certainty. The fact that charges against an alleged kidnapper are dropped due to a lack of evidence will not always be received as just. Especially not by those who consider themselves a victim. However, when we take a closer look at the news item, it would on the other hand lead to undesirable situations when someone can be imprisoned just because he might look like the one who tried to kidnap you. This approach contributes to the idea of legal certainty: you can only be condemned for something that was forbidden at the moment you acted, and the evidence points out that you were the one who committed the act, without doubt. While occasionally this would mean that a criminal will not be punished, this is preferred above the possibility that an innocent man ends up in prison, merely because he has certain looks, or reminds people vaguely of someone who might have committed the act. A fine example of this can be found in the news item.

Legal certainty

A third difference between ethics and law is that law, if it expresses morality in the first place, only expresses the norms and values chosen by those who are in control. In case of ethics, this is clearly not the case. Those who are in control could be a democratically elected legislature, but also a dictator, or the military. This also means that the morality that is expressed by their laws is not automatically the morality that is shared by all individuals within the country they rule. For instance, abortion is prohibited in Chile, and at least 26 per cent of its population disagrees with that (Agnus Reid Global Monitor, 2006).

CBS MIAMI, 13 JANUARY 2017

Charges have been dropped against a Miami man accused of trying to abduct young girls

Marshawn Andrews, 25, was arrested in December after a Miami Police officer noticed him attempt to pick up two females, at two separate locations, within minutes of each other.

It came after similar reports of attempted abductions had occurred in the area on November 10th and December 12th. One girl was 15, the other 17.

On December 23rd, Andrews was seen making a U-turn at N.W. 29th Street, east of N.W. 7th Avenue, stopping his car to talk to a young woman walking on the sidewalk, authorities said. The officer, in an unmarked vehicle, then pulled up behind Andrews to check on her and see if she was alright. She told him that Andrews offered her a ride.

Andrews continued driving westbound. Minutes later, the officer observed him offer another woman a ride who was walking along N.W. 7th Avenue. She would get in. Andrews was soon pulled over and gave a conflicting account of what happened, according to a memorandum from the State Attorney's Office. He told officers that the woman was his girlfriend. The woman, however, admitted that she didn't know Andrews and had been asked if she needed a ride.

1

Fitting the description of the suspect, in both appearance and due to the proximity of the previous encounters, Andrews was arrested later that day.
Investigators would call in the two other victims to the police station, trying to tie Andrews to the previous attempted abduction incidents. They both picked

him out of a photo line-up as the same guy who tried to kidnap them, the State Attorney's Office said.
But this evidence would not be enough for a conviction, prosecutors argued. For one, both victims didn't get a clear look at their attacker.

Finally, it is important to note that in some cases, the legislature deliberately chooses to remain silent on certain matters in which ethics on the other hand plays a very important role. We have seen above that in many countries, cheating is not forbidden by law. Only in some countries, adultery (cheating during your marriage) is forbidden. This means that in most jurisdictions, having an affair is considered a private matter that is not to be dealt with by legislation. Most probably, a majority of the citizens of these countries would consider cheating an unethical thing.

1.6.2   Ethics and theology

Theology

In theology we critically analyse and evaluate the nature of the divine.

Religion, and the study of the divine (theology), shows a strong relationship with ethics. The subject of both disciplines has a lot to do with the question of what is morally right. Many ethical standards are derived from religion and religious writings or thoughts, and consequentially influence the norms and values of many people. Religion in itself is therefore an important source of inspiration for people in determining their morality.

But there are also very essential differences. Norms and values in religion mostly appear in a prescriptive tone. When you follow a certain religion, you have to comply with certain norms to be a faithful believer. For instance, you should fast a certain period, pray at given times of the day, or dress in a particular way. These norms and values are prescribed by, or derived from a holy entity (or holy entities) such as a God. These religious rules are then mostly written down in a widely accepted book, such as the Holy Bible or the Holy Quran. There are usually representatives of this holy entity that have the authority to interpret the norms and values according to their religion, such as a Pope, or an Imam.
In essence, there are many religious norms and values that coincide with theories in normative ethics. The norm 'treat the other as you would like to be treated' is a rule that appears in almost each religion, but is also incorporated in the moral philosophy of Immanuel Kant (Crane & Matten, 2010).
However, while in its appearance this norm is the same, the reasoning behind this norm is fundamentally different. In religion, we treat the other person the way you want to be treated because this is prescribed by a divine authority, where in ethics we do so because we believe it is the right thing to do.

1

The use of contraceptives and the church

A very delicate matter amongst Christians is the usage of contraceptives. The idea is that while using contraceptives, people can experience sexual pleasure and intimacy without getting pregnant. However, this is forbidden by the Vatican as an interpretation of the phrase Be fruitful and multiply and fill the earth and subdue it' (Genesis 1:28): the marital act should be without any reservations because it must be unconditional and an expression of true love.

This is for example aptly stipulated in an encyclical of Pope Paul VI, in which he wrote that: '*the fundamental nature of the marriage act, while uniting husband and wife in the closest intimacy, also renders them capable of generating new life – and this as a result of laws written into the actual nature of man and of woman. And if each of these essential qualities, the unitive and the procreative, is preserved, the use of marriage fully retains its sense of true mutual love and its ordination to the supreme responsibility of parenthood to which man is called*' (Pope Paul VI, Humanae Vitae, 2:6).

Criticism
This viewpoint of the Catholic Church was criticized more than once. Especially in countries in which HIV infection is a serious concern, the prohibition to contraception can lead to a worsening of the situation, in which mostly children born from HIV infected parents are an innocent victim (UN Committee on the rights of the child, 2014).

Considering the example 'The use of contraceptives and the church', the reasoning of Pope Paul VI would not be accepted in ethics. After all, we do not act in compliance with a norm because we consider this the will of God, but instead because we are convinced that something is right or wrong after careful analysis and evaluation. This does not mean that we do not carefully study in theology; the focus is just different.

1.6.3   Ethics and psychology

Yet another related academic discipline we should explore is the study of psychology.

⏐   In psychology we seek to understand and explain human behaviour.   **Psychology**

Where psychology tries to understand and explain behaviour, in ethics we ask ourselves the question whether this behaviour is morally right or wrong.

Carrie Bradshaw and Manolo Blahnik high heels

In the famous series and films 'sex and the city', the main characters are four material girls from New York. Carrie, Samantha, Charlotte and Miranda love fashion, going out, and date good-looking men. The ideal environment for product placement. In the storylines, Carrie is well known as a big fan of Manolo Blahnik high heels. Her boyfriend (Mister Big) even uses such shoes in a wedding proposal, as a substitute to a ring. It is no secret that the appearance of Manolo Blahnik in various episodes of Sex and the City led to a huge boost in their brand awareness. On the other hand, it is also no secret that Manolo Blahnik alongside with some other brands was quite eager to pay significant sums of money for such appearances. According to Sarah

Jessica Parker, the producer of the first movie and actress who plays the character of Carrie, producing the movie would most certainly not be affordable without such deals (Nichols, 2008).

It will be clear that in the case of 'Carrie Bradshaw and Manolo Blahnik high heels' the advertisers expect that showing their products in a popular TV show or movie will affect the purchase behaviour of its viewers. In psychological studies, we try to find out whether such product placement indeed has the intended effect, and may change the buying behaviour of consumers (Waldt e.a., 2007). Such information is very important for companies that are looking for effective ways of advertising.

However, from an ethics perspective we could ask the question whether product placement is a moral thing to do. After all, the viewers of the show are not always aware of the fact that they are not only watching a movie; simultaneously an advertiser is deliberately trying to manipulate their buying behaviour during this show.

So, from the perspective of psychology we could ask ourselves the question whether product placement actually works, where from the ethics discipline we raise the issue whether this is a right thing to do.

1.6.4   Ethics and sociology

Sociology | In sociology we seek to understand and explain social relations.

Social relations are usually defined as relations between social groups, and their behaviour towards one another. Where we try to understand and explain this behaviour in sociology, in ethics we ask ourselves the question whether this behaviour is morally right.

Shell in the Niger Delta

For decades, Shell has employed business activities in the Niger Delta, a region in Nigeria, Africa. This region is well known for its oil resources. In the delta, Shell has negotiated the rights to harvest this oil, but is at the same time strongly opposed by the local inhabitants. They have lived there for ages, and deeply regret that their livelihood is seriously affected as a result of the oil drilling. This has had considerable negative effects on the local fishery and agriculture. To make matters worse, there have been oil leaks in the process, resulting in permanent infertility of the soil of certain regions.

Shell strongly denies that it is responsible for these leaks, and claims that these oil spills are a result of vandalism by angry locals, and not a direct result of any actions of the company (Shell, 2013). However, Shell is opposed by those who claim that the spills are a direct result of negligence caused by Shell (Amnesty International, 2013). In 2013, a Dutch court – using Nigerian law – ruled that four of those spills were indeed a result of vandalism, but two were caused by negligence, and therefore Shell should take its responsibility and pay the awarded damages (District Court of The Hague, 30 January 2013).

From the perspective of sociology, it is interesting to study the way Shell tried to handle this situation. It is striking that Shell, in the Shell in the Niger Delta case, approaches the issue on a very technocratic manner (Shah, 2004). The management of Shell mainly took decisions on the basis of expected results and dealt with the local population accordingly. That resulted in a very corporate way of acting in which the management was mainly focused on realizing the greatest possible oil harvest. If that would require investing in the local infrastructure in order to keep the complaining citizens happy, then that is what should be done. However, the locals could very well sense that Shell did not invest in the infrastructure because they were intrinsically motivated to improve their livelihood, but instead considered this as a necessity to realize their ultimate goal: oil harvest. This way of dealing is typically a Western European approach, in which we try to categorize social actors in 'boxes' and are very much focused on the function of these actors towards our cause. It is then the role of the management to use these 'boxes' in such a way that it turns out to work well for the company.

From a sociological perspective it is interesting to analyse the impact of the rather (Western) European approach of Shell in Nigeria, and explain the relation between this behaviour and the responding behaviour of the local community. More than once, the local inhabitants showed their disdain for Shell, and accused Shell of using them as a means to an end, and most certainly not acting in their best interest (Schram, 2014). As it seems, the approach mustered by Shell worked counterproductive, considering the resulting court trials.

From an ethics perspective, we should ask ourselves the question whether the behaviour of Shell (or the local community) is morally right. For instance, we could discuss the question to what extent it is morally right to use people as a means to an end, or to use sabotage as a way to put pressure on a company when you disagree with them and the company won't listen.

1.6.5 Ethics and economic disciplines

A last related academic discipline to ethics is economics.

> In the economic discipline we seek to explain – and sometimes even predict – how our economy works.

Economic discipline

So, where in the economic discipline we want to explain and predict our economy, in ethics we reflect on whether we think the way our economy works is morally right.

Macro and microeconomics

The essence of economics is usually defined as the production, distribution and consumption of goods and services. These goods and services are not unlimitedly available, due to the fact that resources are – in various degrees – scarce (Sloman & Wride, 2009). While we could hypothetically want unlimited resources, there is always a certain scarcity. This scarcity has an effect on the relation between supply of and demand for a particular product or service. This relation will usually determine the market price in a capitalist market system. For instance, when supply is relatively scarce and demand large, the prices are high, while when the supply is relatively high and demand low, the prices will be low. There are of course other systems than a capitalist system, such as a communist market system, in which the government tries to regulate supply and demand, rather than rely on the effect of supply and demand in itself.

Since the thirties, the economic discipline is subdivided in two main fields: macro and microeconomics. In macroeconomics we study the economy on a national or international level, where in microeconomics, we study the economic behaviour of individuals and organizations (such as a company).

Let's explore macroeconomics first. In this field, we usually discuss general economic theories and phenomena. Famous academics such as Adam Smith, Milton Friedman, Karl Marx, John Stuart Mill, David Ricardo and John Maynard Keynes have developed well-known macroeconomic theories. They have tried to explain how our global economy works from different economic perspectives. In such theories, we usually discuss issues such as inflation, the effects of exchange rates, the impact of government policy on economic growth, imports and exports, employment, the principle of free trade, market protectionism and globalization.

BBC NEWS, 28 OCTOBER 2016

The Poles looking to leave the UK after Brexit

By: Erika Benke

Incidents of hate crime aimed at the UK's Polish community increased after the summer's EU referendum and as a result, some Poles are considering leaving the country.

Joanna Kalinowska believes that the decision to leave the EU was a turning point – when anti-Polish sentiment became increasingly vocalised and continuing to live in the UK became a much less attractive prospect.

'When I first came to England, I thought it would be a big chance for me to have a better life, to learn new skills, to be among nice people,' she says. 'But after more than seven years of being here, I've said that's enough, I don't have to be here any more.'

Joanna lives in Poole and says at times she has been made to feel like a second-class citizen and has even been confronted by a stranger on the street.

'I was talking to my daughter (in Polish), we were joking and laughing. A man passed and said "if you are in England you have to talk in English... otherwise you go back to your country", she tells the BBC's Victoria Derbyshire programme.

'I said to that guy, "I am talking with my child, so I will talk to my child in my language. And this is also my country, and I have equal rights here".'

The man, she says, answered in reply: 'You don't have any rights here any more.'

'That was my experience after Brexit,' she says.

'They think we're invaders.'

Joanna lost her job in a food processing factory four months ago and is now considering moving abroad.

'I don't see any future for me here, especially after what happened after Brexit,' Joanna says.

According to the latest figures, published in August, there are 2.23 million EU nationals working in the UK – an increase of 238,000 on the same period in 2015. An estimated 850,000 Poles live in the UK.

Joanna is keen to challenge the view, held by some, that EU nationals come to the UK to access welfare payments.

'(Polish people) were prepared to come here, work hard and be normal members of society,' she says. 'We integrate very easily and are very willing to integrate with the Brits. But the Brits don't want to integrate with us.'

'They think we are invaders, that we want to take something from them.'
'No,' she says emphatically, 'we don't want to take, we want to give.'

The newspaper article 'The Poles looking to leave the UK' reflects a debate with a macroeconomic origin. After all, most of the debate that preceded the UK referendum that resulted in Brexit was about economics. If the UK would remain a member state of the EU, this would also mean that citizens of other EU countries could move to and reside in the UK and look for a job. This may lead to tensions when for instance people from Poland compete with UK citizens for jobs when there is a certain rate of unemployment, especially when people from Poland are willing to work for a lower wage than the British. Leaving the EU, and making it less easy for foreign workers to find a job in the UK would then protect UK workers looking for a job. On the other hand, we could argue that united countries are stronger. Where on the short term the tensions between Polish workers in the UK and UK citizens could be a problem, trade with open borders on the long term might lead to the most efficient way of allocating resources – including worker – and in the end all will benefit from this. This assumption forms the basis of much international economic cooperation, such as the World Trade Organization (WTO), the North Atlantic Free Trade Agreement (NAFTA), the African Free Trade Zone (AFTZ) and the Caribbean and Common Market Community CARICOM). After all, one of the conditions of a free market economy is the removal of trade barriers between countries, so that trade is not depending on nationality, but rather on the system of supply and demand.

While economists generally agree that the principle of a free market economy will theoretically lead to a more prosperous society on the long term, there are always short term side effects that may be negative for especially those who find it difficult to adapt quickly to the whims of this mechanism of supply and demand. In other words: prosperity is not always fairly distributed. This leads to the question to what extent governments should (or may) interfere in the functioning of this free trade principle, and for instance adopt measures to protect their local markets. And here we need ethics: to what extent do we consider it morally right to depend on a free market economy, potentially leading to the greatest prosperity, and to what extent do we feel the need to protect the interest of those who do not necessarily gain something from this free market economy. In chapter 11, we will discuss this into much more detail.

Translated to the news item, we see a moral dilemma between the 'brexiteers' and the 'bremainers': where the 'brexiteers' urged the UK government to step out the EU and protect the local workers, the 'bremainers' urged their government to remain in the EU, and enjoy the wider and long term benefits of a free European economy. Of course it needs to be noted here that the Brexit debate was much more complicated and encompassed a broader range of issues than the news item reflects.

1

On the micro-economic level we study the individual decisions regarding the production, distribution and consumption of goods and services. These individual decisions are taken by companies that decide to produce and distribute their products and services because they want to meet a certain demand, and by consumers or other businesses who will try to satisfy their individual needs. In microeconomics we predominantly ask ourselves the question what the effects are of these individual decisions on our economy. In ethics, we ask ourselves the question to what extent these decisions are morally right. So, considering the energy drink case, from a microeconomic perspective we could try to understand the effect of Red Bull communicating that their product is not dangerous on the buying behaviour of consumers. From an ethics perspective we ask ourselves the question if it is morally right to set aside the worries of many scientists about the effect of their product on young people, or that Red Bull and other energy drink suppliers especially target this group in their advertisements.

Business administration

Next to macro and microeconomics there are many subjects in the academic circuit that relate to the functioning of companies but do not necessarily seek to explain our economy or individual economic behaviour. We usually find these subjects in applied sciences, in the curricula of business schools. These subjects typically study the functioning of companies and contribute to making companies more efficient and profitable.
For these disciplines we usually apply the term 'business administration', which mainly distinguishes between:
- marketing and sales
- finance and accounting
- organization sciences (such as management, HRM and logistics)

So, where in business administration we try to optimize the functioning of companies, and make them more profitable, in ethics we ask ourselves the question whether this is done in a morally right way. For instance, from a marketing perspective we could analyse whether the various sponsor deals of Red Bull with various sports events have a positive effect on their image or sales. From an ethics perspective we ask ourselves the question whether it is morally right to associate energy drinks with sports achievements.

Business Ethics?

The academic area – where economics and ethics are linked – is sometimes referred to as 'business ethics', thereby suggesting that this is an applied form of ethics in the business context. Some use another popular term to address the same: Corporate Social Responsibility (CSR). These terms have been used many times in many different context and by many different actors, and as a result, its exact meaning is sometimes hard to define (Griseri & Seppala, 2010). For instance, most multinationals claim to 'do' CSR, but in practice their interpretation and the level of incorporating CSR concepts is very different.

The idea of 'business ethics' is criticized by some with good arguments. It is argued that the concept 'business ethics' is an oxymoron: words that are internally contradicting (Collins, 1994). One way or another, a company can only survive when it makes a profit, or at least does not suffer financial loss.

This also means that per definition, in the consideration of a company, money plays a dominant role. This leads to a 'distortion' of ethical decision-making. When ethics and profit go hand in hand, there is no problem, and we can safely talk about business ethics. However, when a company faces a choice between making more profit and acting less in line with their morality on the one hand, and making less profit but acting morally more correct in the other, we can wonder whether the ethical decision-making will be 'pure'.

Energy drinks: giving you wings or making you crash?

Energy drinks are very popular among young people. As a matter of fact, the smell of my lecture hall is drenched with energy drink flavour on a Friday-morning lecture. It is however doubtful whether such drinks are safe to consume.

The World Health Organization warns us for the usage of these drinks, especially by youngsters. In a broad European study, the researchers argue that *'consumption of energy drinks among adolescents is associated with other potentially negative health and behavioural outcomes such as sensation seeking, use of tobacco and other harmful substances, and binge drinking and is associated with a greater risk for depression and injuries that require medical treatment. Recent literature has also found an increasing number of problems with behaviour modification and cognitive capabilities in adolescents who use energy drinks.'*

Especially the caffeine that appears in these drinks seems to be a problem. The researchers firmly hold that…

'The health risks associated with energy drink consumption are primarily related to their caffeine content. A caffeine overdose can cause palpitations, hypertension, dieresis, central nervous system stimulation, nausea, vomiting, marked hypocalcemia, metabolic acidosis, convulsions, and, in rare cases, even death. In adults, there is also an increased risk of arterial hypertension and Type 2 diabetes, as high consumption of caffeine reduces insulin sensitivity. High-caffeine consumption among pregnant women increases the risk of late miscarriages, small for gestational age infants, and stillbirths.

Although some types of coffee can have caffeine levels comparable to energy drinks, coffee is typically consumed hot and consequently more slowly. Further, the proliferation of new brands of energy drinks has included some brands, which contain extreme caffeine levels much higher than mainstream brands as they try to establish themselves in the market. In Europe, the EFSA study showed that the estimated contribution of energy drinks to total caffeine exposure was 43% in children, 13% in adolescents, and 8% in adults. There are proven negative consequences of caffeine consumption among children and adolescents, including effects on the neurological and cardiovascular systems, which can cause physical dependence and addiction' (Breda et al. 2014).

What a difference with the health statement of Red Bull in their FAQ list:

Red Bull Energy Drink is available in 171 countries, including every state of the European Union, because health authorities across the world have concluded that Red Bull Energy Drink is safe to consume. More than 6 billion cans were consumed last year and over 62 billion cans since Red Bull was created more than 30 years ago.

One 250 ml can of Red Bull Energy Drink contains 80 mg of caffeine, about the same amount of caffeine as in a cup of coffee. The European Food Safety Authority (EFSA) concluded in 2009 that the ingredients of energy drinks are of no concern. In 2015, the EFSA confirmed the safety of energy drinks and their ingredients (http://energydrink-us.redbull.com, 2017).

1

Considering the 'energy drinks' case it is probably not surprising that a company such as Red Bull will not communicate things about their products that are too negative. After all, they want to sell it, and are proud to do so. On the other hand, the WHO and the related researchers are an authoritative institution when it concerns health issues. They give us almost desperate warnings about the consumption of energy drinks. Red Bull is very popular amongst its target group, and these youngsters probably do not want Red Bull to change a thing about their advertising, sponsor activities and image. So, Red Bull is facing a certain dilemma here: they have a very successful and popular product, a positive brand image amongst their target group, and an undoing increase in sales. Why would they change a thing in what they do? On the other hand, it seems that the WHO and many scientists believe that their product leads to health issues. Now, can we expect Red Bull to communicate to their target group to please not buy their product too often, because it might be dangerous?
From an ethics perspective, we could very well argue that the value 'health (of our youngsters)' is more important than the value 'profit' of Red Bull.

There is also another 'distorting' factor in ethical decision-making when we consider the concept of 'business ethics'. Companies are mostly legal personalities that are owned and managed by individuals. However, these individuals do not necessarily act in line with their own moral convictions when they act on behalf of this company. It may very well be that the web designer of Red Bull does not like his children to consume energy drinks every day, but simultaneously facilitates the information that Red Bull provides about their products. The fact that companies are not natural persons can lead to a certain institutionalization, which makes it sometimes difficult to distinguish ethical decision-making from calculative profit making.

Does this mean that a phrase such as 'business ethics' is nonsense per definition? Probably not: as long as we are honest and clear of its purpose. Therefore, in this book we make a distinction between ethics and business on the one hand, and business ethics on the other.

> Where in ethics in business we ask the question what is morally correct in our economic behaviour, in business ethics we ask the question how we can make profit in doing the right thing.

In the example 'the marketing success of anti-animal testing', we see that profit and ethics go well hand in hand, as long as they both lead to the same outcomes. The Body Shop is a formula that appeals to consumers. The ethical responsibility has always been their unique selling point, which has led to a worldwide success.

The marketing success of anti-animal testing

In 1976, Anita Roddick sets up a cosmetics company in London. The unique selling point has always been that it supplies cosmetic products while at the same time showing a strongly embedded moral awareness. The Body Shop was one of the first cosmetics companies that fundamentally opposed to animal testing, and therefore would only sell products that were not tested on animals. In addition, the company has always been very active in the field of human rights and environmental protection. The company tries to establish partnerships and is campaigning in this field to contribute to these goals. For these reasons, the Body Shop commits itself: ...*to enrich, not exploit. For us, this means enriching people as well as our planet, its biodiversity and resources. We are committed to working fairly with our farmers and suppliers and helping communities to thrive. Our products enrich, but never make false promises and are never tested on animals. We are proud to be original, irreverent and campaign for what's right; together we can do it.* (www.thebodyshop.com, 2017). This also appeals to the consumer, which is illustrated by the fact that in 2017 the Body Shop is a worldwide brand with more than 3000 establishments in more than 65 countries, and proud winner of the 'business in the community international responsible business of the year' award twice.

We could also consider 'business ethics' as a behavioural study, rather than an ethics discipline, as Crane & Matten seem to suggest (2010). They define business ethics as 'the study of business situations, activities, and decisions where issues of right and wrong are addressed.' This approach would most certainly result in a very interesting perspective, but it is not the approach in this book. As we have seen, the purpose of this book is to structurally analyse and evaluate morality in the context of professionals working in economic professions.

Summary

▶ Ethics is an academic discipline that structurally analyses and evaluates morality. Morality is someone's perception in what is right, and is the combination of norms and values someone seeks to realize.
  • A value is the ultimate goal we seek to achieve by acting in compliance with a norm.
  • A norm is a rule that contributes to the realization of a value.

▶ Norms can be divided into:
  • individual and collective norms (some are even considered to be universal)
  • religious and cultural norms
  • written and unwritten norms

▶ Values can be subdivided in:
  • terminal values, which are essential in life
  • instrumental values, that help us achieving the terminal values

▶ In realizing norms and values, virtue and interest play an important role:
  • A virtue is a certain characteristic that is required to successfully comply with a norm.
  • Our interest is the combination of tangible and intangible things we use to comply with a norm.

▶ We structurally *analyse* morality by using a comparative method: functionalism.
  • Functionalism is the comparison of different solutions to the same problem on the basis of functional equivalence.
  • A functional comparison consists of three steps:
    – determine the moral question
    – map the various ethical viewpoints/answers to this question (norms)
    – explain the selected norms by narrowing them down to values

▶ We can structurally *evaluate* by carefully making a well-informed decision on which ethical viewpoint is to be chosen above all others.

▶ Ethics is closely related to other academic disciplines. It can *deepen* a debate when you explore different viewpoints within an academic discipline, while it can *broaden* this debate when you consider things from various academic disciplines. That is, as long as there is no confusion about which viewpoint comes from which discipline.

- An academic perspective is an approach towards a certain situation exclusively from the perspective of that discipline.
- A viewpoint is a particular opinion within an academic discipline.

▶ In law we ask ourselves the question whether something is legal.
- Law should achieve justice, opportuneness and legal certainty.

▶ In theology we critically analyse and evaluate the nature of the divine.

▶ In psychology we seek to understand and explain human behaviour.

▶ In sociology we seek to understand and explain social relations.

▶ In the economic discipline we seek to explain – and sometimes even predict – how our economy works. The economic discipline can be divided in:
- Macroeconomics, in which we study the economy on a national or international level
- Microeconomics, in which we study economic behaviour of individuals and organizations
- Business administration, in which we study the functioning of companies and contribute to making companies more efficient and profitable

▶ The academic area where economics and ethics are linked is sometimes referred to as business ethics.
- Where in ethics in business we ask the question what is morally correct in our economic behaviour, in business ethics we ask the question how we can make profit in doing the right thing.

Literature

Agnus Reid Global Monitor (2006). *Chileans slowly becoming more liberal.* Agnus Reid.

Amnesty International. (2013). *Bath information, oil spill investigations in the Niger Delta.* Amnesty International Publications.

Breda, J., Whiting, S., Encarnação, R., Norberg, N., Jones, R., Reinap, M. & Jewell, J. (2014). Energy drink consumption in Europe: a review of the risks, adverse health effects, and policy options to respond. Front. *Public Health* 2:134. 14 October 2014.

Collins, J.W. (1994). *Is business ethics an oxymoron?* Business Horizons, Vol. 37, Issue 5.

Crane, W., & Matten, D. (2010). *Business ethics* (3rd edition). Oxford: Oxford University Press.

Donleavy, D., Lam, K. & Ho, S. (2008). Does east meets west in business ethics: an introduction to the special issue. *Journal of Business Ethics* (2008) 79:1–8.

Griseri, P., & Seppala, N. (2010). *Business ethics and corporate social responsibility.* Hampshire: Cengage Learning.

Habermas, J. (1992). *Faktizität und Geltung: Beiträge zur Diskurstheorie des Right und des demokratischen Right Heads.* Frankfurt: Suhrkamp.

Hakker, B. (2016). Het juiste DNA voor de job. *Intermediair magazine.* Vol. 23.

Javidan, M. & Carle D. (2004). East meets West: a cross cultural comparison of charismatic leadership amongst Canadian and Iranian executives. *Journal of management studies,* 41:4 June 2004.

Keith, G. & Iain, W. (1993). Multiple interpretations of the Rokeach value servey. *Journal of Social Psychology,* December 1993, Vol. 133 Issue 6, p. 797 - 805.

Mansfield-Devine, S. (2015). The Ashley Medison Affair. *Network security,* volume September 2015, issue 9, pages 8-16.

Rokeach, M. (1973). *The nature of human values.* New York: Free Press.

Rokeach, M. (1979). From individual to institutional values. In: *Understanding human values, individual and societal.* New York: Free Press.

Schram, E. (2014). 'Peace Negotiations' between Shell and villagers Niger Delta. *One World #5.*

Shah, R. (2004). What a fine mess! Moving beyond simple puzzle-solving for sustainable development. In: A. Henriques & J. Richardson (Red), *The Triple Bottom Line, does it all add up? Assessing the sustainability of business and CSR* (pp. 89-98). London: Earth Scan, UK edition.

Shell. (2013). *Shell in Nigeria, oil theft, tamper and spill.* Shell.

Shell. (2014). *Shell General Business Principles.* Shell International Limited.

Sloman, J., & Wride, A. (2009). *Economics* (7th edition). Harlow: Pearson Prentice Hall.

Stiles, J. (2011). Brain development and the nature versus nurture debate. *Progress in Brain Research,* Vol. 189, 3-22.

The UN Committee on the rights of the child. (2014, 25 February). *Concluding observations carriage on the second report of the Holy See,* CRC/C/barrel/CO/2, para. 56-57.

The UN General Assembly. (1948, 10 December). *The Universal Declaration of Human Rights,* GA resolution 217 A.

Waldt, D. der., du Toit, L., & Speech Handling Huys, R. (2007). Does branded product placement in film enhance realism and product recognition by consumers? *African Journal of Business Management*, May, 19-25.
Wernaart, B. (2013). Methods. In: *The human right to adequate food, a comparative study*. Wageningen: Wageningen Academic Publishers.

Media
Baraniuk, C. (2015, 24 August). Ashley Madison: 'Suicides' over website hack. *BBC news*.
Benke, E. (2016, 28 October). The Poles looking to leave the UK after Brexit. *BBC news*.
Editorial Board. (2017, 13 January) Charges have been dropped against a Miami man accused of trying to abduct young girls. *CBS Miami*.
FIFA, press release (2014, 24 June). Luis Suárez suspended for nine matches and banned for four months from any football-related activity. Retrieved from *www.FIFA.com*.
FIFA, press release (2014, 14 August). FIFA statement on CAS decision relating to Luis Suarez. Retrieved from *www.FIFA.com*.
Kuchler, H. (2016, 14 December). Ashley Madison agrees $1.6m fine for data breach. *The Financial Times*.
Nichols, M. (2008, 15 May). 'Sex and the City' film a marketing dream. *Reuters*.
Rosenberg, M. (2017, 24 March). Virginia court rules for Trump in travel ban dispute, order still halted. *Reuters*.
Weber, J. (2017, 30 January). 'This Is Not a Muslim Ban': Trump Defends Refugee Program Suspension, Temporary Immigration Ban, Says Top Priority Is To 'Protect and Serve' America. *Foxnews*.

Court cases
District Court of The Hague, 30 January 2013, JOR 2013/162, JONDR 2013/651.
United States Courts of Appeals for the Ninth Circuit, 7 February 2017, Trump v. State of Washington & State of Minnesota.

Websites
www.ashleymadison.com
http://energydrink-us.redbull.com
www.shell.com
www.thebodyshop.com
www.power center.nl

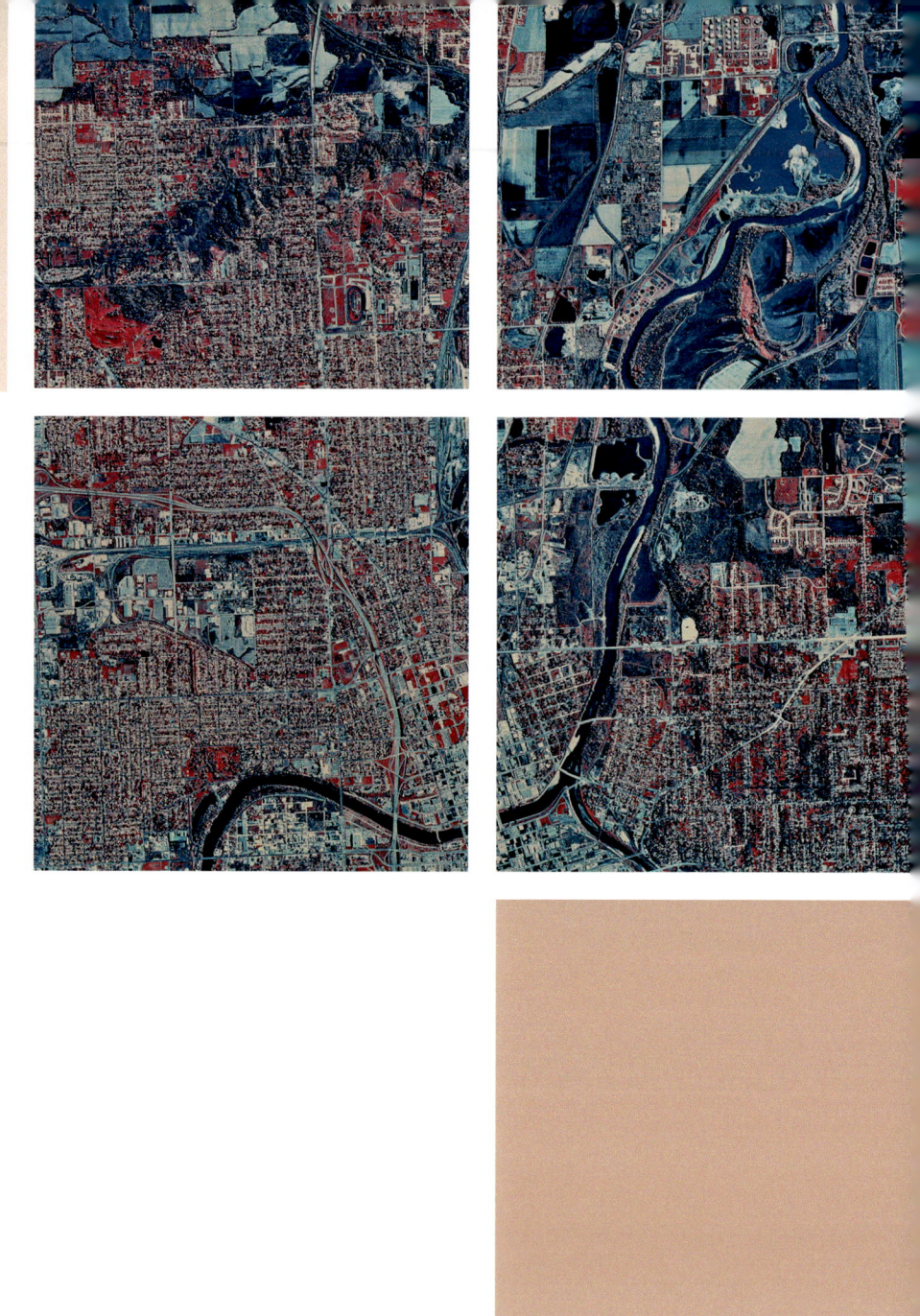

2

Responsibility

2

2.1   **The meaning of responsibility**
2.2   **The ability to take responsibility**
2.3   **Situational factors that influence responsibility**

Discussions in ethics usually emerge when there is a clash of norms and values. When there is such a conflict, we usually address the issue of responsibility. After all, in the pursuit of a certain value, we might stand in the way of other values. The question is then to what extent we feel responsible for the other value we seem to harm, in realizing the first. In this chapter we discuss the various factors that may influence this sense of responsibility in case of conflicting norms and values. These factors are on the one hand factors that affect the ability of taking responsibility, and on the other hand factors that relate to the specific situation of the conflicting values.

2.1 The meaning of responsibility

In the previous chapter we saw that a norm is a way to realize a value. Such a norm is expressed in certain behaviour. When this behaviour does not stand in the way of other norms and values, there will usually not be much of a discussion. However, when it does stand in the way, we are confronted with the moral question to what extent we should take the norms and values we harm as a result of our behaviour into consideration. Phrased differently: to what extent do we feel responsible for other norms and values than the ones we seek to realize?

Responsibility | Responsibility is the way people take conflicting norms and values into consideration.

As you can see in the example 'sipping wine on a beautiful summer day', the norm (sip a glass of wine) in order to realize the values 'pleasure' and/or 'comfortable life' may stand in the way of other norms and values, such as 'safety' of traffic participants, or 'wisdom' and 'intellect' of my students. These norms and values are not necessarily of importance to others, but could also be in conflict with your own morality. Think about the case in which drinking becomes a habit and therefore it stands in the way of my own value 'health'. In case of conflicting norms and values, the issue of responsibility usually pops up. The question to what extent we feel responsible for these conflicting norms and values is influenced by several factors. These factors may relate to the ability of taking responsibility, or are situational factors (figure 2.1):

FIGURE 2.1 Factors that affect responsibility

It is important to point out here that these factors are not laws of nature, but general factors that *may* affect your decisions in ethics. It is however important to recognize such factors and reflect on them, which is exactly the purpose of this chapter.

Sipping wine on a beautiful summer day

In most situations, there will be no problem when I have a cool glass of dry white wine on a sunny summer afternoon, enjoying the view of my garden. In such a situation, the norm 'drink a glass of wine' probably contributes to the values 'pleasure' and 'a comfortable life'.

So far so good. However, things will probably be different when after consuming an entire bottle I step in my car and drive to visit a friend. People around me will hopefully urgently appeal to my sense of responsibility, and ask me not to participate in traffic after drinking a bottle of wine. After all, driving a car in these circumstances will interfere with the value 'safety', not only as a value to other traffic participants but also for myself. Or how about I drink an entire bottle of dry white wine, and then start grading exams of my students. They will most likely feel neglected, or not taken seriously. I may interfere with their values 'intellect' or 'wisdom', since their grading is bias. They will most likely demand a second opinion, and appeal to my sense of responsibility and grade them when I'm sober.

Perhaps I drink this bottle of wine every day and preferably before 10 am. My family will then hopefully emphasize my responsibility towards myself and my own health. After all, I seriously endanger the value 'health' and choose above all else 'pleasure'.

2.2 The ability to take responsibility

Even if we want it, we are not always in a position to take responsibility. To be able to do so, a person must have the necessary kind of freedom, knowledge and conscience. These three prerequisites will affect the way someone is able to express his sense of responsibility.

2.2.1 Freedom

In order to be able to take a certain responsibility a person should have the freedom to do that. That sounds obvious at first, but it is a bit more complicated when we reflect on the exact meaning of the world 'freedom'. Freedom can be understood as physical freedom and autonomy. Both affect the way in which a person may take responsibility.

Physical freedom

In order to be able to take responsibility you will need to have a certain degree of physical freedom.

> Physical freedom is the extent to which an individual is physically able to give expression to his sense of responsibility.

Physical freedom

Harry Potter and the Deathly Hallows

In the last book of the well-known Potter series, Harry, Ron and Hermione are kidnapped by Death Eaters and taken to the house of evil Malfidus. There, Harry and Ron are stripped of their magic wands and detained in a cellar. In the meantime, they hear Hermione being tortured in the living room by Bella Lestrange to get more information about the so-called Horcruxes. Harry and Ron have no other choice than to sit and hear Hermione scream.

In the example of Harry Potter, you would expect Harry, and perhaps even the clumsy Ron, to perform their role as wizard hero. However, our heroes are simply denied any form of physical freedom to save Hermione. Their lack of physical freedom withholds them from taking the responsibility they had in mind. They could not comply with the norm 'help a friend in need', which clashes with the norms and values of Hermoine at that moment: she wanted to 'stay in one piece' and/or 'not give any information'.

Autonomy

In addition to physical freedom you will also need to have a certain degree of autonomy in order to be able to take responsibility.

Autonomy

> Autonomy is the extent to which an individual is able to have a free will to express his sense of responsibility.

A 'free will' sounds great, but is a rather difficult concept to grasp, and is understood rather differently in various regions of the world. The political philosopher Isaiah Berlin gives us some tools to further explore its meaning, and makes a distinction between negative and positive freedom (Berlin, 1996).

Negative freedom

> Negative freedom means that everyone is free to do whatever he wants without interference.

Positive freedom

> Positive freedom means that someone has the possibility to give direction to his life as a result of interference.

Please note that the words 'negative' and 'positive' are not a value judgment. In this context, the word 'negative' means the absence of interference, where 'positive' implies the presence interference. Having a free will probably requires a bit of both: on the one hand we need to be respected in our pursuit of our norms and values, without too much pressure from the outside world so we can act as true autonomous human beings. On the other hand, if no one ever interferes in our lives and helps us to see things from different perspectives, or teaches us in how we can lead a better, healthier and more fruitful life, we will most likely fail in this pursuit, because we simply do not know what norms and values are worth striving for.

This last thought is reflected in the case 'super nanny': you can see that Jo Frost interferes in the life of the child and consequentially prevents the child to do exactly what it wants. This is a typical example of 'positive freedom'. It is usually accepted that a parent or someone else in a pedagogic relationship with the child (for example a teacher) interferes in the life of a child. The reason that someone is raising a child and so occasionally interferes in its life, is that the child will be able to better direct this life in the long term, be economically more independent, and is better able to maintain social relations.

Super Nanny

The television series *Super Nanny* was aired in the UK and US from 2004 to 2012 and later spin-offs were produced in other countries as well (www.jofrost.com). Jo Frost, a pedagogue, visits families in which the parents are unable to handle a child that is seemingly out of control. During the show, Jo gives parenting advise. One of her famous methods is called 'the naughty step'. A particular spot in the house (for instance, the lower bars of the stairs) are designated as a 'naughty step'. When the naughty child does not listen, she gives him a warning first, and informs him about the consequences of misbehaving again. When the child does not listen for the second time, it is punished by sending him to the 'naughty step' for several minutes, so that he can reflect on his behaviour. In the series, this approach appears to work very well, and – together with some other parenting tricks – results in better behaviour of the child. However, it needs to be noted here that not all pedagogues approval of the idea of using punishment as a systematic tool in parenting (Spungin, 2011).

Baby smuggler

Marisa Merico is a young woman who grew up in the Italian Mafia circuit. As a child she was raised by her drugs-smuggling father. Her buggy was frequently used as a hiding place for the stuff her daddy would sell, and she was more than once used as a way of distracting customs officers during border controls. After all, who would suspect drugs on board of the cradle of a newborn? When Marisa is twenty years old she marries a certain Bruno, also a Mafioso. Not surprisingly, she is engaged in criminal activities for years, and is particularly involved in money laundering. She often smuggles drugs money abroad, to put that on a foreign bank account.

Marisa can afford to live a luxury life with bodyguards, expensive gadgets, fashion, and many chic cars. When both her father and husband were caught in a drug deal gone wrong, ending up in prison, she becomes the head of the family, and continues their family business. History seems to repeat itself, since Marisa uses her own newborn the same way she was used by her father: as a distraction in smuggling drugs and drug money. In the end, also Marisa ends up in prison, and there she has some time to reflect on her life. She regrets that as a result of her penalty, she will miss the major part of her daughter's childhood. After her release, she managed to escape the criminal circuit, and moved to England with her daughter. When she looks back at her criminal life, she does not blame her father: *'he did not know better, it was his way of life, since he grew up in the Mafia circuit and could not think of any other way of making a living. Pretty much the same as when I grew up'* (*Grazia*, beauty special 2014).

When there is a misbalance between negative or positive freedom, this most certainly has a significant effect on how an individual is able to take a certain responsibility. For instance, when a child is brought up in accepting (and even expressing) certain behaviour over and over again, the child will see this behaviour as very normal, as we saw 'baby smuggler' case. In this case, the family of Marissa raised her in such a way that it almost seems natural that she becomes a Mafioso as well. While she may have had the physical freedom to lead a more honest life, we can ask ourselves the question whether she would have the necessary autonomy to get rid of her family's lifestyle. It seems that she almost had 'no choice' but to end up as a criminal. In this case we could say that if there would have been more negative freedom during her childhood, instead of her family making her part of criminal activities since being a newborn, she might have taken another direction in life. The fact that she does not blame her father, since he grew up in the mafia circuit as well shows that she does not hold him responsible for this as a result of his childhood. In other words, she seems to accept that the lack of negative freedom and the emphasis on positive freedom reduced her father's autonomy to take responsibility towards her.

Therefore, taking into account our individual backgrounds, the balance of positive and negative freedom influences our autonomy. Also on a larger

Political families

scale, this balance is of great importance. The way a state is governed for instance will affect the way its citizens can be free of mind and act autonomously. However, in politics there are different opinions about how exactly we should establish this balance between negative and positive freedom, as we can see in figure 2.2. Traditionally, right-winged parties usually prefer a government that does not interfere too much in the lives of its citizens. In other words, these parties put more emphasis on negative freedom. On the other hand we have the left wing parties that put more emphasis on government interference in order to create a more desirable and a fairer society. In their view, citizens need a little help in order to be able to pursue their own values, and so they emphasize positive freedom.

FIGURE 2.2 Positive and negative freedom and political families

America: the land of the free and home of the brave

In the U.S., presidential elections are held every four years. This usually results in a campaign in which two parties (the Republicans and the Democrats) nominate a candidate to run for president. During this campaign, the differences in ideology between these parties become very visible, which is particularly demonstrated in two recurring debates: the way healthcare should be organized and the right to bear arms.

In 2013, President Obama – a Democrat – introduced the affordable healthcare act, also called 'Obamacare'. From 1 October 2013, each American was obliged to have health insurance. The motivation of Obama and his supporters is that in many cases the absence of health care insurance could lead to undesirable situations. Earlier, it frequently happened that someone who was very ill could not be properly treated for the simple reason that the individual was not insured. This happened to mostly poor Americans, who could not afford such insurances. By obligating its citizens to have healthcare

insurance, and where needed partly cover the costs, the government actively interferes in the lives of Americans. The Republicans traditionally reject such governmental interference. They hold that this is an undesirable patronizing way of governing, and interferes with the freedom of American citizens to decide how to spend their money. After all, people are very well capable of deciding whether they want to purchase health care insurance, and if so, what kind of insurance suits them best. They don't need a government taking that decision for them.

The other discussion relates to a Constitutional right of the U.S. citizens: the right to bear arms. The Second Amendment to the Constitution of the USA stipulates that: '*a well regulated Militia, being necessary to the security of a free State, the right of the people to keep and bear arms shall not be infringed.*' Each time someone abuses this right – for instance during a so-called school shooting – a debate on the desirability of this right emerges in American politics. On the one hand we have the Democrats, who suggest that this right should be at least restricted so that not every evil person can get a gun just like that, and commit atrocities at will. This requires governmental interference to create a situation in which people can live in freedom. The Republicans on the other hand claim that every person is entitled to defend himself and his loved ones, and should therefore be able to choose to buy guns. In this line, the executive vice president of the National Rifle Association (NRA) Wayne LaPierre argued after a school-shooting in Newton (2012) that: 'the only way to stop a bad guy with a gun is a good guy with a gun.'

2

In the example 'America: the land of the free and home of the brave' we see that the Democrats are a bigger fan of governmental interference compared to the Republicans when it comes to the debate on healthcare and the right to bear arms. On the contrary, the Republicans prefer the government not to interfere, and allow the citizens to make their own decisions in these matters. In other words: the Democrats are a bit more on the positive freedom side, where the Republicans prefer the negative freedom.

This being said, when a government disproportionally favours one version of freedom over the other, we usually see a misbalance and as a result a society we would not want to live in. In the example of Cambodia you see the consequences of extreme ideas on positive freedom, in which the government assumed to be able to create a perfect society in which all is decided for its citizens. In the example of Libya we see the contrary: a society without any effective governmental supervision, resulting in a society in which every individual can do whatever he pleases, without being limited. In both cases we see that this misbalance has a strong and negative effect on the autonomy of its citizens.

The killing fields of Cambodia

The communist Khmer Rouge ruled Cambodia between 1975 and 1979, with what you could call a true reign of terror. Their goal was to create a full communist state in which farm life was embraced and glorified. This Khmer Rouge, under the leadership of Pol Pot, tried to create this society by forcing people to live in a particular manner. Citizens were forced into labour camps and work as farmers in the countryside as equal brothers. Money was abolished: that was not necessary in a self-sufficing agrarian society. To make sure there would be enough descendants to sustain this society, the farmers were married off in forced marriages with random partners in massive ceremonies. These couples were then supposed to make babies as soon as possible. All intellectuals, or anyone who would even slightly appear to be of any intellect by using goggles, were sentenced to death in horrific massacres. The same fate followed for anyone who would even slightly appear to question this regime. All in all this has led to a mass slaughter in which an estimated one quarter of the population was killed.

This way of governance is an expression of extreme positive freedom. Until today, the reign of the Khmer Rouge is a very sensitive issue in Cambodia. In the current government, former Khmer Rouge members are still in office, and the former leaders were hardly punished for their crimes. In fact, some even openly defend what happened in the past. For instance, Im Chem – who had senior rank within the Khmer Rouge – argued on the day that two of her old comrades were tried: 'At the time we tried to protect our country. We tried to help the people to be happy. (…) I just urged people to do farming.' (*Phnom Penh Post*, 9 August 2014).

Anarchy in Libya

For a very long time, Colonel Gaddafi ruled Libya with an iron fist. During his reign, he acted as an absolute ruler. He named his political ideas 'Islamic socialism', and so put an extreme emphasis on positive freedom. Many consider Gaddafi a dictator. His leadership came to an abrupt end during the Arab Spring in 2011 when various groups in Libyan society rebelled against him and overthrew his regime. During this civil war, Gaddafi was killed. In the aftermath of this power struggle, a central government was installed, but quickly lost effective control of the country. The different groups that rebelled against Gaddafi now turned against each other, which resulted in regional power fractions of which even the notorious Islamic State took a portion. In this complete absence of any authority, an opposite situation emerged compared to the Gaddafi reign. From a centrally led totalitarian regime the country turned into complete anarchy, without any effective governance. De facto, we must conclude that this is an extreme manifestation of negative freedom.

2.2.2   Knowledge

In order to take a certain responsibility, it is required that someone understands what is going on. They need to be aware of the relevant facts to form an opinion on what is ethical to do. When there is a lack of such knowledge, it will be hard to feel responsible for any conflicting norms and values. Nevertheless, it is important to notice that in some positions, people are expected to be knowledgeable of certain facts, even if they are not.

> In a case of conflicting morals, knowledge about relevant facts is required or expected to take a certain responsibility.

Firstly, this means that in normal situations the way a person takes responsibility may depend on the knowledge of the case, as we can see in the Kidnapping in Cleveland example.

Kidnapping in Cleveland

No one blamed Charles Ramsey for not acting earlier when he liberated three women from the basement of his neighbour's house in Cleveland, USA. In a TV interview, which went viral, he told his side of the story. One day, he noticed a screaming girl trying to escape his neighbour's house. He offered his help immediately, and found out there were three women hidden in the basement of this house who had been missing for over three years. All this time, they had been kidnapped by his neighbour. He was asked how it was possible that he did not figure out earlier that they were trapped in the house next door. He answered: *'(…)I've barbecued with this dude! We eat ribs and what not, and listened to salsa! (…) Not a clue that the girl was in that house – or anybody else was in there against their will, because of who he is. He just comes out his back yard, plays with the dogs, with potters with his cars and motor cycles and goes back in the house. So he's somebody that you look at and look away because he's not doing nothing but the average stuff. You see what I'm saying? Ain't nothing exciting about him. Well… until today! (…) Bro, I knew something was wrong when a little white girl ran into a black man's arms. Something is wrong here. Dead giveaway. 'cause either she's homeless, or she's got problems (…)'*

Between the lines you can read that of course, Charles would have acted earlier if he would have known that these women were trapped in his neighbour's basement. Without this knowledge, it was impossible for him to take the responsibility towards these women he would have taken with that knowledge.

However, sometimes a person has a certain role or finds himself in a particular situation in which knowledge of certain facts is expected, even if it seems (nearly) impossible. In other words, the one who is expected to be knowledgeable of relevant facts cannot get away with the excuse that he did not, or could not know. It is – so to say – part of the job to know. In the newspaper article about BBC director Entwistle we see a director who was only in charge for two months. He resigned due to the fact that he felt responsible for the content of a documentary that was produced before he got the job, and a scandal that dates back decades before his appointment. It is very doubtful whether mister Entwistle could possibly know all the relevant facts in this context, but still 'takes' his responsibility and resigns. After all, when you are a director general, you are supposed to know such things, even when this is hardly possible, or very difficult. We could say that with power comes responsibility, even without knowing it.

BBC NEWS, 11 NOVEMBER 2012

George Entwistle resigns as BBC director general

The BBC's director general, George Entwistle, has resigned in the wake of the Newsnight child abuse broadcast.

He said that as the man 'ultimately responsible for all content, and in the light of the unacceptable journalistic standards' he would quit.

Mr Entwistle had admitted Newsnight's report, which led to Thatcher-era Tory Lord McAlpine being wrongly implicated, should not have been aired.

The broadcast covered cases of child abuse at north Wales care homes.

BBC Trust chairman Lord Patten, who appeared alongside Mr Entwistle when he delivered his statement, will answer questions on the BBC's Andrew Marr programme on Sunday morning.

Mr Entwistle took up the post of director general on 17 September, and his sudden resignation makes him the shortest serving BBC director general.

In his statement, he said: 'In the light of the fact that the director general is also the editor-in-chief and ultimately responsible for all content, and in the light of the

unacceptable journalistic standards of the Newsnight film broadcast on Friday 2 November, I have decided that the honourable thing to do is to step down from the post of director general.'
(...)
On top of the Jimmy Savile crisis, which was prompted partly by the fact that Newsnight had shelved an earlier investigation into allegations of child abuse, this was particularly damaging to the BBC.
(...)
During his 54 days in charge, Mr Entwistle has also had to deal with controversy over the BBC shelving a Newsnight investigation into former BBC presenter and DJ Jimmy Savile, who police say could have abused as many as 300 people over a 40-year-period.

As a result, an inquiry is examining whether there were BBC management failings surrounding the Newsnight's Savile programme not being broadcast, and another inquiry is diving into the culture and practices at the BBC in the era of alleged sexual abuse by Savile. Sexual harassment policies at the BBC are also being reviewed.
Mr Entwistle's resignation came after he was criticised for his performance during an interview on the BBC's Radio 4 Today programme on Saturday, in which he admitted he had not read a newspaper article revealing the case of mistaken identity involving Lord McAlpine, and that he had not seen the Newsnight broadcast when it aired on 2 November as he 'was out.'

2.2.3   Conscience

A third factor that influences the way in which a person may take responsibility is to what degree someone has a conscience.

Conscience

> Conscience is the psychological ability to develop ethical awareness.

Normally, we assume that every person has a conscious mind in some shape of form, and is therefore able to take a certain responsibility in case of conflicting morality. While the manifestation of that responsibility may greatly differ, it is a result of a conscious consideration, in which an ethical choice was made to take (or not take) a certain responsibility. However, we assume that some people lack a conscious mind, or do not just jet have a conscience. This is usually the case with minors and people with a mental disorder.

THE NEWS NERD, 1 JULY 2014

8-Year-Old Boy Robs Bank with iPad and Gets Away

SOUTH PLAINFIELD – Authorities in South Plainfield, New Jersey are on the hunt for an 8-year-old boy who allegedly robbed a bank with nothing more than an iPad.

The police department says the incident occurred shortly after 12:00 PM Wednesday at the Greater Plainfield Bank & Trust on Harrison Avenue, just north of I-287. Officers quickly arrived at the scene after receiving a phone call from the head of security, alerting them of what he initially mistook as a practical joke, but ended up being a real robbery.

Upon arrival, officers were told by the staff that the child calmly walked up to one of the tellers, handed the unnamed teller an iPad with a typed message that read *'giv me all of th money i hav a gun n my bookbag'*, and fled the building on a motorized scooter with approximately $12,000 dollars in his possession.

The 8-year-old suspect was described as an African-American boy of around 4'3", wearing blue jean shorts and a bright red t-shirt with the words *'TURN DOWN 4 WHAT?'* printed across the front.

Security camera footage showed the boy leaving on the scooter heading west with the bag of money over his shoulder. No witnesses other than the staff were on hand during the time of the crime.

The investigation is ongoing, with police hopeful to find the boy by the end of the day.

Considering the case of the 8-year-old boy robbing a bank, we usually assume that the child does not yet have a fully developed conscious mind, and as a result is unable to take responsibilities comparable to an adult. If the child would have been 24 years old instead, he would face a serious prison sentence, while in this case, the kid will most likely remain a free man (although probably the police will have a very serious chat with his parents).

A difficult issue here is the mental illness. Some people commit atrocious acts we find so offensive that we cannot imagine a sane person would do this. Think about child abuse, violent killing, or human trafficking. When we accept that those who are able to do such things are per definition mentally ill, we also say that they cannot feel the responsibility we would expect a human being to express. In our perception of the meaning of conscience, we must find a careful balance in when we consider someone to consciously act and when not. If it is the first, he is supposed to be responsible for his actions, while if it is the last, he cannot.

2.3 Situational factors that influence responsibility

In the previous section we discussed factors that influence the way we are able to express our sense of responsibility. These factors usually do not always change per situation but are more permanently apparent. In this section we will explore various factors that influence to what degree and towards whom we feel responsible in a given situation. These factors are different all the time, and greatly determine the exact way in which we express our sense of responsibility. In other words: in the previous section we explored factors that influence our ability to take responsibility, where in this section, we discuss situational factors that affect the degree in which we take responsibility.

In this context, four factors play a role:
1   The influence you can have on a situation
2   The causality between you and those who are involved
3   The impact you can have on the situation
4   The relationship you have with those who are involved

It is important to note here that taking a certain responsibility does not automatically imply action, but could also mean that you withhold yourself from acting. In the example 'Topless Kate Middleton' you see a situation in which the Royal Family would have wished that the French photographer would not take the disputed pictures. Taking responsibility here would mean not doing something, instead of acting.

Topless Kate Middleton

In 2012, a paparazzi photographer managed to capture the British crown prince William together with his wife Kate Middleton while they were sunbathing in private. The royal couple was on holiday in the French Provence-Alpes-Cote d'Azur and spent some time on the estate of a family member. A detail worth mentioning is that Kate at that moment was enjoying the sun topless. Although the British media collectively felt that the media would cross a line when publishing these photos, the French tabloid *Closer* decided to publish the scene on their front page. The royal couple was furious, and responded that *'Their Royal Highnesses have been hugely saddened to learn that a French publication and a photographer have invaded their privacy in such a grotesque and totally unjustifiable manner. (…)Their Royal Highnesses had every expectation of privacy in the remote house. It is unthinkable that anyone should take such photographs, let alone publish them.'* The French tabloid, however, released a statement in which they argued that these photos were taken from a public road, and could therefore never be an infringement of the right to privacy. Furthermore, Laurence Pieau, the editor of the magazine, held that *'these photos are not in the least shocking. They show a young woman sunbathing topless, like the millions of women you see on beaches'* (Jones, 2012).

As a direct result of this incident, a wide debate took place concerning the responsibilities of tabloids towards the right to privacy of celebrities. At the core of this discussion was the balance of interest between the freedom of the press publishing things with news value, and the right to privacy of those who are subject of this news. In other words: in what situations should the editor of a tabloid take his responsibility and withhold himself from publishing material that reveals the private life of a celebrity, and in what situations will the freedom of the press prevail?

2.3.1   Influence

Influence | Influence is the extent to which a person's actions (or absence of such actions) can change a certain situation.

We may generally assume that when someone has more influence on a situation that the person's sense of responsibility will probably increase. The influence you have in a certain situation may change per second, but can also be slightly more stable.

'If you want new clothes, you want them to be pretty and affordable'

In April 2013, the Rana Plaza building in Bangladesh collapses, resulting in the unfortunate deaths of over a thousand factory employees, who worked there under very poor labour conditions. It turns out that the collapse was caused by the fact that several floors were added to the building illegally. To make matters worse, very heavy machinery was put on those floors. This garment factory supplied some famous western garment brands, including the Irish based Primark (www.primark.com). Shortly after the disaster, a Dutch newspaper interviewed with a selection of consumers in a Primark store who were asked whether they would change their buying behaviour as a result of the disaster (Van Weezel, 2013).

In general, the interviewees were aware of the disaster and felt saddened about it, but were not planning to change their buying behaviour. For instance, one of the respondents said 'we shop at Primark once every two weeks. We like the clothes and they are very cheap. I did not realize there were so many casualties in that collapse. But even if I would have known the exact number, I would still buy at this place. After all, if you want new clothes, you want them to be pretty and affordable. That is what they have right here!'. Another customer argued that 'it makes no sense to stop buying clothes. If we would do that, they would make no money at all!' Another interviewee claimed that she 'heard about the disaster in Bangladesh, and when I buy these cheap clothes I indeed think about the situation of the employees out there. But let other people take care of these employees: I am involved with the protection of stray animals in Spain. Besides, it could cause a serious problem if these people in Bangladesh would earn more money: they might start eating more meat, which is really bad. Perhaps this sounds cynical, but this is how I see it'.

When such disasters happen as portrayed in the Primark example, we usually see a revival in the debate whether the consumer can or should boycott brands that use employees in developing countries who work for them under inhumane conditions. Elsewhere in this book we will address this debate from a more academic perspective (especially in sections 9.5.3 and 12.3.1). For now, we will argue, rather pessimistically, that consumers will hardly have any influence on the inhumane conditions of the Bangladeshi employees. Let it be noted here that there can also be more optimistic views in this context.

Suppose that you are an ethically concerned consumer, and you feel committed to the fate of these workers, how could you contribute in improving their living conditions? A much suggested approach would be to simply boycott the stores of the companies that allow these poor conditions to exist. On the other hand, this consumer may rightfully doubt whether his boycott will truly change anything. After all, companies such as Primark a so popular, people sometimes have to queue up before entering one of their stores. A boycott will therefore only have any significance when it is widely embraced by a lot of consumers. In other words: one customer will have a very limited influence on that situation.

And even if a large group of consumers would succeed in establishing a wide boycott against one of these companies, would that then lead to the desired results? Perhaps the company will listen and actively start improving the working conditions of the employees of their supplier. However, if that would lead to a higher cost price of their products, the business might lose its comparative strength and in the end will have to withdraw from its activities in the developing country. This might lead to more unemployment amongst those you desire to help, as one of the interviewees also seems to suggest. So again here we could ask ourselves the question to what extent a consumer can make a difference here in using his influence.

In the Primark case, we see an obvious clash between the norms and values of the Dutch consumers (buy cheap and good looking clothes in the realization of the value beauty) and the employees in Bangladesh (work in a good working environment in order to realize the value welfare, safety and health). As we suggested above, due to the factor *influence* – which is very limited – there might be a small chance that the Dutch consumers will feel responsible to do something about the values of the Bangladeshi employees.

2.3.2   Causality

Causality

> Causality is the directness in the relation between your actions (or absence of actions) and those who are involved in a given situation.

In short, the greater the distance between your action and those who are involved, the less responsible you will feel towards them. Or, in reverse, the closer those who are involved get, the more responsible you will feel.

The Primark case offers us a good example of this factor. When you read between the lines of those who were interviewed, we see a certain lack of attention of what actually happened out there at the other side of the world. When you really consider it sad that so many people died, but hey, you want some good looking and cheap clothes, then apparently those who suffer are truly too far away from you to feel responsible for them. However, imagine what would have happened if the Rana Plaza would be located in the Netherlands. Most likely the response of the Dutch interviewees would be less indifferent, since the causality is much more direct.

2.3.3   Impact

Impact

> Impact is the seriousness of the consequences of an action (or the absence of an action) for those who are involved in a given situation.

In other words: the bigger the impact of your actions (or not acting) for someone who is involved, the more responsible you will probably feel towards them.

A baby on wheels

In a London subway station, a woman stalled a baby in a buggy at the bottom of the stairs near the metro railway. While she took the stairs up again to pick up another baby in another buggy, the first buggy was caught by the wind, and slowly rolled over towards the railway. When the woman came down the stairs again, she would find to her horror the first buggy down on the railway. She did not hesitate, and jumped after the buggy, and saved the child seconds before the metro would enter the station (*BBC News*, 2014).

When you find yourself at a London subway station, waiting for a metro, and someone accidentally drops her groceries on the railway, you would probably not easily be tempted to jump on the rails to secure the bag knowing that the metro could enter the station any moment. This might change when that someone does not drop her groceries, but her baby. It will be beyond doubt that the impact of a metro driving into a bag of groceries is not as big as a metro killing a baby. So, therefore, most likely the average bystander will feel more responsible in case of the baby that ends up on the railway compared to the groceries.

2.3.4 Relationship

> The relationship is the particular role you have towards those who are involved in a given situation.

Relationship

The specific role you have towards someone may change your perception of responsibility towards those who are involved, regardless the previous three factors (influence, causality and impact).
In case of the 'baby on wheels', it makes quite a difference when you are a random bystander or the mother of the baby that ends up at the railway. You will probably not assume a similar sense of responsibility towards the baby. Most likely, a random bystander will not risk his own life as quickly as the mother to save the baby. We might even expect the mother to sacrifice her own life to save the baby, which will not be expected as easily from the random bystander.

And what about the security officer, working at the subway station? It is his job to maintain a secure and safe environment at the subway. Perhaps this officer will feel more responsible towards the baby compared to the random bystander, as a result of his work role. When someone wears that uniform we may have different expectations regarding his sense of responsibility than when someone does not wear this uniform.

To sum it up: both the mother and the security officer will probably feel more responsible towards the baby as a result of their role towards the child. In case of the mother, this role is their family tie, where in case of the officer, this role stems from his profession.

Summary

▶ Responsibility is the way people take into consideration conflicting norms and values.

▶ Factors that affect a person's sense of responsibility are divided into:
  • factors that affect the ability to take responsibility
  • situational factors that affect responsibility

▶ Factors that affect the ability to take responsibility are:
  • freedom
  • knowledge
  • conscience

▶ *Freedom*:
  • Physical freedom is the extent to which an individual is physically able to give expression to his sense of responsibility.
  • Autonomy is the extent to which an individual is able to have a free will to express his sense of responsibility. This is divided into:
    – negative freedom, which means that everyone is free to do whatever he wants without interference
    – positive freedom, which means that someone has the possibility to give direction to his life as a result of interference
  Negative and positive freedom are two extremes on a gliding scale.
    – When there is a misbalance between negative and positive freedom, this usually results in less successful societies.
    – The right balance between negative and positive freedom is subject to different political opinions.

▶ *Knowledge* about relevant facts is required or expected to take a certain responsibility.

▶ *Conscience* is the psychological ability to develop ethical awareness. We assume that minors and people with a mental disorder may lack a conscience mind.

▶ Situational factors that affect responsibility are:
  • influence, which is the extent to which a person's actions (or absence of such actions) can change a certain situation
  • causality, which is the directness in the relation between your actions (or absence of actions) and those who are involved in a given situation

- impact, which is the seriousness of the consequences of an action (or the absence of an action) for those who are involved in a given situation
- relationship, which is the particular role you have towards those who are involved in a given situation

Literature

Berlin, I. (1996). *Two concepts of freedom* (Dutch translation). Amsterdam: Publisher Tree.

Spungin, P. (2011). *Childless parenting gurus*. Retrieved from http://drpatspungin.co.uk.

Media

Alam, J., & Hossain, F. (2013, 13 May). Bangladesh collapse search over; death toll 1,127. *The Associated Press.*

Editorial Board. (2014, 11 August). Child in buggy blown on to London Tube station tracks. *BBC News London.*

Editorial Board. (2012, 11 November). George Entwistle resigns as BBC director general. *BBC News.*

Gualtherie Van Weezel, T. (2013, 6 May). Zielig voor die mensen, maar ja... *de Volkskrant.*

Jones, T. (2012, 14 September). Royals launch legal action after topless Kate Middleton photographs in French Closer magazine. *The Independent.*

The news nerd staff. (2014, 1 July). 8-Year-Old Boy Robs Bank with iPad and Gets Away. *The News Nerd.*

Websites

www.jofrost.com

www.primark.com/nl/onze-ethiek

Interviews and speeches

Lapierre, W. (21 December 2012). *NRA Press Conference.*

3

Normative ethics

In the first chapter of this book we established that a norm is a way to realize a value. Acting in compliance with a norm therefore will result in acting (or not acting) from which the outside world may partly deduce someone's sense of morality. In chapter two we discussed that the compliance with your own norms and values might contradict the realization of someone else's norms and values. The word responsibility is then used to find out to what extent we feel responsible towards the conflicting moral.

Since the ancient Greek (and their colleagues in the near and far east), say roughly since 750 BC, philosophers try to answer the question on what norms and values are important to strive for, and in what way we should feel responsible for conflicting norms and values. Their philosophies do not analyse, but evaluate ethics: it prescribes how we should act. The fun fact is that these philosophers hardly agree with one another, and that has led to a varied landscape of different directions in normative ethics. In this chapter we will try to explore the most important ones. These directions may help us in developing our own morality, and we can learn from their strong points as well as their flaws.

⬤3.1 Directions in normative ethics

Normative ethics | In normative ethics we define when something is morally justified.

The word 'normative' means that these theories are not neutral, and instead advise us on what is morally right. We can distinguish two main approaches in normative ethics: ethics for people and ethics from people.

In ethics for people, theories on normative ethics advise us what is morally justified regardless of who uses it. In other words, the theory exists outside the scope of individuals and can be applied by anyone in any given situation. For instance, something is morally justified when it leads to the best outcome (consequentialism) or when we stick to certain principles (deontology). It does not matter what kind of a person applies those theories, since the way these forms of normative ethics are applied will not differ. That is why we choose to label these theories as ethics for people: the theories are rigid and exist regardless the personality of those who adhere to them.

This is different in the case of ethics from people. In these theories, what is morally justified comes forth from the person who uses them (virtue based and post-modernist ethics), or appears from the connection between persons (relation and discourse ethics). In other words: what is morally justified is a flexible concept depending on the individuals who are involved.

FIGURE 3.1 Directions in normative ethics

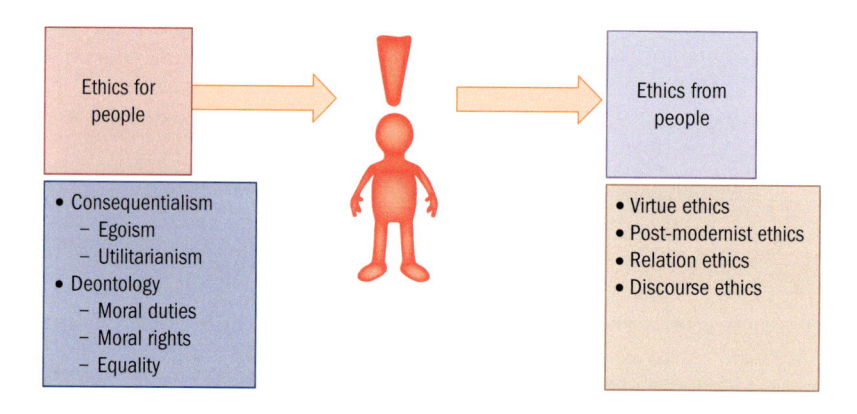

In the upcoming two sections we will explore the most influential theories in normative ethics for and from people.

⬤3.2 Ethics for people

In ethics for people, as we discussed above, theories are rigid, and exist regardless the people who apply those theories. It is – simply put – a 'one size fits all' approach, which should theoretically lead to the most desirable society when applied by everyone who participates in that society. Such theories typically have an origin in the 'Western world', and assume that such a desirable society can be created. The two dominant – and opposing – approaches are consequentialism on the one hand, in which we assume that something is morally justified when it leads to the best possible outcome, and deontology on the other hand, in which something is morally justified when we stick to certain principles, regardless the outcome. What they have in common is that ethics is dominated by rational thinking: what is morally justified can be deduced by reason. Either in assessing what will lead to the best possible outcome, or in the obedience towards certain principles.

3.2.1   Consequentialism

Self-driving cars (1)

The idea of a car that is able to drive autonomously, without a human driver, becomes less and less a fiction that belongs to Batman-like movies. Companies like Tesla, Google and Uber have experimented with cars that can operate with various degrees of autonomy. However, in the product development stage, we encounter some ethical challenges. The car needs to be programmed in a certain way, so that it will know how to act in difficult situations. But how should we programme the car in case of an inevitable accident? What – for instance – should be the choice made by the car when confronted with two unexpected pedestrians on the left side, and five on the right side of the road you drive with 100 km/h, and there is no way to avoid a crash?

> Consequentialism is a direction in normative ethics in which something is considered to be morally right when it leads to the best possible outcome.

Consequentialism

In other words: of all the possible alternatives in a given situation, you should always choose the one which leads to the best consequences. When confronted with a macabre choice as found in the case 'self-driving cars (1)', the programmer should choose the car to go to the left, because this will only lead to two casualties, instead of five. This choice is morally right because it leads to the least amount of casualties and therefore this is the best possible outcome.

However, we can argue about when something is the best possible outcome. In ethics, there are two main approaches in answering that question: egoism and utilitarianism.

Egoism

> Egoism is a form of consequentialism in which an action is morally justified when it leads to the best possible outcome for the actor.

Egoism

3

Self-driving cars (2)

You are the owner of a self-driving car. How would you expect the programmer to programme the software for this car? After all, your car should know what to do in dangerous traffic situations. What if there are three options in a particular traffic situation in which you are bound to have casualties? Again, there are two unexpected pedestrians on the left side, and five on the right side of the road. Option one therefore would be to sacrifice the two on the left. Option two would be to sacrifice the five on the right. However, you might also avoid crashing into any pedestrian by slamming the car in a nearby wall, killing the person sitting next to you. This person could be your mother, for instance. Now, how would you like the car to respond? Sacrifice five or two pedestrians, or perhaps your mother?

When you apply egoism in the second example entitled 'self-driving cars', the result should lead to the best consequences for you: the owner of the car. It will be obvious that the owner of a self-driving car would not like to sacrifice his mother, even though this would lead to the least casualties. You will probably prefer to sacrifice the two pedestrians on the left, and not the five on your right side. In the end, this will most likely lead to the best possible outcome for you. After all, your mother still lives, and your car sacrificed the smallest group of pedestrians, which is likely to be less shocking to watch and easier to live with compared to the sacrifice of the larger group.

In our daily language, the word egoism is mostly used as something negative. When you call someone an egoist, the other person will probably be provoked, since you seem to suggest that he can only think about himself and does not care enough for others. However, in ethics, the word egoist does not necessarily have a negative sound to it. Greek philosophers, especially Plato and Epicurus, already suggested that it is the ultimate goal of a human being to lead 'the good life'. This should be done by always striving to realize personal pleasure or happiness. However, this does not mean that you are antisocial. After all, we could argue that all human action is driven by egoism. We only have to learn to optimize our egoistic thinking, and apply this in our daily decisions.

Plato
Epicurus

Taking care of someone else might at first glance appear to be the opposite of egoism, but when you think of it, you might simply do this out of self-interest. After all, when you do not take care of that other person you feel worse than when you do. For instance, when you donate money to charity, it gives you a good feeling because you feel committed to the goals of this charity organization. And when you help a very old woman to cross the street it gives you a good feeling, and you feel better compared to the situation in which you leave the grandma struggle to cross that street on her own.
However, you will probably not donate money to charity when you really need that money to buy medication for a sick family member, nor would you help the grandma cross the street when your wife is about to deliver a baby and you are in a hurry to make it in time. So, in this reasoning, there is no such thing as altruism: every action is driven by egoism.

Philosophers that assume that egoism is the main driver behind human action have responded rather differently in whether this is a good thing or not, and how we should deal with this notion.

As for Thomas Hobbes, he was not that optimistic. He argued that indeed human beings are egoists by their very nature. As a result, each human being will try to pursue his own interest, if needed by using violence. When we do not restrict ourselves a bit in this pursuit, we end up in a rat race, continuously competing with others to get the best out of it for ourselves. This can only lead to a barbarian society that is dominated with violence and the survival of the strongest only. According to Hobbes, we better give up part of our freedom to pursue our own interest, and appoint a leader that maintains law and order. This could be a king, an emperor, a president or a prime minister, as long as he serves his purpose. One of the main duties of this leader is to protect us against our fellow men, also when this sometimes restricts us in pursuing our own interest. For instance, while it would be in my interest to steal food from my neighbour instead of buying it in a shop, someone should stop me on behalf of this appointed authority, and restore order. This way, a society could be more successful and viable. In section 3.2.2 we will see that Hobbes' solution to egoism can be labelled as deontology based on moral rights.

Thomas Hobbes

Economic philosopher Adam Smith was somewhat less anxious about the egoistic nature of mankind. He assumed that the individual is simply incapable to look beyond the short-term consequences of his actions, and therefore is not in a position to understand the grand schemes of societies. That is why people will only be able to pursue their own short-term goals in life without reflecting too much on the long-term consequences of their actions for society.

Adam Smith

However, Smith was of the opinion that the sum of all egoistic behaviour of people naturally results in the famous 'invisible hand' that ensures that our society will be in balance also on the longer term. As a supporter of free trade, he argued that the forces of supply and demand will always function as a corrective mechanism in a society that is driven by egoism at the individual level.

Invisible hand

Perhaps a short example will explain the above reasoning. When a shop owner sells rubbish, the demand for his products will decrease overtime and despite his short-term profit (which is most likely higher compared to a shop owner that supplies similar products of a better quality) he will eventually go bankrupt. After all, his previous customers will think again to buy something else from his shop, and pursue their own short-term interest by moving on to another shop run by a competitor. No doubt, the competitor will try his best to satisfy these costumers and keep them. In other words: the shop owner is corrected by the forces of supply and demand, caused by the egoistic behaviour of his clients and his competitor.

Utilitarianism

> Utilitarianism is a form of consequentialism in which an action is morally justified when it leads to the greatest happiness for the greatest number of people.

Utilitarianism

Let's go back once more to the example of the self-driving car (2). When applying an egoistic approach, it is obvious you would not sacrifice your mother, but instead the two pedestrians you never heard of before. This will lead to the best outcome for you, and is therefore morally justified. However, if we would apply utilitarianism, the conclusion would be different. You are not so much concerned about your own wellbeing, but about society in general. Choosing between five, two or one casualty is then easy, and you would sacrifice your mother. After all, the total sum up of sorrow that is caused will most likely be the lowest compared to the other two alternatives, and therefore the greatest happiness for the greatest number is preserved. Now, in practice, most people will not be so keen to sacrifice their mother, and therefore utilitarianism will not be so easy to apply as an individual. However, amongst politicians or company leaders, this approach in philosophy is widely used. After all, when ruling over a country or running a business, we expect their leaders to do what is best for the country or the business in general, and not for themselves or other individuals. If they do the latter, we usually accuse them of being corrupt.

Jeremy Bentham
John Stuart Mill

Utilitarianism is mostly known from the works of a group of British philosophers. In particular, Jeremy Bentham and John Stuart Mill developed the utilitarian philosophy during the Enlightenment (17th and 18th century). They also assume that everyone should strive for happiness and pleasure, not at individual level but rather at general societal level. The basic idea is that one's actions should be determined by a detailed consideration of all the possible consequences of the various available alternatives. Eventually, we must choose the alternative that leads to the greatest happiness for the greatest number of people. This is also called the Greatest Happiness Principle (Burns, 2005). The inevitable consequence is that individual pleasure or happiness is inferior to the greater good.

Greatest Happiness Principle

The word utilitarianism is derived from the world 'utility'. Bentham and Mill used this as another word for happiness. So, a decision should lead to the greatest utility for the greatest number of people (Blackburn, 2001).

The pros and cons of consequentialism
The benefits of consequentialism are quite clear: acting in line with this direction in ethics is very practical. All we have to do is carefully balancing various alternatives in a particular situation, and choose the one which leads to the most individual happiness (egoism), or utility for our society (utilitarianism). This creates a certain measurability, which is very attractive for policy makers and business leaders. After all, you can easily show the reasoning behind your action by communicating the various alternatives and demonstrating that your action has to be morally right, due to the fact that it leads the greatest happiness for the greatest number, or leads to the best company result. Even when your action is very negative for a minority or an individual, you can still explain the moral value of it by showing that it does lead to better results for a larger group. The reasoning of a manager, saying 'I'd love to keep you as an employee, but I am bound to fire you since we don't have enough financial resources, and I do not want to put the entire company at risk' is an example of this.

This leads us to the obvious disadvantages (Shaw & Barry, 2007). First, consequentialism says little about what is right or wrong in itself, but merely offers us a way to reason. The mere fact that a certain action leads to more happiness for yourself or the largest group of people, makes it morally right. Suppose that most people in a society usually agree that children, especially girls, could and should get married at a very young age (say around their twelfth birthday), arranged for by their parents. We could then even argue that opposing child marriages would then lead to less happiness in that society,

and would therefore be immoral. But does the fact that a majority in a society agrees on something, makes it something that is automatically morally right? What if there is one girl who has a different opinion in that society, and does not want to get married against her will at this very young age?
Especially in the case of utilitarianism, the minority or individual with a different interest will be unprotected against the will of the majority. For instance, can we torture an alleged terrorist to gather information of a possible future attack? See Ramsay (2006) who is against, and O'Donohue et al., (2014), who under circumstances support torture. Surely the torture will lead to greater happiness for the greater number, especially when this might prevent a terrorist attack from happening. However, does this also mean that the alleged terrorist has no rights at all, especially when his guilt has not been proven yet? The newspaper item on Osama Bin Laden is a good example of this debate.

A second issue is that it is not always easy to measure 'utility' or 'happiness', and make a fair balance between possible outcomes. Surely, when a manufacturer produces highly wanted luxury products, using these products will lead to more happiness in a society. However, in manufacturing these products, a lot of harmful CO_2 pollution is produced. This is not directly tangible to the people in this society, and therefore will not directly affect their happiness on the short term, or even during their lifetime. So, how do we properly balance the effects of CO_2 pollution with the happiness caused by these luxury products?

THE GUARDIAN, 3 MAY 2011

Osama bin Laden's death 'justifies' torture of suspects, former Bush aides claim

Furious debate grips us as White House officials deny ex-Bush aides claim that techniques such as water boarding helped track and kill al-Qaida chief.

A ferocious debate about the use of torture techniques to interrogate terrorist suspects has broken out in America in the wake of the killing or Osama Bin Laden. Some conservatives and members of the administration or former President George Bush have used the death of the terror chief to justify the use of water boarding and other so-called 'harsh interrogation' practices from 2002 to 2006. But critics and current officials have said there is little evidence they produced any single vital break through that led to Bin Laden's hideaway.
In a statement on its website Keep America Safe, which was set up by former Vice President Dick Cheney's daughter Liz Cheney, the group claimed such techniques had helped lead to Bin Laden's death and obliquely criticised their cessation. 'We must continue to provide our men and women in uniform and our intelligence professionals all the tools they need to fight and win this war,' it said. John Yoo, the former justice department official in the Bush White House who helped provide the legal basis for torture techniques, said Bin Laden's death justified such decisions. 'Without the tough decisions tasks by President Bush and his national security team, the United States could not have found and killed Bin Laden,' he wrote on the blog of the conservative American Enterprise Institute (...).

3.2.2   Deontology

Kill the fat man

Imagine you see a car approaching a mob at high speed, and you stand on top of a nearby building, next to a very fat man. The mob is celebrating new year's eve, and the driver of the car obviously wants to commit a terrorist attack by killing as many people as possible by driving his car through the crowd. You know for a fact that when you throw the fat man of the building in front of the car, the car will stop just in time to reach the crowd, and a lot of people will be saved. You also know for a fact that you do not have enough weight to stop the car by sacrificing yourself. So, if you really want to save the crowd, all you have to do is kill the fat man.

Where we focus on the results of our actions in a consequentialist approach, we focus on principles in deontology. Therefore, deontology deals with some of the criticism we could have on consequentialism. After all, it is not the best possible result that counts, but rather the principle we should stick to. If we go back to the torture example, and we choose to apply the principle that people have a right to the integrity of their body, torture is simply a no-go, no matter what the consequences are. A similar reasoning can be applied to the case 'kill the fat man'. Most people would agree that murdering an innocent man is an immoral thing to do. However, when we use a consequentialist approach in this case, the murder of the fat man can easily be justified considering the consequences. On the other hand, when we stick to the principle 'thou shalt not kill', we are bound to stand there and watch the tragedy unfold itself. After all, we don't kill innocent people, regardless the consequences. On top of that, if we would all stick to that principle –including the driver of that car- we would live in a very peaceful world.

Deontology

> In deontology, something is morally justified when we act in compliance with moral principles.

We can argue about which moral principles are worth striving for. In deontology we roughly distinguish three theories on which moral principles we should comply with: the theory of moral duties, moral rights and the principle of equivalence (Jeurissen & Van der Ven, 2007). The idea is that these moral principles are universal norms, and our actions should be driven by these norms.

Moral duties

Immanuel Kant

In his famous work 'Groundwork for the Metaphysic of Morals', the German philosopher Immanuel Kant held that not happiness nor the greatest happiness for the greatest number should be your moral justification. After all, when a burglar has a successful morning and steals money and property from wealthy people, he will probably be happier than before. And perhaps he has a larger family compared to the household he robbed, and so more people are happy with the theft compared to the amount of victims. According to Kant, consequentialist reasoning can justify such crimes, which should be rejected.

Instead, he argues that an action is morally justified when it is driven by duty (Kenny, 2010).

In essence, Kant assumes that each person is a rational human being, and therefore able and obliged to act in compliance with his so-called categorical imperative. This is quite a mouthful, and needs some further explanation. The word 'categorical' means 'unconditional', so this is something you should do in each situation. The word 'imperative' means that you have a duty to do this in each situation. The categorical imperative is composed of three main principles. Every action should stand the test of all three, to make it a morally right action (Crane & Matten, 2010).

Categorical imperative

First, we must ask ourselves the question whether you want your action to be a universal law. In other words: treat others the way you would like to be treated. After all, when you want something to become a universal law, this is how you would like others to approach you as well. This principle is sometimes referred to as the golden rule, since this rule appears – in various wordings – in each religion, and in a large number of theories on normative ethics. By some, this principle is called the principle of reciprocity. If the burglar we met before would apply this principle, he would probably have to conclude that stealing is not a moral thing to do. After all, he will most likely not want stealing to become a universal law, for then it would have to mean that he would perfectly accept people stealing from him as well.

Principle of reciprocity

Second, Kant teaches us that we should treat others as a goal and never as a means to an end. When we use our fellow men as a means to an end, we would use a consequentialist reasoning, since we are driven by the result it brings. A good example can be found in the case 'high school romance', where my former classmate used me to get a date with his crush. Kant assumes that every human being wants to be treated with human dignity and as an autonomous person that seeks to realize its own goals. Where this approach sounds promising and desirable, our economic system will not always allow us to comply, when humans are treated as capital or resources. After all, capital or resources are used to realize something, but are not a goal in itself.

High school romance

During my high school period, I was not exactly the popular football player. Instead, I was mostly losing myself in playing music, reading SF books and writing down whatever crossed my mind. It did therefore came as a surprise that the most popular boy from our class – Willem – asked me to hang out after school, preferably at my place. When we arrived, he insisted on kicking a ball outside, in front of my neighbours' house.

The daughter of my neighbours happened to be the prettiest girl in class. Her name was Martha, and she was the 'cheerleader' type. Willem wanted to hang out with me several times, and consistently asked me to play football on exactly the same spot. This lasted until he got the attention of Martha. When they had their first date, I never heard anything from him ever again.

Principle of universality

Third, Immanuel Kant argues that each time when you act, your action should be a universal law, which is appreciated by all other rational humans. This principle is called the principle of universality. Kant assumes that in the end, all rational human beings will conclude similarly as to what actions are moral and which are not, and we have a duty to act in compliance with these universal laws.

The difference between this principle and the first, is that the first principle relates to your subjective opinion of what should be a universal law, where in this principle, the universal law becomes objective since all rational beings will agree that it is a universal law. The added value of the last principle is that perhaps the burglar will find it a wonderful idea if someone else would steal property and money from him, since he also did this to others. In this reasoning, we comply with the first principle of reciprocity. However, the burglar will never conclude that all rational human beings will appreciate stealing and accept it as a universal law.

Pros and cons

The pros of duty ethics is that it offers us a firm set of rules that are always applicable in any given situation. These rules are not based on result but rather on a duty to act in a moral way. Therefore, the categorical imperative deals with most criticism on consequentialism. For instance, we will never find it morally justified to sacrifice a minority using Kant's theory.

The downside of duty ethics is perhaps that the categorical imperative is a very abstract concept that will not always be easy to apply. When we consider using these principles in our daily lives, it will inevitably lead to a certain vagueness, since we are not all academically trained in ethics.

Perhaps a deontological theory on moral rights might offer us some more clarity in what kind of principles we should comply with in our daily actions. After all, moral rights are – at first glance – a lot more specific compared to the categorical imperative.

Moral rights

In deontology that is based on moral rights, we assume that something is morally justified when we respect the fundamental rights of human beings. Here, we assume that we all have such rights naturally, due to the mere fact that we are human. Therefore, we also call these rights human rights.

The development of moral rights in ethics is closely linked to the emergence of legislation in Europe and America in which fundamental rights for citizens were recognized.

Social contract

A group of philosophers, including Thomas Hobbes (to whom we already referred in the context of consequentialism), Charles de Montesquieu and Jean Jacques Rousseau, advocated a society in which the people would voluntarily give up part of their sovereignty to a ruler, in order to create a safe and fruitful society. In a so-called 'social contract', part of the power of the individual is voluntarily transferred to the ruler. This could be a monarch or a democratically elected statesperson. This is necessary to prevent all individuals to cause harm to one another in their egoistic pursuit of their own desires and goals. It is the responsibility of the ruler to guarantee his citizens a minimum protection against their fellow citizens, by maintaining the law, including human rights.

John Locke reasoned that such a social contract would only work when people could live next to each other in freedom. This freedom should be guaranteed by the State through enforceable rights. In other word: when my neighbour steals my property, I should be able to invoke effective laws so that my property is returned to me. The underlying moral principle is that something is morally justified when you respect the fundamental freedoms of your fellow citizens.

In our recent history we see a strong development in the field of international human rights, in which states agree to respect and progressively realize fundamental rights and freedoms (Wernaart, 2013). We could say that shortly after the Second World War, the U.S. president Franklin Roosevelt's embarks the beginning of this development. Since 1948, the Universal Declaration of Human Rights is a main source of inspiration for drawing and ratifying international human rights treaties, with a global or near-global scope. These treaties – when applied correctly – are the embodiment of moral rights. They can be useful for national legislatures when drafting new laws, or businessmen when confronted with moral dilemmas. In case of the latter, we increasingly see a reference to the Universal Declaration in the code of conducts of companies. The main message then is: whatever you do on behalf of the company, do not under any circumstances act in such a way that it can lead to the violation of human rights.

Human rights

Roosevelt's four-freedoms speech

On 6 January 1941, the American President Roosevelt held his famous 'Four-freedoms speech', in which he emphasized four freedoms that are crucial in realizing a peaceful and meaningful existence. These freedoms were under great pressure by the various totalitarian aggressive regimes before and during the Second World War. Roosevelt argued that:
'In the future days, which we seek to make secure, we look forward to a world founded upon four essential human freedoms.
The first is freedom of speech and expression – everywhere in the world.
The second is freedom of every person to worship God in his own way – everywhere in the world.

The third is freedom from want – which, translated into world terms, means economic understandings which will secure to every nation a healthy peacetime life for its inhabitants – everywhere in the world.
The fourth is freedom from fear – which, translated into world terms, means a world-wide reduction or armaments to such a point and in such a thorough fashion that no nation will be in a position to commit an act of physical aggression against any neighbour – anywhere in the world'
(Roosevelt, 1941).

Traditionally, we subdivide human rights in two categories.
First, we have civil and political rights. In these rights, negative freedom (no interference) is emphasized. For instance, consider the prohibition of discrimination, the right to privacy, the right to physical integrity, the right to political participation, the right to freedom of religion and the right to a fair trial. When you act towards the other, you should predominantly leave that other person be, and not actively interfere with his civil and political rights. Meaning you do not discriminate, physically hurt someone, or violate someone's privacy.

Civil and political rights

Economic, social and cultural rights

Second, there are economic, social and cultural rights. In these rights, positive freedom (interference) is emphasized. We expect someone (mostly a government) to do something in order to realize these rights for others who cannot do this on their own. Think of the right to adequate clothing, shelter and food, health care and education. These are rights in which we expect a government to create an environment in which citizens are helped to realize these rights. This can be done to facilitate an educational system, install social benefit programmes, or provide emergency relief by dropping food packages (Wernaart, 2013).

Pros and cons

The obvious pros of moral rights as normative ethics are first that such human rights are more specific and practical compared to the categorical imperative. Second, they can be used as a moral guide against which you can review your actions. Third, human rights have a strong moral message; we will easily argue about its importance and value.

However, there are also disadvantages First, the human rights codification movement claims to have a universal scope. In practice however, we can say that human rights were mainly built on Western ideas. This explains the cautiousness or even rejection amongst some non-Western countries regarding the human rights agenda, for it is perceived to be a Western occasion, used to be arrogant towards them. Second, human rights are put in the form of codified treaties. The final formulation of these rights is mostly a result of compromise between its signatories. This has had an effect on the clarity of the wordings, leading to vagueness now and then. For instance, does the right to life and physical integrity mean that the death penalty should be banned? This is explained differently amongst the members of these human rights treaties. By some, the death penalty is understood in compliance with these human rights, because punishing a criminal is not the same as willingly inflicting harm on someone. Thirdly, some rights may conflict with other rights. When we go back to the torture example of an alleged terrorist, we could also discuss this from a moral right's perspective. On the one hand, the alleged terrorist has the right to life and physical integrity. Simultaneously, the potential victims of a terrorist attack surely have the same rights. If we would like to stick to this principle, we would still not know what to do. This leaves us to choose between fundamental rights, meaning that some should prevail over others. An example in which this is done can be found in the newspaper item: the right to religion is balanced with the right to freedom of speech. The latter won in this case.

THE GUARDIAN, 14 MARCH 2017

Europe's right hails EU court's workplace headscarf ban ruling

European court of justice says garments can be banned as part of general policy covering religious and political symbols

Politicians on the right have welcomed a ruling by the EU's highest court that allows companies to ban staff from wearing visible religious symbols, as a long-awaited legal judgment ricocheted into the French and Dutch election campaigns. In its first decision on the issue of women wearing Islamic headscarves at work, the European court of justice in Luxembourg ruled the garments could be banned, but only as part of a general policy barring all religious and political symbols. Nor can customers simply demand workers to remove headscarves if the company has no policy barring religious symbols, the court ruled on Tuesday (…).

The principle of equality

Yet another approach in deontology is the principle of equality. This direction is not about rights or duties in itself, but rather about consistently treating people in a similar way, whatever rights or duties you seek to pursue.

For example, students expect a teacher who is grading ethics exams to grade his students in a similar way. The similarity lies in the fact that students with the same type of answer should be rewarded a similar grade. When the teacher is more flexible in the grading of one student, and more rigid in grading the others, he will probably be accused of being unethical since it contradicts the principle of equivalence.

However, we can understand the concept of equality in more than one way, as we can see in figure 3.2. A first distinction is between procedural and distributional equality (Crane & Matten, 2010).

Procedural equality means that individuals have similar access to procedures that allow them to stand up for their rights. This means for example that everyone, without exception, must have access to a court in the event of legal conflict. Another example would be that every employee must be able to propose a candidate for the membership in a participation council, regardless of his position in the company or personal background. This way, everyone has an equal opportunity to make his voice heard in the organization. Unfortunately, procedural equality is not always a matter of course, as we can see in the example 'exchange students properly insured?' We could argue here that exchange students or expats do not have the same access to procedures compared to Dutch people, considering the fact that the procedures in this case were exclusively available in the Dutch language, while in practice predominantly used by foreigners.

Procedural equality

Exchange students properly insured?

Recently one of my exchange students from the Czech Republic came to my office. She was in tears due to the fact that the Dutch National Healthcare Institute slapped a heavy fine on her because she had no Dutch healthcare insurance. However, she had a Czech insurance especially designed for a long stay abroad, practically covering the same as a Dutch healthcare insurance would.

The Dutch law prescribes that a person with a foreign insurer should first file a request at the National Healthcare Institute in order to check whether the foreign insurance is indeed compatible with the Dutch requirements. Only with a permit, someone may indeed use this foreign healthcare insurance during their stay in the Netherlands.

However, my student had no idea she needed such a permit. The Dutch Government did not exactly make it a priority to communicate this to exchange students or expats, and the procedures to get such a permit were exclusively in Dutch. Also the fine she received was in Dutch, without an English translation. This is remarkable, since the target group of such procedures and fines are almost per definition foreigners who temporarily stay in the Netherlands for study or work. They will normally not excel in the Dutch language. All in all, my student had no idea she was breaking any law, while she was well insured and with the intention of being a good citizen.

Effective equality   Effective equality is not about the procedure, but about the effect of equal treatment. In other words: it is not about the route towards equality (procedure) but about the substantial result (effect) of equal treatment. So, for instance we could say that everyone has the right to a minimum guarantee in health care. This right should be applied to each and everyone equally, so that all individuals who are in need effectively are guaranteed this minimum.

In this context it is not always easy to determine the exact meaning of the word equality.

In some cases we want equality to be applied literally, regardless of context and situation. So, we want each person who is 18 years or older to have a right to vote, or we want everyone to have freedom of speech without discrimination. These rights are then applied exactly the same way on each individual in a society. We call this interpretation of equivalence 'egalitarian equality'. The world 'egalitarian' is derived from the French word 'egale', which means 'equal'. We treat people exactly the same.

Egalitarian equality

In some cases however, literally treating everyone exactly the same way will be rather pointless. For example, is it fair to pay each individual a similar salary, regardless his job, educational background, effort or hours of work? In a communist system this is exactly the starting point, where in a capitalist system this approach is rejected. Most economists agree that the communist approach does not really work though.

We can also approach 'equality' in a different way, whereby the specific context determines the way you should be treated. For example, the harder you work, the more money you earn, and the higher the level of education, the higher your salary will be. This is contrary to egalitarian equality, where everyone would earn the same amount of money regardless these factors. On the other hand, when people work in the same job, work equally hard and have a similar educational background, they should earn the same salary. However, when you have more resources (such as income and property), then you are usually bound to pay more taxes.

Or consider a situation in which someone is seriously ill and therefore cannot work: this person will probably rely on social benefits to maintain himself. When you are in perfect health and are able to work this is less likely. So, the greater the need, the more you can make use of a social benefit system.

Proportional equality   In other words: equality is understood in terms of proportionality, and therefore we speak of proportional equality (Jeurissen & Van der Ven, 2007).

As we have explored, we can apply proportional equivalence to someone's needs, effort, productivity or means.

The difficulty here is the way in which you exactly want to apply this. For instance, it is debatable whether it is fair to only judge an employee on result. Shouldn't effort also play a role? And when you are very successful because you work very hard, is it then fair to impose more taxes on your salary? According to Michael Walzer it is extremely difficult to apply the right approach in proportional equality per case, which can lead to a very diverse usage of this theory in our daily lives. This then is often expressed in different political views on how resources (such as money) should be distributed (Waltzer, 1983 & 1994).

FIGURE 3.2 Different approaches to equality

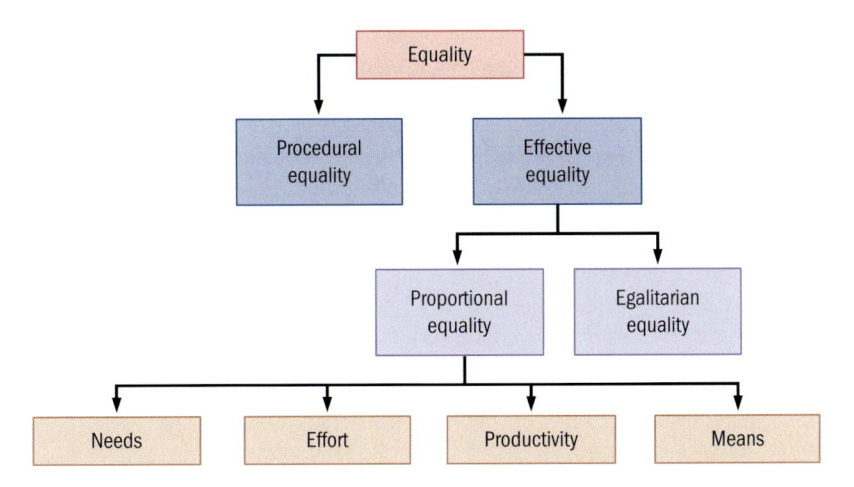

The pros of using equality as a guiding principle in moral actions are that it is perhaps more practical to apply compared to duty or right-based deontology. It is harder to define moral duty or someone's human rights than to assess whether we treat people in a similar way.

The cons of equality as normative ethics is that especially in the context of proportional equality, it is not always easy to determine when we believe people are in a similar situation and should therefore deserve equal treatment. See for instance the case of 'the lazy student'. Another issue is that while equality is considered to be important by many, it is not necessarily the foundation of each society. Instead, some societies are founded on inequality. An example is the Hindu caste system, in which society is divided in various castes. It is a society based on Hindu beliefs is hierarchically divided into various (at least five) different kinds of people. Each caste has its own privileges, rights and duties towards society. The lower the caste, the harsher the life usually gets and the fewer the privileges are. People are usually in their caste for generations, and they are not expected to escape this social structure. To this day, while Constitutionally banned, this caste system is deeply rooted in the Indian social order and culture, which leads to a sharp social debate (Kumar, 2014).

The lazy student

Teachers are very often confronted with students who enter the classroom after starting a lecture. The didactic question here is what to do with such students, and how to encourage them to be on time the next time when you teach them.

Take Eric for instance: a breezy young man who claims that due to the fact that he was born two weeks before his due date, he can justify arriving too late everywhere all the time during his life. To be honest, he is not the most exemplary student and he argues that simply barely passing subjects is not an example of being lazy, but rather an efficient way of spending his time.

Lisa on the other hand is a very bright student, always seated in the front row of classes, paying attention and actively engaging in group discussions. She always arrives on time and never skips a lecture. Except today. She just had a nasty accident on her bicycle and had to see a doctor to make sure she did not break anything. Thankfully, she only had some bruises. In the meantime she sent a message to her teacher to inform her of her situation, and asked if it is possible to still join for the remainder of the lecture (she will obviously arrive too late).

The teacher is now faced with two people who arrive too late: Erik and Lisa. Erik enters first, and the teacher does not allow him to enter until the coffee break. After all, he was late the previous week and the week before, and does not really seem to regret it. Ten minutes later Lisa walks in, and the teacher welcomes her enthusiastically.

The classmates, who are not aware of the situation of Lisa, find this a strange response. They claim that the teacher treats Lisa and Erik unequally. After all, they both arrived too late, and one cannot enter the classroom while the other can. So, obviously, the students are of the opinion that the teacher should have applied egalitarian equality, while the teacher chose to apply proportional equality based on effort.

The situation becomes even more complicated when minutes later another student, Adya enters the lecture hall, and claims that her train was delayed as a result of a large power breakdown. This story can be confirmed by the local news app. What should the teacher do? Should she allow Adya to attend the lecture in line with Lisa, or exclude her in line with Eric?

3.3 Ethics from people

As we have seen in the previous section, we assume in ethics for people that morality is considered a rigid concept, and can be used regardless of the person involved. This is rather different in ethics from people, where morality depends on those who use it. Morality becomes therefore more interactive and flexible. In ethics from people we can distinguish two main approaches. In the first approach, morality comes forth from the person that acts. One can strive to become a virtuous person and as a result do the right thing (virtue ethics) or structurally act in compliance with one's emotions (postmodernist ethics). In the second approach, morality comes forth from the interaction between people. One may seek to continuously improve the relation with those around him (relation ethics), or seek to solve moral conflicts through discourse ethics, in which those who are involved agree to the moral action that should be taken.

3.3.1   Virtue ethics

As we have already seen in the context of egoism, most theories on normative ethics from the ancient Greek assumed that it was the ultimate goal of people to lead the so-called 'good life'. In egoism, we then assume that this can be realized by taking decisions that lead to the best consequences for you. According to the famous philosopher Aristotle this can be done by trying to live a virtuous life. The word 'virtue' says something about the characteristics of a person. Therefore, virtue ethics relates to building a good character to be able to do the right thing. As a result, the right thing comes from you due to the fact that you are a virtuous person.

> In virtue ethics something is morally right when it is done by a virtuous person.

Virtue ethics

According to Aristotle, one would have to develop both moral and intellectual virtues to lead a virtuous life (Kenny, 2010). We can define moral virtues as good characteristics in which is able to find the perfect middle ground between two extremes. This middle ground is sometimes referred to as the golden mean. For instance, between recklessness and cowardice is the moral virtue courage. Aristotle used the example of consuming sufficient food and drink. A virtuous man should not overconsume (greediness), nor starve himself (meanness), but instead eat and drink healthy foodstuff in moderate proportions (moderateness). It is to be expected that Aristotle would disapprove of the models used by Victoria's secret.

Moral virtues

THE DAILY MAIL, UK, 1 DECEMBER 2016

'Don't understand how girls find them inspirational...it's not sexy': Tweeters lash out at 'too thin' Victoria's Secret models as they strut their stuff at annual show in Paris

Every year Victoria's Secret assembles the world's top models for their annual runway extravaganza.

And with the likes of show veterans Alessandra Ambrosio and Adriana Lima walking alongside catwalk newbies Kendall Jenner and Bella Hadid this year, all eyes were on Paris on Wednesday night. But some social media commentators were not impressed with the beauties who strutted down the Grand Palais runway in lingerie and Angel wings – with many hitting out at the 'too thin' models.

Some tweeters slammed Victoria's Secret for, in their opinion, ditching models with curves in favour of more athletic body types.

'I don't really like that Victoria's Secret models are all skinny with no curves. That's not what the average body looks like,' tweeted one.

Another pleaded of the lingerie giants: 'I want a girl with an actual booty to model Victoria's Secret panties. Too much to ask?'

Intellectual virtues

In addition to moral virtues, Aristotle advises you to develop intellectual virtues. These virtues are characteristics that are required to understand the nature of things and apply this understanding in practical situations. Aristotle assumed that when people would rightly develop these virtues, this would ultimately – through rational reasoning – lead to a single understanding of how the world works. It would be the ultimate goal of developing your intellectual virtues to reach this – rather hypothetical – state of mind.

The combination of moral and intellectual virtues can make a person a good person. He emphasized that such virtues could be mastered through practice and education. This also means that he assumed that people were born as a so-called *tabula rasa* (Latin for 'blank slate'). This means that people are not born with characteristic traits, but instead develop them along the way during their lives.

Virtue ethics, as proposed by Aristotle, was later followed up by philosophers such as Thomas van Aquino, David Hume and Frederique Nietzsche. Also in the Far East, virtue ethics has always played an important role in normative ethics. For instance, the teachings of Confucius involve the development of six virtues: humanity, obedience, justice, decency, loyalty and reciprocity.

In a way, we could say that virtue ethics holds a middle position between consequentialism and deontology. In consequentialism we risk that the end justifies the means, where in deontology we risk to stick to principles blindly. In virtue ethics, moral justification is never purely based on outcome nor principles, but depends on the virtuosity of the person. In other words: good virtues lead to moral actions. An important added value of virtue ethics is therefore that the person who wants to act morally does so because he has the intention to do the right thing. This intrinsic motivation to act morally is not necessarily apparent in consequentialism and not always in deontology (except perhaps duty ethics). We can choose the best outcome or stick to a principle without necessarily being convinced that this truly is ethical. We cannot however become virtuous without the inner conviction that this is the right way to live.
When we consider the example 'Slavery: immoral or not profitable?' we could argue that Adam Smith predominantly used consequentialist arguments to end slavery. During the American Civil War, the ban on slavery was considered a principle by the North, where the right to property was considered a principle by the South. The question here can be raised whether the North American truly believed that slavery was immoral, as they claimed, or that it simply was not profitable. Whatever the conclusion would be, we see that both consequentialist and deontological arguments in this context do not necessarily require intrinsic involvement with the situation. Virtue based ethics would, and we could argue in line with Aristotle and Confucius that virtuous men would not enslave each another.

However, there is also criticism with regard to virtue ethics. The main issue is that virtues are often understood as subjective concepts. What is 'decency' for instance? In some cultures it would be very rude to burp during or after a meal, while in other cultures this is considered as a way to show your appreciation of a good meal. Developing the characteristic 'decency' will ultimately manifest itself differently then, depending on which culture you find yourself in. It is very unlikely that 'supermen' with perfect virtues that ultimately lead to only one natural interpretation of what is right and wrong truly exists.

Slavery: immoral or not profitable?

Adam Smith, in his famous book 'The Wealth of Nations' argued that Slavery is extremely inefficient in an industrialized society. On the other hand, free employees would probably be more productive, and would represent a group of consumers that have buying power to which companies can sell their products (Pack, 1996). It is not without reason that he claimed that 'a person who can acquire no property, can have no other interest but to eat as much, and to labour as little as possible' (Smiths, 1776). Besides that, Smith also voiced the opinion that slavery as such was morally wrong.

One of the ideological issues during the American Civil War (1861-1865) was the ban on slavery. The industrial north wanted to ban all slavery, whereas the agricultural south did not want to hear about it. In practice, a ban on slavery in the north would only have a very small impact on the economy, while in the south the wealth of a significant group of landowners was composed of 'human property'. For them, banning slavery would significantly reduce their wealth.

While in theory, in the long term ending slavery in the south would lead to economic progress, it would in the short term disrupt the status quo of that society. One could argue whether the North truly wanted to ban slavery as a principle, or merely because it was no longer profitable.

3.3.2   Postmodernist ethics

Mostly, directions in ethics assume that there is one ultimate truth that can be applied on a universal scale. We have seen this in both consequentialism and deontology: both have theories that should answer everything, and provide a blueprint for each human being on how to live ethically. And even in virtue ethics, originally it was assumed that rational thinking would lead to one type of 'superhuman' who would be virtuous and therefore a good person. In postmodern ethics, such universalism is firmly rejected because such theories deny the real offspring of morality (Rorty, 1979). After all, morality does not come from, for example, rational thinking or universal principles; it comes from one's subjective emotions and impulses.

> In postmodern ethics, morality is found in the subjective emotions and impulses of the individual or small communities.

Postmodern ethics

This direction in ethics is a lot more than just 'relying on your gut feeling'. Especially when considering that this 'gut feeling' is the total sum of your life experiences, things you have learned in the past, and how you've interacted with the world around you. A wonderful example can be found in the book 'In order to live' written by North Korean refugee Yeonmi Park . She finds herself alone in a strange country (China) and has never been taught how the 'real' world works. However, she appears to be able to rely on her gut feeling to tell what is right and wrong.

Not surprisingly, someone's emotions and impulses are very subjective. Post-modernist ethics assumes that there is no such thing as a macro theory on ethics. Instead, it is the individual who has a unique sense of what is moral, and has the right to live accordingly. This means that society as a large construction of organized living together plays no role here. Instead, differences in understanding ethics are an inevitable outcome, which leads to ethical relativism: no one is right or wrong compared to the other. It is only the individual that is responsible towards himself to act morally in line with his emotions and impulses (Bauman, 1993).

At most, local communities have their own shared feelings towards ethics, and will reject people who behave immoral towards their sense of ethics. A post-modernist will therefore only focus on either the individual or small communities, and argue that ethics that moves beyond this level simply does not exist.

The Chinese philosopher Confucius at some point reasons pretty much in line with post-modern approach in his musings about state structure and legislation (Crane & Matten, 2016). Confucius held that people are different from animals because we can experience shame. When we engage in our (local) community, we intuitively feel what is morally acceptable and what is not. When a member of this community behaves unethically, that same community will intuitively correct this behaviour. Think about a stranger entering a pub, or a new member of a team: they will have to get used to the unwritten (and perhaps unspoken) rules of engagement in this small community and in the end will intuitively adapt to the local norms and values. When the new team member wears a T-shirt while everybody else wears a suit, there will be a sense of shame and the team will reject the clothing style. Perhaps not in words, but the new member will surely notice the body language of his new colleagues.
According to Confucius, this is exactly how a society will be at peace and order. He is against codifying standards as universal norms that should be widely applied: this can only lead to a situation in which people blindly follow these rules without understanding their importance or reason, and without feeling intrinsically motivated to act ethically. According to Confucius this can only lead to chaos (Lefande, 2000).

In order to live

'Now I was separated from my mother again, and miserable. Hongwei was broke and frustrated and taking out on me. But as depressed as I was, I realized there was a force inside me that would not give up. Maybe it was just anger, or maybe it was an inexplicable sense that my life might mean something today. I had no word in my vocabulary for 'dignity' or the concept of morality. I just knew what felt wrong, and what I would not accept. This situation was something I could no longer accept. I had to find a way out' (Park, 2015).

The pro of post-modernist ethics is that it fully recognizes personal emotions and impulses as well as the ethical awareness of local communities as the primary source of morality. Ethics comes from within and is not a universal obligation. As a result, people are intrinsically motivated to behave ethically. The con is that this approach towards ethics does not say much about what is right or wrong in itself. When it feels right it is right. This means that there are many understandings of what morality should be, and these understandings may conflict with one another. In post-modernism this is widely accepted and encouraged. However it also makes this approach a radical form of ethical relativism, in which there hardly is any general right or wrong. In other words: it may lack a moral compass, and could potentially be used to morally justify behaviour that would be labelled as immoral in other directions in ethics. For instance, consider a society in which child marriage is generally accepted and even stimulated. A post-modernist would not consider this to be immoral per se, since it depends on the moral perception of that community. Other approaches to ethics will most likely find this phenomenon unethical.

3.3.3 Relation-ethics

Where in virtue based ethics and post-modernist ethics morality stems from the individual, in relation ethics, morality stems from the relationship between individuals. The basic idea is that a person is not an actor in its own right, but always a part of a larger community. Moral behaviour should contribute to establishing and improving relationships.

> In relation-ethics something is morally justified when it contributes to establishing and improving healthy relationships.

Relation-ethics

An example of relation ethics can be found at the core of Buddhist thinking. One of the Buddhist principles is the theory of dependent origination. In short, it is assumed that nothing exists on its own but is interrelated (with the only exception the ultimate state of Nirvana). It is therefore worthwhile to try and understand the complexity of our societies and acknowledge the fact that we are the opposite of independent: we fully depend each other (Nichtern, 2009). Our moral actions should contribute to this aim.

A practical example these days of relation ethics would be the Chinese concept of 'guānxi' (figure 3.3). Although we could argue about whether Guānxi is truly an intrinsic expression of ethics, the example is fitting. Guānxi freely translates as 'relationship building'. It means that mutual trade is based on mutual trust. This trust is the result of a (long) process of building this trust. This building of trust can be done by for instance the exchange of gifts and favours before an actual deal is closed. Western business people are used to a more consequentialist approach, in which not the trading partner, but the particularities of the deal are most important. Furthermore, they may confuse Guānxi with bribery, since the exchange of gifts could take on massive proportions, and as a result overlap with the Western idea of corruption. From a Chinese perspective however, this is an unjust interpretation. After all, we should take some time and invest in building a healthy relationship, also in business. It matters with whom we do business, and whether businesspeople gained each other's trust (Buderi & Huang, 2006).

Guānxi

FIGURE 3.3 The Chinese characters for the word 'guānxi'

Feminist ethics

In western ethics, relation ethics can be found in feminist ethics. In this approach to ethics it is assumed that ethics is generally dominated by male thinkers, and a feminine approach is needed to emphasize the 'female voice' in ethics (Gilligan, 1982). While also within feminist ethics there are many directions (Cole & McQuin, 1992), they have a couple of things in common. First, feminist ethics takes mutual trust as a starting point, and as a counterpoint assumes that each individual has a duty of care towards the other to establish a healthy relationship. Second, someone's life experience should be the moral compass in ethics, rather than consequences and principles (Borgerson, 2007). The latter assumption can also be found in post-modernist ethics, but is now focused on these relations with those around you.

The advantage of relation ethics is that in essence, it is a message of peace: we should build a community that is based on healthy relationships. Moral justification arises from these relations, and as a result we should live together in a harmonious society. Norms and values therefore do not necessarily come from within us, as we have seen in virtue ethics and post-modernism, but are rather determined by our interaction in these relationships.

This disadvantage of relation ethics is that this direction in ethics does not set a moral bottom line, as long as moral behaviour leads to maintaining a healthy relation. It furthermore assumes that people by nature are positive human beings and are willing to trust those around them. Perhaps these are rather high expectations that do not necessarily reflect our daily reality. Furthermore, this direction in ethics emphasizes harmony and mutual trust, but says little about how to deal with the actual conflict that might arise. Perhaps discourse ethics, as we will see below, will solve that last issue.

3.3.4   Discourse ethics

Another direction in ethics in which morality stems from the interaction of people is discourse ethics. The main focus of this approach is that moral action should focus on solving conflicts. The idea is that while people are different and have different norms and values, ethics can be used to find a joint solution to ethical challenges to which all involved actors can agree. However, this can only be done when there is mutual respect for each another's viewpoints.

Discourse ethics

> In discourse ethics, something is morally justified when all involved actors agree to the solution in a conflict.

Theory of communicative action

The German philosopher Jürgen Habermas is one of the founders of discourse ethics. In his famous theory of communicative action he emphasizes that moral justification does not follow from standard norms or rational thinking in itself, but rather evolves when norms and values are applied in action (Habermas, 1992). He considers it most important that actors take a moral decision as a result of discourse. However, this discourse should be fair. This means that the discourse should be free of hierarchical relations, corruption, and other distorting factors, such as a misbalance in expertise and knowledge amongst the participants. Of course, such a discourse is rather hypothetical, but is at least worth striving for.

Parlay in Pirates of the Caribbean

In the popular film series *Pirates of the Caribbean*, the concept of 'parlay' is introduced. The idea of 'parlay' is that in case of a conflict between rivalling groups of pirates, one of them can call for a 'parlay'. In that case, all should cease fighting, and instead face each other on a designated location to solve the issue. The pirates are bound to stay as long as is needed to find a solution everyone agrees to. 'Parlay' stems from the so-called 'pirate code', a sort of self-regulation on ethics amongst pirates.

The advantage of discourse ethics is that is a very practical and applied approach to ethics. Moral justification does not come from complicated standards, but instead follows from the action between the conflicting parties when they resolve a dispute.

This immediately leads to the main disadvantage of this approach. Morality is the result of a process: the solving of a conflict. This says very little about morality itself. After all, as long as the involved actors agree to something, it is considered to be morally right.

3.4 Directions in ethics applied

Let's go back to the first case of this book: 'Leadership? It's in your DNA!'. You are an employee that is asked to participate in such an assessment in which a sample of your DNA is used in a broader range of tests to figure out whether you have the skills to perform well in a job you've applied for within your company. You are very eager to get that job, while simultaneously you are worried about your privacy and physical integrity. What should you do?

In this section, we will give a hypothetical answer from the perspective of the various directions in ethics we discussed in this chapter.

Consequentialism: egoism

'I would take the decision that leads to the best results for me. I carefully balance the alternatives I have, and decide which of them leads to the best consequences for me. If I value my privacy more, I will not do the assessment, while if I value the new job opportunity more, I will go for it.'

Consequentialism: utilitarianism

'I would take the decision which leads to the greatest happiness for the greatest number. Since the assessment is time and energy-saving for a lot of people, I will do the assessment. After all, if I do not do the assessment, alternate tests may have to be performed which are a lot more time consuming. This means extra costs for my company, and more time that will be lost by various actors. Besides that, it will most likely lead to the same conclusion, albeit without the usage of my DNA.'

Deontology: moral duties

'I would examine if participating in these tests should be a universal law:

a   If I would be an employer, would I want my employees to undergo such a test? (principle of reciprocity)

b   Are people treated as a goal in itself, or merely as a means to an end?

c   Is it a desirable situation when all employees in the world would be judged on their DNA composition when applying for a new job? (principle of universality)

Most likely the conclusion is that it is not a good idea to undergo the assessment. While the answer to question (a) will be a subjective one, it is clear people are used as a means to an end, and not considered a goal in itself, and it seems undesirable that from now on, the DNA composition of a human being determines his job opportunities.'

Deontology: moral rights

'I would not undergo the assessment. After all, I have a human right to privacy and physical integrity. If as a result I will not get the job, than that is what it is, for I will not give up my principles.'

Deontology: the principle of equality

'I would only undergo the assessment when all employees are treated equally. When all my colleagues are also asked to undergo the assessment, or all candidates that applied for that job, than I would do it as well.'

Virtue ethics

'I would not undergo the assessment because it starts from the wrong assumption. People are born as a *tabula rasa,* which means that potential or talent cannot be deduced from my DNA. Everything I am I've learned along the way during my life, and in that time I've tried to become as virtuous as possible. My DNA has nothing to do with this.'

Post-modernist ethics

'I would not undergo the assessment. After all, my morality sterns from my emotion and impulses, not my DNA. I have life experience that made me the person I am, and from that life experience I will act. My DNA has nothing to do with this.'

Relation ethics

'I would undergo the assessment, since it will contribute to a healthy relation with my employer. I trust my employer, and therefore I am willing to reveal my DNA in the context of this assessment. There is no need to worry about my privacy. I am sure that my employer also trusts me, and will do anything that he can do to take good care of me in the assessment procedure.'

Discourse ethics

'I would discuss the assessment (and possible alternatives) with all the involved stakeholders, but only as equals. This means in this debate, my employer may not make use of his position as my superior and the assessment company should share all the knowledge about these assessments beforehand so we have equal access to knowledge about the issue. The conclusion is not so relevant, as long as all parties consent to it.'

Summary

▶ In normative ethics we define when something is morally justified.
These normative theories are divided into:
- Ethics for people, in which the content of what is morally correct is determined outside the person. These theories include consequentialism and deontology.
- Ethics from people, morality comes forth from people or their interaction. This includes: virtue based, post-modernist, relation and discourse ethics.

▶ Consequentialism is a direction in normative ethics in which something is considered to be morally right when it leads to the best possible outcome
Consequentialism is divided into:
- Egoism, in which an action is morally justified when it leads to the best possible outcome for the actor.
- Utilitarianism, in which an action is morally justified when it leads to the greatest happiness for the greatest number of people.

▶ In deontology something is morally justified when we act in compliance with moral principles. These moral principles can be found in: the theory of moral duties, moral rights and the principle of equivalence.
- Immanuel Kant argues that an action is morally justified when it is driven by duty. This can be deduced from his categorical imperative, which is composed of three maxims:
  - The principle of reciprocity: treat others the way you would like to be treated.
  - Treat others as a goal and never as a means to an end.
  - The principle of universality: your action should be a universal law that is appreciated by all other rational humans.
- In deontology – which is based on moral rights – we assume that something is morally justified when we respect the fundamental rights of human beings. Human rights are divided into:
  - Civil and Political Rights, with an emphasis on negative freedom
  - Economic, Social and Cultural Rights, with an emphasis on positive freedom
- Equality presupposes that something is morally right when people are treated equally. Equality can be understood in different ways:
  - Procedural equality means that individuals have similar access to procedures that allow them to stand up for their rights.
  - Effective equality means that individuals enjoy the same effects as a result of equal treatment. Effective equality can be understood as egalitarian equality and proportional equality.

- In the case of egalitarian equality, people are treated the same way regardless of the situation.
- In the case of proportional equality, people are treated the same way depending on their needs, effort, productivity or means.

▶ In virtue ethics something is morally right when it is done by a virtuous person. Aristotle made a distinction between moral and intellectual virtues. He also assumed that virtues can be learned in life, since people are born as a *tabula rasa*.
- Moral virtues are good characteristics in which is able to find the perfect middle ground between two extremes.
- Intellectual virtues are characteristics that are required to understand the nature of things and apply this understanding in practical situations.

▶ In postmodern ethics, morality is found in the subjective emotions and impulses of the individual or small communities.

▶ In relation ethics something is morally justified when it contributes to establishing and improving healthy relationships.

▶ In discourse ethics, something is morally justified when all involved actors agree to the solution in a conflict.

Literature

Bauman, Z. (1993). *Postmodernist ethics.* Oxford: Blackwell Publishing.

Blackburn, S. (2001). The greatest happiness of the greatest number. In: *Ethics, a very short introduction.* Oxford: Oxford University Press.

Borgerson, J.L. (2007). On the harmony or feminist ethics and business ethics. *Business Society Review, 112* (4), 477-509.

Buderi, R., & Huang, G.T. (2006). *Guānxi, the art of relationships.* New York: Simon & Schuster.

Burns, J.H. (2005). Happiness and Utility: Jeremey Bentham's Equation. *Utilitas (Cambridge University Press).* Vol. 17. No. 1. March 2005.

Cole, E.B. & McQuin, S.C. (1992). *Explorations in Feminist Ethics.* Bloomington: Indiana University Press.

Crane, W., & Matten, D. (2016). *Business ethics* (4th edition). Oxford: Oxford University Press.

Gilligan, C. (1982). *In a different voice.* Cambridge: Harvard University Press.

Habermas, J. (1992). *Moral Consciousness and Communicative Action.* Cambridge: MIT Press.

Hobbes, T. (2014). *Leviathan.* Hertfordshire: Worldsworth Editions (original publication London, 1651)

Jeurissen, R., & Van de Ven, B. (2007). Values and moral norms in organizations. In: R. Jeurissen (Ed.), *Ethics & Business* (pp. 54-92). Assen: Van Gorcum.

Kant, I. (2002). *Groundwork for the Metaphysic of Morals.* London: Yale University Press (original publication: Riga, 1785).

Kenny, A. (2010). *A new history of western philosophy.* Oxford: Oxford University Press.

Kumar V. (2014). Inequality in India: Newcastle and Hindu Social Order. *Tran Science,* Vol. 5, issue 1.

Lefande, M. (2000). *Aspects or Lega List Philosophy and the Law in Ancient China: The Ch'in and Han Dyna ties and the Rediscovered Manuscripts or Mawangdui and Shuihudi.* www.commonwealthprotection.org.

Locke, J. (2010). *An essay concerning human understanding.* Oxford: Bodleian Library.

Moore, G.E. (1903). *Principia Ethica.* Cambridge University Press.

Moore, G.E. (1912). *Ethics.* London: Williams & Norgate.

Nichtern, E. (2009). *Buddhism 3.0. A universal declaration of reciprocal dependency, Buddhism for the twenty-first century.* Katwijk aan Zee: Panta Rhei.

O'Donohue, W. et al. (2014). The ethics of enhanced interrogations and torture: a reappraisal of the argument. *Ethics & behaviour.* Vol. 24, 2014 - issue 2.

Pack, S.J. (1996). Slavery, Adam Smith's Economic Vision and the Invisible Hand. *History of Economic Ideas,* IV/1996/1-2.

Park, Y. (2015). *In order to live, a North Korean girl's journey to freedom.* Penguin Random House UK.

Ramsay, M. (2006). Can the torture of a terrorist subject be justified? *The international journal of human rights.* Vol. 10. 2006 - issue 2.

Rorty, R. (1979). *Philosophy and the mirror of nature.* Princeton University Press.

Smith, A. (1776). *Book III, Ch. 2. Of the Discouragement of Agriculture in the Ancient State of Europe after the Fall of the Roman Empire*. In: The Wealth of Nations. Wordsworth classics of world literature.

Walzer, M. (1983). *Spheres of justice.* New York: Basic Books.

Walzer, M. (1994). *Thick and thin, moral argument at home and abroad.* Notre Dame: University of Notre Dame Press.

Wernaart, B. (2013). The enforceability of the international human right to adequate food. In: *The human right to adequate food, a comparative study*. Wageningen: Wageningen Academic Publishers.

Media

Burke, J., & Harris, P. (2011, 3 May). Osama bin Laden death 'justifies' torture or suspects, former Bush aides claim. *The Guardian.*

Editorial Board. (1 December 2016). 'Don't understand how girls find them inspirational… it's not sexy': Tweeters lash out at 'too thin' Victoria's Secret models as they strut their stuff at annual show in Paris. *The Daily Mail.*

Rankin, J. & Oltermann, P. (14 March 2017). Europe's right hails EU court's workplace headscarf ban ruling. *The Guardian.*

Speeches

Roosevelt, F. (1941, 6 January). *1941 State of the Union Address; annual message to congress.*

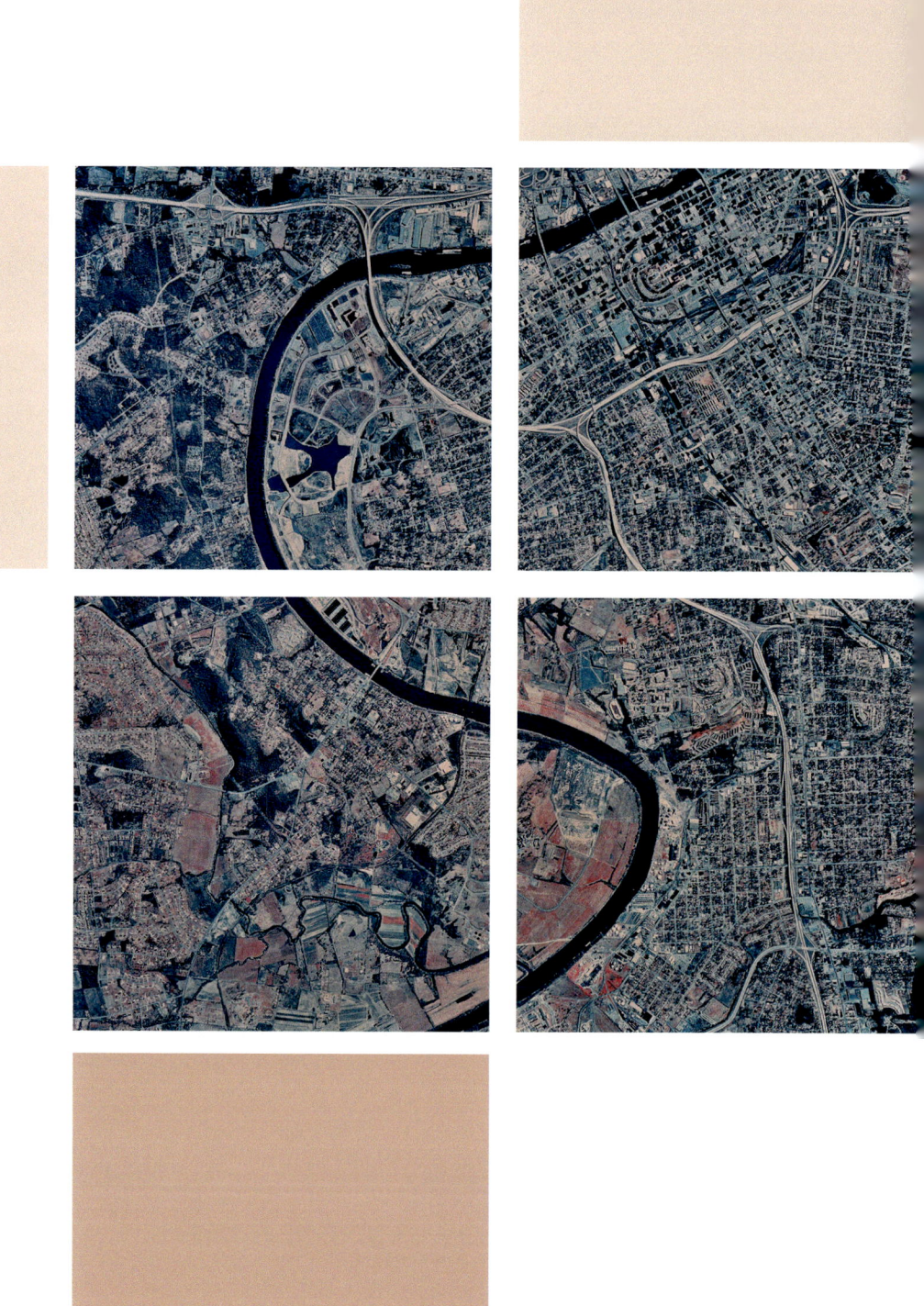

4

A model for ethical decision-making

In chapter 1 we discussed morality, and the underlying norms and values. In the end, we can observe moral behaviour when someone complies with a norm. When there are conflicting norms, we ask ourselves the question to what extent we feel responsible towards the conflicting norm. In chapter 2 we have seen various factors that influence this sense of responsibility. In chapter 3, we explored various directions in normative ethics, in which a position is taken on what norms and values are worth striving for, and how we deal with conflicting norms. In this chapter, we integrate all the above, and formulate a model for ethical decision-making, that should lead to an informed moral choice in case of an ethical dilemma.

4.1 An ethical dilemma

Ethical dilemma

> An ethical dilemma is a situation of conflicting morality, in which a person structurally explores in what way he will act.

We can solve an ethical dilemma through solid analysis and evaluation, as we can see in figure 4.1. In this four step approach, analysis (in which the researcher strives to be objective) and evaluation (in which the researcher is subjective) are integrated. Step 1 – 3 are analytic, step 4 is evaluative.

Step 1: The phrasing of a moral question.
Step 2: The mapping of the moral stakeholders and their morality.
Step 3: The analysis of potential ways of acting, based on functional equivalence.
Step 4: The making of an informed choice: to what extent do you feel responsible towards these stakeholders, and what direction in normative ethics do we use to morally justify our action?

FIGURE 4.1 An ethical decision-making model

	Analysis	**Evaluation**
Step 1	Define a moral question	
Step 2	• Who are involved morally? • What is the morality of the moral actors?	
Step 3	• What are possible alternatives?	
Step 4		Make an informed choice: • For whom do we feel responsible and to what extent? • What normative ethics do we apply?

4.2 Step 1: moral questions

The phrasing of a moral question lies at the core of an ethical decision-making model. It is very important to ask the right question in order to get the solution that is – in your view – the most ethical. While in essence the question greatly depends on the particularities of the conflicting morality, there are some rules of thumb we could use.

- Make sure that the moral question cannot be answered by a simple 'yes' or 'no'. This will almost per definition lead to simplified answers that will not stimulate any further creative problem solving beyond the two options you already imply in the question. An open question typically encourages a less 'black and white' view on matters. Therefore,

preferably phrase your moral question starting with words like 'to what extent', 'what', or 'how'.
- – Do: how should an export manager perform his work in a country where corruption is state of the art?
- – Don't: should an export manager involve himself in corruption in a country where this is state of the art?
- Make sure that the phrasing of your question allows you to explore the dilemma in-depth, and not just superficially.
  - – Do: what measures may Israel take against Hamas in response to the murder of an Israeli teenager?
  - – Don't: may Israel use armed force against its foes?
- Make sure that the phrasing of the question allows adequate room for other – and perhaps not so straight forward – opinions. In other words: do by no means try to force the answer into a certain direction by the formulation of your moral question. At this stage, we do not evaluate but merely provide for an advice.
  - – Do: what should the Dutch government do in response to the international criticism that has been voiced regarding the alleged racist character of Black Pete in the Sinterklaas festivities?
  - – Don't: to what extent is Black Pete a racist character, even when a significant amount of black people say they do not feel discriminated by this character?

With these rules of thumb we at least make sure we do not oversimplify matters or push the decision-making in a certain direction before we even start exploring. An acceptable phrasing of the moral question that relates to the case 'Sophie's Choice' would be:
'What should Sophie do when she is forced to choose between the lives of her two children on arrival in Auschwitz?'

Sophie's Choice

In the famous book of William Styron, Sophie is the main character. The book was later adapted for screen in 1982, featuring Meryl Streep. Sophie is a survival of Auschwitz during the Second World War and tries to get back to a normal life in New York. When the story continues we see several flash backs to the war period.
We see that Sophie was confronted with an impossible choice on arrival at Auschwitz. While waiting in line, already separated from her husband, she stands there huddled with her two children: a son and a daughter. Because she was not a Jew, but also not German (she was a Polish woman), the warden gave her a choice. There was no place for both of her children and therefore she could only bring one. The other would get killed in the gas chambers. If she would not make a choice at all, the guard threatens to kill both of her children. In the end, she chooses to get her daughter killed, and her son to remain alive. She considers that her son will probably be the stronger child, and has a better chance for survival. Unfortunately we learn that her son also dies in that concentration camp as a result of illness, and Sophie is the only one of her family that survives the war (Styron, 1979). This scene in which Sophie makes her choice is very intense to watch, and also the actress could only bear to play the scene once: it was literally filmed in one shot.

4.3 Step 2: moral stakeholders

The second step in an ethical decision model is to thoroughly map the stakeholders that are involved with the ethical dilemma. We refer to them as moral stakeholders. However, merely mapping those who are involved is not enough. We are furthermore interested in their ideas on morality, to make sure we understand the similarities and differences between their norms and values and our own. Answers to these two questions can be found through structural analysis.

Mapping of the moral stakeholders

So, first we map the moral stakeholders that relate to the ethical dilemma.

Moral stakeholders

> Moral stakeholders are actors whose norms and values can be affected by you or who can affect your norms and values in an ethical dilemma.

In the case of Sophie's choice we see that the moral stakeholders – besides Sophie of course – are the warden, the children of Sophie, as well as her husband. Confronted with the demand of the warden, the actions of these stakeholders can affect Sophie's norms and values, or the actions of Sophie can affect their norms and values.

The norms and values of the moral stakeholders

Once we have established who our moral stakeholders are, it is important to assess what their norms and values are in the context of the ethical dilemma. In addition, for a full understanding, it can be helpful to also map the virtue and interest required to comply with these norms and values.

In the example of *Sophie's Choice* this would look as follows:

Warden:
Values: racial purification, purity
Norms: intimidate and exterminate non-Arians
Virtue: determination, ruthlessness
Interest: a gun, a concentration camp

The children of Sophie:
Values: family security, happiness, love, peace, freedom
Norms: try to stay alive
Virtue: courage and determination
Interest: objects that help to hide/defend themselves

Sophie's husband:
Values: family security, happiness, love, peace, freedom
Norms: try to stay alive
Virtue: courage and determination
Interest: objects that help defend his family/access to his family

We can now compare the values of the moral stakeholders with the values of Sophie. Obviously, we do not know yet what her norm(s) will be, since we are using this ethical decision-making model to find out what norm we should comply with if we would be Sophie.

Sophie:
Values: family security, happiness, love, peace, freedom
Norms: to be determined
Virtue: to be determined
Interest: to be determined

In this case, it is not surprising that Sophie's values are at great odds with the values of the warden, and that her values are almost the same compared to her family members.

So, at this stage we know who our moral stakeholders are, and how they perceive morality relating to the ethical dilemma. We also know in what way they are different or similar compared to Sophie's own values.

This gives sufficient input to continue with the next step, which is to assess potential solutions based on functional equivalence.

4.4 Step 3: alternatives

In this step, we assess the potential alternatives for Sophie regarding her ethical dilemma. All alternatives – how radical they might be – are at least functionally equivalent since they all respond to the same moral question. Examples of *Sophie's Choice* could be:

Sophie tries to run away with both of her kids.
While she would only have a small chance of survival, she will not have to choose between one of her children. This alternative would naturally conflict with the values of the warden, who will probably use his gun to stop them. Simultaneously, it would violate her own values, as well as the values of her family members. However, perhaps the value family unity is preserved, because the three of them escape, or all die.

This alternative seems to be inspired by deontology (moral rights): while the consequences are possibly quite severe, at least the family stays together as much as possible, which is in line with the right to family life.

Sophie makes no choice and loses both children.
This alternative would at first sight appear to be contrary to the values of both Sophie, her husband and her children, since now three out of four die for sure, and as a result the values family security, happiness, love and freedom are no longer fulfilled. In addition, the warden will be thrilled because he can actually contribute even more to his value of racial purification.
At the same time we could wonder whether Sophie will ever be able to live with herself when she would choose between one of her children. Also, the remaining child will find it difficult to live with this situation for the remainder of his/her life. Perhaps then an equal treatment is the best way to deal with this situation, not favouring one child over the other.

This alternative seems to be inspired by the principle of equality (egalitarian).

Sophie chooses to let her daughter live.
This alternative would of course conflict with the values of her son. After all, he will never be able to realize family security, happiness, love nor freedom. On the other hand, the daughter potentially might, if she would survive the war. And perhaps the same goes for Sophie, although it is doubtful whether she can live with the memory of such a choice. Imagine Sophie would make that choice because she can identify herself more with her daughter than her son. She acts purely based on emotion, and relies on her gut feeling while making this choice.

This alternative seems to be inspired by post-modernist ethics.

Sophie chooses to let her son live.
This alternative would of course conflict with the values of her daughter. After all, she will never be able to realize family security, happiness, love nor freedom. On the other hand, the son potentially might, if he would survive the war. And perhaps the same goes for Sophie, although it is doubtful whether she can live with the memory of such a choice. Sophie reasons that her son is older than her daughter, and therefore probably will be stronger and has a greater chance of survival in a concentration camp.

This alternative seems to be inspired by consequentialism (utilitarianism): in this reasoning her choice leads to the highest chance of the survival of the largest number of people.

⬛4.5 Step 4: an informed choice

Until now, we used analysis to phrase the moral dilemma, map the moral stakeholders and their moral views, as well as compare different alternatives that could solve the ethical dilemma.

It is time to take a decision and solve the ethical dilemma. This is a subjective decision that is based on our critical evaluation of the possible alternatives we explored. Two things here can help us to substantiate our decision. First, the factors that influence responsibility as discussed in the second chapter. Second, normative ethics, as discussed in chapter three.

Factors that influence responsibility
In step two we analysed who our moral stakeholders are, and how they perceive morality in an ethical dilemma. This does not mean however that we feel equally responsible towards all these stakeholders, for various reasons. The factors that influence responsibility will most likely play a dominant role here. As discussed in chapter two, these factors either relate to your ability of taking responsibility, or relate to the specific situation of conflicting values. As for the first, the following questions may help you:
- *To what degree are your moral stakeholders (including you) free (physically and autonomously) to take on responsibility regarding the other stakeholders?*

- *To what degree do your moral stakeholders (including you) have sufficient knowledge of the situation in order to take responsibility towards the other stakeholders?*
- *To what degree do your moral stakeholders (including you) have adequate moral imagination in order to take responsibility towards the other stakeholders?*

As to the situational factors, the following – reciprocal – questions can help:
- *How much influence do I have on the norms and values of other stakeholders and vice versa?*
- *How close is the relationship with the other stakeholders and vice versa?*
- *How large is the impact you can have on the norms and values of the other stakeholders and vice versa?*
- *What is your specific relationship or role towards the other stakeholders and vice versa?*

In figure 4.2 you can see a schematic representation of factors that influence responsibility between moral stakeholders.

FIGURE 4.2   The structural evaluation of responsibility towards moral actors

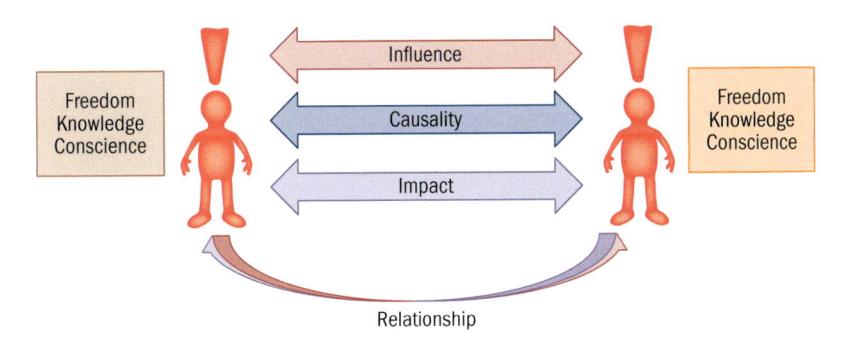

In the example 'Sophie's choice' the situation is truly horrible and perhaps even surrealistic to some. While the norms and values of Sophie and her family are so very different from the warden, and the warden has such a big power position over them, it seems unlikely that we can solve this moral dilemma. However, the evaluative questions on responsibility provide us with at least some insight into the situation on a more analytic level, and we can try to understand what is going on here, and perhaps even how we should act if we would be Sophie. In figure 4.3 you can see a schematic representation of these questions applied to the case of Sophie, in a structural evaluation of our responsibility towards the moral actors.

FIGURE 4.3 The structural evaluation of responsibility towards moral actors

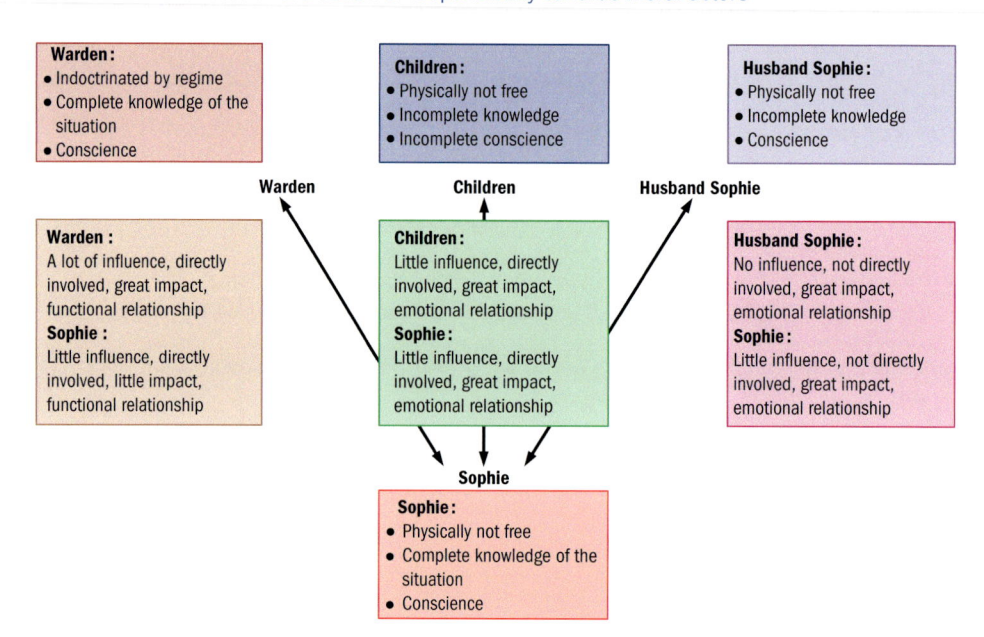

Factors that affect the ability of taking responsibility

When we consider the factors that affect the ability of taking responsibility, it is obvious in this case that Sophie and her family lack the physical freedom to take responsibility towards one another as they would normally do. After all, they are detained in a concentration camp, with armed wardens. In addition, we see that the warden justifies his actions based on a radical doctrine invented by the Nazis, which involves a great deal of positive freedom. The question here would be whether there is a proper balance between negative and positive freedom regarding the warden, or that he is so indoctrinated that he would do atrocious things in the name of Nazi Germany.

We also see that Sophie's children as well as her husband are not fully aware of the situation, or the implications of the choice that is given to Sophie. In other words, we could say they have inadequate knowledge of the situation to take a certain responsibility. Furthermore, we can ask ourselves the question whether the children have the necessary moral imagination to fully understand what is going on here.

Situational factors

When we consider the situational factors we have to conclude that Sophie has very little influence on the warden, while the warden on the other hand has a huge influence on the norms and values of Sophie. The impact of Sophie's choice on the norms and values of the warden is very little, while the choice has a huge impact on all her family members, including herself. It seems that the only influence Sophie has is to make a choice and undergo the consequences.

Needless to say the norms and values of the children and her husband are very close to Sophie, while the norms and values of the warden could not be farther away from her. Lastly, Sophie has a special relation with her husband and children, since they are her family. Especially towards her children therefore we could assume she would like to play a protective role and keep them as safe as possible.

Normative ethics

As we have seen in step three, the various alternatives and reasoning underpinning these alternatives can relate to one of the directions in normative ethics we discussed in chapter three. There is no right or wrong approach here, but a subjective preference. The choice made by Sophie can be classified as complying with one of the theories on normative ethics. We can turn to this direction in normative ethics for the moral justification of the action. For instance, when Sophie chooses to sacrifice her daughter because she thinks that her son is stronger and therefore has a greater chance of survival, utilitarianism can be used to justify this action. After all, it potentially leads to the best possible outcome for the largest number of people, considering the circumstances.

One last remark is that to make sure you took the right decision it always makes sense to check whether indeed your solution responds to the ethical dilemma. In the movie, the ethical dilemma 'What should Sophie do when she is forced to choose between the lives of her two children on arrival in Auschwitz?' is answered with the solution 'Sophie chooses to let her son live'. Despite the horrific solution, this is indeed a solution that solves the ethical dilemma.

4

Summary

4

▶ An ethical dilemma is a situation of conflicting morality, in which a person structurally explores the way he will act.

▶ We can solve an ethical dilemma through solid analysis and evaluation, using a four-step approach. Step 1 – 3 are analytic, step 4 is evaluative.

▶ Step 1: The phrasing of a moral question. There are three rules of thumb:
  • Make sure that the moral question cannot be answered by a simple 'yes' or 'no'.
  • Make sure that the phrasing of your question allows you to explore the dilemma in-depth, and not just superficially.
  • Make sure that the phrasing of the question allows adequate room for other opinions.

▶ Step 2: The mapping of the moral stakeholders and their morality.

▶ Step 3: The analysis of potential ways of acting, based on functional equivalence.

▶ Step 4: The making of an informed choice.
  • To what extent do you feel responsible towards these stakeholders, using individual and situational factors that affect responsibility (chapter two)?
  • What direction in normative ethics do we use to morally justify our action (chapter three)?

Literature

Styron, W. (1979). *Sophie's Choice*. New York: Random House.

4

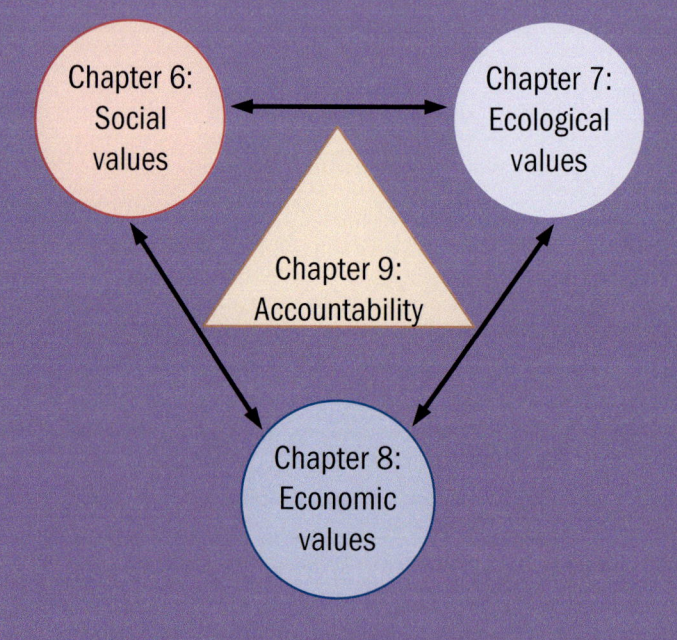

PART 2

Business and ethics

In this part we will discuss ethics at company level.

In chapter 5 we will explore ethics in business from a historical perspective and introduce the idea of the 'triple bottom line', from which we can learn that next to profit maximization, certain values could also play a role in business, and companies could take a responsibility in realizing those values. These are social values (chapter 6), ecological values (chapter 7) and economic values (chapter 8). In addition we will discuss how a company can be held accountable for their behaviour towards these values (chapter 9).

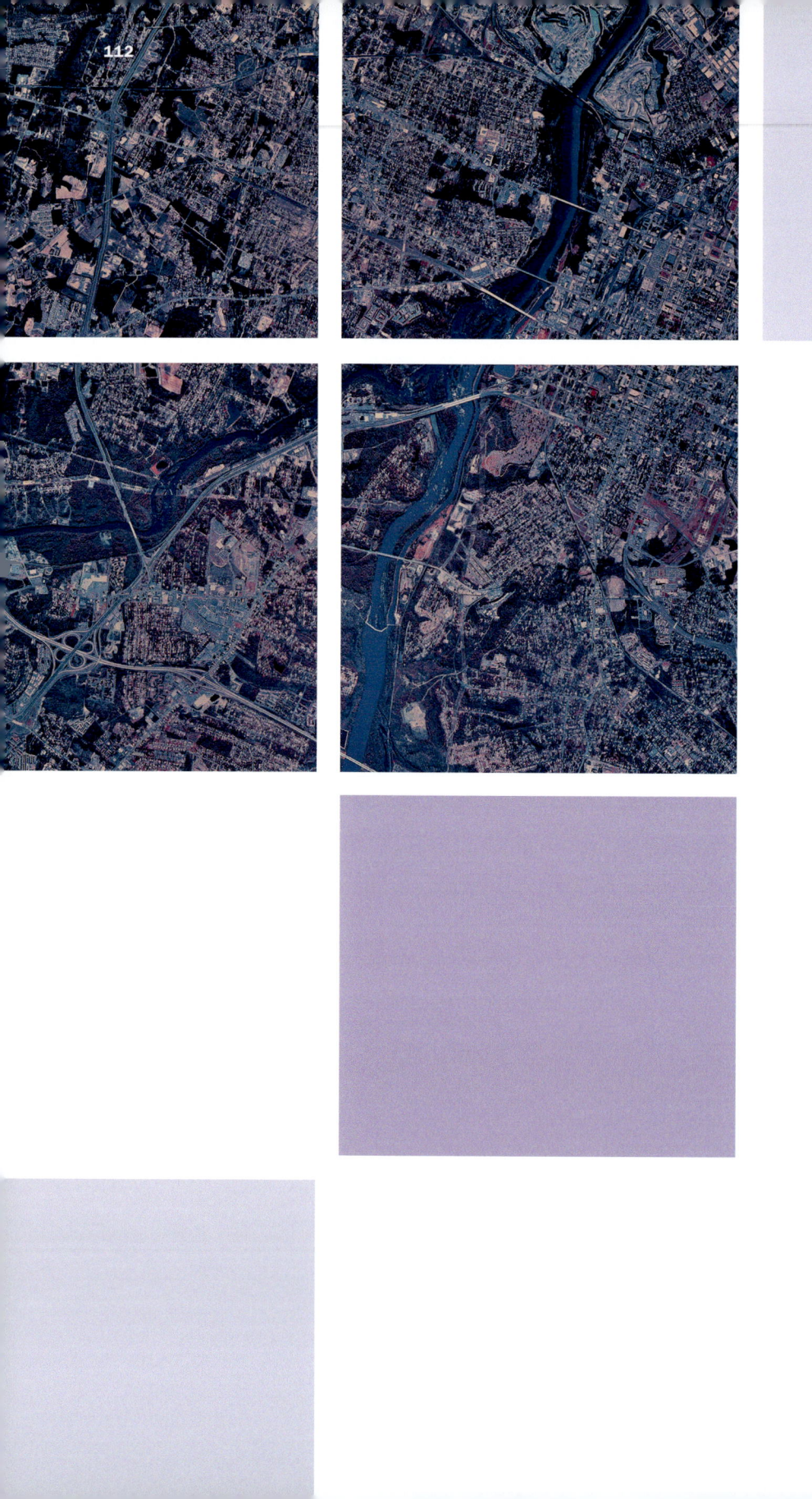

5

A short history of ethics in business

In this chapter we will first discuss the history of ethics at company level. As we will see, ethics has been discussed in this context since the industrial revolution. Secondly, in recent history, we see a renewed interest in ethics in business as a result of certain social trends. Therefore, we will explain these trends in-depth. This modern discussion on ethics in business has led to the emergence of a theory that claims that there is more than just profit: the triple bottom line. In this theory, profit should go hand in hand with taking care of people and our planet. We will critically review this theory with arguments in support of as well as arguments against this approach.

5.1 The industrial revolution

5

A Christmas Carol

The famous book *A Christmas Carol*, written by Charles Dickens (1843), has been adapted to the screen many times. Our favourite is the version featuring the Muppets. In a nutshell, the story involves a wealthy businessman, Ebenezer Scrooge, who simply hates Christmas. To illustrate this, he grumpily rejects an invitation of his cousin Fred to spend Christmas Eve with his family. One day before Christmas, he is confronted with a request of his accountant – Bob Cratchit – to take a day off for Christmas to spend some time with his family. Grumpily, Scrooge agrees but emphasizes that Cratchit has to compensate the free day with working over hours in the next week. The same day, Scrooge shuts the door in the face of a census taker, without giving him anything for charity. All this pretty much characterizes Ebenezer Scrooge: a grumpy and greedy man.

That night, when mister Scrooge comes home and goes to bed, he is haunted in his dreams by three ghosts. The first ghost takes him back to his youth, and we learn that his childhood was far from happy. Scrooge lost his sister when he was very young; she appeared to be the only one that truly cared for him. This past made him the cold man he is today. The second ghost shows him the present, in which we see how the Cratchit family lives in serious poverty. A particularly distressing fact is that Cratchit's son is in poor health, is a cripple and will probably not survive another winter. Finally, the third ghost shows Scrooge his future. They visit his own grave, and see that people seem to welcome his death, and celebrate the fact that this greedy old man is no longer amongst them.

In cold sweat Scrooge wakes up and realizes that this is most certainly not the way he wants to be remembered. He suddenly realizes that his life brought him a lot of wealth, but no luck. From now on he decides to change his life, starting by generously donating to charity, delivers a royal turkey to the Cratchit family (which they could never afford themselves) and celebrates Christmas with his family.

Discussing ethics in the context of companies is not a new phenomenon, but can be traced back to the industrial revolution. This revolution took off in England around 1760 with the invention of the steam engine, and then quickly spread to the rest of Western Europe, the United States and Eastern Asia.

Industrial revolution

> The industrial revolution is the sudden transition from manual production to machine production which took off in Western Europe from 1760.

This metamorphosis of the West European industry had some far-reaching consequences for society: urbanization, income inequality and pollution (Trinder, 2013). These phenomena increasingly led to debates on the responsibility of companies and their ethical awareness. After all, the side effects of profit maximization were not always that positive for the average European citizen. As you can read in the example 'A Christmas Carol', Charles Dickens was one of the first in the 19th century who would critically comment on the large income gap between company owners and employees, and the poor living conditions of the working class. While the 19th century is a long time ago, it is important to learn about the side effects of industrialization, since some countries are currently in the stage of industrializing, and will face (or are facing) similar type of challenges.

As a result of the quick emergence of clustered industrialization in the cities, the countryside was suddenly drained, and people moved to the larger cities in the hope of finding a job. Where before the industrial revolution, West European landscape was mostly dominated by small villages where they would earn a living in the manual production of products, this would all change with the transition from manual to industrial production.

> Urbanization is the development in which people who live in rural areas move to urban regions on a large scale.

Urbanization

With the invention of the steam engine, developed by scientists as Thomas Savery, Thomas Newcomen and James Watt, it was possible to produce much faster and for much lower costs compared to manual production. This certainly played a major role in the textile industry. Family businesses in the countryside, where people would manually produce garments, could simply not compete with the large factories. To be able to still make a living, these people would give up their homes in the countryside, and move to towns in the hope of finding work.

A side effect was that the traditional cottage industry became more or less useless. Where before the industrial revolution all family members (especially women and children) would contribute in small proportions in the production of some clothes, craftwork or foodstuff, and earn some additional income next to the main income of the household, this was not necessary anymore. After all, machines would now be able to produce much more efficiently. So, households would not only lose their primary income, but also their secondary incomes.

Another consequence of the industrial revolution was the ever-increasing income gap between a relatively large part of the population who lived in poverty, and a small part of the population – typically the owners of businesses – who lived in great wealth. This income inequality was mainly caused by the fact that machines were replacing employees. To produce the same amount of products manually would require many more employees compared to the industrial production in a factory. This simply means that the demand for employees went down, while the amount of potential workers went up. The natural economic consequence is that wages go down. Simultaneously, the factory owners would win the competition from manual producers because they could produce for much lower costs. As a result, they would see their profit continuously increasing.

Income inequality

This led to the emergence of a brand new social class in West-European societies: the so called working class. They would live on the edge of the towns in small houses, under very poor conditions. In some growing industrial towns, the sewers were not even in place in these neighbourhoods, and there was inadequate water and electricity supply. These conditions where in sharp contrast with the fact that in most industrialized countries, the Gross National Income (GNI) increased considerably as a result of the success of the industry. However, the profits would go directly to the shareholders, and the average working class citizen would not benefit from the increasing GNI. This situation was labelled as the 'social question' and led to increasing unrest in the industrialized countries (Vercherand, 2014).

Only in the early nineteenth century we see the adoption of social laws that would strengthen the legal position of workers, which includes a ban on child labour, the creation of social security systems, the legalizing of trade unions, and increasing political influence of the working class through labour parties.

The relation of large technological innovation and the labour market is described in an economic theory called the 'Malthusian trap'. Economist Thomas Robert Malthus claimed that when a society is able to use its resources more efficiently and therefore produce more, this will always lead to an increase in the population. After all, products are cheaper and in greater numbers, so society can host more people. However, the living conditions and life expectancy do not improve and may even become worse, since people lose their job as a result of the more efficient allocation of resources. Technological developments therefore always lead to adversity first (Malthus, 1798).

To illustrate, we may find an interesting example of an expected Malthusian trap in our near future when robots are used on a large scale to replace workers (Berriman, 2017), as you may see in the newspaper article 'Watch out America, robots are coming for jour jobs', experts expect a significant impact on our employment and our economies.

Pollution   A third effect of the industrial revolution was the heavy pollution in the cities. The average industry town was flooded with black carbon and waste: a very unhealthy and unhygienic atmosphere to live in. Back then it did not yet occur to people that mass production would have its limits in terms of such pollution. When a lot of people live together in these circumstances, the situation can become very dangerous. For instance, many large industry towns were confronted with cholera outbreaks and other diseases.

When we read the foregoing, we would almost conclude that the industrial revolution only led to negative outcomes. However, that would be a one sided assessment. On the long term, industrialization has led to a far better standard of living in industrialized countries compared to the 19th century. Urbanization also has a strong positive effect: when many people come together, cooperation becomes easier, and new ideas can be nurtured and developed. This has led to great breakthroughs not only in science and technology, but also in other disciplines such as architecture (Trinder, 2013). The steam machine has marked the starting point of an unprecedented technological development, which was later followed by the digital revolution, which took off shortly after the Second World War. The development of computers and other digital tools has led to countless possibilities and applications in our daily life. At the same time, digitalization has also led to more effective production methods, resulting in loss of jobs on the short term (Brynjolfsson & McAfee, 2011).

THE DAILY MAIL ONLINE, 24 MARCH 2017

Watch out America, robots are coming for your jobs: Report finds 38% of US jobs will be automated by 2030

While millions of people fearing a robot-run world, it is Americans who should worry the most.

A new report has found that 38 percent of US jobs will be replaced by robots and artificial intelligence by the early 2030s. The analysis, done by accountancy giant PwC, also revealed that it is financial service jobs that are at most risk of a robot takeover – 61 percent could be replaced by machines.

PwC recently published a report that focused on the UK, but also included details of how Americans will fare over the next 15 years.

The research found that more jobs are at risk in the US compared to other major producing countries around the world – 30 percent of UK jobs, 35 percent in Germany and 21 percent in Japan.

(...)

The development of driverless cars, lorries and vans means workers in the transportation and storage sector are at a particularly high risk.

According to the analysis, around 950,000 of these jobs will be replaced – 56.4 percent of the workforce.

Driverless cars are expected to be on the roads by 2020.

Taxi hailing app Uber is working on building a driverless cab – setting off alarm bells among drivers.

The boom in online shopping is also predicted to lead to a dramatic reduction in the number of high street stores and staff.

Some 2.25 million jobs will disappear in retail and wholesale, more than in any other sector, the report found.

John Hawksworth, PwC's chief economist, said many shops could become more like 'showrooms', where customers look at goods before buying them online.

This would lead to more giant warehouses, such as those operated by Amazon.

Instead of humans, machines will increasingly sort and lift goods before they are delivered to customers in driverless vans, the experts predict.

Self-service tills will also become more prevalent.

More than 1.2 million manufacturing jobs are at high risk – or 46.4 percent of the sector.

And almost 1.1 million jobs – 37.4 per cent – are at risk in administration and support services such as IT.

However, the report said those that have the lowest risk of being replaced by robots include nannies, teachers, white collar workers in the finance industry, and communications staff.

5.2 Current trends in society

As we have seen in the previous section, ethics in business is not really a new phenomenon, and the debate exists ever since the industrialization of our economies. However, we could say that during the last few decades there is a renewed attention for the moral behaviour of companies as a result of certain social trends (Elkington, 1997, Jeurissen, 2007). In this book

we conclude that there are at least five of such trends, which we will explore in this section:
- privatization
- technological and digital innovation
- changes in morality
- economic and financial crises
- globalization

5.2.1 The end of the welfare state: privatization

Privatization

> Privatization is the transfer of public ownership and powers to the private sector.

Since the late eighties, we see a trend that in some West European countries the government took a few steps back in performing certain duties, and instead invited the private sector to take over these jobs. This development has led to various ethical questions and dilemmas.
However, to put all this in the proper context, we first must explore in which way governments performed their duties and took their responsibilities since the industrial revolution. In a nutshell, we see that most governments of industrialized countries balance somewhere in between a night-watchman state and a social welfare state.

Night-watchman state

> A night-watchman state is characterized by a small government that only intervenes in the lives of its citizens where necessary and mostly focuses on maintaining a safe and secure society.

Social welfare state

> A social welfare state is characterized by an active government that takes responsibility for the welfare of its citizens.

To use the terminology of Berlin (see paragraph 2.2.1), a night-watchman state is focused on negative freedom, where a social welfare state puts more emphasis on positive freedom. When the industrial revolution took off, most developed countries were a night-watchman state. However, the negative side effects of industrialization prompted these governments to more actively interfere in their societies. This was mostly encouraged by the labour parties of these countries. As a result, the governments of industrialized countries moved more and more towards a social welfare state, increasingly taking responsibility for the wellbeing of its citizens. This has led to the development of a highly advanced system of social security. However, a social welfare state has its price: due to worldwide economic crisis in the eighties, the average welfare state threatened to collapse under its own weight, and countries feared bankruptcy (Zijderveld, 1999). The fact that unemployment rates kept rising did not help much, and made a social welfare state even more expensive, while simultaneously, tax income went down. As a result, many governments were now forced to cut their budgets dramatically, and implement dramatic economic reforms. One of the solutions was found in privatization.

This leads to ethical dilemmas such as you can see in the news article 'Drug Goes From $13.50 a Tablet to $750, Overnight.' Where we would expect a government to act in defence of public interest, and as a part of that guarantees access to healthcare for all its citizens, some elements of healthcare are entrusted to private parties. In some countries, healthcare insurers are companies, and in most countries, pharmaceutical companies are the main producers and sellers of medication. This could lead to very questionable situations. A healthcare insurer with a profit aim will not likely be very keen on insuring a disabled, elderly or ill person while they need it the most. A pharmaceutical company with a profit aim will not necessarily act in the best interest of public wellbeing, but consider the medicines they sell as a way to make profit. Will you then get the best medicines, or the ones with the highest profit? And will these companies invest serious money in research into medication that can cure very rare diseases, or would they rather go for the medicines that cure something that occurs frequently? These are serious concerns regarding the privatization the health care.

On the other hand, we could say that privatization can lead to a serious improvement of health care, especially because the effects of a market in which insurers and pharmaceutical companies compete. These companies will work as hard as possible to get the best quality for the lowest price, and as a result of the competition consumers have a varied choice of alternatives, instead of prescribed insurance or drugs.

Although privatization is typically a western word, we also find developments of privatizing elsewhere in this world. In China, for example, we see that the Communist Party slowly allows elements of a free market economy in their country, which has led to the gradual transformation of legal forms of a company. Where previously the companies were considered exclusively as public property, run by the government to contribute to public aims, we now see the emergence of new Chinese legislation that allows individuals to own shares in companies. We could say that also here, a public role is transferred to the private domain (Gu, 2006).

THE NEW YORK TIMES, 20 SEPTEMBER 2015

Drug Goes From $13.50 a Tablet to $750, Overnight

By: Andrew Pollack

Specialists in infectious disease are protesting a gigantic overnight increase in the price of a 62-year-old drug that is the standard of care for treating a life – threatening parasitic infection.
The drug, called Daraprim, was acquired in August by Turing Pharmaceuticals, a start-up run by a former hedge fund manager. Turing immediately raised the price to $750 a tablet from $13.50, bringing the annual cost of treatment for some patients to hundreds of thousands of dollars.
(…)

Daraprim, known generically as pyrimethamine, is used mainly to treat toxoplasmosis, a parasite infection that can cause serious or even life-threatening problems for babies born to women who are infected during pregnancy, and also for people with compromised immune systems, like AIDS patients and certain cancer patients.

Martin Shkreli, the founder and chief executive of Turing, said that the drug is so rarely used that the impact on the health system would be minuscule and that Turing would use the money it earns to develop better treatments for toxoplasmosis, with fewer side effects. 'This isn't the greedy drug company trying to gouge patients, it is us trying to stay in business,' Mr. Shkreli said. He said that many patients use the drug for far less than a year and that the price was now more in line with those of other drugs for rare diseases. 'This is still one of the smallest pharmaceutical products in the world,' he said. 'It really doesn't make sense to get any criticism for this.'

This is not the first time the 32-year-old Mr. Shkreli, who has a reputation for both brilliance and brashness, has been the centre of controversy. He started MSMB Capital, a hedge fund company, in his 20s and drew attention for urging the Food and Drug Administration not to approve certain drugs made by companies whose stock he was shorting.

5.2.2   Technological and digital innovation

As we have seen in the previous section, industrialization has led to the capacity to produce on an enormous scale. In addition, digitalization has led to unprecedented connectedness between people, and access to an ever-increasing flow of shared information. Both developments do not come without new ethical challenges for businesses. When technology and digitalization becomes increasingly complex, even a well-educated citizen will probably not fully understand what he is using. The average passenger on a plane will not fully understand the technology used in this plane, and the average social media user will have no clue how the algorithms work that decide what appears in your timeline. This leads to a serious gap in knowledge between the airplane industry or social media platforms on the one hand, and other stakeholders on the other. Only when things go terribly wrong, consumers will start complaining and demand improvement of things preferably through tough legislation. However, at the end of the day, governments will probably also be unable to seriously change the performance of these businesses by using their legislative powers, since also they are not an expert in how these highly complex technological and digital products work. Or in other words: it is very difficult to establish any serious public control over the impact of industrialization and digitalization due to its complexity. This leaves a heavy moral burden on the shoulders of the industry itself, since they appear to be the only one that can seriously use their knowledge to do the right thing (Jasanoff, 2016; Aarts, et al. 2017). The fact that such a company primarily has a profit aim does not always help.

A good example of this phenomenon is the alleged influence of social media on the U.S. elections in 2016. Various stakeholders tried to get 'fake news' across to stimulate the elections results. It was rumoured that foreign entities were also part of this. While no one really can tell what the statistics are of such fake news, and to what extent this may change the minds of voters (Allcott & Gentzkow, 2017), the issue was surrounded by a lot of speculation, as we can see in the news article. Even a hearing in the American Senate involving representatives of Google, Twitter and Facebook did not reveal much of what might have happened (Shaban et al. 2017), nor what these companies will (or can) do to prevent any abuse of democratic systems in the future through their online platforms.

THE GUARDIAN, 22 MAY 2017

How social media filter bubbles and algorithms influence the election

5

With Facebook becoming a key electoral battleground, researchers are studying how automated accounts are used to alter political debate online.

One of the most powerful players in the British election is also one of the most opaque. With just over two weeks to go until voters go to the polls, there are two things every election expert agrees on: what happens on social media, and Facebook in particular, will have an enormous effect on how the country votes; and no one has any clue how to measure what's actually happening there.

'Many of us wish we could study Facebook,' said Prof Philip Howard, of the University of Oxford's Internet Institute, 'but we can't, because they really don't share anything.' Howard is leading a team of researchers studying 'computational propaganda' at the university, attempting to shine a light on the ways automated accounts are used to alter debate online. 'I think that there have been several democratic exercises in the last year that have gone off the rails because of large amounts of misinformation in the public sphere,' Howard said. 'Brexit and its outcome, and the Trump election and its outcome, are what I think of as "mistakes", in that there were such significant amounts of misinformation out in the public sphere.'

'Not all of that comes from automation. It also comes from the news culture, bubbles of education, and people's ability to do critical thinking when they read the news. But the proximate cause of misinformation is Facebook serving junk news to large numbers of users.'(...)

5.2.3   Changes in morality

The digitalization of our societies did not only trigger ethical dilemmas, but also greatly contributed to changing our moral thinking. When we have almost unlimited access to various news agencies, online sources and social platforms, and at the same time can easily contribute to public debates through these media, morality becomes a shared public issue. As Jeurissen (2007) points out: traditional authorities, such as a government, a religious institute, a police officer, or a teacher, have lost their monopoly regarding moral thinking. Instead, we all have the possibility to voice our own opinion on morality, and review this against the opinion of others. As a manner of speaking, social media has become a large debate room in which we can share our moral views on what happens in the world today.

The fact that we do not take traditional moral authority for granted is an interesting development. On the one hand it leads to a wider debate on what is right and wrong, and everyone with access to internet can contribute to this. This 'open access' environment has opened up a brand new digital world for many people, and can lead to serious changes in our societies. For instance, the Arab Spring is nicknamed the 'Twitter revolution' or the Facebook revolution, since the uprising of the people against their governments was triggered by exchanges on social media (Cottle, 2011).

On the other hand, social media is quick and characterized by short messages. This inevitably leads to a decline in thoroughness and encourages sharp communication over modesty and nuance. As we have seen in the previous section, it is not always easy to filter the enormous mass of digital information and assess its accuracy. Fake news is relatively easy to get across, and can be used to manipulate or even oppress people (Spaiser, 2017). When moral authority is more and more owned by the public mass, everything can be questioned. Think about the average discussion on social media on the definition of healthy food. It becomes questionable when established scientific conclusions are rejected by people just because it is their opinion. As we will see in chapter 7, this is a problem in the context of global warming.

This development also has some profound consequences in the field of ethics and business. They are now much more challenged through a public debate to take responsibility for social and environmental values, next to profit maximization (Elkington, 1997). When profit stands in the way of these social and ecological values, there is a risk of public naming and shaming through social media. This has led to behavioural changes amongst companies, in which they focus on how they interact with people through social media and how they get a message across that includes the 'softer' values in the field of social and environmental issues. A good example of this is the case 'Oil disasters and crisis management', in which we observe that in a timeframe of two decades, we see a huge difference in response between the Exxon and BP management regarding an oil disaster. The first is almost authoritarian, not involved and not empathic, where the second seems to be almost the opposite. In Chapter 9 we will further explore approaches in accountability of companies.

Oil disasters and crisis management

On 24 March 1989, an oil tanker of the American company Exxon – Valdez – crashed off the coast of Alaska, and leaked an estimated 250,000 barrels, which comes down to 11 million gallons of oil. The crash was a result of a steering error from a very tired crew member. As it appeared, the ship's captain was sleeping in his cabin at that moment, recovering from some drinks he had the night before. The oil spill had disastrous consequences for the coastal region of Alaska, well known for its unspoiled flora and fauna. Different animal species were severely affected and significantly reduced in population, while some protected nature parks were seriously polluted. Furthermore, the fishing industry of Alaska practically came to a halt. Considering the impact on the environment, we could say this oil disaster was the worst in history (www.evostc.state.ak.us, 2014).

While in Alaska they tried to clean up the mess with all available resources as fast as possible to prevent even more damage to the environment, the management of Exxon did not seem to be in a hurry to take action. The highest board of directors was later accused of being uninvolved, leaving the issue to lower management. Only one week later, some members of the Exxon board would travel to the Alaskan coast to see for themselves what has happened.

The press was initially ignored, and later communication towards the media was very limited, contradicting and unclear. Only after ten days, the company published an apology in some newspapers, although they were still of the opinion not to be responsible for the disaster. Therefore, Exxon did not intend to pay for any damage compensation. This attitude resulted in some considerable image damage to Exxon. In addition, the company was tried in court several times, and were forced to pay significant damage compensation to the victims of the disaster. In the end, Exxon did lose a considerable share in the oil market (Williams & Treadaway, 1992; Holusha, 1989).

Deep Water Horizon
The response of the management of British Petroleum (BP) in the aftermath of the Deep Water Horizon oil spill in 2010 in the Gulf of Mexico was rather different. Within a few days, the highest management assessed the damage done personally, and explored ways in which this could be fixed as soon as possible. Furthermore, they talked to the press frequently, and their responses were more or less coordinated. Also here, BP

considered themselves not fully responsible for the oil disaster (there were more companies operating on the oil platform), but did set up ad-hoc tribunals to make sure that damage compensation was awarded quickly to those who suffered from the oil spill (BP Sustainability Review 2010). Especially the fact that the oil spill went viral on social media caused BP to act quickly in their communication, and come up with a comprehensive strategy to respond to press and social media. While there is some debate about the effectiveness and quality of the initial management statements in the earliest phase of their crisis management (Mejri, 2013) we see a considerable difference compared to the Exxon approach two decades earlier.

5.2.4 Economic and financial crisis

At the end of 2007, the financial markets faced a massive worldwide crisis. Initially, the U.S. financial markets went down, and this affected the rest of the world too, leading to a collapse of the worldwide financial markets. This had an enormous impact on the functioning of our global economy. Some countries were on the brink of bankruptcy and had to take drastic measures, involving major cuts in government budgets, to keep things going. This affected many people negatively.

Part of the explanation of this worldwide crisis was found in the unethical behaviour of financial institutions and companies, as well as failing governmental control over these sectors. Whether or not this is the root cause of the financial crisis, it has stirred a debate about the role of financial institutions, the nature of financial products, and how we can make the sector more sustainable. Furthermore, the relation between the financial markets and governments was debated ever since, assessing the way governments could or should supervise these financial markets, and in what way companies and financial institutes should take a responsibility that goes beyond the making of short-term profits.

On a more macro level, the question is addressed whether our economic system allows these companies and institutions to change their behaviour as such, and whether we should adjust our economic and financial systems in general to create a more sustainable financial environment (Posner, 2011; Westbrook, 2009).

5.2.5 Globalization

Increasingly, our economy will get an international dimension. We could refer to this phenomenon as 'globalization'.

| Globalization is the consequence of fading borders. **Globalization**

Since World War II we see various examples of a step-by-step implementation of a free global market, in which national economies integrate into larger

5

Regulatory competition

markets. Examples are the Mercosur (South America), the North Atlantic Free Trade Agreement, and the South African Customs Union. The most striking example however is the European Union, in which the free movement of goods, services, people, and capital is firmly established and enforced by law. On the one hand, this offers enormous opportunities for exporting companies and multinationals. When companies have equal access to larger markets they can compete fairly, which in theory should lead to more consumer choice, lower prices and faster product innovation. On the other hand, there is always the risk of regulatory competition. The country or region with the most flexible standards will attract most business. After all, a company can cross a border, while national legislation cannot. This means that especially for a multinational, it is easy to establish itself in the country that offers the most flexible tax rules, or labour laws or environmental standards. While essentially this leads to a higher profit for the multinational, and possibly more employment for the selected country, this will not always contribute to the realization of social and ecological values. A famous example is the revealing of the Panama Papers in 2015 and the Paradise Papers in 2017, as we can see in the newspaper item. Rich people and companies use off-shore companies to evade high taxation in other countries. While essentially this is not illegal, it could be considered by some as immoral: the country where you actually live or employ your business is not awarded the taxes it would normally gain.

THE NEW YORK TIMES, 5 NOVEMBER 2017

Paradise Papers Shine Light on Where the Elite Keep Their Money

By: Michael Forsythe

It's called the Paradise Papers: the latest in a series of leaks made public by the International Consortium of Investigative Journalists shedding light on the trillions of dollars that move through offshore tax havens.

The core of the leak, totalling more than 13.4 million documents, focuses on the Bermudan law firm Appleby, a 119-year old company that caters to blue chip corporations and very wealthy people. Appleby helps clients reduce their tax burden; obscure their ownership of assets like companies, private aircraft, real estate

and yachts; and set up huge offshore trusts that in some cases hold billions of dollars. (...)

Regarding the Panama Papers, the Paradise Papers leak came through a duo of reporters at the German newspaper Süddeutsche Zeitung and was then shared with I.C.I.J., a Washington-based group that won the Pulitzer Prize for reporting on the millions of records of a Panamanian law firm. The release of that trove of documents led to the resignation of one prime minister last year and to the unmasking of the wealth of people close to President Vladimir V. Putin of Russia.

5.3 The triple bottom line

In the previous section we discussed social trends that influence our debate on ethics in the business context. From this we can deduce that apparently, society has different ideas on what a company should do compared to a few decades ago. Where before, we would expect a company to focus on making profit within the boundaries of the law, there is an increasing expectation that a company has the responsibility to also peruses different goals. These goals especially relate to social and ecological values. When the business activities of a company move beyond a single bottom-line of making profit, and focuses other values as well, we usually refer to this as corporate social responsibility (CSR).

Corporate social responsibility

To do this, the company will have to consider the interest of their stakeholders next to the profit desire of their shareholders (Freeman, 1984; 2010).

> In a 'stakeholder approach' a company structurally considers the interest of their stakeholders in their business activities alongside the interest of their shareholders.

Stakeholder approach

This approach is in sharp contrast with a shareholder approach, in which a company's actions are purely driven by profit. While this position has an unethical sound to it, there are also interesting arguments to defend this position (Friedman, 1962). After all, there is something unnatural about a company that can only survive by making profit when it pretends to do something more than just that. We will explore the argument into more detail in section 5.3.2.

> In a 'shareholder approach' a company is exclusively driven by the values of their shareholders.

Shareholder approach

5.3.1 The method behind the triple bottom line

When we translate a stakeholder approach to values, we usually consider that instead of a single bottom line (profit) a company should act with a so called 'triple bottom line', in which people, planet and profit are equally important. The founding father of this theory is John Elkington (1997), who came up with these famous three Ps (see figure 5.1).

People, Planet, Profit

> The triple bottom line is a theory that proposes that a company should pursue not only profit but also take responsibilities in the field of social and ecological values.

Triple bottom line

FIGURE 5.1 The triple bottom line

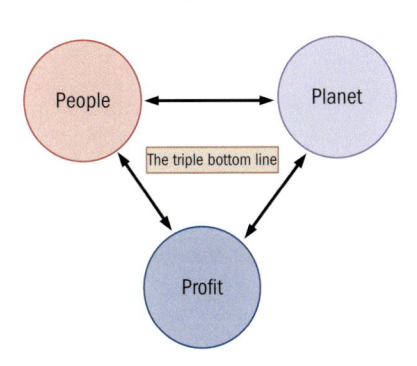

In this section we will further explore and reflect on Elkington's proposition. His theory was later further developed and amended. Three things could be added to make the triple bottom line clearer and slightly more nuanced.

- The term 'profit' or 'profitability' could be changed into the term 'economic values', since this goes beyond mere profit and also includes the overall impact of a company on our economy.
- The connection between the three P's can be regarded as a true triple bottom line as it was originally proposed', but could also be understood as a causal relation, in which investing in social and ecological values inevitably lead to the making of profit.
- The concept of a triple bottom line does not necessarily say anything about long-term thinking, while it seems only reasonable to add this dimension. Adding the dimension 'sustainability' to this triple bottom line adds a long-term element that does more justice to the idea of taking responsibility for social and ecological values.

Below we will explain these three remarks into more detail.

Economic values

We could argue that using the word 'profit', or referring to the value 'profitability' ignores the fact that the actions and decisions of a company do not only affect their own internal financial position, but also affect the (local) economy in which the company operates. If the idea is to consider all stakeholders in company decisions, the interest of the economy affected by the company should then also be captured by the triple bottom line theory. Therefore, some argue to use the wordings 'economic values' instead of 'profit' to do justice to this assumption (Henriques, 2004).

Take the example of the U.S. During the American elections campaign (see website item), the issue of employment was frequently the cause for heated debate. Especially the middle class manufacturing jobs would be vulnerable for so called 'offshoring', meaning that companies would outsource production to countries with lower wages. While this is undoubtedly a good move for the company who is offshoring, it can be disastrous for the local economy.

In politics, there is a fierce debate between those who see market protectionism as a way to protect such local economies, making it harder for companies to leave their country, and those who see open trade as a key to a more prosperous economy. It is not easy to demonstrate the actual effects on jobs when a company offshores its production processes. We could agree with Trump and Sanders, emphasizing that it is not fair when companies offshore jobs, and emphasize the need for local economies to remain intact as they were.

We could instead argue that open trade is to be preferred over protectionism because open borders lead to more import and export, which is beneficial for each and every country. We could also argue that offshoring may lead to progress: while first it institutes a loss of manufacturing jobs, the labour market will inevitably shift from manufacturing oriented jobs to service oriented jobs, meaning that the loss of jobs will be compensated by the creation of different type of jobs (Kovak et al. 2017).

Whichever viewpoint is more convincing is not relevant: when you're a manufacturing employee losing his job it will not help knowing that your local economy will shift towards a service-oriented economy, and you have to either adapt or face the fact that you ran out of luck. This debate has always been a sensitive one, meaning that a lot of people have a strong opinion on the role companies play regarding local economies. Public opinion has an effect on the image of a company, so one way or another, this is something to take into consideration when taking business decisions.

● www.cnn.com

U.S. has lost 5 million manufacturing jobs since 2000

By: Heather Long

Donald Trump claims trade with Mexico and China is killing America's middle class. Corporate America says that's false.
'History shows that trade made easy, affordable and fast...always begets more trade, more jobs, more prosperity,' the founder and CEO of FedEx wrote in a recent Wall Street Journal op-ed.
Who's right? Take a look at what has happened to blue-collar workers.
Manufacturing jobs in the U.S. actually *increased* in the years after the North America Free Trade Agreement with Mexico and Canada went into effect in 1994.
But the story changed dramatically in 2000. Since then, the U.S. has shed 5 million manufacturing jobs, a fact opponents of free trade mention often.

Over 12 million Americans still work in manufacturing
Trump and Bernie Sanders blame China for undercutting American workers with cheap labour (even Trump makes a lot of his suits and ties overseas). But there's another big factor: technology. Robots and machines are also replacing workers. The tech trend would have happened regardless of trade.
Still, manufacturing remains a key part of the U.S. economy. Over 12.3 million Americans are employed in the industry. But it's not the powerhouse it was.
In 1960, about one in four American workers had a job in manufacturing. Today fewer than one in 10 are employed in the sector, according to government data.
Call it the Great Shift. Workers transitioned from the fields to the factories. Now they are moving from factories to service counters and health care centres. The fastest growing jobs in America now are nurses, personal care aides, cooks, waiters, retail sales persons and operations managers.

29 March 2016

A profit model
We could further explore the mutual relation between the elements of the triple bottom line. Elkington suggests that it should truly be about a bottom-line as a principle, meaning that social, ecological and economic values are

all three firm conditions that need to be taken into account when companies act. However, we could also say that there is a causal link between investing in social and ecological values on the one hand, and economic values on the other hand, mustering a more consequentialist approach. In other words: taking good care of people and planet leads to profit (Savitz & Weber, 2014).

As we can see in the example 'Henry Ford and car bottoms' investing in a more environmentally friendly production process in the end leads to a reduction in production costs, and therefore potentially to a higher profit margin. As suggested by McDonough & Braungart (2002) it furthermore leads to less measurable consequences such as less damage to the environment, a better company image, and more satisfied employees.

Henry Ford and car bottoms

One of the most prominent figures in the history of the automobile industry is surely Henry Ford. He has always been in the front line where it concerned product innovation. One of his success stories was his idea of using the packaging materials (metal crates) to ship car components as the bottom floor of the car that would be produced with these components.

This had several advantages. First, he did not have to throw away the metal crates after usage, which would be an economic loss of good basic materials. Second, he would save money in investing in a bottom floor using different materials. Next to these rather concrete and measurable cost savings, it also led to less tangible results. For instance, he was able to slightly limit the negative effects on the environment for upcycling these metal crates instead of considering them as waste. Furthermore, such approaches in production processes were good for the company image. Also, it had an effect on employee satisfaction, since they were happy to work for such an innovative company (McDonough & Braungart, 2002).

Sustainability

The concepts 'people', 'planet' and 'profit' do not necessarily say something about the realization of these values in the long term. When you heavily invest in your employees and give them all a very high salary, but in the end go bankrupt as a result of disproportional expenses, your company decisions do not result in a long-term realization of values. Or when you consider the cheapest way to get rid of your waste and dump it in the ocean, it does lead to short-term profit, but on the long term society pays the bill for a polluted ocean, and with some bad luck you suffer some serious image damage. So, realizing any or the three P's on the short term does not necessarily lead to desirable outcomes. For this reason it could be argued to add the term 'sustainability' to the triple bottom line theory, as we can see in figure 5.2 (Henriques, 2004; Roorda, 2011).

Sustainabilty | Sustainabilty is a value that implies doing business in such a way that it does not stand in the way of the realization of social, environmental and economic values for upcoming generations.

Sustainability therefore involves long-term thinking, and businesses should consider the long-term consequences of their actions in the field of the triple bottom line. That means for instance that we should use energy resources that cannot be exhausted, and therefore we should stop using fossil fuels. This is because future generations will eventually run out of coal, oil or gas, since these sources are not renewable. Moreover, as a result of the large-scale use of fossil fuels, environmental damage is inevitable, which could dramatically change the living conditions of our planet. A sustainable solution would be to use energy resources that can be renewed constantly, also in next generations, such as solar- and wind-power. In chapter 7 we will take a closer look at this issue.

FIGURE 5.2 The triple bottom line, version 2

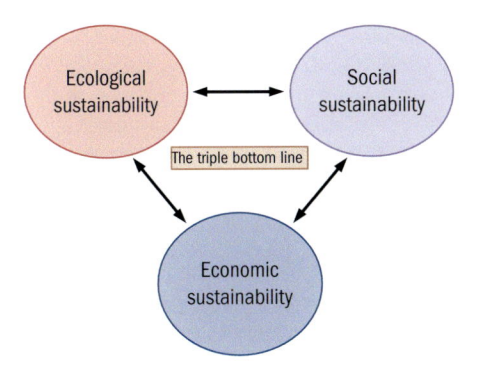

5.3.2   Criticism to the triple bottom line

However, not everyone is enthusiastic about a stakeholders approach or a triple bottom line theory. Already in the sixties, Milton Friedman argued that 'the business of business is business', meaning that it is the social function of a company to make profit, and nothing else. His arguments will be explored into further detail in section 9.2.1 in the context of accountability.

Milton Friedman

For now, the main issue is that it is very unnatural for a company to do something more than making profit. It is therefore very unlikely that a company is able to pursue social and ecological values when this does not go hand in hand with making profit. In other words: a company will not be able to consider social and ecological values as principles, but rather as a means to an end: profit. After all, a company will not survive without profit. As long as this goes well, all is fine, but consider the opposite. What if the realization of social and ecological values leads to a loss for the company, instead of profit? Would in that situation a company still be able to stick to other principles than profit?

Injections that kill

Would you sell injections that kill? Consider these two cases.

Death penalty
In some countries the death penalty exists and is still actively executed. Some U.S States however find it increasingly difficult to execute its death row prisoners since the drugs used in the lethal injections is no longer distributed by European pharmaceutical companies (Death Penalty Information Center, 2013). These companies do not want to be associated with executions. After all, their company image should be about healing people, not taking their lives. For instance, the pharmaceutical company Pfizer states that: *'Pfizer's mission is to apply science and our global resources to improve health and well-being at every stage of life. We strive to set the standard for quality, safety and value in the discovery, development and manufacturing of medicines. Pfizer makes its products to enhance and save the lives of the patients we serve. Consistent with these values, Pfizer strongly objects to the use of its products as lethal injections for capital punishment'* (Pfizer, 2017).

The wrong glue?
In 2015, an employee of the Belgian Based company Terumo blew the whistle in a Dutch television show (EenVandaag). He explained that in some of the needles produced by this company remains of glue could appear, which potentially could end up in the blood of patients, causing serious, possibly lethal diseases such as cancer. According to this whistle blower, this problem was known for years by the management, but was systematically ignored and employees who complained where silenced. After all, the chances of serious consequences would be rather low, and it would not be that easy to prove a causal link between the usage of a needle and a form of cancer.
The negative publications were dramatic for Terumo. Events changed when it appeared that there was no real danger for public health at all, and the allegations were misplaced (RIVM, 2014). Terumo sued the television show for the suffered damage, and won (Court of Amsterdam, 2016).

If we consider the cases in 'Injections that kill' we could ask ourselves what is most important for the involved companies: the values they stick to, or the image they have. Some consider that a company is not a human being, and as a result is not able to show true ethical awareness. But image is important because it can lead to more sales and a higher profit. This makes a discussion on CSR slightly confusing. On the one hand, public opinion encourages companies to invest in triple bottom line thinking. On the other hand, we could ask the question whether a company is able to be intrinsically motivated to be ethical. The whistle blower seemed to suggest that the company deliberately allowed insecure products to be sold on the market, since this would lead to better results and the risk of getting caught was very low. This appeared to be a mistake, and the company did what it could to clear its bad name, including filing a court suit against the television programme.

But would a company act exactly the same when image is not an issue? What if you are an oil company shipping toxic waste that is not accepted in Amsterdam for cleaning, and you want to get rid of it? What if someone at Ivory Coast offers you to get rid of the waste for a ridiculously small amount of money? In the end, this person appears to simply dump the waste in the ocean, instead of really cleaning it according to normal standards, which is something the oil company could reasonably foretell considering the very low amount of money paid. As we can see in the newspaper item, when no one is watching, different things might happen in the field of CSR, and the triple bottom line is not much of a principle, but is merely used as window dressing to create a better image.

THE INDEPENDENT, 23 JULY 2010

Trafigura fined over toxic waste

Oil trading company Trafigura was fined a million euros (£840,000) today for exporting hazardous waste to Ivory Coast and hiding the cargo's dangerous nature when it was unloaded from a ship in Amsterdam.
Prosecutors had asked for a fine of two million euros.

Amsterdam District Court judge Frans Bauduin also convicted a Trafigura employee for his role in the 2006 scandal and the Ukrainian captain of the Probo Koala ship that carried the waste.
Toxic waste made thousands ill in the Ivory Coast capital, Abidjan, in August 2006, although Trafigura insists the waste from the Probo Koala could not have caused serious illness.

The verdict is the first time for Trafigura to be convicted in the scandal.
The company, based in Lucerne, Switzerland, has consistently denied any wrongdoing in the case. But it paid 157 million euros to Ivory Coast to help clean up the waste and another 40 million euros to victims in a British settlement this year.

Under the British settlement, lawyers agreed the waste could not have caused deaths but could have caused short-term, low-level illness.
At the criminal trial in Amsterdam last month, prosecutors accused Trafigura of putting profits ahead of safety by hiding hazardous waste in a ship that docked in Amsterdam in 2006 and then exporting it illegally. The waste was later dumped in Ivory Coast in what became a major environmental scandal.

Presiding Judge Frans Bauduin said Trafigura chose to dump the waste cheaply in Ivory Coast 'for commercial reasons.'
The company employed in Abidjan charged 35 dollars per ton of waste, while in Amsterdam it would have cost almost 1,000 dollars per ton, the court said.
'Under those circumstances, Trafigura – which by that time knew of the exact composition (of the waste) – should never have agreed to its processing at such a price,' the judge said.
The company said it will study the verdicts 'with a view to appeal.'

Summary

5

▶ Since the industrial revolution there is a discussion about ethics in business.

▶ The industrial revolution is the sudden transition from manual production to machine production which took off in Western Europe since 1760. This revolution led to significant technological (and later digital) innovations but also had the following negative side-effects:
1   urbanization, which is the development in which people who live in rural areas move to urban regions on a large scale
2   an increasing income gap
3   pollution

▶ The renewed debate on ethics in business is a result of at least five social trends, which are:
1   privatization, which is the transfer of public ownership and powers to the private sector
2   technological and digital innovation
3   changes in morality
4   economic and financial crisis
5   globalization, which is the consequence of fading borders

▶ Where before, we would expect a company to focus on making profit within the boundaries of the law (shareholder approach), there is an increasing expectation that a company has the responsibility to also peruse different goals (stakeholder approach). When the business activities of a company move beyond a single bottom line of making profit, and focuses on other values as well, we usually refer to this as corporate social responsibility (CSR).
1   In a 'stakeholder approach' a company structurally considers the interest of their stakeholders in their business activities alongside the interest of their shareholders.
2   In a 'shareholder approach' a company is exclusively driven by the values of their shareholders.

▶ Elkington introduced the triple bottom line theory in the context of a stakeholder approach. The triple bottom line is a theory that proposes a company should pursue not only profit but also take responsibilities in the field of social and ecological values: taking care of People Planet and Profit (the three P's).

► The triple bottom line can continue to be nuanced:
1 The term 'profit' or 'profitability' could be changed into the term 'economic values', since this goes beyond mere profit and also includes the overall impact of a company on our economy.
2 The connection between the three P's can be regarded as a true triple bottom line as it was originally proposed, but could also be understood as a causal relation, in which investing in social and ecological values inevitably lead to the making of profit.
3 The concept of a triple bottom line does not necessarily say something about long-term thinking, while it seems only reasonable to add this dimension. Adding the dimension 'sustainability' to this triple bottom line adds a long-term element that does more justice to the idea of taking responsibility for social and ecological values.

► Sustainability is a value that implies doing business in such a way that it does not stand in the way of the realization of social, environmental and economic values for upcoming generations.

► There is also criticism to the triple bottom line theory. Some say that the sole social responsibility of a company is to make profit, and nothing else. We could question the ability of a company to behave ethically, for it is always depending on profit to survive. This means that ecological and social values are per definition a means to an end, and not a goal in itself. This can only lead to CSR being used as window dressing to get a better company image.

Literature

5

Aarts, S., Schouten, G., & Wernaart, B. (2017). Ethiek in onderzoek van de toekomst. In: Wouters, E. & Aarts, S. *Zonder ethiek is het al moeilijk genoeg.* Houten: Bohn Stafleu van Loghum.

Allcott, H, & Gentzkow, M. (2017). Social media and fake news in the 2016 election. *Journal of Economic Perspectives*, Volume 31, Number 2, Spring 2017, pp. 211–236.

Berriman, R. (2017). Will robots steal our jobs? The potential impact of automation on the UK and other major economies. In: *UK Economic Outlook.* PricewaterhouseCoopers (PwC).

Brynjolfsson, E. & McAfee, A. (2011) *Race Against the Machine, how the digital revolution is accelerating innovation, driving productivity and irreversibly transforming employment and the economy.* Lexington: Digital Frontier Press.

Cottle, S. (2011). Media and the Arab uprisings of 2011: Research notes. *Journalism*, 12 (5), 647–659.

Crane, W. & Matten, D. (2010). Shareholders and business ethics. In: *Business Ethics* (3rd edition). Oxford: Oxford University Press.

Dickens, C. (1843). *A Christmas Carol.* London: Chapman & Hall.

Doane, D. *(2004).* Good intentions - Bad Outcome Trial? The broken promise or CSR reporting. In: *A. Henriques & J. Richardson (Red), The Triple Bottom Line, does it all add up? Assessing the sustainability of business and CSR (pp. 81-88). London: Earth Scan.*

Elkington, J. (1997). *Cannibals with forks.* Oxford: Capstone Publishers.

Freeman, E. (1984). *Strategic management.* Cambridge: Cambridge University Press.

Freeman, E. (2010). *Stakeholder theory.* Cambridge: Cambridge University Press.

Friedman, M. (1962). *Capitalism and freedom.* Chicago: University of Chicago Press.

Gu, M. (2006). *Understanding Chinese company law.* Hong Kong: Hong Kong University Press.

Henriques, A. *(2004).* CSR, Sustainability and the triple bottom line. In: *A. Henriques & J. Richardson (Red), The Triple Bottom Line, does it all add up? Assessing the sustainability of business and CSR (pp. 26-33). London: Earth Scan.*

Jasanoff, S. (2016). *The ethics of invention.* New York: Norton & Company Ltd.

Jeurissen, R. (2007). Business ethics and corporate responsibility. In: Jeurissen, R. (Ed.), *Ethics & Business* (pp. 11-23). Assen: Van Gorcum.

Malthus, T. (1978). *An essay on the principle of population.* London: J.Johnson.

McDonough, W., & Braungart, M. (2002). *Cradle to cradle, Remaking the way we make things.* New York: North Point Press.

Mejri, M. (2013). Crisis Management: Lessons Learnt from the BP Deepwater Horizon Spill Oil. *Business Management and Strategy.* ISSN 2157-6068 2013, Vol. 4, No. 2.

Posner, R. (2011). *A failure of capitalism, the crisis of '08 and the descent into depression.*

Roorda, N. (2011). *Basic accounting sustainable development.* Groningen: Noordhoff Uitgevers.

Savitz, A.W., & Weber, K. (2014). *The Triple Bottom Line.* San Francisco: John Wiley & Sons.

Spaiser, V., Chadefaux, T., Donnay, K., Russmann, F. & Helbing, D.(2017). Communication power struggles on social media, a case study of the 2011-12 Russian protests. *Journal of information technology & politics.* Volume 14, 2017, issue 2.

Tokar, B. (1999). *Earth for sale: reclaiming ecology in the age of corporate green wash.*
Cambridge: South End Press.

Trinder, B. (2013). Great cities, old and new. In: *Britain's Industrial Revolution: the making of a manufacturing people, 1700 1870.* Lancaster: Carnegie Publishing.

Vercherand, J. (2014). The 'social question'since the 19th century. In: *Labour.* London: Palgrave Macmillan.

Westbrook, D. (2009). *Out of Crisis: rethinking our financial markets.* Boulder: Paradigm Publishers.

Williams, D. & Treadaway, G. (1992). Exxon and the Valdez accident: a failure in crisis communication. *Communication studies.* Vol. 43, 1992-issue 1.

Zijderveld, A. (1999). *The waning of the social welfare state, the end of comprehensive state succor.* London and Brunswick: Transaction Publishers.

Media

Associated Press (2010, 23 July). Trafigura fined over toxic waste. *The Independent.*

Editorial Board. (2017, 22 May). How social media filter bubbles and algorithms influence the election. *The Guardian.*

Forsythe, M. (2017, 5 November). Paradise papers shine light on where the elite keep their money. *The New York Times.*

Holusha, J. (1989, 21 April). Exxon's public relations problem. *The New York Times.*

Liberatore, S. & Salmon, J. (2017, 24 March). Watch out America, robots are coming for your jobs: Report finds 38% of US jobs will be automated by 2030. *The Daily Mail online.*

Long, H. (2016, 29 march). U.S. has lost 5 million manufacturing jobs since 2000. *www.cnn.com*

Shaban, H., Timberg, C. & Dwoskin, E. (2017 31 October). Facebook, Google and Twitter testified on Capitol Hill. Here's what they said. *The Washington Post.*

Research reports

BP (2010). Sustainability review 2010. www.BP.com/sustainability.

Death Penalty Information Center (2013). The Death Penalty in 2013: year end report.

Kovak, B., Oldenski, L. & Sly, N. (2017). The labor market effects of offshoring by us multinational firms: Evidence from changes in global tax policies. *National Bureau of Economic Research.*

RIVM. (2015, 24 March). Veel gestelde vragen over de veiligheid van Terumo naalden. *Rijksinstituut voor Volksgezondheid en Milieu.*

Press releases

Pfizer. (2017, September). Pfizer's Position on Use of Our Products in Lethal Injections for Capital Punishment. *Global Policy & International Public Affairs, Pfizer Inc.*

Court rulings

Court of Amsterdam, 13 April 2016, GJ 2016/123.

Websites

www.evostc.state.ak.us (Official website of the Exxon Valdez Oil Spill Trustee Council)

6

Social values

In this section we will discuss the friction that could exist between the companies' pursuit of profit and social values in general, and in particular those of its workers and consumers. We will discuss the effects of industrialization on the realization of these social values and explore the related ethical dilemmas. Regarding social values of workers we will discuss various ethical challenges in both developed and developing countries. Furthermore, we will explore various forms of corruption that may affect social values of society. Finally we will discuss the challenges regarding social values of consumers, using the marketing mix as a leading framework.

6.1 The industrial revolution and social values of workers

As we have seen, the industrial revolution influenced our societies in a profound way. Especially the resulting income inequality led to distressing situations in which many families found themselves in poverty and unhygienic conditions. As it seems, economic values stood in the way of and were of more importance than social values.

Social values | Social values are values we pursue to lead a dignified life.

However, we can argue about the exact meaning of the word 'dignified': it can be understood differently in different cultures, as we can see in the example 'the death of a merchant'. In this case, the Dutch authorities had a very different opinion on what dignity would be compared to the Singapore authorities.

The death of a merchant

On 23 September 1994, the Dutch businessman Johannes van Damme was hung in a Singapore prison in execution of his death sentence. He was found guilty of smuggling drugs: in mister Van Damme's luggage, 4.32 kilos of heroin was found on arrival at Singapore Airport. This amount was royally exceeding the legal threshold (15 gram) above which could mean the death sentence in Singapore.

Until his death, Van Damme pleaded innocent, and claimed there was a set up by some Nigerian business partners who put the drugs in the suitcase he was carrying on their behalf. Van Damme was executed despite the repeating attempts to halt this by the Dutch Government, a handful of similar European initiatives and even a desperate plea of the Dutch Queen.

Many human rights organizations, as well as a majority of the countries in Europe, consider the death sentence as an inhumane punishment, and a violation of the right to life. After all, this right is recognized in the Universal Declaration of Human Rights, and in a number of subsequent human right treaties. Interestingly, the Singaporean support the same human rights treaties, but understand the right to life in a rather different way. In an official statement, the Singapore Ministry of Health stated that 'There is no international consensus on abolition of the death penalty. (…). Every country has the sovereign right to decide on its own judicial system. We do not live in a homogenous world. Within certain universally agreed broad parameters, international norms call for the respect of differences of views and beliefs. Singapore does not seek to impose its views on others. We only ask that others do not impose their views on us. (…) Singapore weighs the right to life of the convicted against the rights of victims and the right of the community to live in peace and security. Taking into account our national circumstances, we have made a considered decision to retain the death penalty. It has worked for us, making Singapore one of the safest places in the world to live and work in' (Government of Singapore, 2004).

Furthermore, the context of a region can heavily influence the perception of this word. Consider the case 'Facilities for pregnant women' in which we can see that in a developed country, a debate on paternal leave is in sharp contrast with a debate in a developing country on the actual access healthcare for pregnant woman. A dignified life depends in this case on the state of the economy, whether there is peace, and whether there are basic supplies.

6

Facilities for pregnant women

Norway is famous for its generous parental leave subsidies. Parents are entitled to a total sum up of 46 weeks paid leave (full salary), or 56 weeks on 80 per cent of the salary they usually earn. The mother may take up maternity leave three to twelve weeks before the due date of the baby. The first six weeks after the baby is born are reserved for the mother as well. After that period, both parents can distribute the remaining weeks of their shared leave the way they see fit. However, both the father and the mother should take a minimum of ten weeks (www.nav.no, 2017).

Economic gain for Norway
While this appears to be a costly adventure for the Norwegian State, that for the major part pays these leaves, there are some considerable economic gains. First, this approach stimulates women to keep their job, and even go for a full time job and have a career. The economic participation of women is therefore considerably higher in Norway compared to most other countries, and the economic contribution keeps rising. This leads to a higher tax income for the State, and more employment since these taxes are spent by the government on – for instance – daycare centres. Secondly, it stimulates to have babies at the same time, which is on the long term crucial to avoid a population from aging, leading to an extremely expensive pension fund. When an equal amount of workers enters and leaves the labour market, these budgets are affordable. When there is a misbalance, they become uncontrollable (OECD, 2012). However, when there is a limited parental leave in a country that does not involve the father, parents may not be so keen on having babies, since it will be either not affordable for them, or lead to a serious loss of income during the parental leave (Kerr, 2016).

Maternity death in Africa
The Norwegian situation is in sharp contrast with countries in which public life is gravely disrupted by armed conflict, poverty, a natural disaster, a famine or other humanitarian crises. Africa is a continent with a relatively large number of developing countries with a large record of humanitarian crises. On the continent, we will hardly find something of a social welfare state compared to – for instance – Norway. In an extensive study, the World Health Organization analysed the health status of African Woman in the period 1990-2015, and in particular focused on maternal death. One of the key findings of this report was that: '*the state of maternal health in Africa is dismal, with the Region accounting for more than half of all maternal deaths worldwide, each year; and, sadly, the picture is not improving significantly.*' While HIV related deaths where death cause number one, maternal death is death cause number two in Africa, due to lacking health care or a limited access to healthcare for pregnant women. Some recommendations to improve the situation include information policies on the usage of contraception, funding for primary and local healthcare, and dropping the fees for this kind of healthcare (WHO, 2015).

The inhuman conditions in which workers would find themselves after industrialization slowly led to the realization that this is a dead end. Gradually, in the course of the 19th and 20th century the rights of workers were taken more seriously, leading to legislation and policies to protect these rights, alongside increasing political influence of the working class. While of course these rights are not similarly protected in al industrialized countries, we could say that there is a big gap between the rights of workers in developed countries on the one hand, and developing countries on the other.

It is generally assumed that the countries in Europe and the United States, Canada, Japan, Australia and New Zealand are 'developed countries'. These are basically the countries that were industrialized somewhere in the 19th century. Another name that is mustered for this group is 'western countries', a term we've inherited from the Cold War period, in which we made a distinction between the eastern Soviet-minded countries, and the western capitalist countries. A curious term, since most 'western' countries are on the eastern hemisphere, and a term that reflects a state of the world that is no longer accurate. Therefore we choose a different terminology in this book: developed, developing and newly industrialized countries.

Developed countries

| Developed countries are industrialized countries with a relatively high welfare level.

Developing countries

| Developing countries are non-industrialized countries with a relatively low welfare level.

The term 'developing country' is usually reserved for countries in great poverty. These countries did not industrialize due to various reasons, such as a lack of resources, endless power struggles, humanitarian disasters and other grave conditions. A typical phenomenon in these countries is that often little is regulated for the protection of social values or the rights of workers.

Newly developed countries

| Newly developed countries are countries which recently industrialized, with a moderate welfare level.

In between the welfare level of developed and developing countries we find the newly developed countries (NIC). These countries are in the process of industrialization, and have made a considerable economic growth in the period after the Second World War. These countries are characterized by a moderate level of welfare, and struggle with the immediate consequences of industrialization such as urbanization, an increasing income gap and pollution. In these countries, social values are not as profoundly protected as in developed countries, but are on the agenda. Think in this context of the BRIC countries (Brazil, Russia, India and China), and the so called 'Asian Tigers' (Taiwan, Singapore, South Korea and former Hong Kong). More recently, we could add countries such as the United Arab Emirates, Malaysia, Turkey, Mexico and South Africa to this list considering their considerable economic growth.

We should be cautious in classifying the countries in the world in three rough categories, because it can easily lead to a generalization that does not do justice to the particularities of each country. In this book, the classification is loosely based on the same categorization as used by the United Nations (UN, 2016). The UN uses a slightly different terminology though, in which the terms 'developed economies', 'developing economies' and 'economies in transition' are mustered. In this classification however, some NIC-countries are labelled as developing economies, and not as economies in transition, due to the fact that not only industrialization but also other economic factors are weighted in this classification. Another term that is sometimes used in this context is the world least developed countries to label the poorest countries of our world.

6

6.2 Rights of workers in developed countries

Since the end of the nineteenth century, we can observe an increasing protection of the social values of workers in developed countries. Most importantly, child labour was banned and replaced by compulsory education, workers could increasingly participate in company decisions and politics, social security systems were installed, and human rights were used as a fundament in social values for workers.

6.2.1   Child labour and compulsory education
Before the industrialization in developed countries child labour was very normal. After all, working in the safe environment of the family house contributing a bit to the household income through hand work was considered to be state of the art and not unethical at all. However, things changed when the big factories and their big machines came. First of all, it was very popular to hire very young factory employees, since they would be cheap labour forces. Furthermore, older children would become independent at a very young age, leaving their financial contribution to their younger siblings (Horrel & Humphries, 1995). Increasingly, factories using children in their workforce were criticized, creating a negative image of exploiting children for an extremely low wage.

In most developed countries, child labour came to a halt as a result of compulsory education laws that required children to attend school during their childhood (initially until the age of twelve) (Soysal & Strang, 1989). These laws were introduced in various phases in Europe and the US, most notably in the second half of the 18th century. These systems were mostly facilitated by the state, but the church – and especially the protestant church – did play a major role in the school curricula and provided the teaching staff. Most mass schooling systems were intensified after the Second World War: children would go through a full scale school career until they were fully grown up before they started to work (Martin & Viarento (2009). The role of the church gradually diminished over time.

6.2.2   Participation
Another basic right for workers also greatly helped in strengthening their position by influencing company decisions. We refer to this as 'workers participation'.

Participation is the involvement of workers in decisions regarding their working conditions.

Participation

Participation can be done at the company or department level on the one hand, and on the branch level on the other hand. The first is typically done through a works council, while the second is done through a trade union.

Works council

A works council is a body in a company in which elected workers participate in decision-making of the company regarding working conditions. A works council is usually appointed in medium-sized and large organizations. In smaller companies, a small staff representation usually suffices. Typical decisions in which a works council is consulted are decisions to fire a significant amount of workers, to start a reorganization, to change employment policies, or decisions on work safety. In most countries, the advice of the works council is not binding, however, law may require employers to consult the council first before acting when taking certain decisions. Furthermore, of course, a works council is an effective way to bring a management board closer to the employed workers, and learn what is going on on the work floor.

Trade guilds existed already before the industrialization of developed countries began. However, these guilds predominantly focused on the exchange of craftsmanship and professionalization, not on negotiating with employers. This character profoundly changed as a result of industrialization, when the core values of workers were easily affected as a result of ever-growing companies and the continuous competition for the lowest possible cost prize of a product. Increasingly, trade unions **Trade unions** (also referred to as) were legalized in the second halve of the nineteenth century. Until then, collective actions of workers to stand up for their social values – such as striking – were simply forbidden and punished as a crime. A notable example that changed this approach was the adoption of the British Trade Union Act of 1871 that allowed the existence of Trade Unions not only in Great Britain, but also in most other Commonwealth countries.

Since that time, trade unions are used as a combined effort to collectively negotiate labour conditions with employers to protect these social values. This is typically done through collective bargaining, or – when this leads to no results – collective actions in the sphere of strikes. Trade unions can be established in the context of one company, but we also saw the emergence of nationwide trade unions representing all workers in a particular branch or political background. These nationwide unions do not only engage in a debate with companies and employer organizations, but are also politically involved. After all, a government may initiate legislation that affects the labour conditions of workers in a country, most notably when it concerns workers in the public sector. As we can see in the newspaper item, collective actions do not necessarily focus on a company or employers in general, but may also focus on the government that is about to take a disputed decision.

REUTERS, 9 OCTOBER 2017

France's CGT calls for another strike against labour reform, others refuse

PARIS - France's hard left CGT trade union called a third strike against President Emmanuel Macron's overhaul of employment laws on Monday but failed to get other unions to rally behind it.
Sponsored
The three main unions have been divided over how to respond to the labour law reforms, with the Communist Party-rooted CGT taking to the streets while the more moderate CFDT, now France's biggest union, and the Force Ouvriere preferring negotiations.
France was once a champion of social protest, with unions able to paralyse swathes of the economy and force ministers to back down on reforms. But hard-line unions are now grappling for relevance as strikes become less frequent and less disruptive.
Macron's government spent weeks negotiating with the unions during the summer over measures to give companies more power to set working conditions as well as making it easier to hire and fire workers. Last month, it signed the bill into law by decree.
(...)
Monday's meeting over labour reform action came on the eve of a separate nationwide strike by public sector workers. Strike notices have been lodged in schools, hospitals, airports and government ministries over plans to cut 120,000 jobs, freeze pay and reduce sick leave compensation.
It is the first time in a decade that all nine unions representing 5.4 million public workers have united behind a protest call and will be an important test of public appetite to protest against the reforms. If turnout is low on Tuesday, Macron could feel emboldened as he presses ahead with revamping France's generous unemployment insurance in a bid to spur those who lose their jobs to get back to work more quickly.

6.2.3   Political influence

During the industrial revolution, democracy was a relatively new concept. When the Americans have declared themselves independent from the British after the American War of Independence (1775-1783) on 4 July 1776, they rejected the idea of a monarchy. Since that time, the U.S. is a republic, and its citizens can decide through democratic processes who can wield what power. The U.S. Declaration of Independence would later be a major source of inspiration for many European constitutions in which rights and freedoms of citizens are recognized. One of the most notable principles in this declaration is that: *'we hold these truths to be self-evident, that all people are created equal, that they are endowed by their Creator with certain unalienable rights, that among these are Life, Liberty and the pursuit of Happiness'* (United States Declaration of Independence, 1776).
However, the idea that all people are truly equal appeared to be not self-evident. For instance, it would have to wait until 1920 for white women to have the right to vote, while black and Hispanic/Latino Americans would have to wait decades longer until 1960 (Civil Rights Act of 1960).

In Western Europe, democracy was introduced later, since the European states where led by Monarchs, who were initially not so keen on giving up their power. The nobility was used to their wealth and power, which they usually shared with high-ranking heads of the church. The average citizen was unable to take a bite of this, was uneducated, and did not participate in any public decision-making process.

However, things changed when factories became more and more prosperous as a result of industrialization. The company owners where not necessarily part of the established elite (nobility and the church), which resulted in a brand new middleclass: the bourgeoisie. They wanted a bite of the established power as well, which resulted in some early versions of democratic decision-making, in which citizens could participate in voting when they would pay certain taxes. In practice, this would mean that only the rich bourgeoisie would participate in the voting, and the working class would still be excluded from democratic processes. This phenomenon is also called 'selective suffrage'.

However, as a result of the poverty of the working class and poor living and working conditions, social unrest broke out: the working class wanted to participate in political processes just like their bourgeois fellow citizens. In the end, universal suffrage was introduced in most West European countries. Although this did not happen peacefully everywhere.

French Revolution

A dramatic example of the changes in European politics is the French Revolution, which started in 1789, events cumulated in the storming of the Bastille (14th of July), a prison in Paris that was a symbol for the royal reign of Louis XVI. In the wake of these events, the French nobility was hunted down and preferably executed, including the king. The First French Republic was declared (1792-1804) in which 'normal' citizens would rule. As positive as it sounds, the French Republic is one of the darker chapters in French history: inexperienced people would now wield power and had no idea how to do this properly. The result was chaos and a lot of bloodshed 'in the name of the people'. In the end, Napoleon Bonaparte used these turbulent times to his benefit, and took power after declaring himself emperor in 1804, effectively ending the reign of the people.

The nobility in neighbouring countries were deterred by the events of the French Revolution, and the transition of power from nobility and the church to the people in general came with less bloodshed. The Western-European countries were mostly transformed into republics or constitutional monarchies. In a republic, the president is the head of state, elected by its citizens. In a constitutional monarchy, the country is formally led by a King or Queen without political powers while the country is politically represented by a prime minister who is appointed as a result of democratic processes.

In a way, the events preceding the transition from a monarchy to other state forms is still reflected in the political landscape of most European countries (figure 6.1). Most countries have a right winged party, sometimes referred to as liberal, who traditionally protect the interest of employers, want a small government with a significant proportion of 'laissez faire'-politics. In other words, only governmental interference when really needed; individuals should have the freedom to create their own happiness using their own potential in a free environment. Furthermore, most countries have a left winged party traditionally protecting the interest of the employees. These so-called labour parties consider there will always be unjust elements in our society causing people not to be able to pursue their own happiness. Therefore, wealth needs to be redistributed once in a while, through active governmental interference in the form of policies, subsidies and so on. Labour parties usually have a progressive agenda. Then, we have centre parties that are either conservative, Christian or both. These parties are in between the right winged and labour parties when it concerns the way a government should interfere in the lives of people, and are usually characterized by conservative, traditional principles. Please note that these qualifications are European. In the U.S. for instance the terminology is rather different: conservative is considered to be very much right winged, where liberal is considered to be left winged.

Until today, this political landscape is also reflected in the European Parliament: there we have (with some occasional name changes): the Alliance of Liberals and Democrats for Europe Group (liberal party); European People's Party Group (Christian), the European Conservatives and Reformists (Conservative party), and the Progressive Alliance of Socialists and Democrats (labour party).

More recently, we have seen alternatives on the left and right in politics who question and challenge the established political parties. On the left these are mostly the 'green' parties, who are particularly concerned about the wellbeing of our planet, non-material values and propose a very progressive agenda (Muller-Rommel & Poguntke, 2002). On the right these are the far right nationalist parties, particularly concerned about integration challenges, who propose a very conservative agenda (Mohammadi & Nourbakhsh, 2017).

FIGURE 6.1 Political landscape in Europe after the introduction of universal suffrage

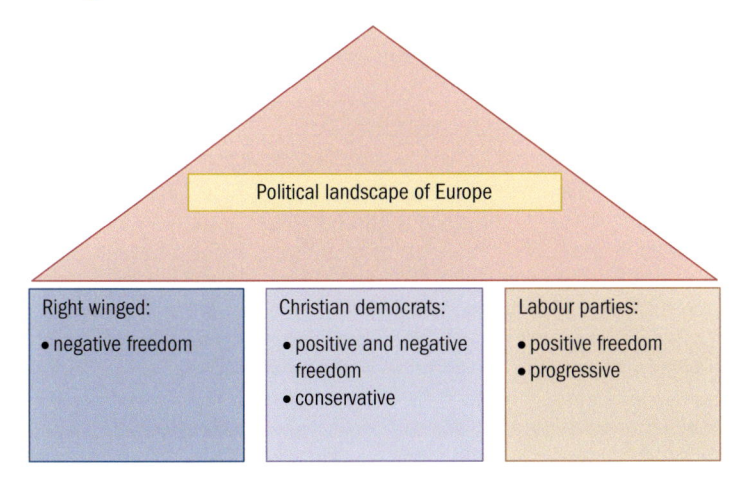

6.2.4   Social security and the protection of workers

As a result of increasing political participation, and resulting creation of welfare states in developed countries, social security systems were increasingly important in protecting the interest of workers.

Social security system

> A social security system is a set of provisions that offers financial means to those in need in order to protect their social values.

A social security system has the primary aim to financially compensate individuals that are not able to provide for themselves. This could be because some people are unable to work as a result of illness or a disability. Furthermore, there could be social benefits for people who are too old to work, such as pensions. Also, there are mostly provisions for those who are for whatever reason unable to find a job.

Next to such compensations, we have seen the emergence of protective laws to guarantee safe working conditions and to avoid exploitation of employees. These are mostly laws concerning the working conditions and working hours of employees, all kinds of bans on discrimination, protection of members of trade unions and works councils, and in some countries a minimum wage was installed.

Political discourse on social security systems is always sharp, since it usually hits the core of what a political party stands for in terms of desirability of government interference. A good example can be found in the discussion about the minimum wage. We can observe convincing arguments against as well as in support of setting a minimum wage in a country. In a nutshell, it can be argued that a minimum wage is a desirable governmental interference because it can have a stimulating effect in the economy since people can spend more and are more secure about their income (Card & Krueger, 2015; Eyraud & Saget, 2005). In contrast it could be argued that this is an undesirable interference, since companies are now forced to hire people for a higher price than market forces would suggest, meaning that the company has a loss which slows down economic growth (Friedman, 2014). It will be not surprising that labour parties usually defend the first, and liberal parties the second argument.

A minimum wage, a good idea?

Those who support the idea of a minimum wage usually refer to the fact that mostly companies try to produce for the lowest possible cost in a 'race to the bottom' as a result of industrialization. In this race, they cut in the costs of wages, which go down unrestrictedly when there is enough labour force on the market, and fewer jobs as a result of the fact that machines replace the manpower. When one would enforce a minimum wage, the working class will most likely spend more money, the economy will improve, and even more jobs will be created. Another effect is that due to the creation of more jobs, the government will have to spend less on social security systems, which encourages the economy in itself. Furthermore, guaranteed minimum income will lead to innovation, because jobs that are not worth minimum wage will disappear and are replaced by more efficient or clever processes. Those who are used to working in such jobs will be more motivated to continue studying.

On the other hand, we could argue that when a minimum wage is set, employers are bound to hire workers for a higher price than their market value. After all, in that case an employee will earn more than the system of supply and demand would dictate. This leads to economic obstruction, the loss of employment, and as a result, more people who depend on social benefits.

Another effect of a minimum wage is that at some point, the consumer price will go up, since the company is bound to pay a higher price for production costs compared to a situation without the minimum wage. When consumer prices go up unnecessarily, sales will drop, and the economy is yet again obstructed.

6.2.5 Human rights

While the issue of human rights was raised long before in some national contexts, the Second World War has been the triggering event to globally address human rights. This has been anchored through the adoption of international declarations and treaties in which fundamental human rights are recognized.

> Human rights are internationally recognized fundamental human rights in order to guarantee human dignity.

Human rights

A first milestone in the creation of a global human rights system was the adoption of the Universal Declaration of Human Rights, shortly after the war (10 December 1948), by the General Assembly of the United nations. The basic idea is the 'recognition of the inherent dignity and of the equal and inalienable rights of all members of the human family.' These rights then apply regardless who you are, as you can see in Article 2 of this declaration.

Article 2 of the Universal Declaration of Human Rights

Everyone is entitled to all the rights and freedoms set forth in this Declaration, without distinction of any kind, such as race, colour, sex, language, religion, political or other opinion, national or social origin, property, birth or other status. Furthermore, no distinction shall be made on the basis of the political, jurisdictional or international status of the country or territory to which a person belongs, whether it be independent, trust, non-self-governing or under any other limitation of sovereignty.

To give more legal body to human rights, various treaties where later added to the international human rights system. Most notably in the context of social values for workers, the International Covenant on Economic, Social and Cultural Rights (ICESCR) was signed by a large number of States in 1966. In that treaty countries solemnly pledged to recognize economic social and cultural rights, which are of particular importance for workers or those who would like to work. These rights mostly imply governmental action in order to support these rights through policies or subsidies, such as

- the right to equality between men and women (including equal payment in similar jobs)
- the right to work
- the right to just and favourable conditions of work
- the right to form trade unions and strike
- the right to social security
- the right to the protection of the family
- the right to an adequate standard of living (including housing, clothing and food)
- the right to health (and health care)
- the right to education
- the right to take part in cultural life, to enjoy the benefits of scientific progress and its applications, and to benefit from the protection of intellectual property

In addition, in the UN context various treaties where adopted in order to protect the values of particular groups that are more vulnerable than others in the realization of their human rights. There is a specific treaty that recognizes fundamental human rights for women, children, indigenous people and people with disabilities.
There are also regional human right treaties with the same goal as the international treaties, but they are adjusted to the particular needs of the involved region. Examples of such rights protecting economic, social and cultural rights are the European Social Charter, and the San Salvador Additional Protocol to the American Convention on Human Rights, or the African Charter on Human and People's Rights (Wernaart, 2013).

An important UN specialized agency is the International Labour Organization (ILO). This organization is a global forum in which employee and employer agencies as well as governments discuss labour rights. In the context of this organization, conventions are drafted to help implementing labour rights worldwide. These conventions can be signed by countries who pledge to uphold the standards recognized within the signed convention. An example of such a convention can be found in the textbox, where a sample is shown of the 1951 ILO Convention on equal remuneration.

Sample of ILO Convention No 100 on equal remuneration, 1951

Article 1

For the purpose of this Convention
- a the term *remuneration* includes the ordinary, basic or minimum wage or salary and any additional emoluments whatsoever payable directly or indirectly, whether in cash or in kind, by the employer to the worker and arising out of the worker's employment;
- b the term *equal remuneration for men and women workers for work of equal value* refers to rates of remuneration established without discrimination based on sex.

Article 2

- 1 Each Member shall, by means appropriate to the methods in operation for determining rates of remuneration, promote and, in so far as is consistent with such methods, ensure the application to all workers of the principle of equal remuneration for men and women workers for work of equal value.
- 2 This principle may be applied by means of
  - a national laws or regulations;
  - b legally established or recognised machinery for wage determination;

c collective agreements between employers and workers; or

d a combination of these various means.

Article 3

- 1 Where such action will assist in giving effect to the provisions of this Convention measures shall be taken to promote objective appraisal of jobs on the basis of the work to be performed.
- 2 The methods to be followed in this appraisal may be decided upon by the authorities responsible for the determination of rates of remuneration, or, where such rates are determined by collective agreements, by the parties thereto.

- 3 Differential rates between workers which correspond, without regard to sex, to differences, as determined by such objective appraisal, in the work to be performed shall not be considered as being contrary to the principle of equal remuneration for men and women workers for work of equal value.

Article 4

Each Member shall co-operate as appropriate with the employers' and workers' organisations concerned for the purpose of giving effect to the provisions of this Convention.

As we said in paragraph 3.2.2, human rights and the worldwide human rights instrument is an expression of deontological ethics. The pros and cons of such an approach have been dealt with in the same section. More specifically in this context it is noteworthy to reflect on the fact that in the global human rights instruments, fundamental rights with a very high moral value are embedded in the legal construct of a treaty. International treaties are not always as easily applied as intended by its drafters. It appears that national governments and courts are not always that keen on using international treaties as norms that are legally binding, or as an authoritative moral document that needs to be effectuated (Wernaart, 2013).

6.3 Challenges in developed countries

The protection of social values of employees in developed countries has changed the wellbeing and position of the working class significantly. However, this does not mean that there are no more challenges. The changes in society as a result of an advanced welfare level has led to new challenges that are sometimes different from the challenges we face in developing and newly industrialized countries. These challenges are found in the context of privatization, discrimination, work-related stress and dismissal procedures.

6.3.1 Privatization

As we have seen in chapter 5, privatization leads to new dilemmas in business. When certain jobs in society were carried out by governmental agencies before, but are now run by companies, there might be reason for concern. Where a government is to a certain degree democratically legitimized and acts in the pursuit of the common good, a company is not subdued to direct democratic control (but should of course obey the law),

and acts primarily in pursuit of profit. Will the end user now get what is best for him, or what is most profitable for the company?
On the other hand, when companies compete in a free market offering services or products that were first provided for by a government, the competition stimulates possibly more product differentiation, quicker innovation, and the lowering of prices.
These two thoughts sum up the average debate on privatization in the context of social (and ecological) values. Since this was also discussed in-depth in chapter five, we will not further explore this here.

6.3.2   Discrimination

Despite the many attempts to ban discrimination by legislation, campaigns and training programmes, it remains a delicate and controversial issue that is not solved that easily.

Discrimination

> Discrimination is the unequal treatment in similar cases based on irrelevant factors.

We can endlessly argue on what factors are relevant and which are not when treating someone differently from others. Take for instance the so-called U.S. Muslim ban (discussed in chapter 1). Supporters would say that a majority of potential Muslim terrorists would come from a certain group of countries, and it can therefore be justified to treat people from these countries differently from people from other countries. In other words: the nationality of a person is therefore a relevant factor for different treatment. Those rejecting the idea might say that individuals from particular countries should not be judged based on characteristics that others might potentially have, and different treatment cannot be justified. Therefore, the nationality of a person is not a relevant factor for different treatment.
According to the ILO, discrimination based on race, colour, sex, religion, political opinion, national extraction or social origin, are irrelevant factors (ILO Convention 111, Article 1). Furthermore, it is observed by the ILO that increasingly, age, sexual orientation, HIV/AIDS status and disability, are protected under anti-discrimination laws (ILO, 2007).

In this section we will further explore the discrimination based on gender, nationality and race, and religion.

There are three different forms in which discrimination can manifest itself: direct discrimination, indirect discrimination and positive discrimination.

Direct discrimination

> Direct discrimination is to explicitly disadvantage someone based on an irrelevant factor.

This is the most outspoken and visible form of discrimination, in which we do not conceal on what grounds we treat someone differently. As we can see in the case 'no Polish employees!' Karl first directly discriminates against Polish workers by literally excluding them in his job description.

Indirect discrimination

> Indirect discrimination is when a non-discriminatory standard or practice disadvantages someone based on an irrelevant factor

This form of discrimination is more hidden. In the example 'No Polish employees!', the farmer introduces a standard for his future employees that does not directly exclude Polish seasonal workers, but will have the practical effect of excluding them. After all, it will mostly be German workers that are able to pass a German writing test and have excellent communication skills in that language.

> Positive discrimination is to explicitly advantage someone who is disadvantaged based on irrelevant factors.

Positive discrimination

6

Sometimes it is accepted to favour certain people because they are obviously outnumbered in a sector or branch. The women's quota, as we will discuss in the next section, is a good example of positive discrimination.

No Polish employees!

Karl is a German farmer who owns a successful asparagus farm. During the harvest season, he needs some seasonal workers. Karl, however, is not so fond of foreigners, especially Polish workers. In his view, the Polish 'steal' the jobs from the German as they invade the country offering their services for very low prices. Initially, Karl wrote a job description in which he was quite clear about his distaste for Polish workers:

We're hiring! We are looking for some skilled workers for our upcoming asparagus harvest. No Polish people please.

Karl was, however, made aware of the usual legal bans on discrimination and came up with a trick to make sure no Polish workers will work on his fields, without directly excluding them.

We're hiring! We are looking for some skilled workers for our upcoming asparagus harvest.
Qualifications:
- *German writing test (GLS 1A)*
- *excellent communication skills in the German language*

While theoretically everyone – including Polish season workers – can apply for this job, in practice only German workers will qualify.

Gender discrimination

In this section we will focus on discrimination against women. The Convention on the Elimination of Discrimination Against Woman recognizes gender equality, and offers a good starting point to explore the various issues that are problematic in today's society. As stated before, discrimination is a worldwide phenomenon, and in developing countries the challenges could be even more fundamental (Morrison & Jütting, 2005; Jayachandran, 2015). Think of challenges in the sphere of unequal access to health care, food, schooling, sexual freedom and free speech. Furthermore, the position of women in conflict areas and disasters is very vulnerable and a reason for concern.

However, industrialization and development in a country does not necessarily end discrimination against women. In most developed countries women still face inequality regarding rather fundamental issues such as wage equality, job opportunities, violence and harassment, and stereotyping. A possible explanation could be that our societies change faster than tradition (Ridgeway, 2011).

Wage equality
Worldwide, women earn less money per worked hour for similar jobs compared to men. In other words: gender is a variable that influences the salary level. This is an example of wage discrimination, since gender is generally believed to be an invalid factor for different treatment. An example of alleged wage discrimination can be found in the newspaper item.

6   **Wage discrimination**

Wage discrimination is unequal payment for similar work based on irrelevant factors.

There is not a single country in the world in which men earn less than women for similar work. However, there are significant differences in this income gap between countries. In their annual global gender gap reports, the World Economic Forum keeps track of the statistics regarding the role of women in – amongst others – our economies (World Economic Forum, 2017). For instance, in their report of 2017, the pay gap is closed in Rwanda (highest on the list) up to 86 per cent, while this is only 40 per cent in Angola (lowest on the list). In comparison, a successfully industrialized country such as the U.S. only closed this gap up to 73 percent, almost a similar percentage compared to Cambodia (70 percent).
According to the European Commission, women earn 16 per cent less than men for the same job in Europe. This is an average of course. Practically, this percentage implies that to earn the same as men, woman would have to work two months more to get the same salary per year. It is noteworthy that the older people are, the bigger this gender gap in payment is. Furthermore, it is worth mentioning that the Scandinavian countries in general score better and are even world leader in reducing this income gap.

The Commission argues that some factors may explain – but by no means justify – this gender gap (European Commission, 2014). Women do significantly more unpaid work, such as housework (thirteen hours per week) or caring for others (twelve hours per week) compared to men (three and five hours respectively). This results in the fact that woman work more part-time compared to men. Furthermore, during their career, women take more career breaks than men, for instance because they are pregnant or temporarily take full time care for her children. The part time working and career breaks are factors that lead to less promotion and career opportunities (Smith et al, 2013). Another factor is the habit of stereotyping of roles of men and women, whereby men are the breadwinner of the family, while women take care of that family. As observed before: this is a tradition that does not change as fast as economic and technological developments in society (Ridgeway, 2011). This sometimes bluntly leads to direct discrimination in which women simply earn less per hour compared to men. This also leads to a habit that in certain industries – in which a majority of the workers is female, for instance in the health sector – the salaries are lower compared to male-dominated industries.

THE GUARDIAN, 7 APRIL 2017

Google accused of 'extreme' gender pay discrimination by US labor department.

By: Sam Levin

Google has discriminated against its female employees, according to the US Department of Labor (DoL), which said it had evidence of 'systemic compensation disparities'.

As part of an ongoing DoL investigation, the government collected information suggesting the internet search giant is violating federal employment laws with its salaries for women, agency officials said.

'We found systemic compensation disparities against women pretty much across the entire workforce,' Janette Wipper, a DoL regional director, testified in court in San Francisco on Friday.

Reached for comment Friday afternoon, Janet Herold, regional solicitor for the DoL, said: 'The investigation is not complete, but at this point the department has received compelling evidence of very significant discrimination against women in the most common positions at Google headquarters.'

(...)

In a statement to the Guardian, Google said: 'We vehemently disagree with [Wipper's] claim. Every year, we do a comprehensive and robust analysis of pay across genders and we have found no gender pay gap. Other than making an unfounded statement which we heard for the first time in court, the DoL hasn't provided any data, or shared its methodology.'

Unequal job opportunities

Another global phenomenon is that in most profit and non-profit organizations, the senior management positions are mostly held by men. A worldwide research in 2014 demonstrates that only 25 per cent of the senior managers are women. However, in Russia this is even 43%, in China 38%, 37% in Eastern Europe, and in Southeast Asia 35 %. This is in stark contrast to the Netherlands, where this percentage is about 10%, slightly higher than Japan with the lowest percentage of 9 % (Grant Thornton, 2014). Therefore – even considering the regional differences – we could say that the boardroom is dominated by men, with hardly any exception.

Another name for this practice is the so-called 'glass ceiling', a metaphor indicating that women should have the same access as men to senior management positions, but are slowed down in their ambition by deeply rooted prejudices (Cotter et al. 2001): women are portrayed as too soft for the job, and too impulsive or emotional to be able to perform management duties on that level.   **Glass ceiling**

Governments and businesses sometimes try to break the glass ceiling by adopting measures to encourage woman to go for a top position. As we have seen above, a career break as a result of pregnancy can slow down the career and place women in a disadvantaged position. Some companies in the digital industry take rather colourful measures to solve that issue by offering their female employees to freeze their ova when they are younger, so they can choose when to have babies when they are older and their career has evolved as planned. You can read more about this in the following newspaper item.

BUSINESS INSIDER, 17 SEPTEMBER 2017

What you need to know about egg-freezing, the hot new perk at Google, Apple, and Facebook

By: Chris Weller

Among the many perks employees enjoy at tech companies like Apple, Facebook, and Google, including extended maternity leave, death benefits, and free beer, oocyte cryopreservation – egg-freezing – is among the most controversial.

The benefit is meant to help younger female employees who may not want kids in their 20s, but don't want all the risks that come with delaying childbirth into their 30s and sometimes 40s. It follows the larger demographic trend of millennial women delaying childbirth to focus on their careers. For the first time in human history, women in their 30s are having more kids than women in their 20s.

'Unfortunately, our hearts' desire and our desire for lifestyle choice is very different than our biology,' Susan Hertzberg, CEO of the fertility company Prelude, told Business Insider.

Recognizing this desire, tech companies happily spend tens of thousands of dollars per employee to offer the perk, claiming the high cost is worth employees' peace of mind. Critics, however, argue the policy sends the wrong message to women – namely, that work is more important than family, and women can't have both at the same time.

Egg-freezing, while well-meaning, perpetuates a broken system that incentivizes women to stay chained to their jobs, these critics claim.

Mostly however, the measures are of a different nature. Both governments and companies have experimented with the so-called gender quota. This means that a certain percentage of senior management should be women. Norway has always been a leading country in using laws to impose a gender quorum on companies. In 2003, the country set a women's quorum of 40 percent for Public Limited Companies that are listed at stock exchange. In academics, we see various opinions on the effects of such a quorum. Some stress the positive effects and long-term changes it brings to society, and underline that legislation is just a tool to bring changes that do not come naturally, and sanctioning a company when they do not comply is the only effective way to work on gender equality in the boardroom (Terjesen et al. 2013). Others are less enthusiastic, and underline that a quorum is hardly effective (Bertrant et al. 2014), or that the short term orientation of companies lead to hastily hiring under-qualified women, which is in nobody's interest (Lindahl, 2015). In Sweden, a woman's quorum did not make it as a law in 2017 due to the fact that a majority of the parliament, despite supporting the cause of gender equality, considered that law would not be the instrument to change this.

Apparently, those who oppose legislation believe that gender equality should be a result of the effects of a free market economy, and companies should be intrinsically motivated to have more female leaders. As a matter of fact, many multinationals currently experiment with gender quota, or systematically measure women's participation at management level. For instance, BP has the ambition to have 25% women group leaders and 30% women senior level leaders by 2020 (www.BP.com, 2017). Apple promotes the fact that they celebrate diversity amongst its personnel, and proudly report that the number of women in a leadership position is increasing every year: 29% of the managers at Apple are women, and 39% of the managers under 30 are women (www.apple.com, 2017).

Violence and harassment
Research shows that 35 percent of all women worldwide have experienced physical and/or sexual violence. The WHO defines these forms of violence as follows:

> Physical violence means being slapped, having something thrown at you, being hit, kicked, dragged or beaten up, being choked or burnt or being threatened with a weapon.

Physical violence

> Sexual violence means being forced to have sexual intercourse, having sexual intercourse because you were afraid of what your partner would might do and/or being forced to do something sexual that you found humiliating or degrading.

Sexual violence

Most of this happens within a relationship, while about 7 per cent of all women have been sexually assaulted by someone else than their partner (WHO, 2013). It is important to note here that apparently voluntary sex is clearly a form of sexual violence when it is done out of fear for negative consequences. An example of this can be found in the case 'the Italian job'.

On the work floor, sexual harassment is a global challenge as well. This became painfully clear when a group of women stood up against sexual harassment in the context of the #MeToo-movement, as you can see in the newspaper item. Sexual harassment is not the same as sexual violence, but is a much broader category. The bottom line is that something is experienced as 'unwelcome' and at some point has a sexual nature. The Australian Sex Discrimination Act defines sexual harassment as follows:

> Sexual harassment is an unwelcome sexual advance, unwelcome request for sexual favours or other unwelcome conduct of a sexual nature which makes a person feel offended, humiliated and/or intimidated, where a reasonable person would anticipate that reaction in the circumstances.

Sexual harassment

In general, 1 out of 5 women in Europe has experienced unwanted touching or kissing. Also new technologies, such as cyber assaulting are a problem: 11 percent of European women has endured sexual harassment online (FRA, 2014). Statistics show that in Europe on average 40 to 50 per cent of working women have encountered some form of sexual harassment in the workplace (UNiTE, 2011). This is where sexual harassment happens the most. In Australia for instance, 88 percent of complaints of sexual harassment are work related. 21 percent of all women have experienced sexual harassment since they were 15, and again 21 percent of all working women have experienced some form of sexual harassment in the last five years (Australian Human Rights Commission 2012).

Also schools can be problematic. In the U.S. for instance, 83 percent of girls aged 12 to 16 experience some form of sexual harassment in public schools (UNiTE, 2011).

Please note that sexual violence or harassment is not necessarily always men against women. It also occurs that men sexually harass other men, or that women are guilty of sexual harassment or violence. However, this generally happens considerably less frequent.

The consequences of sexual violence or harassment are very serious. In the long term it may affect the health of the victim, lead to burn out complaints and serious psychological damage (FRA, 2014).

The Italian job

In 2013, the career of an Italian politician, Luigi Di Fanis, came to an abrupt end. During a corruption investigation, the Italian police accidently found out that mister Di Fanis included some very uncommon terms in a labour contract with his female secretary. In the contract it was stipulated that this lady of 32 years old should have sex at least once a week with mister Di Fanis. The secretary did sign the contract because she was afraid of the consequences if she would not. For a while she indeed had sex with him once a week, until the police discovered the stunning truth during their investigation (Caporale, 2013).

REUTERS, 6 DECEMBER 2017

Time magazine names #MeToo 'silence breakers' as person of the year

By: Susan Heavy

Time magazine has named the social movement aimed at raising awareness about sexual harassment and assault, epitomized by the #MeToo social media hashtag, as the most influential 'person' in 2017, the publication announced on Wednesday. (...)

The recognition comes amid a wave of public allegations of sexual misconduct that have targeted some of the most prominent men in U.S. politics, media and entertainment, leading to multiple firings and investigations.

As more people made their accusations public, other individuals also shared their own stories of assault and harassment, often with posts on social media platforms using the hashtag #MeToo.
(...)
Among the 1,747 American adults surveyed, 17 percent of men and 47 percent of women said they had been abused, according to the Nov. 29-Dec. 4 poll, which had a margin of error of 2.8 percentage points.

The Time announcement comes one day after Representative John Conyers became

the first member of Congress to step down following public allegations of misconduct and amid calls for Senator Al Franken to resign.
Movie mogul Harvey Weinstein and former NBC News anchor Matt Lauer also have lost their jobs amid such allegations. Trump has also been accused of inappropriately touching women and faces related litigation. He has denied the allegations.

Stereotyping
A final problem in the context of discrimination against women is stereotyping.

> Stereotyping is to uphold an incomplete picture of a particular group in which certain characteristics are oversimplified, exaggerated or generalized.

Stereotyping

There are many ideas about the division of roles between men and women. Some believe that women have a different role in society than men, and some believe that gender does not dictate the role one plays in society. Mostly, the position of women in society are driven by culture and tradition. As we have seen above, women do not have the same access to jobs as men worldwide and do not get equal payment compared to men in similar jobs. One of the causes of all this is stereotyping: women are softer, more emotional and more impulsive than men, while men are tougher, more result-driven and have better analytical skills. In science, there is no real evidence that men have different skills than women, and therefore qualify better for certain jobs. At most we could say that women take decisions in a different way than men, and have a different ethical awareness compared to men (Gilligan, 1982). Acknowledging this, and using this, is not necessarily problematic or discriminatory, as we can see in the case of The Hofstede model. However, oversimplifying and exaggerating certain characteristics, and generalizing them as if all women share such characteristics per definition is discriminatory, and a form of stereotyping.

The Hofstede model and gender identity

In analysing cultures, Geert Hofstede created six dimensions that explain differences and similarities between cultures. One of these dimensions is 'masculinity vs femininity'.
'The Masculinity side of this dimension represents a preference in society for achievement, heroism, assertiveness, and material rewards for success. Society at large is more competitive. Its opposite, Femininity, stands for a preference for cooperation, modesty, caring for the weak and quality of life. Society at large is more consensus-oriented' (www.hofstede-insights.com, 2017).

Research shows that the way we educate children has – probably not surprisingly – a huge effect on how they perceive gender identity (Eccles et al. 1990). Media also plays a role of significance in this context: in many movies the hero is a muscled men showing all the stereotyped characteristics we would expect a hero to have: brave, bald, strong, protective and fair. We hardly see women play these roles (with some notable exceptions of course: we have all seen the Tomb Raider movies). Also in commercials we see a deeply rooted stereotyping, in which a girl is supposed to play with pink horses and dolls, while a boy should be cool and play with cars and knights. A similar approach we see in commercials for 'grown ups'. The female is the one cleaning the house using products invented by a clever (male) scientist, and her husband is a guy in a suit who is the successful breadwinner. For companies, this might be a way of 'playing it safe' since they appeal to traditional gender roles that are recognized by a majority of the people, which is in line with established tradition (Brasted, 2010). However, we also see that this form of stereotyping is slowly changing in some countries, and that increasingly we see a more caring man interacting with his children in commercials, sometimes even cleaning the house (Grau & Zotos, 2016).

In the news article we see an example of a garment company trying to oppose gender-based stereotyping by removing 'boys' and 'girls' labels from their products. Such initiatives are usually hailed by some and cursed by others, and touch upon a wider 'gender debate'.

METRO, 2 SEPTEMBER 2017

John Lewis has become the first major department store to ditch 'boys' and 'girls' labels from children's clothing.

By: Tanveer Mann

The chain has also removed 'boys' and 'girls' signs from the childrenswear sections at the store to avoid 'reinforcing gender stereotypes'. From now on, labels on the clothing will say either 'Boys & Girls' or 'Girls & Boys' and will be on all John Lewis clothing from newborn to 14 years. Even dresses with flowers and skirts will carry the unisex labels.
(...)

Caroline Bettis, the head of childrenswear at John Lewis, told MailOnline: 'We do not want to reinforce gender stereotypes within our John Lewis collections and instead want to provide greater choice and variety to our customers, so that the parent or child can choose what they would like to wear.' The department store said it would also be reviewing its online shopping site, which still includes boys' and girls' clothing options. It comes after several retailers were criticised over their sexist clothing ranges.

Discrimination on the basis of nationality and race
As we saw in the example of farmer Karl, discrimination based on someone's nationality or race is a controversial issue. One of the consequences of globalization is that it becomes easier for people to look for a job abroad. When these people can offer their services better, or for a lower price, there will be tension between the immigrants and the locals who fear to lose their job in their own country. For instance, one of the

arguments for a Brexit was fear of losing jobs to foreigners. Another example is the policies of President Trump to slow down immigration in order to protect jobs in the U.S. While market protectionism is questioned by economist as a means to create more jobs (Felbab-Brown, 2017), it is politically a popular tool to give people a secure feeling.

Things become worse when an immigrant minority is linked with a higher degree of criminality than average. According to Trump, the Mexicans did not send their best citizens to the U.S., as we can see in the example. The cause of immigrant minorities ending up at the bottom of society is difficult to explain, and sometimes a 'chicken and egg' discussion.

In Europe we have seen the rise of political parties who strongly oppose immigration and prefer to first take care of the welfare of their own people (Postelnicescu, 2016). These nationalist parties do believe that nationality is a valid reason for different treatment.

Trump on Mexicans

In his speech from the Trump Tower in June 2016, Donald Trump announced that he would run for president. Amongst others, he talked about immigration, and made the following controversial statement:

'When Mexico sends its people, they're not sending their best. They're not sending you.

They're not sending you. They're sending people that have lots of problems, and they're bringing those problems with us. They're bringing drugs. They're bringing crime. They're rapists. And some, I assume, are good people' (Trump, 2016).

When someone feels socially excluded and not valued, he or she will more probably express negative behaviour, such as dropping out of school or ending up as criminals. On the other hand, when someone behaves in a negative way, it can easily lead to social exclusion (Pierson, 2010). Social exclusion of immigrants could result in wage discrimination, or discrimination in job opportunities. This is a downward spiral that is not easily halted. Both interpretations strengthen one another in its effect, as we can see in figure 6.2.

FIGURE 6.2 Social exclusion and negative behaviour

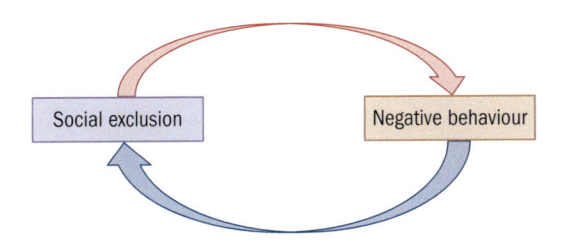

A lot of research was done in the relationship between immigration and criminality. In the UK, there were alarming reports that immigrants would be responsible for a quarter of all crimes in London, mostly committed by people from Poland, Romania and Lithuania (Doyle & Wright, 2012). At the same time, another research demonstrates that crime rates among immigrant workers are not higher compared to English people (Johnston, 2008). Also in the U.S., despite what Trump suggests, a causal link between immigration and crime is difficult to establish (Camarota & Vaughan, 2009, Aaron, 2015) and some researchers even conclude that immigration leads to a decline of crime (Macdonald & Saunders, 2012; Ousey & Kubrin, 2009).

Discrimination based on religion

Discrimination based on religion, and conflict as a result of differences in religion, has been a major theme in the history of mankind. Currently, we see conflicts and religion discrimination on each continent.
Think about:

- the conflict between the Jewish Israel and the Islamic Palestine
- the Coptic Christians in Egypt, who often feel discriminated by the Muslim majority
- the Islamic minority who feels discriminated in Buddhist Thailand
- the Christian minority in Indonesia, who feels discriminated by the Muslim majority
- the Uyghurs Muslim minority in China who feels discriminated by the Chinese authorities
- the Tamils (Christian and Hindu) who feel discriminated by the Buddhist majority in Sri Lanka
- the Muslim Rohingya people in Myanmar, who feel discriminated by the Buddhist majority
- aboriginal people all over the world who feel suppressed in practicing their faith by the 'new' population

Religious minorities are especially vulnerable when the state is not secular, and freedom of religion is not self-evident.

Secular state

> A secular state is a state which is neutral towards religion, and religion has no influence on public decision-making processes.

We could say that a prerequisite for freedom of religion is that a state does not prescribe nor favour a particular religion. In a majority of the conflicts described above, the state in which the conflict emerges is hardly neutral towards religion, and the religious preference of an individual is decisive in how you are treated.

However, a secular state does not necessarily solve all problems, and does not guarantee the absence of religion-based discrimination. One challenge is how to define religion. Can anyone claim to practice a random religion, and should for instance authorities and employers respect and recognize this, and where possible allow people to practice the religion the way they want? An interesting case is the Pastafarian religion (Henderson, 2006), in which a Flying Spaghetti Monster is worshipped (see newspaper item). One of the things Pastafarians do is to wear a colander on their heads. When you are an employer, and you recognize that wearing a headscarf is essential for some people in practicing their religion, should you also allow employees to wear a colander on their head during work? And if not, where do you draw a line?

Another problem is how to find a proper balance between religious freedom and other freedoms (Bijsterveld, 2015). When people do things that are offensive to others when exercising their right to freedom of religion, to what extent do you let freedom of religion prevail? When someone uses hate speech or calls for violence when exercising their religious freedom, when should you stop this person? If you're an employer, can you expect people to wear clothes that are neutral towards religion when they do their job? Do you have to allow religious employees time to pray during office hours? And if you do, what do you do with non-religious employees, do you give them an equal time off? Or, do you have to recognize the fact that your female salesperson – from a religious point of view – does not want to shake the hands of men? And if you do not allow it, is that discrimination, or is it a justified job requirement to do shake hands in your position as a salesperson? All these are questions that are not easily answered; each time it requires a careful balancing of interest. Perhaps an ethical decision-making procedure (chapter four) might help in such cases.

METRO UK, 28 JANUARY 2016

The Netherlands has recognised the Church of the Flying Spaghetti Monster as a religion

By: Amy Willis

The Church of the Flying Spaghetti Monster has finally been recognised as a religion in The Netherlands. Two days ago, pastafarians were told by the country's Chamber of Commerce that they would be granted official status. They had been trying for several years.

Members of the new church obviously celebrated the news with a bowl of pasta. A spokesman for the Dutch arm of the group said: 'The Church of the Flying Spaghetti Monster is since today officially registered as Denomination! Our church stands for equality for all. Therefore, anyone can sign up free of charge and without obligation. To express our faith we put a colander on our heads. Also on official government documents. We come together in local churches and at events. Our services are especially devoted to socialising. So we eat pasta, we drink beer and discuss faith.'

Although a momentous time for the church of FSM – this is not the first time the church has been recognised in some capacity. The Church of the Flying Spaghetti Monster is already recognised in North America after being established by 'prophet' Bobby Henderson in 2005 as a protest against creationism. Pastafarians believe heaven is a beer volcano with a stripper factory, while hell is the same but the beer is stale and the strippers have sexually transmitted diseases. (...)

6.3.3   Work stress

Health is an important social value for employees. Work stress is one of the biggest factors that may negatively affect the health of a worker (ILO, 2016). Globally, the main causes of work-related stress relate either to the content or the context of the work (Crox et al. 2005).

Stress related to work occurs in the sphere of:
- work environment and work equipment, such as unsafe tools or dangerous workplaces
- task design, such as endlessly repeating actions or meaningless work
- workload, such as too much work in too little time
- work schedule, such as shift work, unpredictable hours or work during the night

Stress related to work context occurs in the sphere of:
- organisational culture and function, such as bad communication or a lack of managerial support
- role in organisation, such as carrying a great responsibility for others
- career development, such as a lack of career opportunities
- decision latitude/control, such as too little influence on decision-making processes
- interpersonal relationships at work, such as conflicts or a bad relationship with managers
- home-work interface, such as an insecure situation at home effecting performance at work

In general, we could argue that to avoid work stress, two relations should be balanced: the effort-reward balance and the demand-control balance (Marmot et al. 2009). Please note that this balance may differ per person, in time and per situation. It is the challenge for managers and HRM departments to create an atmosphere in which employees can explore this balance and make sure they can work most effectively without suffering work related stress.

Effort-reward balance

> The effort-reward balance relates to the extent to which a worker is adequately rewarded for his effort.

In particular the combination of hard work and low reward is a common cause of work-related stress, as you can see from the example 'the scheduler and the conductor'. At the same time, receiving a disproportionally high reward for just an average performance can also affect someone's psychological condition, as you can see in the example 'Justin Bieber, drugs and expensive cars'.
Reward does not always have to be expressed in money, although this often will be an important factor. Valuation by career opportunities, improvement of secondary labour conditions or exposure can also contribute to a better effort-reward balance.

Demand-control balance

> The demand-control balance relates to the extent to which a worker has sufficient autonomy in his work.

Autonomy means that an employee has – to a certain extent – influence on how he performs his job. When someone has little autonomy (control), while the employer is extremely strict in what an employee should do (demand), this may lead to work-related stress. We see this very often in low-skilled labour, with repeating tasks that should be done as efficiently as possible to keep the production costs as low as possible. An example in which this balance could be disturbed is the case of casual workers, who are often contracted for a short period to carry out last minute work. In that kind of work there usually is a low autonomy and the temporary worker has to follow the specific instructions of the contractor.

The scheduler and the conductor

At most universities, it is not easy to create a schedule that makes everyone (all teaching staff, students and external experts) happy. The scheduler has to take into account all kinds of individual preferences, specific demands per course and subject, and is limited by the availability of the lecture halls. By teaching staff and students, a schedule is mostly something we take for granted, and consider it self-evident that schedules match our expectations. Only when something is wrong with the schedule, we bother contacting the scheduler. This means that virtually all communication with colleagues or students have a negative message: something is not right. While there will hardly be anything positive in terms of 'thanks for the wonderful schedule, you did a great job!' This results in a job in which the effort-reward balance is easily disturbed.

How different is the job of a conductor. At a performance, the orchestra is already seated on stage, while the conductor waits until he is invited on stage by a speaker. This speaker usually sums up the curriculum vitae of the conductor, summarizing how great he is. After he is invited on stage, the audience applauds and his orchestra stands up out of respect for him. In other words, people are applauding and showing respect for a conductor because he successfully arrived at the job. During the concert, the conductor receives the appreciation of the audience on behalf of the orchestra. After the performance, the conductor receives flowers from the theatre (or wine, or both) and is complimented in the foyer by the audience once more. This results in a job with a relatively high reward in terms of appreciation and secondary labour conditions for a normal working day.

Justin Bieber, drugs and expensive cars

The lifestyle of the rich and the famous can be rather counterproductive, as we have seen many times in case of teenage idols who became superstars in a relatively short period. Take Justin Bieber, for example, who scored hit after hit at a very young age. He is well known for his catchy tunes, his dance moves and his good looks. Girls all over the world are in love with him, and during live performances it is quite normal that groups of girls faint when he hits the lights. When you are put on a pedestal at such a young age, it can only go wrong (Barker, 2014). In essence, Bieber can buy whatever he wants, considering his massive income: he is the proud owner of a bunch of

cars, a private aircraft, and he even bought a monkey as a pet. This leads to an awkward perception of reality, in which Bieber feels that he stands above everything and everyone, including the law. This has led to some disturbing behaviour. For instance, in January 2014 Bieber considered it necessary to participate in a car race through the streets of Miami, without a valid driving license while being under the influence of alcohol and drugs (Stephard et al. 2014). Later that year he would be arrested a second time for crashing a quad and ending up in a fight (Glenza, 2014).

6.3.4 Dismissal

Dismissal law has always been a controversial issue in politics. In most developed countries there is some sort of protection for employees against certain forms of dismissal. In this section we will first explore the nature of dismissal law, and the ethical issues that relate to it. Second, we will discuss collective redundancies and its complications. Third, we will discuss the additional protection that could be offered to whistle blowers, and how dismissal laws may help here.

Security
Employees and employers often have conflicting interests. Usually, employers want to maximize the flexibility in their labour relation with the employees to adapt to the markets as quickly as possible in order to be as competitive as possible. After all, the employer represents those who take the financial risk in entrepreneurship. The employees on the other hand want as much security as possible, since they need to pay their monthly fees and have a family to maintain. Dismissal laws usually try to find a golden mean between these two opposing interests, however there is mostly considerable disagreement as to how exactly do this. The norms and values of employers and employees regarding dismissal law are shown in figure 6.3. In the case 'The American model: employment-at-will' we see an interesting example of this balancing of interest.

FIGURE 6.3 The norms and values of employers and employees in respect of dismissal law

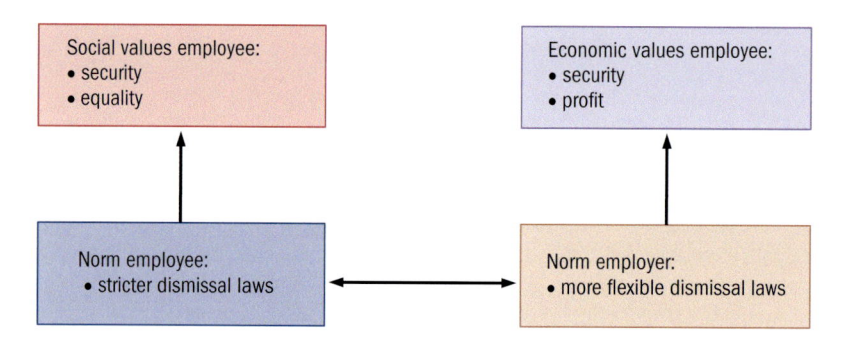

Income security is an important value for employees. When an employee can be fired at will by the employer without any reason on any given moment, this leads to a very insecure situation for the employee. At the core, we consider that the relationship between employer and employee is not equal. After all, the employer mostly represents a large organization that is much more powerful than an individual employee. For that reason, most developed countries adopted certain laws to guarantee a certain degree of income security (Wernaart, 2017). Mostly, there are rules that set a maximum to the amount or duration of temporary contracts. When this threshold is reached, the employee is entitled to a permanent labour contract, meaning that he cannot be fired randomly. Furthermore, we usually see rules to prevent employers using fake constructions to hire people as casual workers while the labour relation has all the characteristics from an employment contract.

The American model: employment-at-will

In the U.S.A. labour agreements are considered 'normal' contracts that govern a private relation. That is, the relationship between the employer and the employee. The idea is that the Government should not interfere with such private relations, since individuals should be entirely free to conduct their own business.

In a landmark ruling, the Supreme Court of Tennessee (1884) held that: 'Obviously the law can adopt and maintain no such standards for judging human conduct; and men must be left, without interference to buy and sell where they please, and to discharge or retain employees at will for good cause or for no cause, or even for bad cause without thereby being guilty of an unlawful act per se. It is a right which an employee may exercise in the same way, to the same extent, for the same cause or want of cause as the employer. He may refuse to work for a man or company that trades with any obnoxious person, or does other things which he dislikes. He may persuade his fellows, and the employer may lose all his hands and be compelled to close his doors; or he may yield to the demand and withdraw his custom or cease his dealings, and the obnoxious person be thus injured or wrecked in business.'

Exceptions

Ever since, this is the starting point in American labour law. However, in some states, exceptions to this principle are accepted (Hackstock & Heyroth, 2002; Muhl, 2001; Summers, 2000).

The first is the public policy exception. This means that a dismissal of an employee may not contradict the public policy of the state. For instance, some rights of employees are publicly protected, such as the protection of whistle-blowers and the duty to notify public authorities about criminal activities within a company.

The second well-known exception is the implied contract. In some labour relations, it becomes obvious that the employee may reasonably expect that his employment will not be terminated 'at will'. This could be deduced from the company's written policy not to fire employees when they function properly, or from oral statements of the employer that the employee may expect to be hired for a particular (or indefinite) period.

A third exception is that all U.S.A. citizens should comply with federal laws. For instance, in the U.S.A., discrimination on gender, disability and age are forbidden at the Federal level. A dismissal that seems to be discriminatory is therefore illegal.

Fourth, in some states the principle of good faith and fair dealing is recognized, which means that an employer may not fire an employee without a valid, legal reason. Especially when they have been employed for a long time. Since this principle restricts the employment-at-will doctrine considerably, it is not widely accepted.

While it is hardly disputed that it is in interest of employees to pursue income security, we can observe various approaches to do so. In this context, we could make a distinction between job security and employability (Jeurissen, 2007).

> Job security means the long-term security of a worker in relation to   **Job security**
> a particular job for the same employer.

In the case of job security there is an emphasis a particular labour relationship between an employer and employee. For the employer, this has the advantage that he can build a deep relationship with the employee, who is truly devoted to his case and is willing to serve almost a lifetime in his employment. The downside is that this also creates a situation of 'business as usual' in which the employee is not intensively motivated to bring in something fresh and new.

Employability | Employability means the long-term security of an employee with respect to work, regardless of the employer.

In the case of employability there is an emphasis on the independent ability of the employee to find employment during his career. This employment is not necessarily one job for one employer; it could be a chain of different jobs in which the employee grows and develops his talents throughout his career. While this offers less security in terms of job security, this so-called 'job-hopping' has various advantages for both the employee and the employer. First, the employer will experience more flexibility in hiring people since there is a permanent coming and going of employees who all bring something new to the organization. Second, the employee feels more responsible for his career opportunities and will actively keep assessing whether he currently works at the right place. This leads to the situation that the employer has motivated people who only do the work they feel comfortable with (otherwise they would leave). The disadvantage could be that the employee is not necessarily loyal to the cause of the employer, and constantly looks for a better job.

While in academic discourse, job security is often labelled as conservative, and employability the way to go, there are some challenges. First, employability might work for highly educated and flexible people, but not always in low-skilled sectors. How would a cab driver invest in himself to make sure he develops his career in a life-long-learning state of mind in cab driving? The other problem is that families are not always that flexible. Not everyone has the luxury of simply moving to another town for work: there are children at school and a partner with yet another job. Lastly, labour law traditionally focuses on job security, and protects the employee against unfair dismissal. The legal environment therefore mostly does not emphasize employability, nor do the governmental policies that support this legislation (Zekic, 2016).

In conclusion, it is likely that the average employer needs a mix of both types of labour relationships: loyal workers who are concerned with the long-term performance of the business, and job-hoppers who bring in the fresh air once in a while.

Collective redundancies

In most developed countries the law imposes certain procedures on employers when they plan to fire a larger group of employees at once. Mostly, collective redundancies are deemed necessary in case of economic slowdown, a merger or a takeover.

In some legal systems, a social plan is required in order to be allowed to fire a group of employees. In this plan, the employer and employees agree on how the employer will facilitate a smooth transition to a new job. This could include some financial support to bridge the time in between jobs, offering some trainings to their dismissed employees to better equip them when looking for another job, or simply to collectively transfer the employees to a befriended company (or company that is in the same franchise).

Social plan | A social plan is a contract in which an employer agrees to support his former employees financially and non-financially in the transition towards a new job.

The extent to which the company supports their former employees depends on the willingness of the company and the potential to close a deal with the relevant trade unions. The strategy towards such a contract differs somewhat per company.

On the one hand we see companies who merely operate within the boundaries of the law, and are not willing to do anything more than that. The social plan will then offer no more protection to the employees than strictly necessary to comply with the relevant legislation. When the company makes sure to inform the employees in the latest possible stage that a round of collective redundancies is planned, the workers will be kept motivated for the longest possible period, and will only feel insecure during the last short part of their employment after the announcement. When the employees are dismissed as quickly as the law allows it, the company carries out the collective redundancies as efficiently as possible.

On the other hand we see companies who are willing to do a lot more than the law prescribes. The company might worry about their good image, or considers that trust in the functioning of the company is important, also in the future when they perhaps can offer more jobs. Besides that, it might even be a more efficient approach to support and help your employees, since it might save the company some litigation, employees are more motivated to help look for a solution, and motivated to work hard for this as 'co-owner' of the problem.

In the newspaper item we see that initially, the Israeli company is reluctant to support their employees and plans to dismiss a significant amount of their factory workers, due to economic slowdown and lack of support of the Israeli government to create a healthy economic climate in the region. In the end, after three months of strikes, an agreement was reached between the company and the trade unions. The company would support voluntary retirements, and pay a compensation to those who would involuntarily lose their job to bridge the period in between jobs. Ultimately, 210 out of the 248 dismissed employees would make use of an early retirement plan. As a result, the number of involuntary dismissals was kept relatively low (ICL, 2015).

Three fundamental values could play a role in social plans: transparency, cooperation and autonomy (figure 6.4).

FIGURE 6.4 Values that play a role in collective redundancies

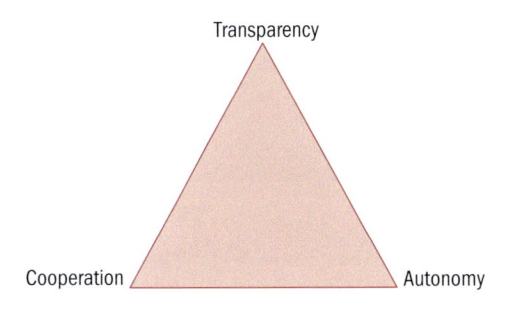

Transparency   Transparency means that a company informs its employees about the financial (and non-financial) situation, and does not leave them unaware about an upcoming round of collective redundancies.

Cooperation   Cooperation means that employees are involved in the decision procedures that relate to their jobs. When employees can contribute in solving problems and use their skills and know-how in the process, resulting solutions are mostly of a better quality and more broadly embraced by all stakeholders. In some countries involving employees in the decisions on collective redundancies is even a legal obligation.

Autonomy   Autonomy means that employees have enough time to make up their own mind regarding their employability, and when necessary can take their own decision about their jobs. This practically means that employees need some time to 'look around' and when they find something that suits them better leave the company voluntarily and start working for the other business.

THE TIMES OF ISRAEL, 17 MAY 2015

Thousands march in Dimona to protest factory layoffs

By: Toi Staff

Opposition leader Herzog calls for government to hold cabinet meeting in south as three cities go on strike in solidarity with workers.

Thousands of people in three southern cities went on strike Sunday in solidarity with Israel Chemicals workers who are facing layoffs, and to protest the bleak state of employment in the Negev region as a whole. In Dimona, Arad and Yeruham, city services were shut down, and some schools were closed and business shuttered in solidarity.

(...)

The protest is designed to draw national attention to what locals and others say is a worsening situation for the working-class towns, where a string of layoffs at nearby plants have hobbled the local economy.

Workers at two subsidiaries of Israel Chemicals – Dead Sea Works in Sodom and Bromine Compounds in Neot Hovav – are facing layoffs, according to reports. Union chairmen at both companies are pressing for agreements for voluntary retirement and early retirement for older workers instead of layoffs, the Hebrew-language news outlet Haaretz reported. Avi Nissenkorn, the head of the Histadrut labor federation, met on Saturday night with Nir Gilad, chairman of the board of Israel Chemicals, to resolve the disagreement as to whether Israel Chemicals has the power to lay off workers as part of its efficiency plan.

(...)

With so many factory closures over the past decade and the accompanying shortage of jobs requiring unskilled labor, those who lose their jobs have nowhere else to go, they say.

The whistle blower

Sometimes an unethical practice within an organization persists. In some cases the company has installed regulations and procedures, possibly supported by a code of conduct, to tackle such unethical practices. Mostly, a code of conduct stimulates employees that observe unethical behaviour to discuss this internally with their superior, and if that does not appear to work with someone from the senior management, or a designated body that is installed to review such observations. If a company wants to encourage its employees to internally discuss unethical practices, it helps to provide them with some safeguards, such as the guarantee that there will be no retaliation actions when someone speaks out, or the possibility to anonymously speak out. A good example of this can be found in the sample from the Code of Ethics of Franklin Resources Ltd.

Sample from the Code of Ethics and Business Conduct of Franklin Resources Ltd, 2017

Questions and Concerns. Described in this Code are procedures generally available for addressing ethical issues that may arise. As a general matter, if a Covered Person has any questions or concerns about compliance with this Code, he or she is encouraged to speak with his or her supervisor, manager, representatives of the Human Resources Department, the Legal Department, the General Counsel of Franklin Resources, Inc. or the Global Compliance Department.

Compliance and Ethics Hotline. If a Covered Person does not feel comfortable talking to any of the persons listed above for any reason, he or she should call the Compliance and Ethics Hotline. (…)If a Covered Person does not feel comfortable stating his or her name, calls to the Compliance and Ethics Hotline may be made anonymously.(…)

Confidentiality and Investigation. The Company will treat the information set forth in a report of any suspected violation of the Code or law, including the identity of the caller, in a confidential manner and will conduct a prompt and appropriate evaluation and investigation of any matter reported.(…)

Protection of Covered Persons. It is a violation of this Code to retaliate against anyone who has communicated to the Company information that such person reasonably believes constitutes a violation of the Code or which is otherwise illegal or unethical. (…)

However, what should the employee do when the company does not solve the unethical behaviour adequately while the consequences of this behaviour can inflict serious harm on people or the environment? Sometimes, there is only one option left, which is to blow the whistle.

> A whistleblower is someone who publicly reveals an alleged unethical practice in an organization.   **Whistleblower**

A whistleblower will find himself in a difficult position. On the one hand there is the potential harm that is inflicted on people or the environment that needs to stop. On the other hand, revealing unethical practices publicly will no doubt damage the good image of the company, and potentially weaken the competitiveness of his employer. This may result in a difficult relation with your employer and perhaps also with your colleagues who might not be too happy with the revelation of the unethical practice since it has consequences for their business and work.
Therefore, a company may seek to protect a whistleblower. In some countries, larger companies are obliged to adopt a whistle blower regulation

with certain minimum safeguards. Three basic values usually play an important role in dealing with whistleblowers, as we can see in figure 6.5: urgency, integrity and protection.

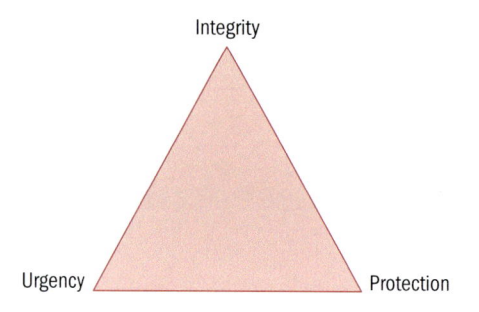

FIGURE 6.5 Values that play a role dealing with whistleblowers

Urgency

Urgency means that a whistleblower should only publicly reveal alleged unethical behaviour when there is no other option left. One should always try to deal with unethical practices internally first. Only when the employee has done everything possible to solve the issue internally and it does not lead to a fitting solution, the whistle should be blown publicly.

Integrity

Integrity means that a whistleblower should only reveal alleged unethical behaviour publicly with the right intentions, and not with conflicting interests. This means that revealing information to settle a personal conflict or to get rid of a manager you do not like is not a good reason.

Protection

Protection means that there should not be any retaliation against a whistleblower for publicly revealing unethical behaviour. The whistleblower should not be fired, discriminated against or otherwise treated differently due to his actions. As you can read in following the newspaper article, this is not self-evident, since there is a huge interest for the company to discourage whistleblowing.

CNN, 21 JULY 2017

Wells Fargo ordered to rehire whistleblower and pay $577,500 in back wages

By: Jacky Wattles

The whistleblower was working as a branch manager in Pomona, California, when she was fired for reporting misconduct related to the bank's fake account scandal, according to findings released on Friday by the Department of Labor's Occupational Safety and Health Administration. Wells Fargo 'terminated the employee turned whistleblower in September 2011 because of concerns raised that the bank's private bankers were opening customer accounts and enrolling customers in bank

products without their knowledge, consent or appropriate disclosures,' OSHA said in a press release.
Federal law prohibits banks from retaliating when an employee reports potentially unlawful activity.
In addition to reinstating the whistleblower's job and awarding her $577,500 in back pay, compensatory damages and attorneys fees, Wells Fargo must clear her personnel file, the OSHA order said. The bank is also required to post notices informing bank workers about federal whistleblower protection laws.

Wells Fargo (WFC) pushed back in a statement issued on Friday and indicated it will appeal the decision.(...)

Wells Fargo has been grappling with the fallout of a massive fake account scandal that became public last year. Wells Fargo has admitted to creating at least 2 million potentially unauthorized checking and credit card accounts between 2011 and 2015 in order to boost its sales figures. Wells Fargo employees have blamed draconian sales targets.
(...) The company has said it's since restructured its sales goals.

6.4 Challenges in developing countries

As discussed in the previous section, we very often see a variety of measures taken to protect the social values of employees in developed countries. In comparison, this is considerably less the case in developing countries and newly developed countries. At the same time, globalization results in the fact that companies can outsource part of their production processes or services abroad. This could lead to ethical dilemmas, since the protection of social values can easily be circumvented by hiring workers in developed or NIC countries, who do not enjoy similar protection compared to the workers in your home country.
This results in the core to two issues:
- To what extent should you make use of the more flexible standards towards the protection of social values in other countries?
- To what extent are you in the position to impose your own norms and values on developing and NIC countries?

6.4.1 The protection of social values for workers

In the example 'Dell and the ICT Hell' we see that there is very little protection for the social values of workers in China. The question is to what extent companies who originate from developed countries – in which these social values are considerably better protected – have the moral obligation to protect such values in a similar way in the countries of their suppliers.

Dell and the ICT Hell
The world's largest ICT factories can be found in Shenzhen City, China. In 2013, the Danish human rights watchdog published a report in which the labour conditions within these factory walls was criticized (Stracke et al. 2013). The information substantiating the report was gathered by conducting risky undercover operations, since the Chinese authorities were not quite cooperative in gathering the relevant data. The report focused on the supplying factories for the American based ICT company Dell, although similar conclusions can be drawn for the suppliers of other ICT companies such as

6

Apple, Samsung, HP, IBM, Fujitsu, Lenovo, Acer, Sony and Toshiba.

Poor labour conditions
There are plenty of examples of poor labour conditions. For instance, employees had to work overtime. Not only because they were forced to by their superiors, but also due to the fact that the salary for a 40-hour working week was inadequate to make a living. Furthermore, the work consisted of very long days of extremely boring production line work. And, the employees were forced to work with dangerous materials without proper protective measures, and were intimidated during work: employees had to ask permission to assume another working position. Next to that, the employees usually lived near the factory, and were housed *en masse* in very small rooms (mostly 8 to 12 employees per room). If an employee wanted to quit their job, she/he risked not to be paid for the previous period. During the summer season, a lot of youngster are also employed in these factories, as an 'intern'. However, in

practice, they simply participate in the production line work, while their school receives a financial compensation for this (DanWatch, 2015).

Dell
Dell stated on several occasions to share the concerns expressed by DanWatch. For instance, in their annual Corporate Social Responsibility Report, the state that: 'According to Verisk Maplecroft's Human Rights Risk Atlas, the information and communications technology industry manufactures in some of the highest-risk countries in the world. Challenges like excessive working hours, insufficient transparency and violations of freely chosen employment standards are systemic and not specific to any one company. Dell continually works to eradicate these and other issues' (Dell, 2015).
Up to now, DanWatch holds that Dell is not living up to their own expectations, and keep pressing their suppliers to lower their prices, instead of improving the labour conditions of the Chinese employees.

Chain responsibility

In chapter 5 we introduced the idea of 'chain responsibility' in the context of globalization. In case of social values this would mean that a company that sells a final product, in the example that would be Dell, is not only responsible for the protection of social values of workers in their own country, but also for these values of workers who are at some point involved in the manufacturing of the product in other countries. This could be in subsidiary establishments owned by Dell in another country, but also in supplying companies that are involved at any stage in the product chain. Therefore, in this context sometimes the term Supplier responsibility is used.

However, all this is easier said than done. There are some serious limitations to what we can reasonably expect from a company in terms of responsibility.

- *Influence*: Depending on the exact market, it will not always be easy to have enough influence and try and make a difference regarding the protection of the social values of workers. When you are the only company that is willing to invest in the wellbeing of people, including the people that work for the supplying companies in developing and newly industrialized countries, you might create a competitive disadvantage for yourself. After all, your competitors do not invest in such values, and as a result are able to offer a lower price for a similar product to the consumer. In highly competitive markets, investing in social values as part of chain responsibility will only make sense when this is a joint action of the most important companies in that market.

- *Causality*: The question could rise why a company selling end products should be responsible for supplying companies as well. After all, it is the primary responsibility of the supplying companies themselves to protect the social values of their workers. A company cannot bear the weight of the world on its own shoulders, and should focus on its own employees first, since they are closest.
- *Impact*: It remains to be seen that the improvement of social values in developing or newly industrialized countries will indeed lead to a better life for the employees over there. After all, when globalization results in regulatory competition, improving the social values in a region may as well put them in a competitive disadvantage. Companies will not be so eager to outsource their production processes or services in that region, and look elsewhere for a region with more flexibility in social standards. The effort could therefore be counterproductive and not automatically lead to the impact that is desired.
- *Relationship*: When social values are not protected adequately in a region or country, it is the primary job of a government to adopt regulations that improve the situation. It is not a healthy situation when a company tries to take over the job of regulator. After all, the relationship between a company and an employee is different compared to the relation between a government and employees. The first hires them for profit, where the second should protect them against unfair and unethical practices.

At the same time there are also good arguments to support the idea of chain responsibility in the context of social values:

- *Impact*: In developing countries or NIC countries, governments are not always able or willing to actively change laws or policies that protect social values of workers. This can be due to a lack of resources, a lack of an effective executive branch, or simply a result of corruption. In such a situation, a multinational can easily take advantage of the flexible approach towards social values, and turn this into a profit. Simultaneously, the developing country in itself, including its government, could be heavily relying on the income generated by the foreign multinationals. If these multinationals would – preferably jointly – set social standards the entire product chain should comply with, this could have considerable impact on the wellbeing of workers in that country. However, as we will see in chapter 9, this can only work when a sound accountability mechanism is installed.
- *Causality*: Where before, companies would mostly produce their products in their own country, in today's globalized world production processes may involve many countries. Preferably countries in which production is possible for the lowest possible costs. As we have seen, this may have its consequences for the social values of workers who are then involved with this production. This work is vital for the success of the company that sells the end product. As a result we could say that the foreign worker employed in a developing or NIC country actually stands very close to the multinational who in the end uses their workforce to their benefit.
- *Impact*: There is a lot to be gained when it concerns the social values of workers in developing and NIC countries. As we can see in the example 'Henry Ford and salary' it could be beneficial to regard workers as economically active citizens instead of a costly matter. It would be

6

interesting to reflect on what would happen when the millions of people around the world who now live below the poverty line, which is around 10.7 per cent of the world population (World Bank Group, 2016), would turn into economically empowered people. The impact would be massive, and obviously multinationals can make this impact.

- *Relationship*: The idea of open trade is that companies can compete on a global market based on the same rules of the game. When social values differ significantly per country, this is a distortion of that system. It would only be fair to expect that the companies who enthusiastically make use of open borders also behave as responsible stakeholders to those who are affected by these open borders. This special relationship cannot be one sided, in which workers have to offer their services for a very low income under poor conditions while the multinational that benefits from this does nothing to improve the situation. With power comes responsibility for this special relationship.

Henry Ford and salary

In this book we will refer more than once to Henry Ford for various reasons. Mostly, he is remembered for his innovative entrepreneurship. In the early 20st century, Ford broke the downward cycle in which companies were engaged in a race to the bottom to get the lowest cost prise for manufactured products, and as a result increasingly lower wages. As a counter-movement, Ford introduced the so-called 'fife-dollar-day' (later even a six-dollar-day), on which an employee would earn twice as much than usual. It was the philosophy of Ford that a worker who earned more would be more motivated and more eager to work harder and more efficiently. Furthermore, a worker with a higher salary would have more to spend, and would be able to allow himself the luxury of buying a (Ford) car. At the same time, Henry Ford managed to still lower the cost prise of his car by optimizing the production process, a talented staff and larger production amounts per car type. Where a Ford-car would still cost $950 in 1920, the price could drop in 1920 to only 355 dollars. Simultaneously, the sales increased enormously: in 1910 the Ford factories produced only 18,664 vehicles, while in 1920, 125,0000 cars were produced. So, in a period of ten years the sales price of a Ford car was about 2.5 times lower while production was 70 times as large. In fact, Ford created an entire new market in which the working class American citizen could afford to buy a Ford car, starting with his own employees who earned enough to proudly ride the vehicles they produced themselves (Ford, 1922).

6.4.2   Imposing norms and values

A well-known English proverb says: 'When in Rome, do as the Romans do.' This means more or less that when you find yourself in another country, behave like the locals, and accept their norms and values. This proverb goes to the heart of a dilemma caused by globalisation: should a multinational adjust its views on norms and values to the local setting in the countries in which they operate, or should they stick to their own? Take the case 'Share a prostitute, then do business'. Imagine you are a foreign export manager invited to a karaoke bar by some potential business partners, and very close in getting a huge deal. Would you give what it takes, and engage in jointly using the services of a prostitute to get things done? Or would you stick to your own principles and walk away, telling your employer you could not get the deal? As we can see in the newspaper item, the Uber management received some bad publicity in the U.S. media after visiting one of these karaoke bars, so apparently 'at home' this kind of behaviour was rejected, while in the country of doing the business, it was not.

Share a prostitute, then do business

In the Far East countries, business is not done overnight. First, business partners should engage in a game of exchanging favours, sharing experiences and in that process form a bond in which the other party can be trusted. In Chapter 3, we already discussed this phenomenon, using the Chinese word Guānxi. When such relationship building is done through innocent gestures, there will hardly be any ethical concerns. However, it may cause difficulties in the international context when foreigners try to do business in – say – South Korea and are confronted with practices that would be considered unethical in their home country.

For instance, in South Korea, it is not unusual to take a business partner to a karaoke bar. Usually, a private karaoke room is hired in which a befriended group can sing, drink and possibly do business. It is also not uncommon that there are prostitutes in a karaoke bar, and it is known that sometimes in the process to get to know each other, businessmen make use of the services of these prostitutes together in that room. After all, when you did something shady together, a bond is created and you feel a togetherness you do not share with someone else. This can be considered as a solid ground for doing business (Chain, 2014).

CNBC, 27 MARCH 2017

Uber employees visited karaoke-escort bar in Seoul, which led to HR complaint, says report

By: Chantel McGee

Several employees at Uber, including CEO Travis Kalanick, visited a karaoke bar known for offering escort services on a trip to Seoul, South Korea, three years ago, according a report in The Information.
A female Uber employee who was with the group expressed her discomfort with the situation, and later complained to the company's human resources chief about

the outing, according to the report. The incident was told to The Information by Gabi Holzwarth, Kalanick's former girlfriend, who was also at the bar.
At the bar, women employed as escorts wore numbers and the employees would call the number of the woman they wanted to sit with, according to The Information. Holzwarth says she left with Kalanick after about an hour, according to The Information report. No allegations of any illegal behavior have been made.

While the prostitution example is about individual behaviour of businessmen, the issue can also be more general. Think about a multinational imposing its own norms and values on an entire product chain in various countries. As we have seen in the previous section, this could greatly contribute in improving social values. On the other hand, it can also have another effect: it could be regarded as arrogant and disrespectful. After all, who are you, as a foreign company, to decide how norms and values should change in other countries where these are mostly part of a long established tradition and firmly embedded in their culture? Mostly, these norms and values should then change alongside the route developed countries took in the past, including 'western' ideas on morality, democracy and freedom.

Kishore Mahbubani (Singapore) frequently addressed this issue in his critical books about developed countries. He argues that the countries which are currently in development do not necessarily want to become a copy of developed countries, and warns these developed countries not to expect that they will be (Mahbubani, 2008). He adds that especially some eastern countries are becoming tired of the attempts of 'western' countries (and companies) to try and change the moral behaviour of other countries while this is a rather biased approach: the western countries themselves have dirty hands on their own, and appear to have double standards. As an example he uses the issue of human rights: some Asian countries (including China) are very often criticized of their poor human right record, while a developed country such as the U.S. opened the doors of Guantanamo Bay, re-introducing torture.
Mahbubani proposes a more open dialogue that is not based on imposing norms and values on others, but rather on creating mutual understanding and respect.

6.5 Corruption

Corruption | Corruption is the abuse of entrusted power for private gain.

This entrusted power is mostly public power in the sphere of governmental positions, or a power position in business. In case of the first, think about a politician that receives money in exchange for a positive vote on certain legislation, or a civil servant that contracts the construction company of his sister to build a new road.
Business can also play a prominent role in upholding corruption. Think of a CEO that outsources services by hiring a company owned by his wife, or an export manager that bribes a local civil servant in order to get preferential treatment and as a result close better deals in that country. It becomes particularly tricky when business interest and public policy becomes intertwined, and public decisions drift away from democratic processes for the sake of private gain.

In general we could say that corruption limits economic growth and leads to more inequality (Moyo, 2010; Hakimi & Hamdi, 2017). While corruption happens everywhere around the globe, it is a much more serious problem in developing countries compared to developed countries (Transparency International, 2017).

It is not easy to define corruption. What all forms of corruption have in common is that the decision maker (public or business) deviates from his normal decision-making schedule as a result of the corrupt action, and decides to do something else in the expectation that he will privately gain something. We distinguish at least the following forms of corruption: bribery and extortion.

Furthermore, it is also not easy to draw a line between corruption and a gesture of good will to someone. Consider the below newspaper item on tobacco companies for instance. Lobbying is part of the usual democratic process in the U.S. Pressure groups try to persuade politicians to adopt (or not adopt) certain legislation that is in their interest. So did the cigarette industry, by sponsoring politicians and trying to influence the top of the U.S. administration. How should we consider this practice? Is it an innocent gesture (after all, other pressure groups do similar things), or does it lead to a deviation in public decision-making, violating the principles of democracy?

THE GUARDIAN, 13 JULY 2017

Tobacco companies tighten hold on Washington under Trump

By: Jessica Glenza

Tobacco companies have moved swiftly to strengthen their grip on Washington politics, ramping up lobbying efforts and securing significant regulatory wins in the first six months of the Trump era.

Day one of Donald Trump's presidency started with tobacco donations, senior figures have been put in place within the Trump administration who have deep ties to tobacco, and lobbying activity has increased significantly.

(...)

America's largest cigarette manufacturers, Reynolds American and Altria Group, donated $1.5m to help the new president celebrate his inauguration. The donations allowed executives to dine and mingle with top administration officials and their families.

Not long after Trump promised to transfer power from Washington to the American people, a wave of spending in pursuit of influence was unleashed. In the first quarter of 2017, tobacco companies and trade associations spent $4.7m lobbying federal officials. Altria, the company behind Marlboro, hired 17 lobbying firms. Reynolds, makers of the Camel brand, hired 13, according to the Campaign for Tobacco Free Kids.

6.5.1   Bribery

Bribery is a form of corruption.

> Bribery means that someone is encouraged to abuse entrusted power for private gain.

Bribery

In the example 'FIFA 2022 in Qatar?' we see that FIFA officials were accused of using their vote in return for money and other luxury: personal gain. If this is proven to be true, we cannot possibly say that these officials used their entrusted power the way they normally would, based on criteria that relate to football. As we can see, there has been widespread criticism towards the selection of Qatar for hosting the World Cup. Amongst others, there were serious doubts about the circumstances under which the football stadia were built. Another concern would relate to the extreme temperatures in which the athletes would have to play the football matches in Qatar. Those opposing the selection of Qatar argue that it is to be expected that such concerns play a role in the selection process of candidate countries in 'bribery free' decision-making.

When this kind of corruption seriously affects public decision-making, we speak of bribery, and it is generally assumed to be unethical. However, when it is done at a lower level, and does not really influence public life **Petty corruption** significantly, we sometimes use the word petty corruption. Think about a small sum of money you pay if you want to pass the customs officer in Tunisia, or the little favour you give to the police officer in Swaziland when you exceeded a speed limit. Here, the situation becomes more complicated from an ethics perspective. While on the one hand, the Tunisian officer abuses his power position and uses his public power for private gain. On the other hand, this is most likely unofficially firmly embedded in the system, and most part of his income may depend on this.

FIFA 2022 in Qatar?

On 2 December 2010, the FIFA announced that the World Cup in 2022 would be held in Qatar. It will be the first time that a country in the Middle East hosts the event. One of the prerequisites for hosting the World Cup is to operate twelve football stadiums with a minimum capacity of 40,000 visitors. Therefore, the choice for Qatar was soon questioned, since Qatar seemed to hastily start these stadia, making wide use of thousands of migrant workers (mostly from Nepal), who had to construct these buildings under dire, sometimes even life-threatening-conditions. While it is difficult to give accurate numbers due to inaccessibility of data, Human Right Watch consistently reports hundreds of deaths per year amongst the migrant workers (Human Rights Watch, 2017).

Another issue was the expected heat during the planned period of the World Cup. However, this problem was easily resolved by rescheduling the Cup to a cooler season.

A third issue was the alleged bribery preceding the selection for Qatar. The British newspaper *The Sunday Times* received from an anonymous tipster millions of documents that would prove corruption (Calvert & Blake, 2014). These documents revealed that Mohammad Bin Hammam, former FIFA official, had set up a fund to pay bribes to a couple of African officials. In addition he would have arranged meetings in Asia with FIFA officials, and treated them on luxury diners. It would also appear that the former vice-president of FIFA, Jack Warner would have received 1.2 million US dollars from a company related to Qatar. In addition, his son also received a considerable sum of money: approximately 750,000 dollars (Newell et al. 2014). All this to make sure Qatar would be voted to host the World Cup in 2022.

Up to now, Qatar strongly rejected such accusations, and argued that this is a typical example of envy from the rest of the world. Interesting detail is that the FIFA did not allow the publication of the original report of an official investigation to the alleged bribery, conducted by Michael J. Garcia. Only the interpretative note in this report written by the President of the FIFA Ethics Committee was released. In this release, we read that Qatar is innocent of any of the allegations, and has rightfully won the selection of hosting the World Cup. Whether or not this is true, some major sponsors have withdrawn their sponsorship since then, including Emirates, Sony Electronics, Castrol, Continental Tyres and Johnson & Johnson (Pfanner, 2014).

6.5.2 Extortion

Another form of corruption is extortion.

> Extortion means that someone is put under pressure to abuse entrusted power to prevent negative private consequences from happening.

Extortion

6

In case of bribery, the one who is being bribed can gain something in the private sphere when he abuses his entrusted power. In case of extortion, the one who is extorted will not lose something or avoid negative things from happening in the private sphere, when he abuses the entrusted power. Where bribery is something we typically (but not exclusively) notice in the sphere of public positions, extortion happens in the public sector as well as business life. Another – more popular – word for extortion is 'blackmail'.

In the business sector, blackmailing will mostly aim at tapping into the financial resources of the business. If the company does not pay a certain amount of money, something negative will happen to the business. We distinguish a least four different types of extortion (Leiden et al. 2007):

- Product extortion: The blackmailer threatens to sabotage the functioning of the company by threatening to damage products or other business property. The newspaper item about IKEA is an example of product extortion.
- Protection money: The blackmailer threatens the company that it needs protection against violence. If the company will not pay a certain amount of so called 'protection money' the blackmailer will inflict harm on the company. If the money is paid, the violence is bought off. In some regions of the world, this is how the mainstream Mafia earns money, and how companies survive in these regions. Think about the famous Italian Mafia (Ndrangheta), the American Italian Mafia, the Japanese Yakuza, the Russian Bratva or the Hong Kong Triads (Varese, 2014).
- Cyber extortion: The blackmailer threatens the digital environment of the company, until the company buys off the threat. For instance, in 2014, online video provider Vimeo was taken offline by a DDos attack (Denial of Service). This means that the site was taken offline as a result of a data overflow. The blackmailers would only stop the attack after a significant payment (Perlroth, 2014).
- Extortion of a private person: The blackmailer threatens to harm a person or his family if they don't pay a certain amount of money. Mostly, this happens to wealthy people. This often happens in the world of wealthy people. For instance, in 1984 Katsuhisa Ezaki, the CEO of the Japanese-based food business operator Glico, was kidnapped from his house, in front of his family. A ransom of more than 4 million American dollars was demanded in exchange for his freedom (The Japan Times, 1999). Perhaps good to know that mister Ezaki managed to escape on his own, and continued his job as CEO for a very long time afterwards. Please note that extortion of a private person also regularly happens outside the domain of business. Cyber bullying and sexting are increasingly used as extortion tools, and not only to get money. Take the Miss Teen U.S.A. case for instance, in which a hacker got access to her private webcam, took pictures and filmed her while she was naked, and used this material to get more of such images and films.

CBC NEWS, 8 OCTOBER 2011

2 Poles arrested for IKEA store bombings

By: Associated Press

Two Polish men have been arrested and charged with a string of bomb attacks at IKEA stores across Europe and trying to extort millions from the Swedish furniture giant, authorities said Saturday.

The arrests shed light on a mysterious spate of bombings that had prompted the evacuation of spooked shoppers and forced the retailer known for its affordable self-assembly furniture and bright blue-and-yellow stores to beef up security around the continent.

A handful of homemade bomb attacks occurred from May to September in France, Belgium, the Netherlands, Germany and the Czech Republic.

Two people were lightly injured in the German attack but there were no fatalities. Some of the bombs were potentially lethal, though not all detonated.

Polish officials said they have significant evidence incriminating the two men for planting the explosives and trying to extort $6 million Cdn from IKEA. The arrests were made after a manhunt involving investigators from across Europe.

(...)

After the last attack, in Prague, the men demanded that IKEA pay them $6 million and threatened more attacks if the money wasn't paid quickly (...).

CNN NEWS, 27 SEPTEMBER 2013

Arrest made in Miss Teen USA Cassidy Wolf 'sextortion' case

By: Greg Botelho

A college student was arrested Thursday for allegedly hijacking the webcams of young women – among them reigning Miss Teen USA Cassidy Wolf – taking nude images, then blackmailing his victims to send him more explicit material or else be exposed. Jared James Abrahams, a 19-year-old computer science student from Temecula, California, surrendered on Thursday to the FBI on federal extortion charges, the agency announced. Authorities say he victimized young women surreptitiously, by taking control of their computers then photographing them as they changed out of their clothes.

Abrahams appeared in court later in the day, then was released 'on intensive pretrial supervision and home detention with electronic monitoring' after his parents signed bond agreements totaling $50,000, FBI spokeswoman Lourdes Arocho said. U.S. District Judge Jean Rosenbluth ruled that he could use a single desktop computer at his parents' home for school only, albeit only after monitoring software is applied.

When he admitted what he'd done in June, Abrahams said he had 30 to 40 'slave computers' – or other people's electronic devices he controlled – and has had as many as 150 total, according to a criminal complaint.

6.6 Social values of consumers

While the promise of fair and free competition is that consumers will get more choice and better products, this does not always seem to work like that. Especially when consumers do not always make an informed choice, or are not able to do sue due to the complexity of the product or product chain. The ongoing race amongst companies to create the lowest possible cost prise for their products and services, or to get the highest possible profit margin to strengthen their competitiveness does not necessarily lead to the best products for consumers. In some cases, this effect may even negatively affect the social values of consumers. Therefore, in this section we will discuss the ethics challenges that come with marketing products and services to consumers. It only seems fitting to use the well-known marketing **Marketing mix** mix as a framework. While the variety in 'P's differs per author who writes about this mix, we use the four traditional keywords that are most generally used: product, price, promotion and place.

6.6.1   Product

An interesting question could be who primarily bears the responsibility of a product or service.

In the famous movie *Lord of War* (Niccol, 2005), we are introduced to a weapon supplier who argues that men will always be at war, and he merely fulfils an ongoing need in supplying them with arms. And did we not already consider in chapter two that 'the only way to stop a bad guy with a gun is a good guy with a gun'. It is the bearer of the arms that can be right or wrong, not the arm in itself nor its supplier (LaPierre, 2012).

However, not everyone agrees with this point of view, and considers that the weapons industry is (at least to a certain extent) responsible for the effects of their products, and should take their responsibility towards the social (and possibly also ecological) values that are negatively affected as a result of their products (Perlo-Freeman, 2016). As we can see in the example 'no more nukes!' investment agencies are increasingly aware of the consequences of funding the production of weapons of mass destruction, and act accordingly.

No more nukes!
In January 2018, it was reported that Europe's biggest pension fund (ABP, seated in the Netherlands) would undertake to stop investing in companies that produce nuclear arms or tobacco. The fund did not want to be associated with weapons of mass destruction, and promised to sell over 3.3 billion euros of holdings in companies that at some point contribute to either the production of tobacco or nuclear weapons (ABP, 2018). ABP's strategy was fully in line with a more general trend in Europe, in which funds sell holdings hat can be traced back to the production of tobacco or weapons of mass destruction.

The case of weapons production and responsibility shows the various approaches we could have towards product responsibility. On the one hand we could see a company as merely an agency that fulfils the needs of consumers. It is the responsibility of the consumer to make an informed choice about what they buy, and bear the ethical consequences of their purchase. This idea is caught in the Latin phrase 'caveat emptor'. Freely translated this means   **Caveat emptor** something like 'the buyer should be aware of what he buys'.

However, we could also consider that to a certain extent the seller of a product also bears a responsibility towards the products or services he sells. We could call this a duty of care. Both views are visualized in figure 6.6.

Duty of care

FIGURE 6.6 The responsibility of the consumer vs. the responsibility of the company

As a matter of fact, most industrialized countries adopted some degree of product legislation, which stipulates that the producer of a product or supplier of a service is liable for any damage that is suffered if the product/service does not comply with the quality standards or characteristics that can reasonably be expected by the consumer. Also in the B-to-B relation, such standards (albeit less firmly embedded) can be found between a seller and a buyer. Furthermore, states may adopt laws that impose certain quality standards on the industry, for instance hygiene and labelling rules in the food business sector, or privacy laws in case of social media services. However, such product legislation mostly implements a certain minimum requirement as to the reasonable functioning of a product or service. As we have seen in chapter one, product innovation and product legislation do not always develop at the same pace, or can tap into the same technological resources. This could lead to outdated laws that do not necessarily catch up with the latest product or service developments. Also, consumers sometimes find it hard (or do not want to) make an informed choice regarding the products or services they buy.

What to think of tobacco products or unhealthy food for instance? It is the free choice of people to purchase these products, while the long-term consequences of consuming these products are negative for both the consumer and those around him. At most, governments could adopt legislation to discourage consumers to buy unhealthy products. They could for instance impose higher taxes on tobacco products, or adopt labelling laws to force companies to inform people about what it is in their junk food. But yet again, these are minimum standards, and not necessarily a guarantee to a healthy lifestyle. The company that produces unhealthy products will try to sell those at the end of the day, and encourage people to buy their wares.

In ethics, we could wonder what the exact responsibility is of such companies towards the social values of consumer (that is, a healthy life). In the example 'supersize me!' we dig into this a bit deeper, and see a shift in how fast food companies deal with their responsibility towards consumers over time.

Supersize me!

A Cambridge University study shows that in the UK in the period 2002-2012 unhealthy food was persistently cheaper than healthy food, and the price gap between them increased consistently (Jones et al. 2014). This implies that people with a lower income will find it harder to maintain a healthy lifestyle compared to richer people, and could be – amongst other factors – an explanation why obesity is a bigger problem for low-income families compared to richer families (Jolliffe, 2011). Such families are an easy target for fast food companies, who are more than once criticized for their commercial activities, promoting unhealthy food for a very low price. A popular example is the movie *Super Size Me* (Spurlock, 2004), in which the harmful (and addictive) effect of fast food is criticized. However, increasing awareness amongst consumers on healthy food habits resulted in the trend that fast food companies became more transparent on the composition of their food, and introduced new slightly more healthy alternatives to the traditional fast food products (Hearst et al., 2013).

6.6.2 Price

Extreme high or low pricing could have a negative impact on the social values of the consumer.

For instance, a company could hold a dominant position on a market and make use of that position to lower prices and dump its products temporarily at a market in order to destroy the remaining competition. Another strategy could be to force the consumer to accept other products or services that are unrelated to the original deal. In some legal systems this is called tying. The practical result of tying is that competitors offering the 'side' product are blocked from the market because it is included in a contract for non-related products provided for by the market leader. This eventually will lead to less consumer choice and slower product innovation. In the case 'A player with media players' we can see some examples of tying and alleged tying. As we can see, there is a thin line between legal and illegal practices here. All the more reason to consider this from an ethics perspective as well.

Abuse dominant position

A player with media players

A notorious case dates back to 2004, in which Microsoft was accused of tying: the purchase of the operating system Windows could not be made without receiving Windows Media Player for free. These two were in essence unrelated, since an operating system is not the same as a media player. At first glance this seems like a friendly gesture towards the consumer. However, the practical result of offering Windows Media Player as an inextricable part of the Windows software was that software competitors were practically blocked from the market. After all, why would consumers pay for such software when they would get this for free when using Windows. At that time, Windows software was used by the vast majority of computer owners, meaning that competing software producers where simply banned from the market. This will eventually lead to less consumer choice, and slower product innovation. This abuse of power led to a huge fine for Microsoft, imposed by the European Commission of around 497 million euros (EU Court of Justice, 2007).

Years later, Apple was accused of tying as well. The complaints concerned their media

6

services. Especially in the period 2009-2014 (Montgomerie & Roscoe, 2013), various competing music distributors complained that they could not sell music through Apple's I-pods, since Apple did not want to allow them access to their technology. This means that when consumers would buy an I-pod, they could only buy music from Apple. Also, the I-tunes store was frequently criticized for blocking music distributors that would not accept the Apple conditions, including the fixed prices per song or download, resulting in a situation that artists or record labels could no longer decide on sales prices for themselves. Mostly however, such claims were dismissed since it is not easy prove that Apple has indeed a dominant position on the market since there is plenty of competition that successfully competes with Apple.

Cartel   Another strategy could be to form a cartel with other companies, and together secretly agree to increase pricing of the products or services, so that all companies can have a higher profit margin. In most legal systems, cartels are forbidden because they distort normal competition, unless they represent an insignificant market share. However, a secret cartel is not always easy to prove (Wernaart, 2017b). The consumer literally pays the price for such a cartel.

6.6.3   Promotion

A company will of course try to convince its potential customers to buy their products or services. In marketing jargon one speaks of 'potentials' or even 'targets'. Some companies are more aggressive than others in their enthusiasm of selling their sales ware. But how far can promotional activities go, and when do we cross a line that makes advertising unethical?

In most industrialized countries, the law will set some boundaries to what companies cannot do in promoting their products. Think about deliberately misleading consumers, using hate speech or violating someone's privacy. However, the companies are mostly allowed a wide margin of appreciation in how they want to advertise, since they also enjoy freedom of speech. To make sure the legislature does not unnecessarily censor advertisements whilst on the other hand companies cannot unrestrictedly say whatever works to sell their products and services, self-regulation is used. As we can **Advertising code**   see in chapter nine, in many industrialized countries advertising codes are adopted in which we can find ethical standards for advertisement (EASA, 2016). While the wordings of such codes may differ, two main principles play an important role: autonomy of the consumer and public morality.

Autonomy of the consumer

Autonomy means that a consumer is able to use his buying power freely and can take an independent decision on what products or services are in his best interest to purchase. When this freedom of choice is disproportionally affected by advertising, this principle could be violated.

This is clearly the case when companies disguise their commercials, and the consumer is not aware of that fact. Think about product placement in **Subliminal advertising**   popular tv shows (see section 1.6.3), or true subliminal advertisements. The company tries to influence the subconscious of the consumer by showing them an advertisement in a context in which the consumer does not recognize the message as advertisement. Especially subliminal advertising is considered to be a violation of the autonomy of the consumer. An example can be found in the 'McDonald's Iron Chef'. Whether or not such subliminal messages truly work is debated in psychological sciences. Research shows various results, although it can be argued that when a consumer is in a particular situation, already in need for a particular type of product and unaware of the subliminal influence, the choice for the product brand could be influenced by subliminal advertising (Randolph-Seng & Mather, 2009). Whether or not subliminal messaging works is from an ethics perspective perhaps less relevant: the fact that a company tries to influence the subconscious of the consumer while the consumer does not know. This in itself is a violation of their autonomy.

6

McDonald's and Iron Chef

For a long time, *Iron Chef America* has been a very popular TV show in the U.S. The idea is simple: two chefs compete with each other and are challenged to serve a first class culinary dish in only ninety minutes. However, in a broadcast on 27 January 2007, a McDonald's logo suddenly appeared on the screen as a very short 'pop-up'. This was discovered by an American teenager, who played the episode in slow motion by accident. Therefore, the average viewer would not notice the logo. According to McDonald's however, they did not try to broadcast a subliminal message, but instead the pop-up was a result of a technical error. Then, the show was corrected for further airings (Silverberg, 2007).

From consumer behavioural studies we can learn that companies try to persuade consumers in three ways: by means of affective, cognitive and conative influence (Hilgard, 1980; Eagly & Chaiken, 1998). In short, affective relates to how we feel, cognitive to what we know, and conative to how we behave.

> Affective influence occurs when advertising appeals to the emotion of the consumer.

Affective influence

In particular companies that focus on strong brand awareness among their customers will use affective influence to persuade their potentials to buy their products and services. The message will most likely not be 'our product is better' or 'our product is cheaper', but instead 'our product is really cool'. When consumers are loyal to a brand, the brand may become part of their lifestyle. For instance, regular beer is a product in which companies typically use affective influence. While the differences in taste between beer brands may be noticeable, they are not huge. Instead, the brand awareness may really make a difference in the buying behaviour of a consumer. There is nothing wrong with trying to create a strong brand with a clear message that fits into a lifestyle of a cool person. However, it may become problematic when in these attempts, the drinking of alcohol is associated with something we rather not see in combination with alcohol. Think about driving a car, work, young people or sport. We could ask ourselves the question whether sponsorship of worldwide top-sport events, such as the World Cup in football or national competitions, is such a good idea. Consider the newspaper example about the English Football competition: the question here is raised whether a beer producer and a gambling office are the right companies to be the main sponsor of this top sport event.

BBC NEWS, 5 MAY 2017

FA 'considering' relationship with gambling and alcohol firms

By: Greg Clarke

The Football Association is 'considering' its relationship with gambling firms and alcohol companies, says the governing body's chairman.
Greg Clarke has ordered a report into whether it is appropriate to have official partnerships with gambling and betting. 'The sport has a duty to consider and ask itself what is right,' Clarke told The Times. The FA board is expected to make a decision this summer.
It has commercial agreements with the alcoholic drinks companies Carling, Budweiser and Carlsberg, as well as a long-term deal with betting firm Ladbrokes.

In April, Burnley midfielder Joey Barton was banned from football for 18 months after admitting charges in relation to betting. The 34-year-old was fined £30,000 and warned about his future conduct after being charged with breaking FA rules for placing 1,260 bets on matches over a 10-year period.
But Barton questioned the FA and said it should 'look at its own dependence on the gambling companies' instead of 'blaming' the players.
Clarke added: 'We are actively considering what our position will be and should be. It is right we consider it and then make a positive decision on what we are going to do or not.' (...)

Cognitive influence

| Cognitive influence occurs when advertising appeals to the knowledge of the consumer.

The consumer is convinced by rational arguments. The message will most likely be 'our product is better' or 'our product is cheaper' compared to our competitors. Cognitive influence violates the autonomy of the consumer when the facts that are portrayed are unclear or simply not true. After all, if the consumer would have known the accurate facts, he would probably have made another decision. We call this misleading advertisements

The autonomy of the consumer is affected in cases where the information contained in the advertisements prevents incorrect or cannot be verified.

The anti-age cream of L'Oréal
In 2012, L'Oréal launched a new advertising campaign, starring Rachel Weisz. This actress had won an Oscar in 2006 for Best Supporting Actress in the film *The Gardener*. Back then, Weisz was 41 years old, but in the L'Oréal ad she looked like

she was in her twenties. This of course would be the result of using the anti-age cream. However, the British Advertising Standard Authority ruled that it was clear that the images in which Weisz was shown were edited and did not represent her true looks. This was misleading the consumer, and as a result the campaign was banned. (*The Guardian*, 2012).

> Conative influence occurs when advertising appeals to peer pressure.

Conative influence

Where affective and cognitive influence are not directly related to the social context of the consumer, conative influence does. The conative element in this context addresses the actual intention to act. Various factors, such as peer pressure, may interfere with the original intention to buy something, even though the consumer desires something (affective) or knows that something is the best thing to buy (cognitive). Think about sponsorship of popular people. When you are a famous singer, you probably have a contract with a fashion company, exclusively wearing their clothes. The company is eager to sign such sponsor contracts in the expectation that the fans of the popular singer will change their normal buying behaviour and are pressured to buying the same brand. This is an accepted idea, however, conative influence should not interfere with the normal process of identity formation of especially young people. Think about a teen idol that is totally adored by a certain group of youngsters. Companies can of course make use of that adoration and try to link products to this idol in the expectation that the fans will also buy them. However, the company should not abuse this adoration, and facilitate a situation in which the teenagers only want to look like their idol and do not develop their own characteristics in a healthy way.

Public morality
It is generally acknowledged that advertisements should not violate public morality. The perception of public morality will of course differ per region. Think about using sex related topics, or barely dressed people in the promotion of products or services. Some countries are more flexible with such things than others. However, some approaches are simply so shocking that they are instantly banned. Think about a Korean instant noodle commercial in which we see a Korean girl's face suggesting she is having oral sex with someone. When the camera zooms out it appears to be that she is eating noodles. Such commercials are generally speaking against public morality.

6.6.4   Place/distribution
The place where products or services are sold and the way in which they are to be distributed can negatively influence the social values of consumers.

Place
As we have seen in chapter 5, globalization is one of the reasons why ethics in business is high on the agenda. One of the effects of open trade is that companies have access to foreign markets, can outsource production activities abroad, and can sell their products in other legal systems, which may offer more flexible rules on product standards. An example of the latter

can be found in the newspaper item. The issue of chain responsibility has already been discussed in this chapter.

THE INDEPENDENT, 28 JANUARY 2001

Britain put 69 countries at the risk of BSE

By: Paul Lashmar

Britain could have spread BSE to 69 countries by selling them meat-and-bone cattle meal knowing that it might have been contaminated with the disease. Britain could have spread BSE to 69 countries by selling them meat-and- bone cattle meal knowing that it might have been contaminated with the disease. The revelation, in previously unpublished Ministry of Agriculture documents, shows the extent of Britain's exports of the potentially contaminated material. Between 1988, when meat-and-bone meal (MBM) was banned in Britain and 1996, thousands of tons were sent to European nations such as the Netherlands, France and Germany. Israel imported more than 31,000 tons, and Russia more than 3,000 tons.

Large amounts were sent to developing countries, particularly after European countries banned British MBM feed. Indonesia imported 60,000 tons from Britain between 1991 and 1996 and Kenya imported 521 tons between 1987 and 1996. The figures include some poultry feed, which continued to be sold legally after 1996. Britain also exported more than three million live cows to 36 countries between 1988 and 1996. (...)
Some experts fear that the exports will lead to BSE epidemics in some of the poorest countries in the world. Stephen Dealler, a clinical microbiologist and BSE expert, said: 'Exporting MBM feed that was potentially BSE-infected was like selling boxes of blank bullets containing a few live ones and saying it's not your problem if someone gets shot.'

Distribution

A common discussion about the distribution of products and services is to what extent a bonus system can be counterproductive towards social values of consumers. If a salesperson gets a bonus when certain products are sold in given amounts, the question is raised whether this results in whether the consumer will buy the products that are best for him, or best for the sales agent. In the example of the lazy real estate agent, we see an example in which a reward system stands in the way of delivering outstanding quality for his clients.

The lazy real estate agent

A real estate agent earns one percent of the total purchase price of the real estate that he sells on behalf of a client. So, when a house is sold for 200,000 euros, he will earn 2,000 euros. For the owner of the house, it will make a great difference if the real estate agent could sell the house for a slightly higher price, say 210,000 euros.

However, this would mean hours of extra work for the real estate agent, for only 100 euro extra. In that time, he can also sell another house for 200,000 euros. We could ask ourselves the question what real estate agent would walk the extra mile for his clients, if the reward system works like this.

Summary

▶ Social values are values we pursue to lead dignified life. The meaning of the word dignified depends on the context of the region.

▶ As to the level of their development, we could classify the countries in the world into three categories. The ethical challenges in business may differ per category.
1 Developed countries are industrialized countries with a relatively high welfare level.
2 Developing countries are non-industrialized countries with a relatively low prosperity level.
3 Newly developed countries are countries which recently industrialized, with a moderate welfare level.

▶ In developed countries, the rights of workers were recognized in different areas:
1 A ban on child labour, and compulsory education.
2 The participation of employees in decision-making of the company regarding work conditions through works councils and trade unions. The usual influence tool of trade unions are collective bargaining, collective actions and ultimately strikes.
3 Political influence of workers through political parties.
4 The establishing of a social security system: a set of provisions that offers financial means to those in need in order to protect their social values.
5 The recognition of human rights.

▶ Challenges in respect of workers in developed countries are:
1 The effects of privatization.
2 Discrimination, which is the unequal treatment in similar cases based on irrelevant factors. Discrimination of workers can be – among other things – on the basis of gender, nationality, race and religion. Discrimination can be direct, indirect or positive:
   • Direct discrimination is to explicitly disadvantage someone based on an irrelevant factor.
   • Indirect discrimination is when a non-discriminatory standard or practice disadvantages someone based on an irrelevant factor.
   • Positive discrimination is to explicitly advantage someone who is disadvantaged based on irrelevant factors.
3 Work-related stress: the main causes of work-related stress relate either to the content or the context of the work. In a healthy work environment, two relationships must be balanced:
   • The effort-reward balance relates to the extent to which a worker is adequately rewarded for his effort.

- The demand-control balance relates to the extent to which a worker has sufficient autonomy in his work.

4 In most developed countries there is some sort of protection for employees against certain forms of dismissal, balancing the opposing interests of the employer and the employee in this regard.
  - Income security is an important value for employees. In this context we could distinguish between job security and employability:
    - Job security means the long-term security of a worker in relation to a particular job for the same employer.
    - Employability means the long-term security of an employee with respect to work, regardless of the employer.
  - A whistleblower is someone who publicly reveals an alleged unethical practice in an organization. In the proper dealing with whistle blowers, three values may play an important role: urgency, integrity and protection.
  - In case of collective redundancies, in some legal systems a social plan is required in order to be allowed to proceed. A social plan is a contract in which an employer agrees to support his former employees financially and non-financially in the transition towards a new job. Three fundamental values could play a role in social plans: transparency, cooperation and autonomy.

▶ Challenges for companies that do business in developing countries are twofold:
  1 To what extent should you make use of the more flexible standards towards the protection of social values in other countries?
  2 To what extent are you in the position to impose your own norms and values on developing and NIC countries?

▶ Corruption is the abuse of entrusted power for private gain. There are two forms of corruption:
  1 Bribery means that someone is encouraged to abuse entrusted power for private gain.
  2 Extortion means that someone is put under pressure to abuse entrusted power to prevent negative private consequences from happening.

We distinguish a least four different types of extortion:
1 Product extortion: the blackmailer threatens to sabotage the functioning of the company by threatening to damage products or other business property.
2 Protection money: the blackmailer threatens the company that it needs protection against violence.
3 Cyber extortion: the blackmailer threatens the digital environment of the company, until the company buys off the threat.
4 Extortion of a private person: the blackmailer threatens to harm a person or his family if they don't pay a certain amount of money.

▶ Social values of consumers play a role in the four areas of the marketing mix:

1 Product: to what extent is the consumer responsible for his buying behaviour (caveat emptor) and the businesses responsible for the products/services they sell (duty of care)?

2 Price: to what extent can extreme high or low pricing negatively affect the social values of consumers? Abuse of a dominant position or the establishing of a cartel may distort natural competition and negatively affect consumer choice or slow down product innovation.

3 In the context of promotion, two main principles play an important role in advertising: autonomy of the consumer and public morality. The autonomy of the consumer could be violated by:
   - product placement or subliminal advertisement
   - affective influence (when advertising appeals to the emotion of the consumer) when there is an unethical association between product and image
   - cognitive influence (when advertising appeals to the knowledge of the consumer) when advertisements are misleading
   - conative influence (occurs when advertising appeals to peer pressure)

4 Place: Due to globalization companies can make use of more flexible standards abroad. In that process, social values of workers and consumers could be negatively affected.

5 Distribution: The question is asked to what extent a bonus system is in the interest of the consumer.

6

Literature

Aaron, C. (2015). The Long-run Effect of Mexican Immigrants on Crime in U.S. Cities: Evidence from Variation in Mexican Fertility Rates. *American Economic Review* 105(5). Pp. 220-225.

Australian Human Rights Commission. (2012). Working without fear: results of the sexual harassment national telephone survey. Australian Human Rights Commission.

Bertrand, M., Black, S., Jensen, S. & Lleras-Muney, A. (2014). *Breaking the Glass Ceiling? The Effect of Board Quotas on Female Labor Market Outcomes in Norway.* Bonn: Institute for the Study of Labor.

Bijsterveld, S. (2015). Religion and the Secular State in the Netherlands. In: Martínez-Torrón, J.; Durham, W.C.; Thayer, D. (ed.), *Religion and the Secular State: National Reports,* pp. 542-558. Madrid: Complutense Universidad de Madrid.

Brasted, M. (2010, 17 February). Care Bears vs. Transformers: gender stereotypes in Advertisements. *The SocJournal.* Alleging www.sociology.org.

Camarota, S., & Vaughan, J. (2009). *Immigration and crime: assessing a conflicted issue.* Center for Immigration Studies.

Card, D. & Krueger, A.B. (2015). *Myth and Measurement, the New Economics of the Minimum Wage.* Princeton University Press.

Cotter, D., Hermsen, J., Ovadia, S., & Venneman, R. (2001). The glass ceiling effect. *Social Forces*, 80 (2), 655-682.

Cox, T & Griffiths, A. (2005) The nature and measurement of work-related stress: theory and practice. In: Wilson, J.R. and Corlett, N. (eds.) *Evaluation of Human Work, 3rd Edition.* Abingdon: Routledge.

DanWatch. (2015). *Servants of servers Rights violations and forced labour in the supply chain of ICT equipment in European universities A Journalistic investigation.* DanWatch.

Eagly, A., & Chaiken, S. (1998). *Attitude structure and function, handbook of social psychology.* Boston: McGrow Company.

EASA. (2016). Annual report 2016. *European Advertising Standards Alliance.*

Eccles,J.S., Jacobs, J.E. & Harold, R.D. (1990). Gender Role Stereotypes, Expectancy Effects, and Parents' Socialization of Gender Differences. *Journal of social issues.* Volume 46, Issue 2, summer 1990, Pp. 183–201.

European Commission. (2014). *Tackling the gender pay gap in the European Union.* Luxembourg: Publications Office of the European Union.

Eyraud, F. & Saget, C. (2005). *The Fundamentals of Minimum Wage Fixing.* Geneva: International Labour Office.

Felbab-Brown. (2017). The Wall: the real costs of a barrier between the United States and Mexico. *Brookings Institution.*

FNV. (2009). *Law on works councils.* Stichting FNV Compressed.

Ford, H. (1922). *My life and work.* Harvard University Press.

FRA. (2014). *Violence against women: an EU-wide survey.* Luxembourg: European Agency for Fundamental Rights.

Gilligan, C. (1982). *In a different voice.* Cambridge: Harvard University Press.

Grant Thornton. (2014). *Women in business: From class room to boardroom.* Grant Thornton International Business Report 2014.

Grau, S.L. & Zotos, Y. (2016). Gender stereotypes in advertising: A review of current research. *International Journal of Advertising.* August 2016, 35(5): 761-770.

Hackstock, A. & Heyroth, A. (2002). Employment at will: the legal perspective. *Values-Based Leadership, Section 2/Houston April 24, 2002.*

Hakimi, A. & Hamdi, H. (2017). Does corruption limit FDI and economic growth? Evidence from MENA countries. *International Journal of Emerging Markets,* Vol. 12 Issue: 3, pp. 550-571.

Hearst, M. O., Harnack, L. J., Bauer, K. W., Earnest, A. A., French, S. A., & Michael Oakes, J. (2013). Nutritional quality at eight U.S. fast-food chains: 14-Year trends. *American Journal of Preventive Medicine, 44*(6), pp. 589-594.

Henderson, B. (2016). *The gospel of the Flying Spaghetti Monster.* New York: Villard Books.

Hilgard, E. (1980). The trilogy of mind: Cognition, affection, and conation. Journal of the history of the behavioural sciences. Volume 16, Issue 2 April 1980 pp. 107–117.

Horrel, S. & Humphries, J. (1995) 'The Exploitation of Little Children': Child Labor and the Family Economy in the Industrial Revolution. *Elsevier: Explorations in Economic History,* Vol. 32, October 1995, Pages 485-516.

ILO. (2007). *Equality at work: Tackling the challenges, report of the Director-General, Global Report under the follow-up to the ILO Declaration on Fundamental Principles and Rights at Work.* Geneva: ILO.

ILO. (2016). *Workplace stress: a collective challenge.* ILO cataloguing in publication data.

Jayachandran, S. (2015). The Roots of Gender Inequality in Developing Countries. *Annual Review of Economics*, Vol. 7, pp. 63-88, 2015.

Jennissen, R.P.W., & Blom, M. (2004). Immigrant and indigenous suspects of various types of offense. *Cahiers*, 2007-4.

Jeurissen, R. (2007). Handling corruption and gifts. In: R. Saturday's qualifications went well (Ed.), *Ethics & Business* (pp. 199-211). Assen: Van Gorcum.

Jeurissen, R. (2007). Responsibility toward and or employees. In: R. Saturday's qualifications went well (Ed.), *Ethics & Business* (pp. 166-183). Assen: Van Gorcum.

Jolliffe, D. (2011). Overweight and poor? On the relationship between income and the body mass index. *Economics and human biology*, 2011, December, 9(4), pp. 342-355.

Jones N., Conklin A, Suhrcke M, Monsivais P (2014) The Growing Price Gap between More and Less Healthy Foods: Analysis of a Novel Longitudinal UK Dataset. *PLoS ONE* 9(10): e109343.

Kerr, S.P. (2016). Parental Leave Legislation and Women's Work: A Story of Unequal Opportunities. *Journal of policy analysis and management.* Volume 35, Issue 1 Winter 2016, pp. 117–144.

Leiden, I., De Vries, E., Ferwerda, R., & Ferwerda, H. (2007). *Your company or your life. Nature and approach of extortion of business.* Amsterdam: Publisher SWP.

Lindahl, B. (2015). Norway's female boardroom quotas: what has been the effect? *Nordic Labour Journal*, 21 May 2015.

MacDonald, J.M. & Saunders, J. (2012). Are Immigrant Youth Less Violent? Specifying the Reasons and Mechanisms. *The Annals of the American Academy of Political and Social Science.* 641(1): Pp. 125-147.

Mahbubani, K. (2008). *New Asian hemisphere: the irresistible shift of global power to the east.* New York: PublicAffairs.

Marmot, M., Sieg Rist, J. & Theorell, T. (2009). Health and the psychosocial environment at work. In: M. The Marmot & R. Wilkinson, *Social Determinants or heath.* Oxford: Oxford Scholarship online publications.

Martin, F. & Viarengo, M. (2009). The Expansion and Convergence of Compulsory Schooling in Western Europe, 1950–2000. *Economica.* Volume 78, Issue 311, July 2011, pp. 501–522.

Mohammadi, M.J. & Nourbakhsh, S.D. (2017). Examining the Social Basis of the Far-right Parties in Europe. *Journal of World Sociopolitical Studies*, Vol. 1, No. 1, July 2017, pp. 139-174.

Montgomerie, J. & Roscoe, S. (2013). Owning the consumer – getting to the core of the Apple business model. *Elsevier: Accounting Forum 37 (2013) pp. 290-299.*

Morrison, C. & Jütting, J. (2005). Women's discrimination in developing countries: A new data set for better policies. *World Development,* vol. 33, issue 7, July 2005, pp. 1065-1081.

Moyo, D. (2010). *Dead Aid, why aid is not working and how there is another way for Africa.* London: Penguin Books.

Muhl, C. (2001). The employment-at-will doctrine: three major exceptions window. *Monthly Labor Review,* January 2001.

Muller-Rommel, F. & Poguntke, T. (2002). *Green parties in national governments.* London: Routeledge.

Ousey, G.C. & Kubrin, C.E. (2009). Exploring the Connection Between Immigration and Violent Crime Rates in U.S. Cities, 1980-2000. *Social Problems* 56(3): 447-473.

Perlo-Freeman, S. (2016) Special treatment: UK Government support for the arms industry and trade. *Campaign Against Arms Trade (CAAT).*

Pierson, J. (2010). Racism and social exclusion. In: *Tack Ling social exclusion.* Abingdon: Routledge.

Postelnicescu, C. (2016). Europe's New Identity: The Refugee Crisis and the Rise of Nationalism. *Europe's Journal of Psychology.* 2016, Vol. 12(2), Pp. 203–209.

Randolph-Seng, B. & Mather, R. (2009). Does subliminal persuasion work? It depends on your motivation and awareness. *Sceptical Inquirer,* Sept-Oct 2009.

Ridgeway, C.L. (2011). *Framed by gender: how gender inequality persists in the modern world.* Oxford: Oxford Scholarship Online.

Smiths, M., Agnieszka, P., Burchell, B., Rubery, J., Rafferty, A., Rose, J. & Carter, L. (2013). *Women, men and working conditions in Europe.* Luxembourg: Publications Office of the European Union.

Soysal, Y. & Strang, D. (1989). Construction of the First Mass Education Systems in Nineteenth-Century Europe *Sociology of Education* Vol. 62, No. 4 (Oct., 1989), pp. 277-288.

Stracke, S., Lendal, N., & Johannisson, F. (2013). *IT workers still pay the price for cheap computers, case study or labor conditions at 4 Dell suppliers in China.* DanWatch.

Summers, C.W. (2000). Employment at will in the united States: the divine right of employers. *University of Pennsylvania Journal of labor and employment law.* 2000. Vol. 3:1.

Terjesen, S.A., Aguilera, R. & Lorenz, R. (2013). Legislating a woman's seat on the board: institutional factors driving gender quotas for boards of directors. *Journal of business ethics,* forthcoming.

Transparency International. (2017). Corruption Perceptions Index.

UN. (2016). World Economic Situation and Prospects 2016. Un.

UNiTE. (2011). *Violence against women.* UN department of public information.

Varese, F. (2014). Protection and extortion. In: Paoli (edt), *The Oxford Handbook on Organized Crime.* Oxford: Oxford University Press.

Wernaart, B. (2013). *The human right to adequate food, a comparative study.* Wageningen: Wageningen Academic Publishers.

Wernaart, B. (2017). Labour Law. In: *International law and business, a global introduction.* Groningen: Noordhoff Uitgevers.

Wernaart, B. (2017). The European Union. In: *International law and business, a global introduction.* Groningen: Noordhoff Uitgevers.

WHO. (2013). *Global and regional estimates of violence against women: prevalence and health effects of intimate partner violence and non-partner sexual violence.* WHO Library cataloguing-in-publication data.

WHO, regional office for Africa. (2015). *Addressing the Challenge of Women's Health in Africa Report of the Commission on Women's Health in the African Region.* AFRO Library Cataloguing-in-Publication Data.

6

World Bank Group. (2016). *Taking on inequality, poverty and shared prosperity 2016*. Washington: World Bank Group.

World Economic Forum. (2017). *Global Gender Gap Report 2017*. Geneva: World Economic Forum.

WTO. (2014). *The H4+ partnership joint support to improve women's and children's health Progress Report-2013*. Geneva: WTO Publications.

Zekic, N. (2016). Job security or employment security: What's in a name? *European Labour Law Journal*, 7(4), 549.

Media

ABP. (2018, 11 January). Press release: ABP Pension fund excludes tobacco and nuclear weapons. *ABP*.

Associated Press (2011, 8 October). 2 Poles arrested for IKEA store bombings. *CBC news, Canada*.

Barker, O. (2014, 23 January). Justin Bieber has reached point or alarm', experts say. *USA Today*.

Botelo, G. (2013, 27 September). Arrest made in Miss Teen USA Cassidy Wolf 'sextortion' case. *CNN News*.

Calvert, J., & Blake, H. (2014, 1 June). Ploy to buy the World Cup, huge email cache reveals secrets of Qatar's shock victory. *The Sunday Times*.

Caporale, G. (2013, 19 December). 'Farai sesso con me una Volta a serri mana'. Il contratto shock tra assessore e segretaria. *La Republica*.

Chain, G. (2014, 22 September). In South Korea, Real Business Gets Done In Brothels And Karaoke Joints. *Business Insider*.

Clarke, G. (2017, 5 May). FA 'considering' relationship with gambling and alcohol firms. *BBC news*.

Doyle, J., & Wright, S. (2012, 18 February). Foreign nationals were accused or a quarter of all crimes in London. *The Daily Mail*.

Editorial Board. (2012, 1 February). L'Oréal advert featuring Rachel Weisz banned for being 'misleading'. *The Guardian*.

Editorial Board. (1999, 24 February). Clock ticking on Glico-Morinaga cases. *The Japan Times*.

Glenza, J. (2014, 2 September). Justin Bieber assaulted and arrested for dangerous driving in Canada. *The Guardian*.

Heavy, S. (2017, 6 December). Time magazine names #MeToo 'silence breakers' as person of the year. *Reuters*.

Human Rights Watch. (2017, 27 September). Qatar: Take Urgent Action to Protect Construction Workers FIFA, National Associations Should Press Qatar on Heat Risks, Preventable Deaths. *Human Rights Watch*.

ICL. (2015, 29 May). Following agreement with union, ICL to implement operational excellence and efficiency plan at Israel plants. *ICL Press release*.

International Trade Union Confederation ITUC,. (2013, 27 September). Qatar 2022 World Cup risks 4000 lives, warns International Trade Union Confederation. Alleging www.ITUC-csi.org.

Johnston, P. (2008, 16 April). Immigration and crime: the real results. *The Telegraph*.

Kuijk, L. Van (2004, 23 August). 'Van Damme is verraden door zijn echtgenote'. *Trouw*.

Lashmar, P. (2001, 28 January). Britain put 69 countries at the risk of BSE. *The Independent*.

Levin, S. (2017, 7 April). Google accused of 'extreme' gender pay discrimination by US labor department. *The Guardian*.

Mann, T. (2017, 2 September). John Lewis has become the first major department store to ditch 'boys' and 'girls' labels from children's clothing. *Metro*.

McGee, C. (2017, 27 March). Uber employees visited karaoke-escort bar in Seoul, which led to HR complaint, says report. *CNBC*.

Newell, C., Watt, H., Duffin, C., Bryant, B., & Good, A. (2014, 17 March). Qatar World Cup 2022 investigation: former Fifa vice president Jack Warner and family paid millions. *The Telegraph*.

OECD. (2012, November). Women in work: The Norwegian experience. *OECD Observer* No. 293 Q4 November 2012.

Oster, S. (2014, 4 March). President Xi's anti-corruption campaign biggest Since Mao. *Bloomberg*.

Perlroth, N. (2014, 19 July). Extortion tally or Cyber attacks on Tech Companies grows. *The New York Times*.

Pfanner, E. (2014, 25 November). Sony pullovers World Cup sponsorship. *The Wall Street Journal*.

Reuters Staff. (2017, 9 October). France's CGT calls another strike against labour reform, others refuse. *Reuters*.

Silverberg, D. (2007, 22 January). Is McDonald's Adding Subliminal Advertising to Its Marketing Arsenal? *Digital Journal*.

Staff, T. (2015, 17 May). Thousands march in Dimona to protest factory layoffs. *The times of Israel*.

Stephard, W., Hamacher, B., & Van Oot, T. (2014, 24 January). Justin Bieber charged with DUI, Resi Ting judgment in Miami Beach drag-racing incident: cops. *NBC Miami*.

Stoop, M. (2007, 6 June). Merchant and Reverend in India. Based on *World Broadcasting.nl*.

Wattles, J. (2017, 21 July). Wells Fargo ordered to rehire whistleblower and pay $577,500 in back wages. *CNN*.

Weller, C. (2017, 17 September). What you need to know about egg-freezing, the hot new perk at Google, Apple and Facebook. *Business Insider*.

Willis, A. (2016, 28 January). The Netherlands has recognized the Church of the Flying Spaghetti Monster as a religion. *Metro UK*.

Legislation, regulations and case law

African Charter on Human and People's Rights, June 1981.

Civil Rights Act of 1960, U.S. Public law 86-449, May 6, 1960, 74 Stat.

European Social Charter, 18 October 1961.

EU Court of Justice, 17 September 2007, Microsoft Corp. v. Commission. ECLI:EU:T:2007:289.

ILO Convention 100 on equal remuneration, 1951.

ILO Convention 111, Discrimination (Employment and Occupation) Convention, 25 June 1958.

Parliament of Singapore. (1973, 7 July). Arose within the Act (Chapter 185, revised edition).

San Salvador Additional Protocol to the American Convention on Human Rights, November 1988.

Sexual Discrimination Act, Australia, 1984.

Supreme Court of Tennessee, 81 Tenn. 507, (Payne v. Railroad company).

United States Declaration of Independence, 1776.

Press release

Government of Singapore. (2004, 30 January). The Singapore Government's response to Amnesty International's Report 'Singapore – the Death Penalty: A Hidden Toll Or Executions'.

Code of conduct

Code of Ethics and Business Conduct of Franklin Resources, approved at 14 June 2017, available at: www.franklinresources.com

Websites
https://www.apple.com/diversity
https://www.bp.com/en/global/bp-careers/working-at-bp/diversity-inclusion.
   html#gender
https://www.hofstede-insights.com
www.mcdonalds.nl: www.mcdonalds.nl/faq/kilocalorieen
www.nav.no, consulted at 27 November 2017
www.stopwapenhandel.org

Movie
Niccol, A. (2005). *Lord of War.*
Spurlock, M. (2004). *Super-size Me.*

Interviews and speeches
Friedman, M. (2014, 1 February). A conversation on minimum wage.
Lapierre, W. (21 December 2012). *NRA Press Conference.*
Trump, D. (2015, 16 June). Announcement of presidential bid at the Trump Tower, New
   York.

6

7

Ecological values

7.1 **The tragedy of the commons**
7.2 **Towards a circular economy**

In this section we will discuss the tension between economic values and ecological values. For ecological values we will address the consequences of industrialization. As we will see, the desire to control the environment and produce on a massive scale can be devastating for our ecology. This is exactly why we need to explore alternatives to combine economic and ecological values in a sustainable manner. This can be done by moving towards a circular economy through implementing ways of producing that are eco-efficient.

7.1 The tragedy of the commons

Ecological values | Ecological values are values that contribute to a sustainable environment.

An environment that is truly sustainable is an environment in which future generations can continue to live without the need to adjust their lifestyle or ways of producing due to exhaustion of resources or health risks. In other words: our economy should run in such a way that we can continue to do so forever. Examples of ecological values are health, preservation, and (bio) diversity. This means for instance that – as a definition – the usage of fossil fuels or any acts that lead to a reduction in bio diversity are unsustainable. As we have seen in chapter five, industrialization has led to great progress in our production processes but also to significant challenges in the sphere of social and ecological values. Especially the desire to produce for the lowest possible costs in order to beat the competition has led to a very short sighted race to the bottom, which negatively affects the realization of ecological values.

The economist Hardin explains why this race to the bottom can be profitable on the short term, but is inevitably destructive on the long term (Hardin, 1968). In his article 'the tragedy of the commons' he explains that natural resources are not unlimitedly available and will not reappear once exhausted. However, the pressure of day-to-day competition does not always allow a company to take that into consideration. The example of salmon fishing is loosely based on his argument. For one fisherman who tries to make a living it sound like a good idea to catch some more fish per day, in order to offer a lower price per piece and as a result be more successful in selling the fish. The bigger picture however is that when all fishermen do the exact same thing, this will ultimately lead to fishing habits that do not allow the salmon population to recover and in the end will cease to exist. This practically means that you drive your own trades ware to extinction, which on the long run negatively affects your economic values. It is not easy to solve this dilemma. After all, imagine what would happen if you would be the only fisherman that sticks to a certain fishing quota to avoid overfishing, while all your colleagues do not. You will ruin your own business since you are not able to compete with those who do not stick to that quota.

The tragedy of the commons: salmon fishing

Mike Stubborn is a fifty-year-old experienced fisherman. He specialized in catching salmon in the North Sea. On average, he is able to catch 600 salmons a day. This means that he can sell the fish for 0.50 U.S. dollar per piece. However, when he urges his crew to work harder in the same amount of hours, and uses bigger nets, he is able to catch 800 salmons a day, while bearing the same costs. This means that the catch is not very precise, so Stubborn also catches crabs and other species he is not interested in. This also means that he can drop his sales price slightly (0.38 U.S. dollar per piece) and beat his competition.

Of course that same competition will not await their bankruptcy and on their turn adjust their own catching methods to be able to catch up with Stubborn. This will result in a situation in which the entire branch catches more in the same hour, prices keep dropping, and increased collateral damage is done to the environment. On the long run, the salmon will not be able to restore themselves in the same pace as the fishermen take them out of the ocean. The result is that the salmon species is greatly damaged, as well as the salmon trade that will inevitably suffer the consequences.

In their famous book *Cradle to Cradle* (2002), McDonough and Braungart explain into detail some of the consequences of this 'tragedy'. The effects are twofold: on the one hand, it leads to a persistent desire to control our environment, which is probably not possible and even counterproductive. On the other hand it has led to very unsustainable production processes that perhaps indeed lead to a lowest possible cost price, but not to a lowest possible effect on the environment.

As it seems, there is an underlying ethical dilemma. We have to balance economic values with ecological values for various reasons. First and foremost because our planet is unique, and it is our home. It would be a very stupid idea to inflict serious harm to our home for the sake of short-term profits. In the second place – also in light of economic values – we need to be careful not to damage ecological values, since it may be catastrophic for the realisation of economic values in itself in the long run, as we have seen in the 'tragedy of the commons' case.

7.1.1 Controlling the environment

With industrialization came the idea that people could not only control massive production processes, but even mother nature herself. As a result of the impressive breakthroughs in technology, uncultivated nature was considered to be something alien, savage and even hostile. This mindset is vividly at the forefront in the book *The Mysterious Island,* written by Jules Verne (1874).

The Mysterious Island, Jules Verne

In 1874, the famous French science fiction author Jules Verne wrote *L'Île mystérieuse* (in English: *The Mysterious Island*). This book gives us a good impression of how we considered environmental values after industrialization.

The book tells us the incredible story of five men who fled a prison during the American Civil War by means of an air balloon. When they find themselves above the Pacific Ocean, they encounter a heavy storm and crash down on a seemingly uninhabited island. Luckily, there is an engineer among them: Cyrus Smith. He comes up with wild ideas on how to cultivate the island, and make it a place they can call 'home' for a while. However, it is striking that one of the first things the gentlemen undertake is to cut down most of the trees, shoot down wild animals, build a factory and produce agricultural equipment. After a while, they manage to produce building stones, pots, and later even dynamite and a house. Eventually, the men are able to create a vessel to explore the surrounding ocean.

While this attitude dates back to the 18th and 19th century, it is also recognizable in today's societies: we strongly desire to manage and cultivate the environment in a way that is most favourable to us. In that process, the preservation of our planet is not the primary consideration. The most pressing issues in this context are deforestation, the artificial modification of plant and animal species, and the wellbeing of animals.

Deforestation

Deforestation is an ongoing process in which mankind takes away more forest than it gives back or nature can restore. The motivation to cut trees is diverse. For instance, wood can be used as basic materials in products and fuel, and the space that was occupied by trees can be used for agricultural purposes. In case of the latter, forests disappear for the sake of agricultural expansion, which leads to various ethical dilemmas as we can see in the case 'deforestation in Malaysia'. While the landscape changes visibly, there are long term effects that are not so easy to measure. As a result of deforestation, there is a decrease in bio-diversity and the process of photosynthesis (creating oxygen) is slowed down. The result is that the quality of the air we breathe deteriorates (Tscharntke et al. 2010). Ultimately, forests function as a natural barrier against desertification, because forests feed the soil. Desertification means that deforested soil gradually turns into desert (Linde, 2011).

Deforestation in Malaysia

South East Asia – and most notably Malaysia and Indonesia – is blessed with a unique flora. Ancient primeval forests that date back to before the ice Age (a rarity) widely cover these countries. However, since two decades, these forests are replaced by palm trees for the benefit of the ever-expanding palm oil industry.

The primeval forests of Malaysia
Take Malaysia: between 2000 and 2010, the country lost 230,000 hectares of primeval forest per year, while at the same time the hectares of palm trees expanded from 3,467,000 to 5,230,000. This comes down to an average increase of 176,300 hectares per year (Gunarso et al., 2013; Hansen et al. 2013). A trend that did not significantly change in the period 2010-2017 (Li et al, 2017).
Unfortunately, the effects of deforestation are noticeable in many respects. First, the Malaysian landscape changed notably. Considering the fact that 50 per cent of the flora and fauna species lives in primeval forests, replacing these forests with only one species has a devastating effect on the bio-diversity of Malaysia.

Second, we see an increase of CO_2 pollution. In comparison to primeval forests, palm trees contribute far less to the process of photosynthesis: the conversion of CO_2 to O_2 (oxygen). This means that as a result of deforestation, less O_2 is produced, and more CO_2 remains in the air. Furthermore, the end product (palm oil) is partly used as biofuel, producing even more CO_2. And last but not least, the cheapest way to cut primeval forests is by burning it down. This is done on a large scale, and in itself leads to additional CO_2 pollution. So, growing palm trees does lead to a triple negative effect in CO_2 pollution.

Thirdly, deforestation has serious consequences for the livelihoods of the original inhabitants of Malaysia, who prefer to maintain their old ways of living deep in the rainforests. Their living space literally shrinks.

Wild animals that live naturally in the ancient forests have a similar problem: their natural habitat is shrinking, which leads to massive problems. Think about the living area of the Asian elephant. Increasingly, wild elephants are spot nearby rural areas where people live. To protect humans against wild elephants, the elephants are replaced, shot to death or housed in so called 'elephant farms' (accessible for tourists).

The welfare of Malaysia
Opposite these negative consequences of deforestation, the Malaysian economy showed unprecedented growth and the gross national income of Malaysia has increased significantly. When we consider the period 2000-2010 once more, the GNI of Malaysia increases from 93.74 to no less than 247.53 billion American dollars (data.worldbank.org, 2018). In other words, in a very short time Malaysia changed from a developing country to a newly industrialized country. It opens many possibilities for its people because it leads to significant improvement in the area of living standards, business opportunities, education and health care.

Artificial modification of plant and animal species
As a result of technological progress we are increasingly able to modify our environment and adapt it in line with our needs or desires. This is done by genetic engineering and artificially regulating the population of species.

In the case of genetic engineering, we change the DNA structure of living beings to enhance or change certain features. This is done on a large scale in case of fruit and vegetables. These are then called 'genetically modified organisms' (GMOs). At first glance, changing foodstuff to improve the quality seems to be a good idea, and not necessarily something we need to discuss in the context of ethics. After all, what is wrong with tomatoes that become juicier and more reddish while the taste becomes more intense? Or how about mushrooms that become larger and therefore easier to handle in the kitchen? We can even add vitamin C to rice, which could offer a very accessible solution in some regions in the world that cope with unhealthy diets due to a lack of resources. In other words, the promise of GMOs is huge, and through genetic engineering we could theoretically contribute to solve serious issues in the world such as malnutrition and hunger.

GMOs

But there are also concerns. From especially religious groups the question is raised whether it is ethical to change living things, who after all were created by a divine figure for a certain reason or purpose.
Another concern relates to ownership. Techniques of genetic engineering can be owned as intellectual property (mostly patents or breeders rights). This means that a company can obtain an exclusive right to use certain applications in genetic engineering. In practice, only a handful of companies own the intellectual property rights on GMOs. This may lead to ethical dilemmas. For instance, can such an exclusive right prevail in urgent scenarios in which people are at risk of dying from malnutrition, or should other producers also be able to use such GMO techniques to end the food crisis? It would not be the first time that food aid is rejected out of fear from patent claims. Or what about ownership in itself? Is it ethical when companies can practically own certain food species due to their exclusive rights to genetic engineering techniques? And if so, where do we draw the line? Scientists are increasingly successful in cloning living species by copying their DNA structure. As we can see in the newspaper item, Chinese

scientists were able to clone monkeys, which is considered one step closer to the cloning of human beings (Liu et al. 2018). If we would hypothetically be able to clone people, would the cloner then also be able to own his creation?

One last issue relates to the purpose of GMOs. Considering its potential, we would perhaps expect genetic engineering to be used to improve quality of life or solve problems such as malnutrition and hunger by increasing food production and food quality. However, research shows that a majority of the genetic engineering techniques are focused on optimizing the production process of foodstuff to make sure the products can be produced for lower costs and improve the competitive position of the companies owning these techniques (Ziegler et al. 2011).

7

XINUANET, 27 JANUARY 2018

Researchers overseas hail China's first monkey clones as advance for better human disease research

By: Lu Hui

BEIJING, Jan. 27 (Xinhua) - The first two cloned monkeys created by Chinese researchers have recently caught much spotlight on the international stage, as experts abroad praised the study as a technical advance with the potential of furthering human disease research.

'It's a landmark work,' said Jun Wu, assistant professor at the University of Texas Southwestern Medical Center, who had participated in the creation of the first human-pig chimera embryos and the altering of the genes of a human embryo in the United States.

'Monkeys are the primates closest to humans and the biggest contribution of this work is to produce non-human primate models for human disease,' noted the professor.

Echoing his perspective, Darren Griffin, professor of genetics at the University of Kent in Canterbury, England, called the study 'very impressive technically.'
(...)

More specifically, Robert Desimone, Director of McGovern Institute of Brain Research at Massachusetts Institute of Technology in the U.S., labeled the study as 'a significant advance' for disease research, as the cloning methods may be 'particularly useful for combining several disease-related mutations in the same animal.'
(...)

Yet, Griffin warned that the first cloning of a non-human primate would raise ethical concerns, with critics arguing that this could possibly be 'one step closer to human cloning.'

'Careful consideration now needs to be given to the ethical framework under which such experiments can, and should, operate,' he said. 'Cautious optimism is my personal response to this study. The study itself is very impressive technically.'

Artificially regulating the population of species

Another issue is the artificially regulating of the population of species. Most of the times this is not too problematic when done in a thoughtful way. We could for instance breed fish in fish farms to satisfy our needs instead of fishing the 'wild' population. In this way we will reduce the effects of overfishing. However, we could raise questions regarding the wellbeing of the fish in such farms, as we will discuss below. Besides that, when breeding species is not done in a thoughtful manner, taking into account the particularities of eco-systems, it can go radically wrong. A painful example is the case of Lake Victoria in Tanzania, where fishing companies introduced the Nile perch in a closed ecosystem. The results were devastating, since the entire ecosystem was disrupted. The population of the Nile perch expanded in an extreme pace, and literally consumed most other species that would originate from this lake. The biodiversity was affected, which resulted in major ecological damage (Goldschmidt, 2004).

The wellbeing of animals

In general, it can be assumed that men feel superior to animals in many ways. We enjoy wildlife on a holiday trip, look at them in a zoo, keep them as a pet for company, and breed and consume them as food. Our relationship with animals is therefore complicated and diverse, as we can see in the example 'the chicken murders'. The general ethical dilemma we could distil from this is to what extent we have a moral obligation to take into account the wellbeing of animals in our relationship with them. There is no single right answer to this, and people deal with this dilemma rather differently. In this chapter we focus on particular issues that relate to this dilemma: food production and animal testing.

The Chicken Murders

In the village where I live, some youngsters committed an atrocious act around New Year's Eve. They sneaked into a local chicken farm, tied fireworks to the beak of some of the sleepy chicken, and blew them to pieces. Apparently this gave them a thrill, because they did this once more at another chicken farm. This cruelty was the talk of the town for a couple of days. When I went shopping for my groceries I overheard a conversation between two ladies. They were talking about the chicken murders in horror, and strongly condemned the actions and motives of the perpetrators. They felt sorry that these poor chicken had to end up like this.

It struck me that at the same moment they put chicken wings in their shopping bags, ready to eat.

In the case of food production the aim to produce as much as possible for the lowest possible cost price has led to major dilemmas in respect of the welfare of animals. While some people choose not to consume meat, fish or use products in which animals are used, humans are omnivorous by nature, and most cultures have a long tradition of consuming animals, or use parts of their bodies in craftwork or clothes.

Food production

Centuries ago, this would mean that we had to hunt for animals in their natural habitat. People would travel around in nomadic groups in a continuous search for new food and supplies.

In various places in the world, people gradually changed their way of living from nomadic to agricultural. While there is some debate about the exact reason behind this, it is assumed that the milder climate after the Ice Age and the resulting more fertile ground was a fruitful combination for agricultural settlements. During a very broad period (11,000 BCE to 500 CE) in at least six regions of the world, the agricultural revolution took off independently. These regions are: the Fertile Crescent (including the Nile delta and Syria), Turkey, South East China, the Indus Valley (covering parts of Pakistan, Afghanistan and Northern India), Peru (Andes region) and Mexico (Barker & Goucher, 2015). From these regions, the agricultural revolution spread gradually throughout the entire world. Until the industrial revolution, farms were relatively small scaled with a local focus. However, industrialization dramatically changed the agricultural sector in which farms and factories could mass-produce foodstuff.

Factory farming

When animals are used in massive quantities in food production, this is called factory farming or industrial farming. From many perspectives, factory farming is promising. It leads to more food production for a lower price, meaning that a larger population of the world has access to protein-based foodstuff. Furthermore, breeding animals on a large scale for the sake of mass production in the food-business industry also means that we can leave wild species alone.

Besides these beneficial characteristics, there are also concerns that relate to both human and animal welfare (Anomaly, 2015). First, factory farming means that animals are kept en masse in crowded and closed facilities. This significantly increases the chance of disease outbreaks, such as influenza (the flu), which also affects humans. To prevent these animals from sickness, they are usually treated with antibiotics beforehand. The ongoing consumption of treated foodstuff can also lead to resistance against antibiotics amongst humans. Furthermore, the breeding of some animal species is particularly damaging to the environment. Study reveals that the production of beef is disproportionally bad in terms of land and water usage and CO_2 output (Eshel et al. 2014). Last, and perhaps most important in this context, is the wellbeing of animals themselves. Leading a life in the confinement of bio industry can easily lead to cruelty against animals. Think about overfeeding chickens so they grow as quickly as possible, and slaughtered as soon as possible to reduce costs and optimize efficiency. Or think about the stress it causes to be kept in overly crowded farms without any fresh air.

This leaves the main question: do we have the moral obligation to take into consideration the wellbeing of animals in food production? We could think of various answers to this question.

Arguments

One – pretty straightforward – answer could be a simple 'no'. Animals are different from humans, and therefore we do not have the same moral responsibilities towards animals compared to fellow humans. Animals do not have the same level of self-awareness and experience or remember pain in a different way. Next to that, humans are natural omnivores, and naturally at the top of the food chain. This natural argument morally justifies we take advantage of animals, and consume them without a need to take care of their wellbeing.

A different argument is provided by the Australian philosopher Singer (1975). He argues that from a utilitarian point of view the greatest happiness for the greatest number is wrongly exclusively applied to human beings. He holds that animals and humans to a certain extent have the same interest or desires. Both humans and (some) animals are able to suffer pain, so why would we not accept a human being suffering, while we would accept animals to suffer? The argument that humans are more self-aware than animals does not hold, according to Singer, since we also no not let babies suffer, who may have a similar level of self-awareness than some animals. Therefore, the greatest happiness for the greatest number should also take into consideration that animals suffer too. When we apply this reasoning to factory farming, the conclusion should probably be that this does not lead to the greatest happiness for the greatest number.

Yet another argument is provided for by Regan (1983). He argues that both humans and some animals are self-aware, and therefore are able to feel pleasure and pain, as well as remember where they came from or where they would go to in the near future. He calls this a 'psychological identity'. He believes that at least (and not exclusively) mammals show these characteristics. He argues that from a rights-based approach, entities who have a psychological identity have fundamental rights, including the right not to be hurt.

In both the reasoning of Singer and Regan, we have the moral obligation to take into consideration the wellbeing of some animals: those who are able to experience pain or are self-aware. As we can see in the newspaper item, it is not always easy to draw a line between animals who do and do not show those characteristics. As a result of academic research (Magee & Elwood, 2013), Switzerland legally banned the boiling of lobsters, since it was established that they are able to experience pain.

7

CNN TRAVEL, 12 JANUARY 2018

Switzerland bans boiling lobsters alive

By: Francesca Street

Lobsters are a delicious delicacy loved by coastal dwellers across the world – but is boiling them alive inhumane?

In a new law, the Swiss government has banned the common culinary practice of throwing the crustaceans into boiling water while they are still conscious.

The move is a response to studies that suggest lobsters are sentient with advanced nervous systems that may feel pain.

From March 2018, lobsters being prepared in Switzerland will need to be knocked out before they're put to death, or killed instantly. They'll also get other protections while in transit.

'Live crustaceans, including the lobster, may no longer be transported on ice or in ice water. Aquatic species must always be kept in their natural environment,' says the new law, according to Swiss Info.

'Crustaceans must now be stunned before they are killed.'

The new edict comes in the wake of a recent Italian law that decreed lobsters can't be kept on ice in restaurant kitchens. Switzerland's decision is applauded by Professor Robert Elwood, emeritus professor in ecology, evolution, behaviour and environmental economics at Queens University, Belfast.

Animal testing

In the case of animal testing things become slightly more complicated. We usually use animals as test subjects for four reasons: for scientific research, for educational purposes, for testing medication, and for testing cosmetic products. An example of the first is injecting an artificial heart valve into a pig to find out whether the valve holds and the heart keeps beating. These studies could in the end contribute to the creation of a stable heart valve that can help to save the lives of children with heart abnormality.

An example of animal testing in education would be when veterinary science students need to practice how to administer injections on real animals. An example of testing medication on animals would be when scientists develop treatment for human diseases such as cancer or ALS and need to be sure whether it is absolutely safe to use them on humans. In the past, animals where used on a wide scale for testing the effects of cosmetics. This is now forbidden in some (but not all) industrialized countries, and in these regions, cosmetic companies found alternatives to improve their products (Adler et al, 2010).

The question we could raise here is: when is animal testing morally right? If we use the reasoning of Regan, sacrificing self-aware animals for the wellbeing of humans would be considered immoral from a principle point of view. After all, we also do not sacrifice our fellow humans to test drugs or use living humans to practice surgery. However, when we would approach this from a utilitarian perspective, we could ask ourselves the question when the benefits of animal testing outweigh the costs, which includes the sacrifice of the animal. We could consider that if it could really cure a human disease, it is worth the life of several test animals, since the outcome will lead to the greatest happiness for the greatest number. We could even increase the amount of general happiness by making sure the test animal is taken care of in a very generous way, leading a life of a much higher quality compared to his fellow-species, until the day he is sacrificed (Haynes, 2010).

As we can see in the newspaper item, Pamela Anderson rejects the idea of animal testing in finding a cure for ALS from both a principle point of view and a utilitarian perspective (according to her, the benefits do not outweigh the costs).

● www.news.com.au

Pamela Anderson says she won't do ice bucket challenge because of ALS animal testing

By: Network Writers

The ice bucket challenge has taken Hollywood by storm, but Pamela Anderson has issued her own challenge to ALS researchers.
The former Baywatch star instead called on ALS researchers to end animal testing, which she said is cruel and has a high failure rate.
(…)

It's all for a good cause – raising money and awareness for motor neuron disease, or Amyotrophic lateral sclerosis (ALS), and has raised more than $15 million.
However, not every celeb is jumping on the bandwagon.
(...)
'Sorry – I can't bring myself to do your Ice Bucket Challenge,' she wrote.
'I thought instead I'd challenge ALS to stop Animal testing.'

The actor and animal rights activist went on: 'Recent experiments funded by the ALS Association, mice had holes drilled in their skulls, were inflicted with crippling illnesses, and were forced to run on an inclined treadmill until they collapsed from exhaustion. Monkeys had chemicals injected into their brains and backs and were later killed and dissected.'
'What is the result of these experiments (other than a lot of suffering?)'
Anderson went on to say that animal experiments are outdated and almost never work when the treatments are transferred to humans.
(...)

22 August 2014

7.1.2 Unsustainable production

A second effect of industrialization is unsustainable production. In our ongoing efforts to optimize our production processes for the lowest possible costs with a maximum output we have been able to establish industries of mass-production. However, such a way of producing can have serious consequences for the realization of ecological values. If producing as much as possible for the lowest possible costs is the ultimate goal, this inevitably leads to standardizing of products. Furthermore, it leads to what we would call a linear economy, in which basic materials are distracted from our planet, transformed into products, consumed, and end up as waste after consumption. This economy type ultimately results in problems that are larger than life and cross generations, such as global warming. In the upcoming section we will discuss these issues in-depth.

Standardization of products
The promise of mass production is that due to the enormous quantity of products the fixed costs per produced unit are very low. And, the more we produce, the lower these costs will get. This inevitably encourages producers to create standard types what are applicable in as many situations as possible so that they need to design only one product. A 'one size fits all'-principle. At first glance, a safe choice, since standardized products are predictable and simply do what the consumer expects them to do. However, at the same time, products that are designed this way are a permanent waste of basic materials since they do more than necessary for their particular usage, as we can see in the example 'Let's eat some chemicals?'.

A larger product differentiation or more sustainable production processes could lead to more 'tailor-made' products, in which the usage of basic materials is limited to what is strictly needed, and the negative impact on environmental values will be reduced.

Let's eat some chemicals?

Perhaps not surprisingly, a producer of laundry detergent wants his product to perform well under all circumstances worldwide, regardless the water type that is available that is used in washing machines. Depending on the region, but also on incidental circumstances, water can be 'hard' or 'soft'. The hardness of water relates to how effective soap can be. In hard water we find more calcium related ions. The practical effect of such ions is that they reduce the effect of soap. This means that we need to soften the water by adding chemicals that kill the calcium. These chemicals are acid to a certain degree (that is why you should not drink washing detergent).

Now, if a producer wants to produce laundry detergent that works everywhere in the world, he will probably put as many chemicals in the product as necessary to make the product function in the hardest water type used in households. This also means that per definition, a lot of chemicals are used in regions with a softer water type where this is totally unnecessary. From an ecological perspective, it would be recommendable to limit the usage of chemicals as much as possible (or stop using them at all). A solution in this case would be to either invest in research to come up with an alternative to the usage of such chemicals, or at least produce different types of detergent in which different levels of chemicals are used to combat the calcium, compatible with the various water types we usually have per region. However, this would involve larger production costs, lead to an increase in the production costs, and as a result harm the competitive position of the company

producing the laundry detergent. Only in the long term, will there be a breakeven point in which the reduction in costs of using fewer chemicals in general outweighs the additional production costs of a larger product differentiation (McDonough & Braungart, 2002).

The effects of chemicals in the St. Laurence River

As it seems, water is not always filtered or cleaned before it ends up in a river or sea. The consequence of this is that the flora and fauna of a river or sea can be seriously affected by the chemicals that end up in there. Not only households spill chemicals in water as a result of using washing determent, also companies use them a lot in their production processes.

A dramatic example of this relates to the fate of the white dolphin in the Canadian St. Laurence River. This dolphin species has been threatened with extinction for years. Despite the fact that the white dolphin is a protected animal since 1979, and is therefore not being hunted, it did not succeed to recover yet. The main cause is the rapid growth of the industry at the riverside. The companies located there are responsible for the increase of chemicals that end up in the water. Unfortunately, the dolphins swallow these chemicals. As a matter of fact, their prey also consumed them – mostly aquatic invertebrates – so the dolphin is affected twice. To make matters worse, the eel also lives in the natural habitat of the white dolphin. While the eel is much more resistant to chemicals, they bring these chemicals to less contaminated areas and as a side effect help spread the chemicals (Elkington, 1997).

A linear economy
The industrial revolution has resulted in a linear economy.

> In a linear economy, products (including energy) end up as waste after usage.

Linear economy

The practical implication of this is that the basic materials that are used to create the products are only used in one product cycle, and are then considered waste. This is very often a lucrative way of producing, since it leads to the lowest costs on the short term. After all, producing one-size-fits-all products that are quick and easy to use, and easy to dispose of, are mostly the easiest to produce at the lowest costs. Alternatives to linear production mostly require an investment and change of attitude in which a company has to focus on the long term instead of short-term profits.

However, a linear economy is anything but sustainable. It means that you have to keep tapping into your resources of basic materials, while such resources are not unlimited. Simultaneously, the waste should go somewhere, and does not magically disappear. Even when it is burned for energy recovery, there is CO_2 pollution, which is waste in itself. This also implies that one day, there will be a shortage of basic materials since the resources are exhausted, and there is a surplus of waste that cannot go anywhere. This means we have two problems: one that relates to the location from which basic materials are derived, and one where the product ultimately ends up as waste.
A good example of this can be found in the case 'linear production: from tin to e-waste'. On at least two locations the production of these devices causes serious social and environmental problems. First, these are the mining areas of tin, because the mining is devastating for the local flora and biodiversity, where in the meanwhile the soil is exhausted. Second, the (informal) landfills in some developing countries cause serious problems, where the e-waste belt is growing every day.

Linear production: from tin to e-waste
The last decade, the information and communication technology sector was characterized by a huge increase of innovation, new possibilities, and a growing amount of people using devices such as smartphones, laptops and tablets. While on the one hand, individuals increasingly own more than one device, the so-called replacement cycle of these devices becomes shorter due to rapid innovation.

Unsustainable tin mining
One of the raw materials used in the manufacturing of such devices is tin. In every smartphone we need approximately two grams, and in each tablet approximately four grams of tin. It is estimated the one third of the world's tin supply is mined on two Indonesian islands: Banka and Beli Tung. While this has led to a flourishing local economy, with the lowest poverty rate in Indonesia, there are serious concerns about social values (workers' rights) and ecological values. To focus on the latter: the rich and bio-diverse flora of Banka and Beli Tung are replaced by a moonlike landscape filled with tin mines, and the waste that is produced in mining is dumped in the nearby coastal regions. This leads to a destruction of nature, and a serious loss of bio diversity. (Ginting et al. 2014). If nothing is done, it would take hundreds of years

before the flora on Banka and Beli Tung will restore itself (Oktavia et al. 2015).

E-waste
The rapid increase of information and communication technology has also led to an unprecedented waste problem. It was estimated that there was a worldwide e-waste quantity of over 44.7 million metric tonnes per year in 2016 and this number is expected to increase to 52.2 million metric tonnes in 2021. Only 20 percent of this e-waste is properly recycled. The end destination of the other 80 per cent is mostly undocumented. However, a large part of this ends up in developing countries, where workers try to (manually) strip the second hand devices of useful components for resale. The remains end up in unofficial landfills (Baldé et al. 2017)

Global warming
Industrialization has led to a worldwide challenge: global warming.

Global warming
> Global warming is the process through which the earth's atmospheric temperature gradually increases as a result of the greenhouse effect, causing changes in our climate.

Greenhouse effect
> The greenhouse effect is the effect of atmospheric radiation heating the planet's surface above the temperature it would have without an atmosphere.

In essence, the greenhouse effect is vital for human existence, and not a negative thing. After all, the earth would be much cooler without the greenhouse effect, making life as we know it impossible. This greenhouse effect is stimulated by particular gasses that we naturally have on our planet. Examples are CO_2, Chlorofluorocarbons (CKC's), Methane (CH4) and Ozone (O3). However, when we artificially generate much more of such gasses as a result of industrialization, the earth's temperature is bound to change and will gradually warm up.

One of the problems resulting from industrialization is the widespread usage of fossil fuels to create energy. Fossil fuels are a relatively inexpensive way to produce energy because there is no need for complicated techniques to achieve this.

Fossil fuels
> Fossil fuels are fuels that are incinerated in order to generate energy, releasing greenhouse gasses.

Examples of such fossil fuels are oil, gas and coal. The problem with such fuels is twofold: first, in contributes to global warming, and second, they are non-renewable resources.

The last few decades there has been a broad international debate on the possible warming of the earth. We can divide this debate into three different questions:
1 Does global warming exist?
2 Is global warming man-made?
3 What will be the long-term effects global warming?

This discussion has always been a difficult one. In the first place due to the complexity of the matter. It is very difficult to measure the extent to which the earth is warming up, and what exactly is causing this. It is even more difficult to precisely forecast what the consequences will be on the long term. Climate is dependent on so many factors that interact and are interdependent. In the second place due to the fact that instead of a purely academic debate, the discussion became more and more political. There are sometimes huge differences between the views of leading academics on global warming compared to what politicians think and say, as we can clearly see in the newspaper item.

CNBC, 29 DECEMBER 2017

Climate scientists blast Trump's global warming tweet

By: Michael Sheetz

President Donald Trump's tweet suggesting that the nation's cold snap disproves global warming has raised an outcry in response from climate scientists.
(...)
Trump made his latest blast against global warming in a tweet Thursday.
'In the East, it could be the COLDEST New Year's Eve on record. Perhaps we could use a little bit of that good old Global Warming,' Trump wrote.
Climate scientists agree that global warming is real and that the driver is carbon dioxide and other greenhouse gas emissions from human activity.
Shaena Montanari, a paleontologist and member of the American Association for the Advancement of Science, tweeted that Trump was using circular reasoning, comparing his thoughts on the weather to issues of starvation and poverty.
The possibility of record low temperatures in some parts of the United States has drawn mass attention. Christopher Kucharik, an atmospheric scientist at the University of Wisconsin-Madison, said more context is necessary, tweeting that 'memory is short.'

University of Georgia meteorologist Marshall Shepherd noted that there were 'far more record highs than record lows in 2017.'
(...)
This is far from the first time Trump expressed skepticism about climate change. In 2012, he called global warming a 'hoax' that the Chinese created in an effort to hurt the American economy. Vox in June collected 115 times Trump tweeted skepticism about climate change, saying his consistency matched with his decision at the time to withdraw from the Paris climate accord, which aims to curb carbon emissions.
According to the National Ocean and Atmospheric Administration, the 10 hottest years ever measured were in the last two decades – with the top three being 2014 through 2016. Shepherd told USA Today that weekly weather patterns 'say nothing about longer term climate change.'
'The clothes that you have on today do not describe what you have in your closet but rather how you dressed for today's weather. The range of clothing that you have in your closet is climate,' Shepherd said.

In this book, we rather stick to science. And science is very clear on two things: yes, there is global warming, and yes, it is manmade. The only thing academics seem to argue about is the exact impact it will have in the future.

The International Panel on Climate Change summarized the most important research that has been done in this field. The Panel concludes that *'human influence on the climate system is clear, and recent anthropogenic emissions of greenhouse gases are the highest in history. Recent climate changes have had widespread impacts on human and natural systems.'* Furthermore, the Panel established that *'anthropogenic greenhouse gas emissions have increased since the pre-industrial era, driven largely by economic and population growth, and are now higher than ever. This has led to atmospheric concentrations of carbon dioxide, methane and nitrous oxide that are unprecedented in at least the last 800,000 years. Their effects, together with those of other anthropogenic drivers, have been detected throughout the climate system and are extremely likely to have been the dominant cause of the observed warming since the mid-20th century'* (IPCC, 2014).

As stated above, scientists are not in agreement regarding the exact long-term consequences of this manmade global warming. While there is a general consensus that such consequences are hazardous for mankind, some academics (a minority that is) argue that we should not be too pessimistic, and nuance the ominous warnings of their colleagues (Lewis & Crok, 2014). Such academics are more than once referred to by climate change deniers. However, Lewis and Crok also argue that man-made global warming exists and we should take it seriously and do something about it.

The calculations amongst academics regarding the long-term consequences of manmade global warming vary between an average worldwide increase of temperature of 2.0 to 4.5 degrees Celsius. However, there is more than just an increase of temperature. Other consequences are inevitably the rise of the sea level (and therefore floods), desertification, more extreme weather conditions, a decrease of the quality of oxygen, and further reducing our biodiversity. For this reason politicians might ask themselves the question whether they can afford themselves to take the risk these consequences become a reality, instead of having an outdated debate on whether global warming is real or manmade (Wernaart, 2013).

Paris Agreement   In 2015, at the 21 Conference of the Parties of the United Nations Framework Convention on Climate Change, 197 countries consented to the Paris Agreement. This agreement reflects a worldwide ambition of *'...holding the increase in the global average temperature to well below 2°C above pre-industrial levels and pursuing efforts to limit the temperature increase to 1.5°C above pre-industrial levels, recognizing that this would significantly reduce the risks and impacts of climate change'* (Art. 2 (a) Paris Agreement). The Member States of this Agreement are bound to undertake ambitious efforts to meet this goal, through setting their own 'nationally determined contribution'. This means that the Paris Agreement works 'bottom up', and countries are responsible for and determine their own goals to contribute to limit climate change. There is no mechanism that can force countries to truly commit to these goals. At most, there is a reporting procedure through which countries engage in dialogues to discuss their internal goals. While these are the legal aspects to it, this does not necessarily reflect the politics that are involved, as we can see in the newspaper item. The motivation given by Trump to consider stepping out of the Paris Agreement is from a legal perspective rather remarkable.

THE GUARDIAN, 1 JUNE 2017

Donald Trump confirms US will quit Paris climate agreement

By: Oliver Milman, David Smith and Damian Carrington

World's second largest greenhouse gas emitter will remove itself from global treaty as Trump claims accord 'will harm' American jobs.

Donald Trump has confirmed that he will withdraw the US from the Paris climate agreement, in effect ensuring the world's second largest emitter of greenhouse gases will quit the international effort to address dangerous global warming.

The US will remove itself from the deal, joining Syria and Nicaragua as the only countries not party to the Paris agreement. There will be no penalty for leaving, with the Paris deal based upon the premise of voluntary emissions reductions by participating countries.

'In order to fulfil my solemn duty to the United States and its citizens, the US will withdraw from the Paris climate accord, but begin negotiations to re-enter either the Paris accords or a really entirely new transaction, on terms that are fair to the United States,' the US president told press in the White House rose garden on Thursday.

'We will start to negotiate, and we will see if we can make a deal that's fair,' Trump said. 'If we can, that's great. If we can't, that's fine.'

But Italy, France and Germany issued a joint statement shortly after Trump's speech saying they believed the treaty could not be renegotiated.

Trump told the crowd outside the White House: 'The fact that the Paris deal hamstrings the United States while empowering some of the world's top polluting countries should expel any doubt as to why foreign lobbyists should wish to keep our beautiful country tied up and bound down ... That's not going to happen while I'm president, I'm sorry.'

The Paris Agreement could be hailed as a historic agreement to seriously do something about Climate Change. It's predecessor, the Kyoto protocol (1997) hardly worked (Rosen, 2015). While its main goal, to establish a reduction of 4.2 percent greenhouse gas emissions, was well met by the contributing countries, it remains doubtful whether this really helped. First, the top-down approach and fining system did not seem to work; scaring important countries who greatly contribute to pollution such as the United States, China and India, who never committed to the binding nature of the treaty, and Russia, Japan and Canada not joining a second commitment period (Canada even withdrew to avoid a large fine for non-compliance). Secondly, there was a complex mechanism to do some creative accounting with so-called emission rights. Countries who polluted less could sell them to countries who polluted too much. For most industrialized countries it would be cheaper to buy those emission rights than to invest in clean energy (Olivier et al., 2011). As it seemed, climate change grew worse during the Kyoto Protocol terms, and further measures would be needed to reduce emissions of greenhouse gases (Kutney, 2014). This would eventually be the Paris Agreement.

Kyoto protocol

We could criticize the Paris Agreement for a procedural and a substantive reason. The procedural is the non-binding nature of the Agreement. Countries can get away with non-compliance without any consequences. On the other hand, as we have seen in light of the Kyoto Protocol, a top-down approach did not seem to work either, which explains the new bottom-up approach. Besides that, in international law, binding global treaties with an effective enforcement mechanism are a rarity, and we should perhaps consider such documents more as a political than a legislative effort (Wernaart & Van der Meulen 2017). From a substantive perspective we could ask the question whether the goal to hold the increase in the global average temperature to below 2°C will be a realistic one. At least the short-term commitment goals of participating countries do not give the impression that this goal will be met (Schleussner et al. 2016; Clemençon, 2016).

Role of business

Therefore, the role of business (especially multinationals) is considered to be increasingly important to contribute to the Paris Agreement ambition without the explicit legislative urge from states. They can do this through innovation, taking chain responsibility and giving account to their impact on society. They can furthermore encourage their State legislatures to take the ambition of the Paris Agreement seriously, as we can see in the newspaper item.

CNN MONEY, 2 JUNE 2017

Top CEOs tell the CEO president: You're wrong on Paris

By: Julia Horowitz and Jethro Mullen

Dozens of top executives urged Trump not to pull the U.S. out of the Paris climate agreement. Now that he's decided to do it, many are voicing their displeasure. 'Disappointed with today's decision on the Paris Agreement,' Immelt said Thursday on Twitter shortly after Trump's announcement.

'Climate change is real,' he wrote. 'Industry must now lead and not depend on government.' The criticism of Trump came from executives across many industries, and it was a sign of just how damaged the Trump brand has become, said presidential historian Douglas Brinkley. Brinkley said the broad criticism of a president from so many CEOs, who by nature are cautious in their public comments, was very unusual.

7.2 Towards a circular economy

Many scientists, public authorities, companies and interest groups are interested in alternatives that lead to a more sustainable production, while at the same time continuing to fulfil economic values. Moving towards a circular economy (McDonough & Braungart, 2002) may unite ecological and economic values.

FIGURE 7.1 A linear economy and a circular economy

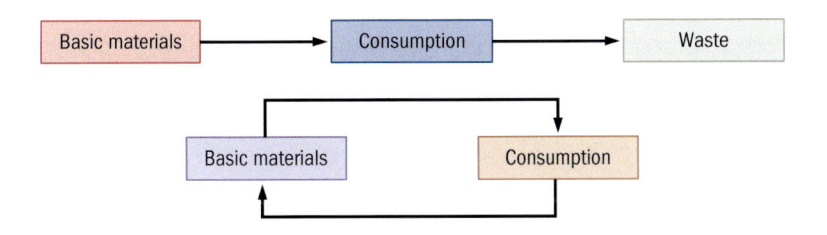

| A circular economy is an economy in which waste does not exist.

In figure 7.1 we can see the difference between a linear and circular economy.

As we have seen in the previous section, moving towards a circular economy means that we have to rethink the way our production processes work. This usually requires redesign in our way of doing business, and an investment in new technologies. In markets with fierce competition, this may be difficult to realize for companies, while it could create an advantage on the long term due to the fact that sustainable producing leads to a situation in which there is no longer a need to continuously purchase new basic materials.

7.2.1   Three pressure waves

Already since the seventies there is a global concern regarding our ecological values. Elkington (1997) argues that there were at least three periods in which governments and companies in industrialized countries responded to these concerns in increasing awareness and action. He labels these periods as 'pressure waves' through which public pressure has led to changes in governmental policies and company governance towards ecological values. Each wave has a peak that usually leads to these changes, but also a decline in which the public concern is waning.

The first pressure wave is called 'limits', and peaked around 1969. After the Second World War, the former warzones – including Europe – were rebuilt. During the war, factories were seriously damaged and therefore also the industry was rebuilt, but this time the factories were bigger than ever before. The joy of peace led to a growth of the population, and consumers consumed all kinds of new products with great enthusiasm. However, soon enough people became aware that unlimited growth and use of basic materials was a destructive way to go. A milestone book fuelling these concerns was Silent Spring, written by Rachel Carson (1962). She addressed the issue of using pesticides in agriculture, and accused the chemical industry of producing irresponsible products affecting human health and causing serious damage to the environment. In the U.S. her book triggered the adoption of environmental laws, including a ban on the usage of the very polluting dichlorodiphenyltrichloroethane (DDT). This wave was met with strong opposition from companies, who tried to block such legislation. At this stage, the business response to environmental concerns was mainly to stick to the laws that were imposed on them. This reflects the traditional

Limits

view on the relation between the public and private sector, in which the public sector should take responsibility for social and environmental issues by creating a legislative framework in which the private sector should operate.

A current problem is that countries who are in the process of industrializing may face similar problems and pressure waves, but at a later stage. For instance, in the industrialized areas of China, smog is a serious threat to human health (Hallquist et al, 2016), and as we can see in the newspaper item, the government is currently trying to limit air pollution by adopting environmental policies. A dilemma here is that industrialized countries blame the industrializing countries for polluting the air, while they did exactly the same thing a few decades ago. Why can't the industrializing countries enjoy the benefits of mass production just like the industrialized countries did in the past, or are they expected to skip the process of pollution and turn to more innovative ways of producing straight away?

REUTERS, 11 SEPTEMBER 2017

Northern China smog cuts life expectancy by 3 years versus south: study

By: David Stanway

SHANGHAI (Reuters) - Air pollution caused by coal-fired winter heating has slashed life expectancy in northern China by more than three years compared with the south, according to a new study, underlining the urgency of Beijing's efforts to tackle smog.

Researchers with the Energy Policy Institute at the University of Chicago (EPIC) said average lifespans north of the Huai river, where China supplies mostly coal-fired winter heat, were 3.1 years lower than in the south, which is not covered by the state heating policy. EPIC's study cites long-term smog exposure as a primary cause of the difference.

In a statement, EPIC said its study examined pollution and mortality data in 154 cities from 2004 to 2012, and found higher death rates were due entirely to increases in cardiorespiratory illnesses. EPIC didn't give an absolute number for average life expectancy, but said its study was the first to focus on differences in air quality north and south of the Huai river. 'We know on highly polluted days more people die and more people are sick, but what this study helps to isolate are the consequences of long-run sustained exposure,' said Michael Greenstone, EPIC director and one of the report's authors. China is in the fourth year of a 'war on pollution' designed to reverse the damage done by decades of untrammeled economic growth and allay concerns that hazardous smog and widespread water and soil contamination are causing hundreds of thousands of early deaths every year.

According to EPIC, if China were to comply with World Health Organization air quality standards, its people could live 3.5 years longer on average.

Green

A second pressure wave is called 'green' and peaked around 1990 during a period of huge environmental disasters. Amongst them we could count the Tsjernobyl nuclear disaster (1986), the Exxon Valdez oil disaster (1989, see also section 5.2.3) and the Bhopal gas disaster (1984), the biggest industrial disaster in history, as we can see in the Bophal disaster case. These disasters came at the same time while there were public debates and concerns about the hole in the ozone layer, acid rain and the massive cut down of rainforests. This led to the realization that limiting the use of basic materials or limiting pollution in itself was clearly not enough. Instead, we need to rethink our ways of producing and strive for more sustainable solutions. This led to an encouraging role for governments to stimulate companies to become more sustainable and come up with innovative and alternate production processes. The role of companies changed from passive (obey the law) to active (compete with sustainable products), and took the lead more and more.

The Bhopal disaster

In Bhopal (India), a large pesticide plant was built by Union Carbide India Limited. The U.S. based Union Carbide owned a majority of the shares of this offshore company, and was settled as a result of new policies adopted by the Indian government to encourage foreign investments in the Indian industries. The company produced – amongst others – pesticides for the Southeast Asian agricultural markets. On December 3, 1984, the biggest disaster in industrial history occurred: around 40 tons of methyl isocyanate gas was leaked into Bhopal while most of its inhabitants where asleep. This has led to the death of at least 3800 people, which included entire families and their children.

The disaster not only ends up in the history books as the biggest industrial disaster ever witnessed, no one truly took responsibility for the disaster either. Attempts to sue the U.S. mother company failed, and the U.S. Courts referred the trial back to the local courts in India. Eventually, a settlement was reached before the Indian Supreme Court and the company had to pay 470 million U.S. dollar to compensate for the harm that was done. This was mostly perceived as a very small sum compared to the long-term damage that was done. The mother company was accused of actively trying to evade all forms of responsibility by withholding vital information and spreading fake stories of sabotage, and gradually withdrew from the Indian company (Fortuin, 2001; Broughton, 2005). Until today, this remains a disputed issue, since Union Carbide still denies such accusations, and emphasizes they have every reason to believe the leak was caused by sabotage, and the company was hindered in taking its responsibility immediately after the disaster by the Indian authorities, who shut down the company site (Browning, 1993).

A third wave is called 'globalization', with a peak around 2002. During this wave, there were serious public concerns about the downside of globalization, such as the functioning of the most important economic institutions (WTO, the G8), or the effects of complicated product chains. Most importantly, the role of global governance was discussed, and the responsibility of companies who operate internationally was high on the agenda. The effects of globalization were already discussed in the previous two chapters, and will also be discussed in-depth in chapter 11.

Globalization

7.2.2   The waste pyramid

What all three waves have in common is an increasing awareness that product chains should be reconsidered, and sustainable industries are required. In other words: we need to move from a linear to a circular economy.

In their groundbreaking book *Cradle to Cradle,* McDonough and Braungart (2002) explain how production processes can be structurally redesigned towards a sustainable economy. The basic idea is that waste no longer exists and is always new basic material in itself. This leads to an endless circle in which all materials are kept in our economy. This also means that such materials should be suitable for sustainable usage. This means per definition that resources that are non-renewable are unsustainable. According to McDonough and Braungart, this implies that our production processes should be as eco-efficient as possible.

Eco-efficiency

> Eco-efficiency is to optimize the efficiency in the production process and to minimize the impact on ecological values.

In other words, eco-efficiency is the key to move towards a circular economy, as we can see in figure 7.2.

FIGURE 7.2 From a linear to a circular economy through eco-efficiency

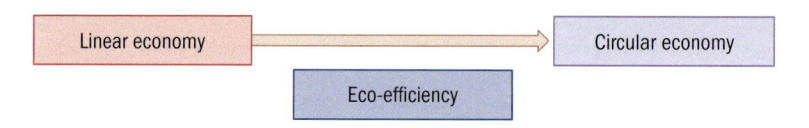

In essence, the process of eco-efficiency focuses on how to deal with waste. In this light, the Dutch politician Ad Lansink introduced the 'Ladder of Lansink', categorizing various ways to deal with waste in production processes, from most preferred options to least preferred options (figure 7.3) (Bree, 2005). This 'ladder' was later adopted for a more international audience, and now widely used the 'waste hierarchy' or 'waste pyramid' (Hyman, 2013, European Parliament and Council, 2008). While there are some variations, the elements of the waste hierarchy are mainly: prevention, reuse, recycling, recovery and disposal. In short, prevention is considered to be the most preferred option. Then, reuse and recycling, since this leads to another loop in the economic cycle of products. Least desirable are energy recovery and disposal, since they lead to waste, and cause the problems we discussed in the previous section.

Ladder of Lansink

Waste hierarchy

Prevention

Prevention

> Prevention means to avoid production or the usage of energy.

The idea is simple: if something does not exist it cannot lead to waste. The initiative may of course come from the consumer, who chooses to reduce its consumption and as a result contribute to more sustainable product chains. An example could be ecotourism, in which a tourist decides to travel without harming the environment at all, to fly CO_2 neutral, and consume only that which is needed and only when it is produced in an environmental friendly way. Consumers who choose this way of travelling mostly do so

FIGURE 7.3 The Ladder of Lansink: various gradations in waste management

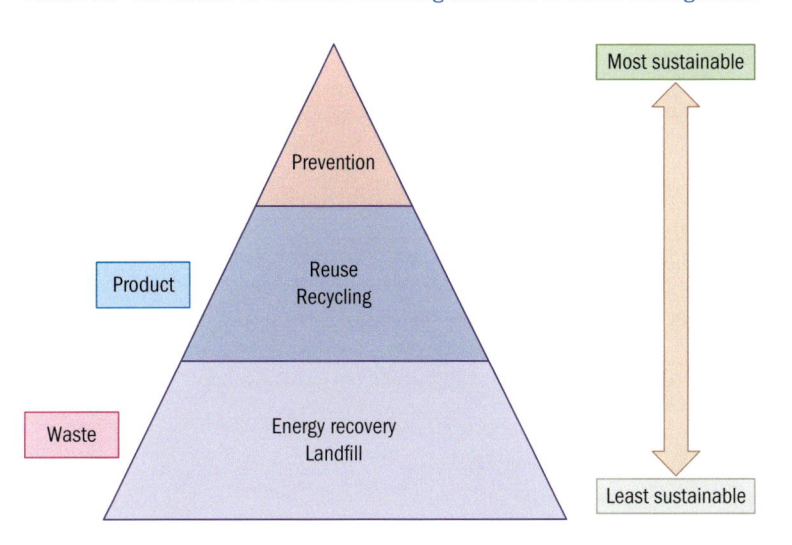

because they feel a principle-based responsibility as a result of their own moral convictions. However, there could also be a financial motivation when consumers decide to consume less. Think of energy-friendly alternatives that lead to a cost reduction in the household, such as energy-saving lights, or better isolation of the house.

The initiative can also come from the government perspective. A serious global environmental issue is the plastic that is disposed in the oceans and ends up in our food chain. (Andray, 2011; Van Sebile, 2015). For this reason, around the world, many countries at some point restricted or forbade the use of plastic bags in shops, as we can see in the newspaper example below. The result is simple: less plastic is used in the retail sector, contributing to a reduction of the use of plastic.

REUTERS, 28 AUGUST 2017

Kenya imposes world's toughest law against plastic bags

By: Katharine Houreld, John Ndiso

NAIROBI (Reuters) – Kenyans producing, selling or even using plastic bags will risk imprisonment of up to four years or fines of $40,000 from Monday, as the world's toughest law aimed at reducing plastic pollution came into effect.

The East African nation joins more than 40 other countries that have banned, partly banned or taxed single use plastic bags, including China, France, Rwanda, and Italy.
Many bags drift into the ocean, strangling turtles, suffocating seabirds and filling the stomachs of dolphins and whales with waste until they die of starvation.

'If we continue like this, by 2050, we will have more plastic in the ocean than fish,' said Habib El-Habr, an expert on marine litter working with the U.N. Environment Programme in Kenya.

Plastic bags, which El-Habr says take between 500 to 1,000 years to break down, also enter the human food chain through fish and other animals. In Nairobi's slaughterhouses, some cows destined for human consumption had 20 bags removed from their stomachs.

'This is something we didn't get ten years ago but now its almost on a daily basis,' said county vet Mbuthi Kinyanjui as he watched men in bloodied white uniforms scoop sodden plastic bags from the stomachs of cow carcasses.

Kenya's law allows police to go after anyone even carrying a plastic bag. But Judy Wakhungu, Kenya's environment minister, said enforcement would initially be directed at manufacturers and suppliers.

(…)

Big Kenyan supermarket chains like France's Carrefour and Nakumatt have already started offering customers cloth bags as alternatives.

While it is assumed that prevention of production is the most eco-efficient way to deal with waste, we could argue that companies may – at first glance – not admire such an approach. After all, it would simply mean they would have to produce less. On the other hand, that might not necessarily be a problem since it could also create new opportunities. As we have seen, there is a consumer demand for product avoidance, or there could be governmental policies that demand the prevention of using certain products. Companies could fulfil that demand by developing clever solutions and offering new products and services that contribute to such prevention. Think about those energy-saving light bulbs, cleaner cars so less gasoline is used, or vegan alternatives to meat.

It needs to be noted here that prevention is not only about the quantity that is produced. It could also be about the quality of the products. This means that products could be redesigned in such a way that the amount of non-renewable basic materials is reduced, and the amount of renewable resources is increased. This would reduce the usage of damaging materials (so, in that sense prevention), and encourage reuse or recycling. An interesting example of qualitative prevention is the creation of dye that absorbs solar energy and can be used to light roads during the nights, as we can see in the example 'Smog free towers and energy absorbing paint'. Due to this innovation, there is no longer a need for light posts and energy to make them work.

Reuse

Reuse

> Reuse is the re-use of the same product or energy source for the same purpose.

The terms 'reuse' and 'recycling' are sometimes used in our common language as if they are interchangeable, while actually they are very different. When we reuse a product, it is simply used again in the same function, while when we recycle, the product is decomposed and turned into something else, which is then used.

The economic lifespan of a product is sometimes much longer than the average duration of usage. In such cases, it makes sense to resell the product and offer it another life. Think about second-hand stores, or online sales of second hand products between consumers. In the B-to-B setting we could think of leasing equipment instead of buying them, so that the equipment can be reused over and over again by various companies to maximize the use during the economic lifespan of the product, and therefore minimize the need for new products.

Unlike waste hierarchy suggests we could argue that re-cycling is a better option than re-use, because re-use could still lead to energy recovery or disposal in the end, where recycling keeps materials in the economic cycle. After all, reuse does not guarantee the absence of waste, where recycling in potential could, as we will discuss below. The reason why in the waste hierarchy reuse is favoured over recycling is most probably that reuse leads to reduction of producing, which is the most favoured option.

Recycling

> Recycling is the usage of waste as new basic materials.

Recycling

As a matter of fact, we can distinguish two types of recycling: upcycling and downcycling (McDonough &Braungart, 2002).

> With upcycling the new basic materials can generate a higher value compared to the recycled product.

Upcycling

An example of upcycling has already been given in Chapter 5, in which the metal crates to ship car components were later used as basic material for the bottom floor of these cars. A modern innovator in this area is the Dutch entrepreneur Daan Roosegaarde, as you can see in the example of the smog free tower, in which greenhouse gas emissions are converted into clean air, and basic materials for jewellery and bicycles.

Smog free towers and energy absorbing paint

Daan Roosegaarde is a Dutch artist and innovator, and frequently hits the headlines with his clever innovations that contribute to more sustainable products. For instance, in 2014, he patented his technique for positive ionization of smog (mostly CO_2), and used this in giant 'smog vacuum cleaners'. One of such cleaners is a giant smog-free tower. Experiments with such a tower were undertaken in the Netherlands, Poland and China. This tower cleans 30,000 m3 per hour, works on green energy and is produced using environmentally friendly materials. The particles that were filtered from the air are compressed and used as basic materials for jewellery or bicycles. In other words: the greenhouse gas emissions (in particular CO_2) are converted into clean air and jewellery. Another innovation created by Roosegaarde and his team is the development of paint that can charge itself during the day using solar energy, and as a result glows by night. This is an energy-saving alternative for lampposts. In Nuenen, the Netherlands, this paint is used to light cycling roads during nighttime, using the colours of works from the famous Dutch painter Vincent van Gogh. Art meets upcycling in its purest form! (www.studioroosegaarde.net).

Downcycling

> With downcycling the new basic materials generate a lower value compared to the recycled product.

An example of downcycling is the recycling of paper, glass or metal. Existing products are decomposed and reduced to new raw materials. Unfortunately we need a larger quantity of 'old' materials in order to generate 'new' materials. Throughout the process therefore the value slowly decreases each time products are downcycled. However, it is better than the alternative: energy recovery or simply disposal.

Energy recovery

Energy recovery

> Energy recovery is the generation of energy by waste incineration.

While this is obviously an environmentally unfriendly alternative, it is to be chosen above disposal because at least energy is recovered that has an economic value and can be used as electricity supply. Energy recovery usually leads to pollution. However, the seriousness of the pollution depends on what we incinerate exactly. Therefore, in the production process we could take this into account and focus on using basic materials that are less polluting when burned.

Disposal

Disposal

> Disposal is the dumping of waste.

In the case of energy recovery, it needs to be noted that the pollution that results from this process is a form of disposal in itself. After all, the pollution is dumped in the air (or below the surface) and lingers around forever.

In case of products, disposal would be to dump it in a landfill. This is then the final destination of the consumed products. Earlier in this chapter we saw the devastating effects of e-waste. Next to some cities in developing countries, huge landfills emerged without any prospect of alternative ways to deal with the amount of waste. Poignant examples are landfills in Managua, Jakarta, Phnom Penh and Mexico City. As we have seen above, the ocean is also a landfill in its own right, in which large quantities of plastics float around.

Summary

► Ecological values are values that contribute to a sustainable environment.

► Industrialization has led to a situation in which economic values stand in the way of ecological values. This is particularly the case when:
1 Humans try to control the environment by:
   • deforestation
   • artificial modification of plant and animal species
   • neglecting animal welfare
2 Unsustainable production processes are implemented, which results into:
   • the standardisation of products
   • a linear economy (products -including energy- end up as waste after usage)
   • global warming (the process through which the earth's atmospheric temperature gradually increases as a result of the greenhouse effect, causing changes in our climate)

► A circular economy is an economy in which waste does not exist. This is a sustainable alternative to a linear economy and can be achieved by eco-efficient production processes.

► Eco-efficiency is to optimize the efficiency in the production process and to minimize the impact on ecological values.

► According to John Elkongton, the public awareness of the need for eco-efficiency came in three pressure waves:
   • Limits (peak around 1969): realization that there cannot be unlimited growth, followed by state legislation, company compliance.
   • Green (peaked around 1990): realization that production processes needed to be redesigned, followed by government encouragement towards companies, and increasing sustainable product differentiation by companies.
   • Globalization (peaked around 2002): realization that global institutions and actors have a strong influence on the environmental challenges of our planet, followed by a call for action at the address of these actors.

7

▶ The ladder of Lansink/waste hierarchy helps us in analysing our production processes in order to produce more eco-efficiently. It categorizes five alternatives to waste management that are listed from most to least preferred options.
- Prevention means to avoid production or the usage of energy:
  - Quantitative prevention aims at producing fewer amounts.
  - Qualitative prevention aims at producing with more sustainable basic materials.
- Reuse is the reuse of the same product or energy source for the same purpose.
- Recycling is the usage of waste as new basic materials:
  - With upcycling the new basic materials can generate a higher value compared to the recycled product.
  - With downcycling the new basic materials generate a lower value compared to the recycled product.
- Energy recovery is the generation of energy by waste incineration.
- Disposal is the dumping of waste.

Literature

Adler, S., Basketter, D., Creton, S. et al. (2011) Alternative (non-animal) methods for cosmetics testing: current status and future prospects – 2010. *Archives of Toxicology*. May 2011, Volume 85, Issue 5, pp. 367-485.

Andray, A. (2011). Microplastics in the maritime environment. *Maritime Pollution Bulletin*, vol. 62. Pp. 1596-1605.

Anomaly, J. (2015). What's wrong with factory farming? *Public Health Ethics*, Volume 8, Issue 3, 1 November 2015, pp. 246–254.

Baldé, C.P., Forti V., Gray, V., Kuehr, R., Stegmann,P. (2017). *The Global E-waste Monitor – 2017*. Bonn/Geneva/Vienna: United Nations University (UNU), International Telecommunication Union (ITU) & International Solid Waste Association (ISWA).

Barker, G. & Goucher, C. (edts.) (2015). *The Cambridge World History, Volume II, a world with agriculture, 12.000 BCE – 500 CE*. Cambridge: Cambridge University Press.

Bree, M. The. (2005). *Waste and innovation, how waste companies and government can interact to stimulate innovation in the Dutch waste industry*. Amsterdam: Berghauser-pont.

Broughton, E. (2005). The Bhopal disaster and its aftermath: a review. *Environmental Health*, vol. 2005; 4: 6.

Browning, J.B. (1993). Union Carbide: disaster at Bhopal. *Union Carbide Corp*.

Carson, R. (1962). *Silent Spring*. Boston: Houghton Mifflin Harcourt.

Clemençon, R. (2016). The Two Sides of the Paris Climate Agreement, Dismal Failure or Historic Breakthrough? *The Journal of Environment & Development*, vol. 25 issue 1, pp. 3-24.

Elkington, J. (1997). *Cannibals with forks*. Oxford: Caps Tone Publishers.

Eshel, G., Shepon, A., Makov, T. & Milo, R. (2014). Land, irrigation water, greenhouse gas, and reactive nitrogen burdens of meat, eggs, and dairy production in the United States. *National Academy of Science* (U.S.) vol. 111 no. 33 11996-12001.

Fortuin, K. (2001). *Advocacy after Bhopal*. Chicago University Press.

Ginting, P., Budi, R. & Khalid, K. (2014). *Grim portraits of Banka Belitung Tin Mining, demanding global, national and local responsibility*. Friends of the earth.

Goldschmidt, T. (2004). *Darwins Hofvijver een drama in het Victoriameer*. Amsterdam: Bakker.

Gunarso, P., Eko Hartoyo, M., Agus, F., & Killeen, T.J. (2013). Oil palm and land use change in Indonesia, Malaysia and Papua New Guinea. *Reports from the Technical panels of the 2nd Green House Gas Working Group or the Round Table on Sustainable Palm Oil (RSPO)*.

Hallquist, M. et al. (2016). Photochemical smog in China: scientific challenges and implications for air-quality policies. *National Science Review*, vol. 3, issue 4, 1 December 2016, pp. 401-403.

Hansen, M. et al. (2013). High-Resolution Global Maps of 21st-Century Forest Cover Change. *Science*, 15 Nov 2013: Vol. 342, Issue 6160, pp. 850-853.

Hardin, G. (1968). The Tragedy of the Commons. *Science*, Vol. 162.

Haynes, R. (2010). Animals in research, in: Comstock, E. (edt). *Life science ethics*. New York: Springer.

Hyman, M. (2013). Guidelines for national waste management strategies, moving from challenges to opportunities. *United Nations Environment Programme.*

IPCC, 2014: Climate Change 2014: *Synthesis Report. Contribution of Working Groups I, II and III to the Fifth Assessment Report of the Intergovernmental Panel on Climate Change.* IPCC, Geneva, Switzerland.

Kutney, G. (2014). *Carbon politics and the failure of the Kyoto Protocol.* Taylor & Francis.

Lewis, M., & Croc, N. (2014). *A sensitive matter, how the IPCC buried evidence showing good news about global warming.* The global warming policy foundation.

Li, L., Liu, J., Long, H., Jong, W. de & Youn, Y. (2017). Economic globalization, trade and forest transition-the case of nine Asian countries. Elsevier: *Forest Policy and Economics.* Issue 76 (2017) pp.7-13.

Linde, B. (2011). *Deforestation and desertification, find out what can be done to keep the world 'green'.* New York: Benchmark Education.

Liu, Z., Cai, Y., Nie, Y., Zhang, C., Xu Y., Zhang, X., Lu Yong., Wang, Z., Poo, M. & Sun, Q. (2018). Cloning of Macaque Monkeys by Somatic Cell Nuclear transfer. *Elsevier: Cell,* 16 January 2018.

Magee, B. & Elwood, R. (2013). Shock avoidance by discrimination learning in the shore crab (Carcinus maenas) is consistent with a key criterion for pain. *Journal of Experimental Biology,* 2013; 216 (3).

McDonough, W., & Braungart, M. (2002). *Cradle to cradle, Rema king the way we make things.* New York: North Point Press.

Oktavia, D., Setiadi, Y. & Hilwan, I. (2015). The comparison of soil properties in heath forest and post-tin mined land: basic for ecosystem restoration. Elsevier: *Procedia Environmental Sciences* vol. 28 (2015) pp. 124 – 131.

Olivier, J., Janssens Gerdemann, G., Peters, J., & Wilson, J. (2011). *Long term trend in CO_2 emissions.* The Hague: Plan Agency for the environment.

Porrit, J. *(2004).* Locating the government's bottom line. In: A. Henriques & J. Richardson (Red), *The Triple Bottom Line, does it all add up? Assessing the sustainability of business and CSR (pp. 59/69).* London: Earth Scan, UK edition.

Regan, T. (1983). *The case for animal rights.* Berkeley: University of California Press.

Rosen, A. (2015). The Wrong Solution at the Right Time: The Failure of the Kyoto Protocol on Climate Change. *Politics & Policy,* Volume 43, No. 1: pp. 30-58.

Schleussner, C. et al. (2016). Science and policy characteristics of the Paris Agreement temperature goal. *Nature Climate Change* volume 6, pages 827–835 (2016).

Schluepa, M., Hageluekenb, C., Kuehrc, R., Magalinic, F., Maurerc, C., Meskersb, C., Muellera, E., & Wang, F. (2009). *Recycling: from e-waste to resources.* United Nations Environment Program (UNEP) & United Nations University (UNU).

Sebile, E. van. (2015). The ocean's accumulating plastic garbage. *Physics today.* Vol. 68. Pp. 60-61.

Singer, P. (1975). *Animal Liberation: A New Ethics for Our Treatment of Animals.* New York: HarperCollins.

Stocker, T.F., Qin, G.-K., Plattner, M., Tignor, S.K., all, J., Bosc Hung, A., Nauels, Y., Xia, V., Bex & Midgley. P.M. (Ed.) (2013). Summary for policy makers. In: *Climate Change 2013: The Physical Science basis. Contribution or Working Group I to the Fifth Assessment Report of the Intergovernmental Panel on Climate Change.* Cambridge/New York: Cambridge University Press.

Tscharntke, T., Leuschner, C., Veldkamp, E., Faust, H., Guhardja, E., & Bidin, A. (Ed.) (2010). *Tropical Rainforests and Agro forests under Global Change.* New York: Springer.

Verne, J. (1874). *'L'Île mystérieuse.* Paris: Pierre Jules Hetzel.

Wernaart, B. (2013). Proposition 6. In: *The human right to adequate food, a comparative study.* Wageningen: Wageningen Academic Publishers.

Wernaart, B. & Meulen, B. van der. (2017). The Right to Food in International Law with Case Studies from the Netherlands and Belgium. In: Steier, G. & Platel. K. (edt). *International Food Law and Policy*. New York: Springer.

Ziegler, J., Golay, C., Mahon, C., & Way, S. (2011). *The fight for the right to food, lessons learned.* Hampshire: Pall Grave Macmillan.

Media

Horowitz, J. & Mullen, J. (2017, 2 June). Top CEOs tell the CEO president: You're wrong on Paris. *CNN Money*.

Houreld, K. & Ndiso, J. (2017, 28 August). Kenya imposes world's toughest law against plastic bags. *Reuters*.

Hui, L. (2018, 27 January). Researchers overseas hail China's first monkey clones as advance for better human disease research. *Xinuanet*.

Milman, O., Smith, D. & Carrington, D. (2017, 1 June). Donald Trump confirms US will quit Paris climate agreement. *The Guardian*.

Network Writers. (2014, 22 August). Pamela Anderson says she won't do ice bucket challenge because of ALS animal testing. *News.com.au*.

Sengers, F. (2014, 13 November). Climate Agreement China and America is warning for Europe. *Elsevier*.

Sheetz, M. (2017, 29 December). Climate scientists blast Trump's global warming tweet. *CNBC*.

Stanway, D. (2017, 11 September). Northern China smog cuts life expectancy by 3 years versus south: study. *Reuters*.

Street, F. (2018, 12 January). Switzerland bans boiling lobsters alive. *CNN travel*.

Legislation and regulations

Directive 2008/98/EC of the European Parliament and of the Council of 19 November 2008 on waste and repealing a number of directives.

Paris Agreement, UN, 12 December 2015.

Kyoto Protocol, UN, 11 December 1997.

Websites

http://data.worldbank.org

www.studioroosegaarde.net

7

8

Economic values

In this chapter we discuss economic values and how they relate to social and ecological values. We will discuss one of the most obvious economic values: profitability. We will address the concept profit from a business administration perspective, and discuss alternative ways to measure business performance through external cost-accounting. We will conclude with arguments why a company has a moral obligation to be profitable.

8.1 Economic values

Economic values | Economic values are values that contribute to prosperity.

Examples are 'profitability' 'stability' and 'growth'. The word 'prosperity' is perhaps a rather vague concept and is often interpreted in different ways. Generally we could say that it indicates the fact that people are doing fine because they have adequate resources in order to live. Usually, access to those resources is gained by means of money. Therefore, we use the following definition to specify prosperity:

Prosperity implies | Prosperity implies that people have sufficient financial resources to provide in their needs.

As we have seen in the previous chapters, such needs could relate to social and ecological values. For example, in order to implement social security systems, or a system of courts before whom employees can bring complains about discrimination we need financial resources. Or think about an investment that is required to find sustainable solutions in production processes, or resources to protect animal- and wildlife: to realize all this we need money.

At the same time we argued that the desire to make profit has led to a race to the bottom between companies, seriously harming those social and ecological values.

This expresses the dual relation between economic values on the one hand and social and ecological values on the other hand. Economic values may contribute to the realization of the other values, but can also tear them down (figure 8.1).

FIGURE 8.1 The relationship between economic values on the one hand, and social and ecological values on the other hand

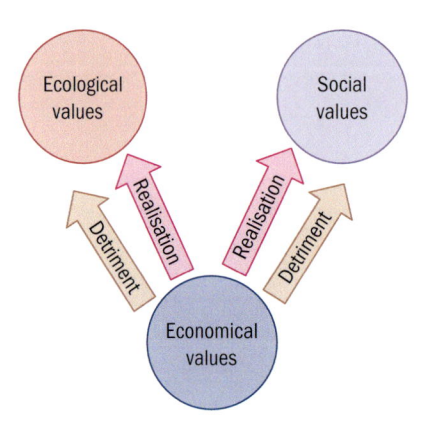

As you can see in the example 'dead aid', the success of the malaria net factory is decisive in how people in Nigeria can prevent a malaria infection. The development aid generated by the rock-star does help a lot of people on the short term, but not necessarily on the long term. The effects are that the factory cannot compete with the (well intentioned) development aid, and faces bankruptcy. As a consequence, the dependency on such development aid grows, and entrepreneurship is not encouraged. Some scholars believe that for this reason, development aid should either focus on emergency relief, or the encouragement of entrepreneurship. Giving away things for free does not help but instead has a devastating effect on the local economy. Dambisa Moyo (2010) argues that such development aid has put some African countries in a very depending and vulnerable position, making them 'addicted' to aid, paralyzing the local economies, and keeping corrupted governments where they are. She believes that traditional development aid should be abolished altogether, and instead the involved countries should focus on a stable, corruption-free and sustainable economic growth.

An often suggested solution could be the provision of micro-credit, or microfinancing: relatively small loans with low interests to people in a developing country so that they can start running their own business. Such ways of providing money can potentially lead to a positive economic flow, enabling people to fulfil their own needs instead of relying on development aid, as we can see in the case 'The pros and cons of micro-credit'. This is a bottom-up attempt to improve the local economy, contrary to the development aid as described above. As we can also see in the case, the success of microfinance depends on the conditions towards the customer, and whether or not there is a positive environment for the user of these financial products, including (gender) equality, the absence of corruption, respect for human rights, and opportunities for (business) education.

Microfinancing

8

Dead aid

A famous rock star feels very involved with the healthcare situation in Nigeria: the country is facing the highest number of malaria victims in the world (WTO, 2017). As with most things, prevention is better than curing, and therefore sleeping under an impregnated malaria net can truly make a difference. For that reason, the famous rock star organizes a benefit concert to raise money that can be used to provide as many Nigerians with such a malaria net as possible. The event is huge, and is broadcast on radio, television and live-streamed on the internet. A serious amount of 1 million euros is collected, and used for the purchase of a huge amount of malaria nets. In Nigeria, several aid agencies distribute the nets for free to those who claim to sleep without one.

But there is also a downside to this: in the capital of the country – Abuja – a local entrepreneur runs a malaria net factory, supplying the entire country. She has fifty employees on the payroll. In recent years,

the economy of Nigeria is in a positive flow, and the country has the largest GDP of the African continent (IMF, 2016). That also had its positive effects on the factory. Within three years, the number of employees grew from twenty to fifty, and production capacity quadrupled. The effect was that more and more people in the capital would purchase a malaria net, sleeping relatively safe from the threat of a malaria infection.

However, as a result of the free malaria nets that are distributed by charity organizations, the factory is facing a huge setback, and in the end declared bankruptcy. In the short term this means that fifty people have to look for a new job. The long-term effects are even more disastrous: the capital now does not have a malaria net producer anymore, and depends on these nets from elsewhere. Since importing these products will lead to a high sales price, the people in Abuja become dependent on development aid and will have to wait until the next rock-star sponsors a shipment of malaria nets.

The pros and cons of micro-credit

In a developing country, not all inhabitants have adequate resources to provide for themselves and as a result are bound to live in poverty or extreme poverty. To break the cycle of poverty, a small sum of money can help to establish a business to guarantee a more permanent source of income.

Think what the purchase of a sewing machine or a cow could do in a very poor region: the owner can now guarantee his household a permanent income in producing clothes or milk products. With some entrepreneurial skills, the generated income will exceed the money that needs to be paid to pay off the small loan, and eventually the debt is repaid. This may result in an entire family that can provide for themselves. When this is done more permanently in a particular region, the money earned will also be spent, and a new generation of customers is born. This leads to a boost in the local economy.

However, banks are usually rather hesitant in providing people such loans. First, because the loan sums are too small (twenty to a hundred euros) to be interesting for a bank. Second because there is no pledge to the bank that can be used when the debt is not paid off, which is a potential risk to a bank.

Despite the seemingly unfavourable conditions for banks, the idea of micro-credits became a worldwide phenomenon and a big success in 2005. The Bangladeshi economist Muhammad Yunus founded the Grameen Bank with the sole aim to provide small loans to the poor. He noticed that many of the established banks would not lend money to the poor, and as a result a large population would never have access to financial products that would be essential to combat poverty. At the same time he considered that all people, poor or not, are responsible for their own lives. Just giving them money would work counterproductive, but a low-interest loan would work as an encouragement to spend the money wisely and think through their entrepreneurial strategy. For their achievements to combat poverty, Muhammad Yunus and his Grameen Bank were awarded the Nobel Peace Prize in 2006. According to the committee, peace can only prevail when people are lifted up from poverty (The Norwegian Nobel Committee, 2006).

Since then, microfinancing became increasingly popular. On a global level, the UN as well as global financial institutions such as the World Bank and the International Monetary Fund promote microcredits as a way to combat poverty (Kota, 2007). However, there is also a downside to it, which is increasingly addressed amongst academia.

A first issue is the commercialization of microfinancing. Since the idea became successful, also conventional banks engaged in microfinancing, leading to less favourable clauses and higher rates for clients. These rates are for most users of such financial products impossible to repay. Even the Grameen Bank, where the idea of micro-credit began, was accused of unethical practices (Karim, 2017). Instead of reducing poverty, it could therefore even increase property by making people depending on such loans, putting them in a downward financial cycle.

Second, microfinancing alone will not combat poverty. The environment should be an encouraging one, in which there is enough (gender) equality, absence of corruption, respect for human rights, and (business) education to guarantee successful entrepreneurship. In the absence of such an environment, microfinancing can work counterproductive, lead to biased power relations and in the end do more harm than good (Rooyen, Stewart & Wet, 2012).

It is suggested that in its core, microfinancing could work when it is supervised in an effective way (Ghosh, 2013), and the microfinancing sector should stick to ethical standards, such as the Basel Principles of Effective Banking (Bank for International Settlements, 2010).

8.2 Profit

It is generally accepted that profit contributes to prosperity.

| Profit is a value expressing that someone realizes a valuable return.   **Profit**

The exact meaning of a valuable return could be debated. When you are a skater participating at the Olympics, a golden medal will be the most valuable return you can get. When you are a teacher and your students pass an exam or graduate, this could be considered a valuable return. However, in economics, and in particular in business administration, a valuable return is most often understood as a financial return. Most often, as we will see below, non-financial achievements could also be considered as a valuable return.

8.2.1 The measuring of profit

In specifying the financial returns, we traditionally make a distinction between 'turnover', 'pre-tax profit' and 'after-tax profit'.

| Turnover is the revenue of the sales of products or services in a certain period.   **Turnover**

| Pre-tax profit is the turnover of a company minus all the expenses from sales except taxation. This is also called gross profit.   **Pre-tax profit**

The added value of analysing the pre-tax profit performance of a company is that it gives the most honest impression of the company's performance. After all, if a company gets a tax reduction, or is confronted with unexpectedly higher taxation, this has an effect on the after-tax profit, but says nothing about the performance of the company in itself.

| After-tax profit is the pre-tax profit minus taxation. This is also called net profit.   **After-tax profit**

The added value of analysing the after-tax profit is that it gives an impression of what the company actually earns form their business activities: the financial return generated by the sales of goods and/or services.

In figure 8.2 we see the relation between turnover, pre-tax profit and after-tax profit.

In most countries, companies with limited liability (companies with shares) are legally obliged to publish their financial achievements annually. This is done by publishing a so-called 'annual financial statement'. This statement mostly includes a balance sheet on assets and liabilities, a report on profit (or loss), a statement of changes in equity, a cash flow statement, a summary of significant accounting policies and a statement when in retrospective items of previous financial statements are changed (IAS 1, Art. 10). Since this data focuses on the internal financial achievements of a company, this way of reporting is also called 'internal cost-accounting'.   **Financial statement**

FIGURE 8.2 The relation between turnover, pre-tax profit and after-tax profit

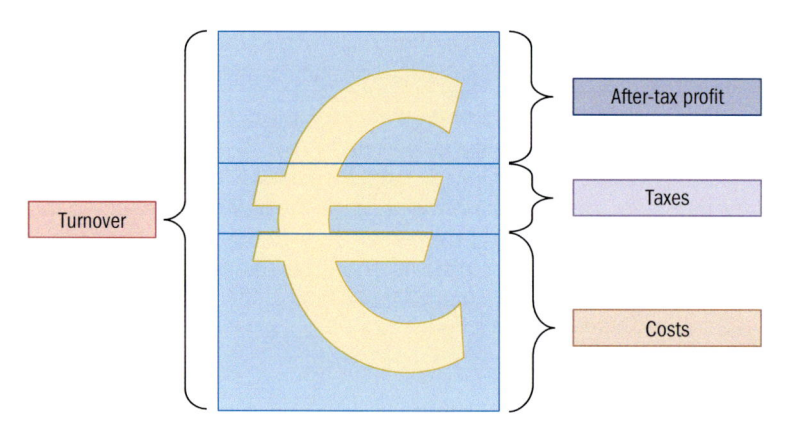

8

Based on these reports, various stakeholders can assess the achievements of the company on an annual basis. For instance:
- For tax agencies this is important in order to verify the amount of tax that should be paid.
- For shareholders (or potential shareholders/future owners) this is important to see how their shares are doing and what they can expect in the near future.
- For employees this is important to consider the stability of their employer, and therefore their job security.
- For managers this is important to show how effective they run the business (and in some cases their annual bonus depends on these achievements).

As we can see, a lot of interest relates to these annual financial statements, and it could be beneficial for a company to present the figures as positive as possible.
When net profit is based on the simple calculation of sales in the last year, minus the actual costs to generate these sales, minus taxes that were paid, things are pretty straightforward. However, the seemingly simple calculation of net profit can be rather complicated and open for interpretation, especially when companies operate in multiple countries, own shares of various subsidiary companies, or are engaged in various long-term contracts. The situation may be so complicated that profit becomes a matter of interpretation. When a company takes advantage of this, it may paint a rosy picture when presenting its financial achievements, misleading the various stakeholders.

One issue that can be used for creative accounting is the way we can value assets and liabilities. On the one hand it does not make much sense to account assets for a historic purchase price when the market value of the same assets has changed. It makes more sense to account for the current market value in order to paint a realistic picture of the company's financial **Fair value accounting** performance. We call this approach fair value accounting or mark-to-market accounting. However, as we can see in the example 'what is fair value?', the limits of fair value accounting can be overreached and this could lead to deceiving the readers of a financial report. This is in particular the case when the value of assets or liabilities changes rapidly, or is uncertain in the near future.

The International Accounting Standards Board (IASB) is an agency that adopts global accounting standards for companies that are obliged to present annual financial reports (Mirza & Ankarath, 2015). These standards are known as the International Financial Reporting Standards (IFRS), formerly known as the International Accounting Standards (IAS). In many countries, including all the EU countries, these standards are obligatory codes for companies to comply with. For instance, one of these standards give more detailed rules on how to measure a fair value of assets and liabilities (IAS 13).

Accounting standards

International Financial Reporting Standards

On a national level we see the adoption of Generally Accepted Accounting Principles (GAAP) that are set by the domestic authoritative body. For instance, well known GAAP rules are set in the U.S. by the Financial Accounting Standards Board (FASB), and are sometimes considered as the counterpart of the IAS used in Europe. While both are different, a convergence project was started in 2002 by the signing of the Norwalk Agreement. This means that the U.S. GAAP and the standards issued by the IASB are gradually converged. This also had an impact on GAAP elsewhere in the world. For instance, the Chinese GAAP (Peng & Van der Laan-Smith, 2010) are increasingly altered in the direction of the U.S. and European counterparts.

Generally Accepted Accounting Principles

8

However, as we can see in the newspaper item, accounting scandals still shake the financial world once in a while, despite the adopted codes in this field.

What is a fair value (the Enron case)?

When a company owns immovable property, it is reasonable to assume that the market value of this property can go up or down, and the value of these assets should change accordingly. So, when a building was purchased for 400,000 U.S. dollar in 2016 and the estimated market value of the building increased to 430,000 U.S. dollar, it makes sense to account for the building for the latter amount, and not the amount that was actually paid for. After all, if the company would hypothetically sell the property right now, the building would be sold for 430,000 dollar, and not 400,000 U.S. dollar. There is probably not much disagreement on this reasoning.

However, how do we measure the exact market value of the building? Which numbers do we believe to be true considering the data we can find on

financial trends in immovable property? If we want the company to look more successful, we take the more optimistic statistics, while if we need another image, we take the more pessimistic view. There is room for interpretation, so to say.

Things become blurry when a company owns shares of various other entities, and the value of these shares change per day. How do we account for the value of these shares in a proper way? Do we literally take the exact value of the share at the last day of the accounting year, the average value of the last year, or the estimated value of the coming year? There is even more room for interpretation here.

The Enron case
Or what to think of a situation in which a company closes a deal that covers more than one year (say, seven years), with a

guaranteed sale of a certain amount of services and connected products. Such a deal should at some point be reflected in the financial statements, since it certainly influences the financial achievements of the company and the overall value of the company. However, how do we account for this deal when we do not know for sure what the future cost price of supplying the services and goods will be, or the returns in a fluctuating market? It will most probably be an educated guess based on a certain forecast.

Things become extremely complicated when the company owns various subsidiary entities, and is engaged in several joint ventures with other companies, sharing the risks and profits. To what extent should the performance of these entities also be reflected in the annual financial report of the mother company? Again, room for interpretation with not a single right answer. The last two challenges were problematic in the famous Enron case, in which the company tried to present itself as an extremely successful business and a global market leader, claiming to have realized a revenue growth from 13.3 billion U.S. dollar to 100.8 billion U.S. dollar in only four year time. This has led to the deception of their stakeholders and eventually its bankruptcy (Healy & Palepu, 2003; Dharan & Bufkins, 2008).

THE FINANCIAL TIMES, 23 FEBRUARY 2016

Valeant incorrectly booked revenues from pharmacy chain

DRUGMAKER'S RESTATEMENT OF EARNINGS FUELS ACCOUNTING FEARS

By: David Crow

Shares in Valeant Pharmaceuticals rallied on Tuesday morning, even after the besieged drugmaker said it would have to restate its earnings for two years because it had incorrectly booked revenues from a pharmacy chain accused of accounting fraud. Valeant said roughly $58m of sales to Philidor, a network of pharmacies with which it had close ties, was booked when the company delivered its drugs to the vendor, but should only have been recognised when the medicines were received by patients. The error would shave 10 cents off earnings per share for 2014 under generally accepted accounting principles or GAAP, Valeant said, while adding 9 cents to EPS for 2015. The overall hit is quite small – Valeant's EPS on the GAAP measure were $2.57 in 2014 – but the revelation threatens to reignite concerns over the company's accounting standards and its relationship with Philidor.(...)

Also at the macro-economic level, we measure valuable returns. We could do that by analysing the profitability of a country. This could be expressed in the Gross Domestic Product.

Gross Domestic Product | The Gross Domestic Product is the total value of all the goods and services of a country.

The Gross Domestic Product (GDP) is usually calculated per calendar year. There are various ways to calculate a country's GDP, all with their own challenges in data finding (Landefeld, Sesking & Fraumeni, 2008). Accepted methods are:
- to calculate the income generated in a country by each group that participates in the economy
- to calculate the total expenses by each group that participates in the economy of a country
- to calculate the value that is generated by producing goods and services in a country

While the results should be more or less similar, the data collected per chosen method gives different insights. For instance, calculating the added value of production leads to detailed insights in how industries perform, where a focus on income is interesting from a taxation point of view, while a focus on expenses gives us more insight in the buying power.

The GDP focuses on territory, and all value that is generated within the boundaries of a country regardless the nationality of the involved economic actors. This is increasingly considered problematic, since in a globalized world, the profit of a Chinese company operating in Brazil can hardly considered to be a Brazilian achievement. Therefore, as an alternative, we increasingly see the calculation of the Gross National Product (GNP), focusing on the nationality of the economic actors, regardless where they are operating.

> The Gross National Product is the total value of all the goods and services of the citizens of a country.

Gross National Product

What the GDP methods and GNP have in common is that they all exclusively focus on profitability: there is no measurement of the wellbeing of a population, or the biodiversity of the flora and fauna of a country. For instance, when we take a look at the Malaysian case in chapter 7, we see an ongoing increase of the country's GDP that goes hand in hand with an ongoing decrease of the biodiversity of the country. Another challenge could be that GDP or GNP data only express the general economic revenue that is generated, but remains silent on how this is distributed. A country can have a very high GDP while large groups of people live in extreme poverty when the means of production are in the hands of a small lucky few who earn all the money.

8.2.2 Alternative ideas about profit: internal and external cost-accounting

As we have seen, a valuable return of a company is mostly expressed in profit, which is perceived as a monetary concept. This is then reported annually to the outside world in an annual financial statement. This reporting is internally focused, and only reflects on the financial achievements of a business. Increasingly, we see alternatives to this internal cost-accounting, in which companies experiment with ways of reporting on their non-financial achievements. These achievements relate to social and ecological values, and are mostly perceived to be less tangible compared to internal cost-accounting. The reporting of non-financial achievements is called 'external cost-accounting'.

Internal cost-accounting

In the previous section we discussed the annual financial statement of companies. Such a statement reflects the financial achievements of the company.

Internal cost-accounting

> Internal cost-accounting is the reporting of the financial achievements of a company through an annual financial statement.

When we consider the average balance sheet, which is part of such an annual statement, we have to conclude that at first glance, these achievements are mostly tangible, since the segments on the sheet reflect assets, liabilities and equity. This gives insight in what the company owns (assets), what it owes to other parties (liabilities), and what is invested by the shareholders (equity). If reported correctly, the assets should equal the sum of liabilities and equity, as we can see figure 8.3.

FIGURE 8.3 Segments of the balance sheet: internal cost-accounting

However, as we have seen in the previous section, there is room for interpretation in a financial statement, depending on how an accountant wants to present the achievements of a company. 'Hard' numbers are more flexible than we would consider at first glance, especially in the context of more complicated business structures or products/services. Increasingly, we see that the financial performance of a company is not only measured by tangible achievements and also intangible elements find their way in a balance sheet. Examples are the value of the know-how and goodwill of a company. Know-how reflects the knowledge and experience of the company. Goodwill reflects the value of the good image of a company, including the good image of a brand name or company name (Brand Finance, 2018). While in essence, these things reflect nothing more but thin air and are intangible, they nonetheless alter the company value significantly, as we can see in the newspaper item. After all, if someone would hypothetically buy the company right now, years of experience in a particular branch or a good company image will inevitably boost the actual sum that is paid for the takeover. For this reason, both items are generally accepted terms in a balance sheet.

THE IRISH TIMES, 1 FEBRUARY 2018

Amazon overtakes Apple and Google as most valuable brand

By: Charlie Taylor

Amazon has leapfrogged Apple and Google to become the world's most valuable brand in a new ranking dominated by technology-related firms. Valued at $150.8 billion (€121 billion), Amazon saw its value increase by 42 per cent from $106.4 billion over the last year on the back of its takeover of Whole Foods, its increased presence in the home, and rising revenues from its cloud infrastructure business.

Apple remained in second place in the Brand Finance Global 500 study as its value rebounded following a 27 per cent decline last year. The brand's value rose 37 per cent year on year to $146.3 billion from $107.2 million. However, the report's authors described its future as 'looking bleak' as it has failed to diversify and grown over-dependent on sales of its flagship iPhones.

Apple's 'increasing focus on what are effectively luxury products may cost the brand a fair share of the global mass market, limiting the potential for brand value growth,' they said.

Internet giant Google dropped from first to third place last year as its brand value rose by just 10 per cent to $120.9 billion. 'Google is a champion in internet search, cloud and mobile OS technology but, similar to Apple, its focus on particular sectors is holding it back from unleashing the full potential of its brand,' the report authors said.

Technology firms claim the top five places with Samsung taking fourth spot with a 39 per cent in growth to $92.3 billion, and Facebook in fifth, with its value growth jumping 45 per cent to $89.7 billion. Microsoft was in seventh place overall.

External cost-accounting

From the intangible segments we accept in a balance sheet in internal cost-Accounting, it is not such a giant step to also focus on the less tangible effects a company may have on social and environmental values. While these are not internal (where know-how and goodwill definitely is), performing well in those areas could have a positive internal effect as well. For instance, reducing pollution in the production process may have a positive effect in the value of the goodwill of a company. Or contributing to the wellbeing of your employees may result in better motivated and highly performing personnel. For this however we need to shift our focus from internal to external. We call this, not surprisingly, 'external cost-accounting'.

> External cost-accounting is the reporting of the non-financial achievements of a company regarding the impact on social and environmental values.

External cost-accounting

Only considering internal cost-accounting can be counterproductive and dangerous, since it only gives a very one-sided impression of a company's performance. The effects on society are perhaps not that tangible or interesting from a financial perspective, but do complete the full picture of how a company is performing. Take the Haber-Bosch process case.

Undoubtedly, the German-based company BASF generated a massive valuable return in terms of profit by selling their fertilizers. However, we could ask ourselves the question whether the company performed well considering the side-effects of their product on the environment, or the other applications of the chemical process that were later used in warfare.

The Haber-Bosch Process

In 1909, the chemist Fritz Haber discovered a chemical reaction through which ammonia could be created from natural nitrogen. This chemical process was later patented in 1910 and purchased by the German-based company BASF. Under the supervision of Carl Bosch, the company further developed and adopted the invention by optimizing its efficiency. Interestingly, this invention could be used in various applications, which led to both the saving and the destruction of lives (Elkington & Zeitz, 2014).

Ammonia can be used as an application for agricultural fertilizers. Previously, agricultural fertilizers were made naturally, and would end as biodegradable waste. However, with natural fertilizers, the agricultural production capacity would be relatively low, while using ammonia would substantially increase the productivity. This simply means that using the chemical reaction in agriculture would result in more food, and more people who can be fed. The Haber-Bosch process was even hailed as a potential solution to the world's hunger problem, and the application was even rewarded with Nobel Prize in chemistry (The Norwegian Nobel Committee, 1920).

A dark side
However, there is also a dark side to this invention. In the first place because the same chemical reaction would later be used in the production of gas weapons during the First World War. Furthermore, the chemical reaction was used in creating the dreaded Zykilon B-gas, which was used in the gas chambers of the Nazi Germany in the Second World War. Currently, the chemical process is still used in creating explosives for warfare. All these applications have led to the deaths of millions of people.

Another effect of the Haber-Bosch process is that the exponential growth of the agricultural sector as a result of ammonia fertilizers also created the possibility of population growth. In some regions of the world this has simply led to a serious overpopulation of people. It is estimated that more than 80 per cent of the proteins in a human body can be traced back to food that is processed using the Haber-Bosch process (Howarth, 2008). In other words: we almost fully depend on this invention in our food chain. At the same time, ammonia is not exactly environmentally friendly. In creating ammonia, we make use of natural gas and other fossil fuels, and ammonia in itself causes groundwater contamination and contributes to global warming (Smil, 1999).

In accountancy, the word 'materiality' is a core principle. The IASB gives the following definition (IAS, 2010):

Materiality

> Information is material if omitting it or misstating it could influence decisions that users make on the basis of financial information about a specific reporting entity.

In other words, a financial annual statement should include all information that is valuable for their direct stakeholders in order to use the statement as a basis for decision-making. After all, there would not be much added value of such a statement when it lacks or misrepresents decisive information for those who use it. Increasingly, we accept that intangible information is 'material' in annual reporting.

An interesting development in this context is the reporting on natural capital.

| Natural capital is the value of natural resources.   **Natural capital**

Our planet provides for us in many ways (Costanza et al. 1997). This includes the provision of basic materials, the cleaning of our air and water, the provision of livelihoods, and the supply of energy, as we can see in the example 'the value of Canadian forests'. When a company makes use of these services they do not bear the consequences of consuming these resources. For instance, when a company pollutes, the CO_2 pollution causes damage the company does not account for, or only to a very limited extent when a government imposes fees on more polluting production processes. This means that a company can be very successful considering its net profit, while at the same time destroy natural capital on a large scale.

The value of Canadian forests

In 2005, scientists published an estimate of the value of the largest ecosystems of Canada (Anielski & Wilson, 2005). They concluded that this natural area represents a potential market value of 37.8 billion dollar per year. That is approximately 4.7 percent of the value of the entire Canadian domestic market. The value of the forests is based on various factors. First, the raw materials it supplies, including wood, oil, natural gas and coal. Second, the forest regions are a supplier of energy that comes from hydropower plants. Third, the forest regions provide services, such as natural water purification and cleaning the air we breathe through the process of photosynthesis. Fourth, the forest regions provide for the livelihoods and resources of large groups of indigenous people, and are additionally used for recreation purposes for eco-tourists.

The scientists furthermore estimated the costs of damage done to the forest regions by cutting trees and pollution, and deduced this amount from the value that was generated by the forest regions.

This is not only damaging to our environment, but also creates a huge potential risk. When companies are overly dependent on using non-renewable natural resources, or can only be successful when they pollute the air, there are serious long-term risks to consider (KPMG et al. 2013). The company may quickly run out of basic natural materials, or will be closed on behalf of a government because it affects human health. Considering a bigger picture, the ongoing loss of bio-diversity and the decline of ecosystems seriously reduce the potential of our planet to provide for natural capital, which will have a profound effect on the ways companies can continue their business (Bishop, 2012). It is not always easy to measure the effects of a company or sector on the environment, especially since threats to our environment are mostly not directly visible and have long-term effects rather than short-term consequences. Therefore, the need to structurally monitor the impact of company behaviour on the environment was considered to be increasingly urgent (Boyd & Banzhaf, 2007).

Company level

As we can see in the example 'Puma: a pioneer in external cost-accounting', some companies embraced reporting on their impact on the environment on their own initiative. A common approach is to monetarize the impact of the company (including the entire product chain) on the environment. To put it simply, it is calculated what the company takes away from the environment and what they give back in return. Usually, the amount a company takes away surpasses the amount of what is given in return. This gives a pretty good insight in what elements of the production process are the most damaging to the environment, and need to be improved to avoid the risks that come with the loss of natural resources.

Branch level

On a meso-level, we see that academics and environmental organizations undertake studies to measure the impact on the environment of branches and markets. For instance, Trucost – an organization that generates data on a global level to understand the economic consequences of natural capital dependency – concludes that some industries in general even gain a smaller financial revenue compared to the environmental costs their business activities create (Trucost, 2013). One of their ranking lists is led by the coal power sector in Southeast Asia, with an ecological impact of 452 Billion U.S. dollar per year, generating a revenue of 443.1 Billion U.S. dollar.

Global level

Various reporting initiatives exist where companies are invited to – voluntarily – report on their emissions or environmental impact. Examples are the Corporate Disclosure Project (CDP) in which companies are asked to fill in enquiries in the context of climate change (CDP, 2016), or the Global Reporting Initiative (GRI), covering a broader scope of environmental issues (GRI, 2015). The willingness to do so seems to increase amongst companies. For instance, research shows that North American enterprises (predominantly Multinationals) increasingly report on their CO_2 emissions, and the quality of their data is improving (Werner & Bolton, 2018).

National level

At the national level, a system of environmental-economic accounting has been developed. This accounting method measures the impact of a country on the environment by calculating the used natural capital in the domestic economy (natural inputs) and the residuals that are returned to the environment, including pollution and used water (UN, 2014). The data that is generated using this methodology can be used to complement statistics on GDP or GNP, and paint a more realistic picture on the welfare of a country.

Puma: a pioneer in external cost-accounting

Puma is a German company well known for their sportswear. They were one of the first companies that would structurally report on their externalities. In 2010, the company published a revolutionary report in which the impact of their production processes was expressed in monetary results (Puma, 2010).

The total impact of the business on ecological values was estimated at 145 million euros per year. In other words: these were the costs Puma did not pay for directly, but they represented the value of natural capital that was used and not returned to society. Two main segments represented a particularly high value: the use of water and CO_2 emissions (both estimated 47 million euros).

The value of CO_2 emissions was based on the social consequences of each ton of CO_2 that was polluted by the company somewhere in their product chain. This was practically translated to 66 euros per ton, considering the threat of Global Warming and other negative consequences for humans and their environment.

The value of water usage was based on the scarcity of water per the region where Puma exploited business activities. The scarcer the water, the higher the social costs for using water for producing sportswear. Puma practically accounted for 0.81 euros per m^2 of used water. In the end, it was calculated that society would bear the external costs of 6.70 euros per produced pair of shoes.

The external cost analysis of Puma is not limited to the company in itself, but represents the entire product chain, including all suppliers. Interestingly, but perhaps not surprising, is that most of the external costs were caused by the suppliers and not by Puma. This kind of data can be easily used to help optimize the product chain, and analyse where exactly in the production process most externalities are created.

Since their initial report in 2002, Puma has experimented with various ways of reporting on their impact on society. An alternative to separately calculating the costs of externalities is to calculate the tons of pollution or water used per million euros of turnover, and focus on reducing this amount. This way, Puma increasingly integrated their annual financial report with their external accounting (Puma, 2016).

Although mostly external cost-accounting focuses on ecological values, it is not necessarily an exclusive focus. As we have seen in chapter 6, the behaviour of a company may have serious impact on the realization of social values. Also here, a company may use or create resources it does not directly account for in an annual financial statement, while reporting on these resources could be considered 'material' in assessing the overall performance of a company. In this context we could speak of human capital.

> Human capital is the value of the wellbeing and talent of the persons involved in the production of a company.   **Human capital**

We have already considered that know-how can be a segment on the balance sheet expressing the value of knowledge that companies have on board or can tap into. Employees are not only an expense, but also generate value. In this light, the wellbeing of employees can be an important feature to consider the long-term stability of the company. When working conditions guarantee a safe and healthy work environment, and employees enjoy a balanced workload, this contributes to more sustainability in the workforce of a company. Also the coaching of employees in developing skills as well as talent management contribute to this.

Some companies take this one step further, and aim at social values in general, not necessarily limited to their employees. They consider contributing to the realization of human rights in the regions in which they operate as one of their social goals. Of course this could contribute to the good image of the company, or raises brand awareness in return. In the newspaper item we see an example of a controversial commercial in which a company addressed discrimination based on sexual preferences as part of their social values agenda.

To this end, as a part of external cost-accounting, companies may report on the health of their employees, salaries paid, promotions earned, safety requirements set, HR programmes installed, and their human rights record (Bassie et al. (2014). The external cost-accounting of Puma could serve as an example here as well. Puma has set KPI's and performs self-assessments in a variety of fields, such as child labour, fair remuneration, integration of minorities and corruption (Puma, 2016).

BUSINESS INSIDER, 22 FEBRUARY 2018

A suit startup's new ads features two men kissing – and some people are furious

By: Dennis Green

Most companies try to avoid controversy. With its newest ad campaign, however, Suitsupply dove right into it.
Founded in 2000 in Amsterdam, the European suit-maker has quietly made a name for itself as the place where convenience, quality, and price all meet. (…)
The social-media backlash was swift, fierce, and expected. The campaign launched on Wednesday, February 21, and by Thursday the suit-maker's Instagram account had lost 12,000 subscribers, the company said.(…)
The response has not caught the Dutch company off-guard, however – CEO Fokke de Jong said he expected it. He also pointed to some of the more positive reactions the ads have received.
'We do not aim to and cannot control the reactions, however, the new followers and positive messages that have been prominent in our social media is a good indicator that this campaign has been well received and has impacted many people positively. It's amazing what one kiss can do,' de Jong said in a statement to Business Insider.
De Jong says the campaign was motivated by inclusivity and celebrating all kinds of relationships. He said an ad campaign featuring gay imagery was 'long overdue.'
De Jong also dismissed the criticism that Suitsupply is targeting the gay community. 'The message of this campaign is love, attraction and passion. We are a fashion company and we sell clothes but it was not targeted to commercialize the gay community. It was to show the message of love and attraction stylized by Suitsupply,' he said.
Some in Suitsupply's social-media comments praised the company for its courage in going forward with the campaign while knowing it would provoke backlash. (…)

Social capital | Social capital is the value generated by the social relations in and of a company.

When a company is built on healthy social relations, this is usually a sign of a healthy and sustainable organization. In other words: the value of the social capital influences the chances of success of a company (MacGillivray, 2004). Reporting on social capital can therefore also be considered 'material'. These relations could be internal: employees who share a strong bond, or an accessible CEO that has a good relationship with both his shareholders and his employees. These relations could also be external: the network of the company. When the business maintains a healthy social relationship with all its stakeholders, this leads to mutual trust. After all, when a company is known to be trustworthy and a reliable partner, this leads to cost-reduction and perhaps interesting partnerships generating more creativity and mutual solution based approaches towards business challenges. In the long term, both internal and external relations can be valuable for the success of a company, and could therefore be evaluated in the form of social capital.

It can be argued that a company should focus on creating internal social value first in order to be successful in their external network. Research shows that a CEO that overly focuses on external relations and overlooks internal relations is bound to fail. Instead, a CEO that understands the organization will be able to successfully build an external network. In other words: internal social values are a necessary condition to build healthy external relations (Barrosso-Castro et al. 2016).

8.2.3   The pros and cons of external cost-accounting

The obvious advantage of external cost-accounting is that social and environmental values are structurally included in the assessment of company performance. As a result, the annual reporting of the company includes externalities that could be 'material' in measuring the performance of a company, as we have argued above. When such data is published alongside (or even included in) the annual report on the internal financial performance, there is a bigger chance the relevant stakeholders – including shareholders – will emphasize the importance of social and ecological values. This might be encouraging in realizing the necessary innovative steps for companies to become truly sustainable and socially responsible actors. Also, it may be very helpful as a risk management tool. Externalities may become internalities when it leads to a bad image, when basic materials are exhausted or when governments set a price to those externalities by adopting new tax laws.

Pros

In academics, it is argued that companies who are involved with the realization social end ecological values perform better financially (Margolish & Walsh, 2001). For instance, in a 2014 Corporate Disclosure Project report, a link between climate change management and profitability was found amongst North American enterprises (CDP, 2014):
'Our analysis shows that, on climate change management, S&P 500 industry leaders:
- generate superior profitability: ROE 18% higher than low scoring peers and 67% higher than non-responders
- with more stability: 50% lower volatility of earnings over the past decade than low scoring peers
- grow dividends to shareholders: 21% stronger than low scoring peers
- exhibit value attributes attractive to equity investors.'

The same organization concluded that when companies would put a price tag on CO_2 pollution in their annual reporting, the overall company performance was better compared to companies who did not (CDP, 2016).

There are also cons to external cost-accounting. First, suggesting that companies that report on their externalities perform better could also be a

Cons

chicken-egg debate. Which was first: a well-performing company, or the external cost-accounting? It could very well be that companies who have the luxury in being involved with external cost-accounting have the budgets and resources to do so. When a company finds itself in an environment of fierce competition, this is doubtful. The causal link is difficult to truly establish.

Second, the valuing of externalities can be very random. As we have seen, some companies have experimented in monetarizing the externalities and report this alongside their annual financial statement. However, how exactly do we measure intangible things such as pollution, wellbeing of employees or the realization of human rights? Whatever method is used, there is always some randomness in valuing intangible externalities. Take the initial external cost-accounting report published by Puma. Why does the company account for a ton of CO_2 a financial amount of 66 euros and not – say – 75 euros? Such a seemingly minor detail would greatly affect the conclusions of the external cost-accounting report. When companies account for externalities based on their own methodology they might be easily tempted to make their accounting rules in such a way that they are in line with the message they want to get across to society. This leads to conclusions that do not necessarily reflect a realistic course of affairs.

This problem could be solved by unifying accounting rules on external cost-accounting. As we have seen above, this is done by some organizations at meso level. While the companies report based on fixed guidelines, they have to reveal the data voluntarily. As we will see in the next chapter, there are still risks involved that could lead to the misrepresentation of facts. However, we could also worry about the methods used at meso level. While it most certainly is a more neutral way of external cost-accounting, and companies cannot use their methodology for window dressing, also on this level cost-accounting can fail, as we can see in the example BP: a sustainable company or a disaster waiting to happen? The methodology used is decisive in the perception of the external performance of the company. This could lead to the remarkable situation in which good performance on some indicators can be used to trade off bad performance on other indicators. The bad performance is then covered up, because the general outcome of the evaluation is positive, or sometimes even labelled as 'sustainable' (Richardson, 2004).

BP: a sustainable company or a disaster waiting to happen?

In 2010, BP was involved with the Deepwater Horizon oil spill (see also Chapter 5: Oil disasters and crisis management). Interestingly enough, at that time, BP was considered to belong to the top 10 percent of most sustainable companies in the oil and gas branch, using the SAM methodology. The data generated by SAM (Sustainable Asset Management) is used to compose the Down Jones Sustainability Index. Analysis shows that various factors could contribute to the perception that BP was labelled as 'sustainable'. First, SAM acknowledges the fact that it is impossible to assess the external performance of a company in each sector the same way, and therefore uses different approaches per sector. This also results in ranking sustainable companies per sector. Where oil and gas could be considered as unsustainable by nature, within that unsustainable sector there can be more and less sustainable companies. Second, it was analysed that in the weighting of that various indicators, a stronger emphasis was put on economic factors compared to environmental factors (Fowler, 2007). Third, the final score of BP was an aggregate overview of its overall external performance, but did not map any risks related to particular indicators. In this case, BP scored very high on transparency (reporting initiatives) and their pledge to invest in renewable energy innovation. The fact that safety assessments were underperforming is then quickly overlooked by the positive end result of the SAM assessment (Murtha & Hamilton, 2012).

In contrast, an investment company (Domini Social Investments) did not include BP in their investment funds long before the Deepwater Horizon disaster. This was decided after a thorough assessment of the company's external performance. However, the methodology used was different from the SAM method. Domini used a method in which health and safety played a more prominent role, and the relation with all stakeholders of the company was included in the analysis. In other words: the method focused on the quality of the network and relation with business stakeholders. This led to the alarming conclusion that BP did communicate their great intentions towards the environment very well, but at the same time had a troubled relation with various governmental institutions (they received various fines for safety incidents that occurred before), and the relationship with employees was questionable, resulting in a culture in which efficiency was more important than safety (Fay, 2012).

Summary

8

▶ Economic values are values that contribute to prosperity.

▶ Prosperity implies that people have sufficient financial resources to provide for their needs.

▶ Profit is a value expressing that someone realizes a valuable return.

▶ In business, prosperity is mostly expressed in monetary terms. The following concepts are generally accepted and used:
  • Turnover is the revenue of the sales of products or services in a certain period.
  • Pre-tax profit is the turnover of a company minus all the expenses from sales except taxation. This is called also called gross profit.
  • After-tax profit is the pre-tax profit minus taxation. This is called also called net profit.

▶ In most countries, companies with limited liability (companies with shares) are legally obliged to publish their financial achievements annually:
  • This is done by publishing a so-called annual financial statement.
  • This way of reporting is also called internal cost-accounting.
  • Based on these reports, various stakeholders can assess the achievements of the company on an annual basis.

▶ Also on the macro-economic, we measure valuable returns. We could do that by analysing the profitability of a country. This could be expressed in the Gross Domestic Product (GDP) or the Gross National Product (GNP).

▶ External cost-accounting is the reporting of the non-financial achievements of a company regarding the impact on social and environmental values. This is done at the company level, branch level or per country.

▶ Information is material if omitting it or misstating it could influence decisions that users make on the basis of financial information about a specific reporting entity. It could be argued that this includes externalities, such as natural, human and social capital.
  • Natural capital is the value of natural resources.
  • Human capital is the value of the wellbeing and talent of the persons involved in the production of a company.
  • Social capital is the value generated by the social relations in and of a company.

► There are pros and cons to external cost-accounting.
  • Pros:
    – Sustainable companies are also profitable companies.
    – Externalities may have internal effects or become internalities.
  • Cons:
    – It is hard to measure externalities properly.
    – The methodology of external cost-accounting is not always water-proof.
    – Measuring externalities can lead to a situation in which companies weigh up their total external performance, allowing bad behaviour to persist.

Literature

Anielski, M., & Wilson, S. (2005). *Counting Canada's Natural Capital: assessing the real value of Canada's boreal ecosystems.* The Canadian Boreal Initiative & The Pembina Institute.

Bank for International Settlements. (2010). Microfinance activities and the core principles for effective banking principles. *Bank for International Settlements.*

Barrosso-Castro, C., Villegas-Perinan, M., Casillas-Bueno, J. (2014). *How boards internal and external social capital interact to affect firm performance.* Strategic Organization, 2016 Vol. 14 (I) pp. 6-31.

Bassie, L., Creelman, D., & Lamber t, A. (2014). *The smarter annual report: How companies are integrating financial and human capital reporting.* Creelman Lambert & McBassi.

Bishop, J. (2012). *The Economics of Ecosystems and Biodiversity in Business and Enterprise.* London and New York: Earthscan.

Boyd, J. & Banzhaf, C. (2007). What are ecosystem services? The need for standardized environmental accounting units. Elsevier: *Ecological Economics,* Vol. 63, Issues 2-3, August 2007, pp.616-626.

Brand Finance. (2018). *Global 500 2018, the annual report on the world's most valuable brands.* Brand Finance.

CDP. (2014). *Climate action and profitability, CDP S&P 500 Climate Change Report 2014.* CDP.

CDP. (2016). *CDP Climate change report 2016, CEE edition.* CDP.

Costanza, R., Arge, R. 'D., large, R., Farberk, S., Grasso, M., Hannon, B., Limburg, K., Naeem, S., Neal, R. 'o., Paruelo, J., Raskin, R., & Suttonkk, P. (1997). The value or the world's ecosystem services and natural capital. *Nature,* Vol. 387, 253-260.

Crane, W., & Mats, D. (2010). Suppliers, Competitors and Business Ethics. In: *Business Ethics* (3rd edition). Oxford: Oxford University Press.

Dharan, B.G. & Bufkins, W.R. (2008). Red flags in Enron's Reporting of Revenues & Key Financial Measures. *Social Science Research Network, pp. 97–100.*

Elkington, J., & Zeitz, J. (2014). Apply true accounting principles. In: *The break through challenge. 10 ways to connect today's profit with tomorrow's bottom line.* San Francisco: Jossey-Brass.

Fay, C. (2012). Domini and BP. In: Krosinsky, C, (edt.). *Evolutions in Sustainable Investing.* Hoboken: John Wiley & sons Inc.

Fowler, S.J. (2007). A Critical Review of Sustainable Business Indices and their Impact. *Journal of Business Ethics,* December 2007, vol. 76, issue 3, pp. 243-252.

Ghosh, J. (2013). Microfinance and the challenge of financial inclusion for development. *Cambridge Journal of Economics,* Vol. 37, Issue 6, 1 November 2013.

Healy, P.M. & Palepu, K.G. (2003). The fall of Enron. *Journal of Economic Perspectives,* Vol. 17, No. 2, Spring 2003, pp. 3–26.

Howarth, R. (2008). Coastal nitrogen pollution: a review of sources and trends globally and region ally. *Harmful Algae, 8,* 14-20.

IMF. (2016). World economic outlook, subdued demand: symptoms and remedies. *WTO.*

Karim. L. (2017). The scandal of Grameen: The Nobel Prize, the Bank and the State in Bangladesh. In: Bateman, M. & McClean, K. (edts). *Seduced and betrayed, exposing the contemporary microfinance phenomenon.* Santa Fe: School for advanced research press.

Kota, I. (2007). Back to basics, banking for the poor. *Finance and development*, June 2007, Volume 44, Number 2.

KPMG, Flora and Fauna International & ACCA. (2013). *Identifying natural capital risk and materiality*. KPMG.

Landefeld, J.S., Seskin, E.P. & Fraumeni, B.M. (2008). Taking the Pulse of the Economy: Measuring GDP. *Journal of Economic Perspectives*, Vol. 22, Number 2, Spring 2008, pp. 193-216.

Lybaert, N., & Jans, M. (2006). Profit control of Belgian companies through the facilities policy. *Accountancy & Business Administration*, *26*(5), 3-18.

MacGillivray, A. (2004). Social capital at work: a Manager's Guide. In: A. Henriques & J. Richardson (Editors), *The Triple Bottom Line, does it all add up? Assessing the sustainability of business and CSR* (pp. 121-130). London: Earth Scan, UK edition.

Margolish, J., & Walsh, J. (2001). *People and Profit? The search for a link between a company's social and financial performance.* Oxford: Taylor & Francis.

Mirza, A. A. & Ankarath, N. (2015). *International trends in financial reporting under the IFRS, including comparisons with the U.S. GAAP, Chinese GAAP and India Accounting Standards*. Hoboken: John Wiley & Sons.

Moyo, D. (2010). *Dead aid, why aid is not working and how there is another way for Africa.* London: Penguin Books.

Murtha, T.O. & Hamilton, A. (2012). Sustainable Asset Management. In: Krosinsky, C, (edt.). *Evolutions in Sustainable Investing*. Hoboken: John Wiley & sons Inc.

Peng, S. & Van der Laan-Smith, J. (2010). Chinese GAAP and IFRS: An analysis of the convergence process. Elsevier: *Journal of International Accounting, Auditing and Taxation*. Vol. 19. Issue 1. 2010. pp. 16-34.

Richardson, J. (2004). Accounting for Sustainability: Measuring Quantities or Enhancing Quali Ties? In: A. Henriques & J. Richardson (Editors), *The Triple Bottom Line, does it all add up? Assessing the sustainability of business and CSR* (pp. 34-44). London: Earth Scan, UK edition.

Rooyen, C. van, Stewart, R. & Wet, T. de. (2012). The Impact of Microfinance in Sub-Saharan Africa: A Systematic Review of the Evidence. *Elsevier: World Development*, Vol. 40, Issue 11, November 2012, Pp 2249-2262.

Smil, V. (1999). Nitrogen cycle and world food production. *Nature*, 400:415.

Trucost. (2013). *Natural capital at risk: the top 100 externalities of business.* Trucost.

Werner, B. & Bolton, S. (2018). *Corporate Carbon Disclosure in North America.* S & P Dow Jones Indices.

WHO. (2017). *World malaria report 2017.* Geneva: World Health Organization.

Media

Crow, D. (2016, 23 February). Valeant incorrectly booked revenues from pharmacy chain. *The Financial Times.*

Green, D. (2018, 22 February). A suit startup's new ads features two men kissing – and some people are furious. *Business Insider.*

Taylor, C. (2018, 1 February). Amazon overtakes Apple and Google as most valuable brand. *The Irish Times.*

Press release

The Norwegian Nobel Committee. (2016, 13 October). The Nobel Peace Prize for 2006. *Press release.*

The Norwegian Nobel Committee. (1920, 1 June). Award ceremony speech by Doctor Å.G. Ekstrand.

8

Annual reports

Puma. (2010). *Puma's Environmental Profit and Loss Account for the year ended 31 December 2010*. Puma.

Puma. (2016). *Momentum, Annual Report, 2016*. Puma.

Business codes

CDP. (2016). *CDP 2016 Climate change scoring methodology*. CDP.

GRI. (2015). *G4 Sustainability Reporting Guidelines*. GRI.

International Accounting Standard Board (IASB). (2010). *The Conceptual Framework for Financial Reporting 2010*.

International Accounting Standard Board (IASB). (2001). Presentation of financial statements. *International Accounting Standard 1*.

International Accounting Standard Board (IASB). (2011). Fair value measurement, *International Accounting Standard 13*.

United Nations (UN). (2014). System of environmental-economic accounting 2012.

9

Accountability

In this chapter we explore the meaning of accountability. After defining the concept, we will discuss three different ideas on accountability. The first view is that a company's only responsibility is to make profit. A second view is that a company should do more, and express its accountability towards social and environmental values voluntarily. A third approach would be to enforce companies to be accountable for their impact on social and environmental values. As we will see, all three approaches have their positive aspects but inevitably also their flaws. Therefore, we will explore a compromise between voluntary and mandatory accountability: collective self-regulation. In illustration of the latter a case study was added on the Bangladesh Accord.

9.1 Transparency and compliance

As we have seen in the previous chapters, we could argue about the exact responsibilities of a company regarding social, ecological and economic values. Whatever these responsibilities are, they are meaningless when we only talk about them. Only discussing company values and responsibilities could easily lead to using CSR terminology as window dressing, using it as a marketing instrument rather than a means to actually undertake serious efforts to act in a morally responsible way. Therefore, some authors argue that companies should say what they do, and do what they say. In other words, a company should be transparent towards and comply with their norms and values, and the corporate responsibilities they imply (Elkington, 1997; Henrique & Richardson, 2004). We usually refer to these two goals using the broader word 'accountability', not to be confused with cost-accounting, which we use in the context of finance (see previous chapter).

Accountability

> Accountability means that a company is transparent with regard to their corporate responsibilities and act accordingly.

As we can see, 'accountability' is composed of two essential components: transparency and compliance (Henrique, 2004). These two terms are difficult to see in isolation since they are complementary. After all, without communicating the social and environmental responsibilities, people will not know what kind of compliance we can expect from a company. And vice versa, when we can only expect a company to be compliant towards certain norms and values, when we are aware of the responsibilities a company pledges to embrace (see figure 9.1).

FIGURE 9.1 Accountability: transparency and compliance

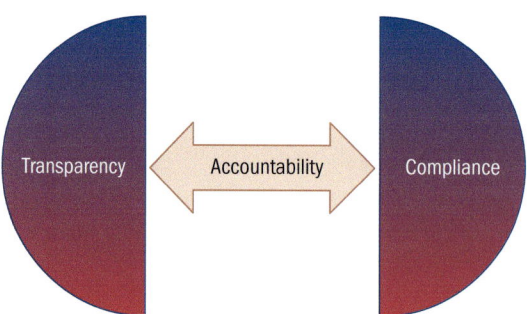

The Wells Fargo case perfectly demonstrates that transparency and compliance are crucial in the realization of CSR related goals. As we can see, the company indeed uses CSR terminology and emphasizes the importance of ethics in their daily work. However, even after various whistle blowers and external reports pointing out that there where unethical practices, this was never fully acknowledged by the management board. The board was not transparent on what was actually going on. Furthermore, it seems that the compliance mechanisms – such as an ethics hotline – did not work properly, and did not result in an improvement of the situation. This has led

to a long lasting and large scale fraud-scandal amongst Wells Fargo
employees, driven by an obscure bonus system.

The Wells Fargo Bank: how financial incentives ruined a sustainable image

The Wells Fargo Bank is one of the oldest banks in the U.S. (founded in 1852) and became one of the biggest banks in the world. The bank survived the economic crises of 2008 without many problems, and had built a trustworthy, sustainable and responsible image. This was mainly due to the fact that the bank did not invest in the obscure financial products that led other banks to bankruptcy during the crisis (Pastin, 2017). The ethics statement of the company looked promising and hands-on: 'we believe in values lived, not in phrases memorized. If you want to find out how strong a company's ethics are, don't listen to what its people say, watch what they do.' Furthermore, the company had a so-called 'ethics hotline' installed through which employees could report unethical practices.

A new bonus system
Since 2011 however, the bank adopted a new reward system for its employees, strongly encouraging to sell as many financial products as possible, preferably through cross selling. Cross selling is to make sure existing (or new) customers buy more financial products. For instance, customers were encouraged to get another credit card, or open multiple bank deposits or savings. At some point in time, the target was set to sell at least eight products to each existing customers (it was reported that the random number of eight was picked by the CEO, Mr. John Strumpf because it would rhyme with 'great'). Sometimes the targets were even set per day or even by the hour, creating a very unhealthy working atmosphere. After all, the targets set for each sales department were almost impossible to meet, and if not met, the remaining paycheck for an average employee was simply not enough to pay their daily expenses (Glazer, 2016; Warren, 2016).

In the end, it was established that employees of the bank, under pressure of these financial incentives, engaged in fraudulent behaviour on a massive scale. The U.S.A. Consumer Financial Protection Bureau fined the Wells Fargo bank for 185 Million U.S. dollar for the illegal creation of 1,534,280 deposit accounts and 565,433 credit card accounts without the consent of the involved customers. These accounts were used to meet the targets set by the company (CFPB, 2016).

Red flags
Some red flags were raised during the period in which the unauthorized accounts were created, but mainly ignored by the management board. For instance, there were whistleblowers who called the ethics hotline, and employee satisfaction research showed that employees felt uncomfortable with the bonus structure. As it seems however, lower management tried to cover up these signals, and as it turned out even fired some of the whistleblowers in retaliation for using the ethics hotline (Egan, 2017).

John Strumpf
Eventually, Wells Fargo fired 5.300 employees for unethical or illegal behaviour. The CEO at that time, John Strumpf persisted in explaining that these employees only represented 1 per cent of all employees of the bank, and suggested that the problems where local and decentralized. Interestingly, the highest management board of the bank did initially not resign but instead took another bonus, which was broadly criticized. Furthermore, the Board of Governors of the Federal Reserve System (a financial watchdog) held mister Strumpf personally responsible for missing the signs that point in the direction of widespread unethical behaviour, adopting an unhealthy reward system causing this

behaviour, and not taking responsibility for this. Amongst others, the Board held that:
'In the past year and a half, it has emerged that there were many pervasive and serious compliance and conduct failures ongoing during your tenure as Chair. These include the sales practices that led to the issuance of the Consent Orders from the Office of the Comptroller of the Currency and Consumer Financial Protection Bureau in 2016. (…) In addition, according to the April 10, 2017, Sales Practices Investigation Report (Report), you were aware of specific sales practice problems over the years in your management capacity at the firm. However, as Chair, you did not ensure that the full board received detailed and timely reporting from senior management. (…) You also continued to support the sales goals that were a major cause of the problem, and the senior executives who were most responsible for the failures, and, as detailed in the Report, you resisted attempts by other directors to hold executives accountable even when the other directors had become aware of the seriousness of the compliance and conduct issues' (Board of Governors of the Federal Reserve System, 2018).

Not everyone understands accountability in the same way, resulting in at least three main viewpoints regarding the essence of transparency and compliance, as shown in figure 9.2 shows. We could firstly argue that accountability does not help at all, and stands in the way of the social function of a company in our society. We could secondly argue that accountability only works if companies voluntarily implement strategies to support transparency and compliance. We can thirdly hold the position that all this can only lead to using CSR as a marketing tool, and the only way to make companies open up and comply with social and ecological values is to enforce them to do so. In the next sections we will explore these various viewpoints in more detail.

FIGURE 9.2 Accountability regarding social and ecological values

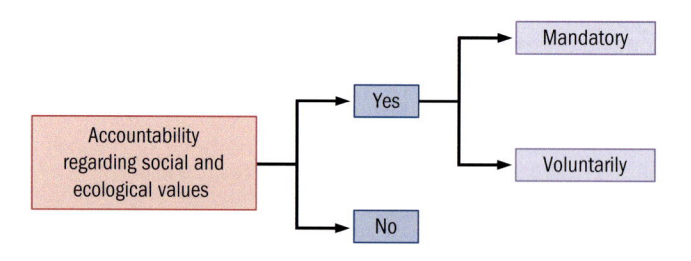

9.2 The business of business is business

In the sixties and seventies, economist Milton Friedman thoroughly argued that the only moral responsibility of a company was to maximize its profits. He summarized his viewpoint with the catchy phrase 'the business of business is business' (Friedman, 1970). When we read the average book on CSR or related topics, this viewpoint is mostly unceremoniously rejected and considered as an unethical approach. After all, it does not seem to consider the importance of social and ecological values. However, this simply is drawing conclusions too hastily. We could still defend this position with good arguments (Jansen, 2012), and it would be worthwhile to explore the exact arguments used to support this idea. In contrast, and to paint a full picture, we will also explore the most arguments to reject Friedman's theory. Both pros and cons are summarized in figure 9.3. While Friedman's theory is about rejecting CSR in general (see section 5.3.2), we discuss his arguments in the context of accountability, since transparency and compliance are typically means to truly implement CSR policies, which he seems to oppose at the core.

FIGURE 9.3 Arguments in support of and against the theory of Milton Friedman

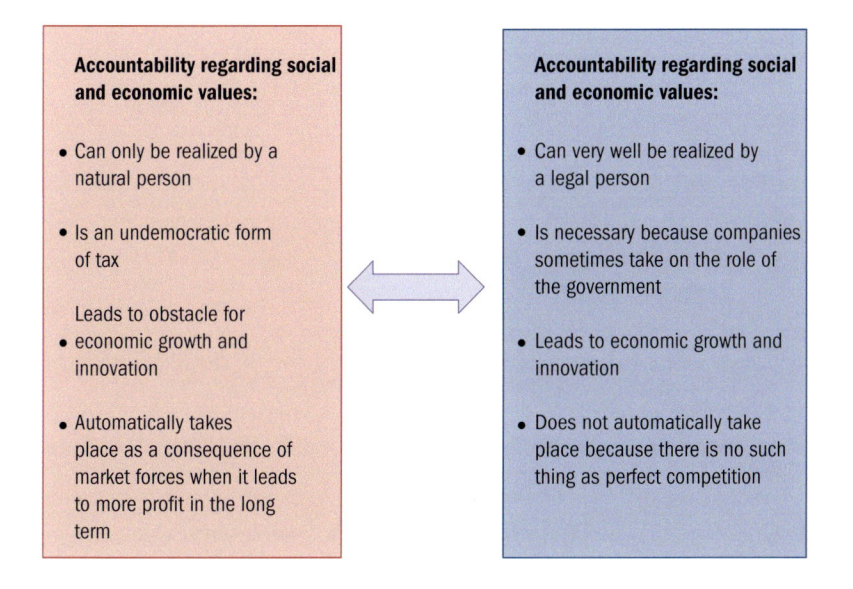

Accountability regarding social and economic values:

- Can only be realized by a natural person

- Is an undemocratic form of tax

Leads to obstacle for
- economic growth and innovation

- Automatically takes place as a consequence of market forces when it leads to more profit in the long term

Accountability regarding social and economic values:

- Can very well be realized by a legal person

- Is necessary because companies sometimes take on the role of the government

- Leads to economic growth and innovation

- Does not automatically take place because there is no such thing as perfect competition

9.2.1 Why Milton Friedman could be right

In this section we will narrow down Friedman's approach towards CSR and accountability to four main arguments.

Argument 1: Only real people can be accountable for the realization of social and ecological values.
Friedman argued that a company owned by shareholders is not a person. In his view, such a company is nothing more than an empty shell in which real people (natural persons) act. These people are employees, who produce the products and services the company offers, and the managers, representing the shareholders and those who are responsible for optimizing the profits. The profit in itself can be used to (re-)invest in the company, or paid to shareholders as a return of their initial investment. Figure 9.4 shows a simplified version of these actors in the shell of a company.

FIGURE 9.4 The company with shareholders, managers and employees

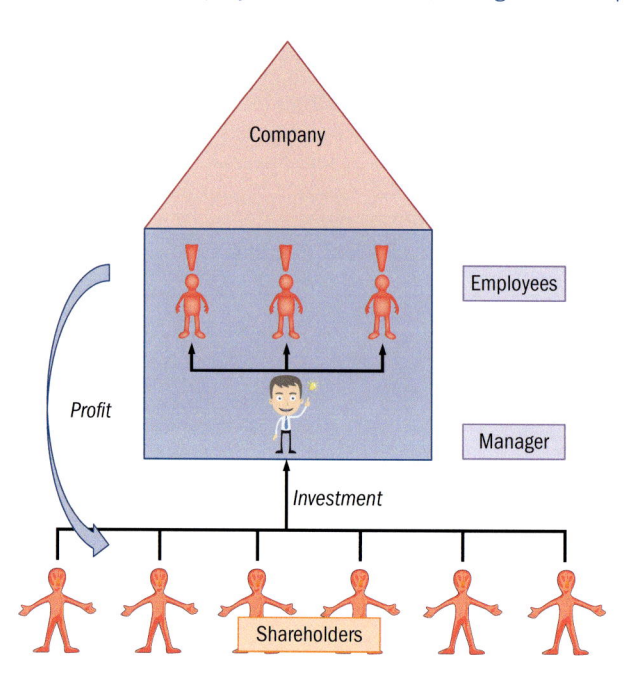

The idea that a company has its own norms and values is rejected by Friedman. He argues that not the company but the individuals who work in the context of that company have a moral imagination. Speaking of business ethics is therefore meaningless since it cannot possibly exist.

According to Friedman it is only natural that it is in the interest of a shareholder to maximize the profits of the company, since he invested in the company at his own risk, and wants the return of his investment to maintain himself and his family. He therefore hires a management in order to allocate the financial resources in such a way that it leads to the most financial success over a longest possible period. In other words: the company is a vessel for profit maximization that was created with that initial purpose.

It could very well be that a manager or an employee is particularly concerned about a certain social or ecological issue. However, contributing in realizing this issue cannot possibly be done using the company capital when this does not contribute to the goal of making profit. This would be a misuse of the money invested by the shareholders. If the manager or employee wants to contribute to these social and ecological values, they should use their own money or employ their own private efforts to do so, and leave the company out of it.

This argument of Friedman is further explained in the grocery shop example.

The grocery shop

In support of his argument, Friedman discusses a small grocery shop owned by a local entrepreneur. Friedman argues that anyone will understand that this entrepreneur will do his utmost best to generate a decent income for himself and his family. Hardly anyone will expect that the entrepreneur spends part of his business capital on social or environmental issues just because he happens to be an entrepreneur. Instead, people will understand that the investments made by the entrepreneur should primarily contribute to the success of his business.

How different is the perception of people regarding the responsibilities of a business when the organizational structure changes. When the same grocery shop is owned by a number of shareholders, the store is led by a management staff and employees are hired to sell the products, people have different expectations. Suddenly, the company is supposed to be concerned with social and ecological values, and we expect the company to dedicate parts of its budget to contribute the realization of such values.

Friedman is surprised about this, because he sees no difference between the first and the last situation. In both cases, someone is willing to invest his capital in a company at his own risk. In the first case, this is the private capital of the entrepreneur, in the second case the combined value of the shares is paid by the shareholders. Both use this investment to generate income by means of a return of their investment when the company is successful.

According to Friedman a company owned by shareholders hires a management to allocate the financial resources in an optimized way for profit maximization. Part of the management's job is to hire employees who contribute to that goal. In the view of Friedman it would make no sense when this management would use the financial resources invested by someone else for a different purpose than profit maximization. In essence, the manager would deviate from the job he was hired for (Friedman, 1970).

Argument 2: Accountability towards social and ecological values constitutes an undemocratic form of taxation.
Friedman argues that there is a clear difference between the social role of a company and that of public authorities. A company is established to pursue private interests where public authorities are established to pursue the public interest. Social and ecological values are mostly considered values that are in the interest of everyone who is part of a society. After all, we all want to live in a society in which we have access to housing, food, healthcare and education in a clean environment, and can raise or children in a safe environment. According to Friedman, this is the exclusive domain of public institutions that use the powers entrusted to them as a result of democratic procedures to realize these values. The way public authorities should contribute in the realization of these values then depends on how the people use their voting power. Public authorities can finance their policies by collecting taxes. This way, all participants of society contribute more or less to the realization of social and ecological values in a way that a majority of the people prefers.

Friedman holds that it is the responsibility of businesses to pursue the interest of their shareholders, who did their investments at their own risk. This means that a company should focus on profit maximization, and public authorities should restrict any company behaviour that stands in the way of the realization of their policies to achieve social and ecological values. This can be done through legislation (Legislature), the adoption of policies and execution of laws (Government) or if need be in the courtroom (Judiciary). In other words: a business should focus on making profit, where public authorities should determine the rules of the game in making profit, to guarantee social and ecological values.

According to Friedman it would be rather strange when a company also wants to contribute in realizing these social and ecological values, and invests in this domain. He considers this investment that does not lead to a visible return on the investment a hidden tax. After all, the money has to be paid by someone. This could be the shareholder who will lose a part of his returns, the consumer who pays a higher price for the same product, or an employee who will receive a lower paycheck. Friedman considers this an unethical practice, since all of them already pay their taxes, and are now taxed twice. One governmental tax that is visible, and one company tax, that is hidden. Besides that, he continues, when a company spends money on social and ecological values, the money is not spent in a democratic way. Where the electorate can have a say in how public budgets are spend by voting, we cannot vote for the management of a company.
Finally, Friedman suggests that companies are good at marketing and making profit, and not necessarily in realizing social and ecological goals. This could lead to counterproductive actions, since they do not always have the experience and know-how in solving public issues. They are built to be profitable, not social. An interesting example where this might lead to unfortunate partnerships is the so-called 'pinkwashing' where companies market products that should raise awareness and funds to fight breast cancer (King, 2008), as we can also see in the newspaper item.

THE HUFFINGTON POST, 22 OCTOBER 2014

Breast Cancer Awareness Month Brings the Usual 'Pinkwashing' and Unethical Cause-Marketing Partnerships.

By: John BrothersEach

October brings Breast Cancer Awareness month, where millions of dollars are raised in the support of a cure for the disease. Often the most visible aspect of the month is the number of products that are recolored pink to bring awareness and donations to the cause. While most would assume that this expression through cause marketing brings a number of great benefits including awareness and resources, a growing number of people and organizations are challenging the idea that these areas are actually bringing real benefit – calling this trend 'pinkwashing'. In a 2013 ABC News story, pinkwashing was defined as 'a company or organization that claims to care about breast cancer by promoting a pink ribbon product, but at the same time produces, manufactures and/or sells products that are linked to the disease.' An example of pinkwashing can be seen in the recent relationship between the Susan G. Komen Foundation and a firm called Baker Hughes. According to a recent

article by Mother Jones, Baker Hughes is a leader in the fracking world and has agreed to give Komen a $100,000 donation and sell 1,000 pink drill bits that are commonly used for fracking. The issue with fracking, as cited by the magazine, is that the fracking process 'injects possible and known carcinogens, including benzene, formaldehyde, and sulfuric acid, into the ground and surrounding environment.' These elements have been closely linked to the causes of cancer, chemicals that have even been highlighted on Komen's website as 'common chemicals that may be associated with breast cancer.' According to Breast Cancer Action, an advocacy and watchdog group looking at the cancer world, called the partnership between Komen and Baker Hughes as 'the most ludicrous piece of pink sh*t" they've seen all year.'
(...)
In looking at those challenged with their corporate relationships and as the skepticism towards pink grows, hopefully the attention of the breast cancer world can move the focus away from the partnerships and marketing efforts that may have pushed away the mission of the work – finding a cure.

Argument 3: Accountability towards social and ecological values creates limitations to economic growth and innovation.
As hard as it sounds, massive redundancies are mostly a side effect of progress. We have already discussed the Malthusian trap in Chapter 5 that explains why we can expect economic downfall as a result of technological progress. Friedman seems to agree with this, but also considers this a good thing that will in the end be better for society in general.
As a result of innovation, old products and services become superfluous, and are replaced. This could indeed lead to massive redundancies when it leads to the bankruptcy of companies that were specialized in the old products and services, and were unable to compete with the improved products and services offered elsewhere.
Friedman observes that mostly established larger companies, who are market leader for quite some time, are then challenged by new, small start-up companies with progressive and innovative ideas. The start-up company will progress and become the market leader in its own right, and be part of the 'establishment' waiting to be overthrown by yet another start-up challenger.
It is not always easy for the larger, established market leader to keep up with the pace of the challenging start-up. The company will have its own bureaucracy, company tradition in which a certain way of working is valued, and a long history in doing things in a particular way. This could stand in the way of the sometimes radical changes that would be necessary to keep up with the upcoming competition of the smaller challengers (Tripsas, 1997). This means that in many industries, the old market leaders will simply disappear. This is a phenomenon we call 'creative destruction'.

> Creative destruction is the process in which new companies challenge existing companies by creative innovation, often at the expense of the existing companies.

Creative destruction

The fact that a market leader disappears will inevitably lead to the loss of many jobs. However, according to Friedman this is only a short-term effect. On the longer term, the newly emerged market will attract more and more employees by creating new types of jobs. According to Friedman, any (governmental) efforts to avoid the loss of jobs by keeping the old market leader up and running is a waste of capital and leads to a slowdown in innovation, while at the same time this loss of jobs cannot be avoided.

The smartphone industry is a good example of how creative destruction works: the rapid progress in this industry has led to a continuous race among businesses to innovate and to develop new products. The new challengers in the industry became a market leader on their own, but would also be replaced by yet another newcomer in due time.

Creative destruction in the smartphone industry

In 1928, The Galvin Manu Frac Turing Company was founded in the U.S. A company that would later specialize in the development and production of car radios and other portable communication tools. In 1947, the company changed its name in the brand name they already owned: Motorola. In 1973, Motorola created their first cell phone, under the supervision of the famous inventor Martin Cooper. The device weighed 1.1 kilo, was almost 30 cm long, and it took over 10 hours to charge its battery, enabling the user to have a wireless phone conversation for half an hour (Goodwin, 2013). It would have to wait until 1983 when Motorola introduced a commercial version of their cell phone. Owning a cell phone was not for everyone, since the purchase price was almost 4,000 U.S. dollar.
Since 1990 however, Motorola was challenged by the Japanese NEC and Finnish Nokia. Especially Nokia was able to produce much smaller cell phones that were affordable for a wider audience. This resulted in the fact that at the end of the nineties, Nokia became market leader in the field of mobile phones. However, in 2012 their position was overthrown by the South Korean company Samsung (Williamson, 2012).

At the same time, an entirely new market was created in which smart technology was integrated, and one device would be multifunctional: the smartphone and tablet. Users could use the same product to access the internet, send messages, use social media, and have a phone conversation. In the period 2012-2014, Samsung and Apple competed for market leadership. The old market leaders were forgotten and on the edge of bankruptcy. To survive, parts of Nokia were sold to Microsoft, and Motorola was taken over by Google.

Argument 4: The markets will automatically correct unethical behaviour
Friedman argues that it is nonsense to assume that a company will engage in CSR activities from an altruistic point of view. When a company claims to be involved with social and ecological values, this will only be the case when there´s something in it for the company's profit. Friedman therefore assumes that so-called 'transparency' regarding CSR will most likely be just another form of marketing, and a company will only comply with CSR goals when it suits their needs.
Friedman also reasons the other way round: a company will be corrected by their own markets when they behave in such a way that it damages social or environmental values. Governments may restrict the behaviour of a company, as we already saw before in this chapter, and consumers may use their buying power to send a message to the company that is misbehaving. A striking example is the newspaper item. A bakery that refuses to sell a

wedding pie to a lesbian couple due to their religious perspective is bound to close their shop. First, because they are fined by a court for discriminating based on sexual orientation, and second because they lost a significant part of their customers due to the negative publicity.

THE DAILY MAIL, 3 JULY 2015

'He's doing this to the wrong Christian': Bakers hit out after court rules that they must pay $135k to lesbian couple after they refused to make them a wedding cake

By: Belinda Robinson and Christopher Brennan

The owners of a Portland-area bakery who refused to bake a wedding cake for a gay couple and were ordered to pay them $135,000 in damages have hit back at the ruling.

Aaron and Melissa Klein, the owners of Sweet Cakes by Melissa bakery were ordered to pay $60,000 in damages to Laurel Bowman-Cryer and $75,000 in damages to Rachel Bowman-Cryer for emotional suffering.

But they say that they're being discriminated against because their views are being silenced by Oregon Labor Commissioner Brad Avakian.

Aaron Klein told The Blaze: 'He [Avakian] wants to silence anyone who opposes his point of view. Unfortunately, he's doing this with the wrong Christian, because I fight back.'

(…)

Administrative Law Judge Alan McCullough issued a proposed order last week that meant that they must pay a bill of $135,000.

But Klein said he and his wife will 'request a stay' in an effort to delay the judge's order that they must pay damages to the two women.

'It has the potential to financially ruin our family … [Avakian] knew that full well going into this. He did not seek business assets, he sought personal property.'

(…)

Oregon prohibits businesses from discriminating based on sexual orientation and the Christian bakers were found guilty of discrimination earlier this year.

A ruling issued by the Oregon Bureau of Labor and Industries saying that the Kleins discriminated also rejected their argument that she did not discriminate against the couple because she had previously sold Rachel Cryer a cake for her mother's wedding.

Bowman-Cryers filed a civil rights suit in the case, which has joined a series of similar proceedings in a national debate about anti-LGBT discrimination and religious freedom.

They said during compensation hearings that they had received death threats and were worried about losing their two foster children after the case received widespread attention, according to Oregon Live.

The Kleins, who closed their store in 2013 amid attention drawn to the discrimination and now operate it from their home, have said that they and their five children are struggling financially.

9

9.2.2   Why Milton Friedman could be wrong

Most authors in the field of ethics and business reject the ideas of Friedman, and argue that companies have a broader responsibility than only being profitable. Friedman's arguments could be rejected by the following counter-arguments.

Argument 1: A company can very well be accountable in the field of social and ecological values, since it creates a shared morality that transcends the individual.

In law, a company with shareholders is a legal personality. In most legal systems, a legal personality is considered to be equal to a natural person. After all, a legal personality has the capacity of participating in trade, can own property, is obliged to pay tax and can commit crimes.

Of course a legal personality is not really a natural person. However, does this then automatically mean that a legal person cannot have its own morality? According to Friedman the answer was yes. However, we could also argue that the answer should be no. After all, individuals who work on behalf of the company may be driven by different norms and values compared to their own, as we can see in the Dirty Disney example. This means that a company sets forth a new moral consciousness that exists apart from and is not necessarily similar to the morality of the individuals that relate to the company (Crane & Matten, 2016).

9

Dirty Disney

Disneyland Paris is a widely known theme park inspired by (and owned by) the Walt Disney Company. When visitors walk around in one of the two main parks, you can bump into many well-known Disney Characters. The employees who perform these characters are carefully instructed by their management: make sure that especially the kids who visit the parks are enchanted by all that happens, and have a day filled with magic and wonder they will never forget. Lindsay is one of those employees, and plays the character of Jasmine (Alladin). One day, she is confronted with a seven-year-old boy who had the cheek to slap her bottom. The parents of the child appear to find this particularly amusing and even encourage the child to do this once more.

Lindsay is not so amused, and would rather have the parents correct the child and raise him properly. But Lindsay – bearing in mind her mission on behalf of the company – grabs the hands of the child and performs a silly dance with him before she quickly leaves the scene. The boy, annoying as he might be, should have a great day.

The situation would probably be different if Lindsay would not be dressed up as Jasmine, and not represent her company. What would have happened if she would be waiting for a bus, and the same child would slap her, while the parents laugh. Most likely, Lindsay would not perform a silly dance, but instead confront the parents with the behaviour of their son.

Argument 2: Accountability towards social and ecological values is necessary as a result of privatization.

As we have seen in Paragraph 5.2 privatization is one of the trends in society that triggers an increased attention to ethics in business. Friedman assumes a strict division between the public and the private sector. While this may have been more accurate at the time of writing his works, we see an increasing merge of the public and private sector. When companies assume duties that were earlier performed by public authorities, we cannot possibly say that the company should just focus on making profit, nor can we speak of a hidden undemocratic tax. When public authorities privatize some of their functions, they expect the effects of a free market to be more promising than when it is performed by tax funded public actors. This should – at least theoretically – involve a cost reduction instead of a double taxation as is suggested by Friedman.

Argument 3: Accountability in respect of social and ecological values will lead to economic growth and innovation.
As we have seen in chapter 8, a causal relation is suggested between companies that undertake external cost-accounting and profitability. When companies consider themselves an actor in a web of various shareholders, instead of a profit driven entity on its own, different kinds of products and services are created. These products and services are profitable but also solve social issues. This integrated approach is more sustainable, also when it relates to profitability, as we can see in the example 'eating crickets and upcycling carbon'. However, this requires not only an internal focus on profits, but also an external focus on partnerships, social and environmental issues, and long term strategy over short term strategy.

Eating crickets and upcycling carbon

Sustainia is an advisory group promoting business solutions in the field of social and ecological values. Each year, they publish a list of sustainable solutions. These are often products, services or processes that improve social and ecological values in a very creative way. For instance, in their Global Opportunity Report 2018, the organization explores the potential of using insects as a protein food source. Protein bars made of insects (such as crickets) are much more nutritious compared to chicken or meat, while its production leads to considerably less pollution. The organization predicts that the market value of insect protein food will rise to 772.9 million U.S. dollar in 2024. The organization also points out that this would require a change of mindset amongst producers, consumers and also legislators in the field of food law.

In the same report, various applications of CO_2 are explored in which CO_2 is no longer considered as pollution but as a valuable basic material in production processes. It reminds us of the inventions of Daan Roosegaard as discussed in chapter 7. Here, the CO_2 is suggested to be integrated in existing production processes, and can be applied in the production of certain chemicals in an ongoing circle. The market potential for these kinds of innovative techniques is estimated to be 800 billion to 1.1 trillion U.S. dollar, using up to ten percent of the worldwide annual CO_2 emission as basic material.

Argument 4: The markets will not automatically correct unethical behaviour because there is no such thing as perfect competition.
Friedman argument assumes there is such a thing as perfect competition.

Perfect competition means that all market participants compete on equal footage, have equal access to markets, offer similar products at a price that exceeds the cost prize.   **Perfect competition**

Although the exact meaning of this concept is disputed, it is based on the works of the French economist Léon Walras (Dardi, 2012). In general we could deduce four assumptions of a market with perfect competition:

1 Perfect competition means that there are a lot of small and medium-sized companies who have comparable market seizes. Monopolists do not exist. Therefore, the companies cannot influence market effects on their own and depend on the mechanism of supply and demand (the invisible hand).
2 Perfect competition means that there are no limitations to enter a market. The already existing competition cannot block a new player at their markets.
3 Perfect competition means that companies offer similar products. Consumers can therefore choose to purchase one product from different suppliers, and most likely buy the product from the supplier that is able to offer the lowest prize or the best quality. In other words: consumers know what they buy and will purchase the product that best suits their needs.
4 Perfect competition assumes that the selling price exceeds the cost prize, and therefore companies do not dump their products or services at a market.

If such markets would really exist, Friedman might be right in assuming that companies are concerned about their ethics when this is in their best interest, and consumers might use their buying power to correct unethical behaviour from companies. After all, it is easy for these consumers to purchase similar products elsewhere from a company that does not behave unethically. However, such markets in which there is perfect competition hardly exist due to several reasons (Ven & Jeurissen, 2007).

1 Most markets are not equally shared by medium sized companies. On the contrary, in a lot of markets there is a handful of market leaders occupying a powerful position in that market. In some cases there are even monopolists. In those situations, consumers are limited in their options if they would buy a certain product or service, and cannot unlimitedly use their buying power in correcting unethical behaviour.

OPEC and powerplay

Worldwide, there is only a limited number of countries that export oil. Fourteen of these countries are united in the Organization of Petroleum Exporting Countries (OPEC). One of the main goals of the OPEC is to 'devise ways and means of ensuring the stabilization of prices in international oil markets with a view to eliminating harmful and unnecessary fluctuations' (OPEC, 2012). One of the means of doing this is to limit production of oil when prices drop to make sure they stabilize and go up again. The only reason why OPEC countries can once in a while successfully correct the oil prizes is that they possess more than 70 percent of the worldwide oil reserves. This means that the oil companies in these countries have a rather dominant position in the global oil market, and those branches that depend on oil do not have that many alternatives to buy oil products elsewhere. The OPEC position becomes even more powerful when they are backed by other serious players in the oil market, such as the Russian Federation, who is not an OPEC member (see newspaper item).

REUTERS, 22 DECEMBER 2017

Russia backs gradual, managed exit from oil cuts with OPEC

By: Oleysia Astakhova

MOSCOW (Reuters) – OPEC and Russia will exit from oil production cuts very smoothly, possibly extending the curbs in some form to avoid creating any new surplus in the market, the Russian energy minister told Reuters.

Alexander Novak also said in comments cleared for publication on Friday that he saw no direct connection between the oil cuts and Saudi Arabia's plan to list Saudi Aramco, the world's top oil producer. 'Everyone in the market is interested in achieving balance,' Novak said in response to a question on whether Saudi Arabia could abruptly exit the cuts as soon as it lists Aramco sometime in 2018. The share sale promises to be the world's biggest.

The Organization of the Petroleum Exporting Countries and other large oil producers led by Russia agreed last month to extend until the end of next year their deal to cut a combined 1.8 million barrels per day of output.

The move is aimed at clearing a global stocks overhang and propping up oil prices.

Russia and Saudi Arabia have significantly improved bilateral ties this year, resulting in a visit to Moscow by Saudi King Salman accompanied by a large political and business delegation.

Oil is a key source of budget revenue for both countries and Novak said he expected prices to fluctuate at $50-$60 per barrel next year.

2 The result of powerful market leaders is that sometimes they are able to successfully ban newcomers from their market. This means that there is not always unlimited access to markets by anyone who wants to compete. This can be done by dumping a product by temporary selling it below cost prize. It can also be done by tying a product to another unrelated product as we have seen in the Microsoft case. In both cases it will be really hard for a newcomer to enter the involved market.

The mediaplayer case

In chapter 6 we saw the case of Microsoft automatically adding Windows Media Player to their basic software package. This resulted in a de facto blocking of all new market participants who wanted to sell media players or similar type of products. Microsoft could manage to do this as a result of their dominant market position in the operating system software branch.

3 Consumers do not always make a rational decision in their 'customer journey' before they purchase a product. We would at first glance perhaps expect that a consumer will not buy an unethical product, and use his buying power to correct the unethical behaviour by purchasing a likewise product from a competitor that is not unethical. However, this will hardly work this way, since it seems that a person behaves differently in his role

Citizen-consumer-hypothesis

as a citizen compared to his role as a consumer (Batley et al. 2001). This phenomenon is called also called the 'citizen-consumer-hypothesis' (Curtis & McConnel, 2002). As we can see in the example, an individual might feel very much concerned about and involved with the wellbeing of farmers in developing countries, but at the same time in his capacity as a consumer not use his buying power accordingly. It has been proven that we can encourage consumers to use their buying power more often in line with their ethical reasoning as a citizen by providing them with accurate information about products and production processes (Gielissen, 2010). However, the vast majority of consumers will still choose with his wallet and not with his conscience.

Market research and Max Havelaar

In 1988, the Max Havelaar coffee label was introduced to the Dutch market. The idea was simple: give farmers in developing countries a fair prize for their coffee beans. One of the effects of the fierce competition in the coffee branch has always been that the farmer in developing countries was underpaid by the big coffee companies. Max havelaar should put an end to this practice, and become the first 'ethical' coffee brand on the Dutch markets, paying 10 percent more to the farmers than the average competitor would.

Before the brand was introduced, an extensive market research was done, from which the conclusion was drawn that Max Havelaar could expect to occupy 7 to 15 percent of the coffee market after its introduction: a very high percentage for a new coffee brand. However, the real numbers were disappointing: the market share appeared to be not even two percent after one year after introducing the concept. It appeared that the market research gave a false impression of the potential of the new brand. People filled out the questionnaires in a socially desirable way. Of course everyone was concerned about and involved with the fate of poor farmers in developing countries. And of course it would be reasonable to pay a little extra for a pack of coffee, knowing that the farmer would then receive a fair prize for his products. However, once in the supermarket, these concerned citizens started to behave like consumers, buying the cheapest, and not necessarily the fairest coffee (Roozen & Hoff, 2001).

4   A consumer is not always aware of what he buys. As we have already discussed in chapter 5.2, products and services become increasingly complex, as well as their product chain. This means that a consumer is not always aware of the exact (ethical) implications of the products or services he buys.

Consumer awareness and buying behaviour

When you walk into a shop and you see very young children under poor hygienic conditions performing tough labour, you will probably walk away and not buy anything in that shop. However, this hardly will be the case, as the shop in which you buy the end product will look fresh and clean, with nice and well-dressed salespeople looking to help you. That the children mentioned earlier might have been involved somewhere in the production process somewhere on the other side of the world is something you will probably never know. You buy the product, unaware of the

external implications the production process brings in the field of social (or ecological) values.
Or take the bakery that closed due to the negative publicity resulting from their refusal to sell a pie to the lesbian couple. The consumers who boycott the bakery might as well buy a lot of products that were produced abroad. Possibly in countries where homosexuality is a crime and punished accordingly. However, it is not doable to perform an extended research to each product you buy and carefully consider the origin and implications of the product. As a result, the consumer will be unaware of his own double standard in his buying behaviour.

In conclusion, we can establish that companies hardly compete on an equal footing with small and medium enterprises, and consumers are hardly aware of the ethical implications of the products and services they buy. It is therefore unlikely that that the system of supply and demand automatically corrects unethical company behaviour.

9.3 Voluntary accountability

Some authors hold the position that transparency and compliance should come from within the company voluntarily: an intrinsically motivated responsibility (Elkington, 1997; Henrique & Richardson, 2004). Driven by the social trends explained in chapter 5, we see an increasing amount of companies opening up en discuss how they comply with their goals in the field of social and ecological values. Internally, this is typically done by adopting an ethics code of conduct, sometimes accompanied by a body that should oversee the compliance with this code (for instance, and ethics committee). In the external relations, this is mostly done by implementing an external cost-accounting report cycle, in which the company shows to the outside world how it believes to comply with its own external goals.

9.3.1   Internal codes

An internal code is a company directive expressing social and environmental values that should be complied with within the organization.

Internal code

In practice, these internal codes have rather different names, and these names are mostly used as synonyms. However, we could argue that an ethics code, a values statement or business principles is a document predominantly expressing basic values that should serve as a solid basis for all company behaviour, where a code of conduct is a document specifying what behaviour is expected in realization of these values. In other words: the first express values where the second type stipulates norms. An example of a value-oriented statement can be found in the Philips case. An example of a norms/behaviour-oriented statement can be found in the Coca Cola case.

Philips General Business Principles (sample)
Fair Employment Practices

'We believe a diverse workforce and an inclusive work environment are essential to a thriving innovative business. We strive to attract employees from a wide range of backgrounds. We do not discriminate on the basis of race, color, age, gender, gender identity or expression, sexual orientation, language, religion, political or other opinions, disability, national or social origin or birth. We promote a workplace that is free from physical and verbal harassment. We do not tolerate any conduct that creates, encourages or permits an offensive, humiliating or intimidating work environment.

We do not make use of child labor or forced labor.
We recognize and respect the freedom of our employees to associate with any employee organization of their own choosing under local law without fear of reprisal, intimidation or harassment. Where employees are represented by a legally recognized union, we establish a constructive dialogue and engage in negotiations or consultation as required with their freely chosen representatives. We aim to maintain a healthy, safe and productive work environment' (Philips, 2014).

Code of business conduct, Coca-Cola Hellenic Bottling Company
Relatives and friends

'Many employees have relatives who are employed by or invest in or have substantial financial or commercial relationships with customers or suppliers of the Company. These financial interests do not create a conflict under the Code unless:
- you have discretionary authority in dealing with any of these companies as part of your job with the Company; or
- your relative deals with the Company on behalf of the other company.

In either of these situations, you must notify your Code Compliance Officers in writing, and you must renew this notification annually. If your relative is employed by a competitor of the Company, you must also notify your Code Compliance Officers, and renew it annually. You may have friends who are employed by, or have ownership interests in, customers or suppliers of the Company. If you deal with such a customer or supplier, take care to ensure that your friendship does not affect, or appear to affect, your ability to act in the best interest of the Company. If you are uncertain whether your friendship may create an issue, consult your manager or your Code Compliance Officers. In addition, personal relationships at work must not influence your ability to act in the best interest of the Company, and must not affect any employment relationship. Employment-related decisions should be based on qualifications, performance, skills and experience' (The Coca-Cola Company, 2015).

Next to value and behaviour-oriented codes, we could distinguish process-based and hybrid codes (Oakley & Buckland, 2004). A process-oriented code is not about the substance of ethics, but about the process or procedure that should lead to ethical behaviour. An example can be found in the IKEA case. Hybrid codes have elements of all the above. In practice, companies will have to use value, behaviour and process oriented codes to fully implement their ethics in the organization.

IKEA IWAY Standard

The IKEA Supplier shall always comply with the most demanding requirements whether they are relevant applicable laws or IKEA IWAY specific requirements. Should the IKEA requirement contradict national laws or regulations, the law shall always be complied with and prevail. In such cases, the Supplier shall immediately inform IKEA (IKEA, 2016).

Internal codes are initially nothing but written statements. Having a code does not say too much about the effectiveness of the code, as we have seen in the Wells Fargo Bank case. The way a code is implemented makes the difference. Of course, the better the quality of the codes and the supervision on compliance with that code, the better the outcome (Erwin, 2011). Research has shown that the way a code of conduct is communicated is crucial in the effect of such a code (Adam & Rachman-Moore, 2004). Most companies put their code on a website and notify the employees through their regular channels (for instance, by email or an internal website) alongside all other paperwork. This way, a code is easily ignored and only consulted when something bad already happened. A more active way of communicating and training is required to actually make sure the code is complied with.

Furthermore, from a sociological perspective, the code should be accepted in the company culture. The attitude of the management is crucial here. It is important that they act like a role model when it concerns internal codes, and make sure that non-compliance is not tolerated (Stevens, 2009). When unethical behaviour is tolerated this inevitably leads to skepticism amongst employees, creating a downward spiral in which the internal code gradually loses its importance (Nitsch et al. 2005).

9.3.2 Voluntary external cost-accounting

In chapter 8 we have already discussed external cost-accounting in detail. We have seen that companies can choose to undertake this kind of reporting. This is therefore mostly a voluntary form of accountability. The reporting in itself may be realized at company level, based on a methodology and criteria invented by the company (as we have seen in the Puma case). It could also happen at branch level, when an organization offers a forum through which companies can communicate their external reporting based on the same methods and criteria, as we have seen in the context of the Corporate Disclosure Project.

However, it is still the company that decides what data is revealed and how it is presented. This approach has obvious pros and cons.

The advantage is that companies are intrinsically motivated to report on their externalities, and how they comply with social and ecological values. The initiative comes from within, and if done in an honest way, it may lead to a learning curve and ongoing improvement of the company performance in the field of these externalities. As we have seen in the previous chapter, successful companies are sustainable companies. All the more reason to undertake external cost-accounting and enjoy its benefits.

The disadvantage is that voluntary accountability means that a company mostly judges its own performance. After all, the company decides what data is published (and perhaps more importantly what data is not), and how this data should be understood. It is therefore easy to paint a rosy picture about the company's performance regarding its externalities, and use it as a marketing tool (Farache & Perks, 2010).

This could lead to remarkable situations in which a company promotes its CSR to the outside world, while internally they do not practice what they preach. As we have seen in the previous chapter, a company like British Petroleum was considered as a relatively sustainable company using the SAM methodology. As it appeared, the fact that BP widely communicated their pledge to become a leader in clean energy played a significant role here. This is data the company chose to promote. When we consider the BP Sustainability report 2010, published in the year of the Deepwater Horizon disaster, we see a report in which BP does apologize for the harm caused, but furthermore continues to list the wonderful things the company did so far to correct the damage done. Only limited space is used to reflect on the incident and how to improve the business organization to prevent future incidents from happening (BP, 2010). This approach towards external

Greenwashing   cost-accounting is by some referred to as 'greenwashing' (Cherry & Sneirson, 2011).

The question could be raised whether it is meaningful when a company who produces unsustainable products promotes their CSR policies. Would an external cost-accounting report of a company producing oil products, cigarettes or even weapons (see example) make sense? On the one hand we could argue that we'd rather have a weapons producer who is concerned with ethics than one who does not care. On the other hand, we could argue that it is very likely that when a weapons manufacturer reports on their social and environmental standards and goals, this is just a way to cover up their bad behaviour.

BEA Systems and 'corporate responsibility'

The British company BEA Systems has a comprehensive code of conduct, subtitled 'doing the right thing' (BEA Systems, 2018). The company annually reports on how they contribute in the realization of social and environmental values. In support, the company established an ethics helpline that can be consulted by anyone who works in the organization who is confronted with an ethics dilemma. The CSR areas of focus are:

1 the development of an inclusive, diverse workplace to drive innovation and performance
2 instilling responsible behaviour to be a trusted partner
3 supporting customer confidence in our business by continuously improving standards of safety for employees and those using our products
4 proactively managing the environmental impacts of our facilities and products to improve efficiencies and cost savings (BAY Systems, 2016)

Minimizing environmental impact
In the context of the latter, the company reported in their 2016 annual report that: 'We are committed to minimising the environmental impact of our operations. Resource efficiency is an important measure of business effectiveness at BAE Systems and is embedded within our Environment Policy. As a major manufacturer, our operations have an impact on the environment – from the energy and resources we use to the waste that we generate. Minimising this impact shrinks our environmental footprint and

reduces our operating costs. Each of our businesses sets annual targets to use resources as efficiently as possible with a focus on energy, water and waste. We are improving energy efficiency and de-carbonising our energy supply to reduce greenhouse gas emissions. The nature of our business, with large-scale projects and fluctuations in orders, makes it challenging to set a global emissions reduction goal. We set energy targets at business level that contribute to an overall reduction. The majority of our greenhouse gas emissions come from the energy we use across our facilities. The Group's total greenhouse gas emissions decreased by 4% in the 12 months to 31 October 2016.'(BAE, 2016)

CEO statement
The company CEO stated in the code of conduct that: 'Being a responsible business is about doing the right thing – legally and ethically – in a way that continually earns us the trust of all our stakeholders. This is absolutely fundamental to everything we do, particularly given the sensitive nature of the work we are entrusted with and our vital role in helping to defend national security and prosperity' (BEA, 2018).

Perhaps you wonder what exactly this company produces? BEA Systems manufactures products and services in the field of defence, aviation and security. In other words: it is a weapons manufacturer.

9.4 Mandatory accountability

As we have seen in the previous section, some may argue that voluntary accountability is meaningless, and just a marketing tool. One of the reasons why voluntary accountability would not work is that there are hardly any consequences in case of non-compliance, which is at odds with the grave impact a company can have in the field of social and ecological values. Therefore, some authors argue that accountability should be a mandatory thing, enforced by legislation (Bennet & Van der Lugt, 2004). This would lead to a situation in which each company is assessed the same way, faces similar consequences in case of non-compliances, and these consequences are serious enough to take them into due consideration when acting. Problem solved, we might think. However, things are not as simple as they seem. While this might work at national level, on a global level this would be problematic. There are two major problems with this approach reducing it to mainly a theoretical option, and not a very practical one: it has proven to be very difficult to agree on international laws, and even more difficult to find appropriate enforcing mechanisms.

On a global level there are many different perceptions on what is morally right and wrong. The political differences here are often simply too complicated to bridge. Unanimous agreement on how things should progress in this world has proven to be very difficult to achieve regarding social, environmental and economic values. For instance, the adoption of human right treaties in which social values are globally recognized has always been the result of lengthy negotiations, leading to political compromises rather than a clear set of rules (Wernaart, 2013). We also saw in chapter 7 that it has proven to be impossible to agree on specific outcomes or CO_2 reduction in a climate agreement as the Paris Agreement. Another striking example of how global decision-making processes seem to be complicated is the negotiations in the context of the world's largest trade institution: the World Trade Organization. Since 2001, all major negotiations to further liberalize markets and level the playing field for market participants are stuck and countries are hardly willing to move away from their initial position (Fergusson, 2008; Cho, 2010), as we can see in the newspaper item below.

THE NEW YORK TIMES, 1 JANUARY 2016

Global Trade After the Failure of the Doha Round

By: The editorial board

After 14 years of talks, members of the World Trade Organization have effectively ended the Doha round of negotiations. That was not unexpected given how fruitless these discussions have been. Now, world leaders need to think anew about the global trading system. Countries had hoped that the talks, named after the capital of Qatar, where they began in late 2001, would substantially lower trade barriers, contribute to development in poor nations and tackle difficult issues like agricultural subsidies that were not resolved in earlier pacts, like the General Agreement on Tariffs and Trade. Failure to achieve this ambitious agenda has undermined the credibility of the multilateral trading system and hurt the least-developed countries, which are desperate to export more of their goods to richer countries.

At a meeting of the W.T.O. in mid-December in Nairobi, trade ministers from more than 160 countries failed to agree that they should keep the negotiations going. In recent years, it became clear that the talks, which were originally supposed to conclude in 2005, were paralyzed because neither developed economies like the United States and the European Union nor developing countries like China and India were willing or able to make fundamental concessions (...).

The enforcement of international rules is often even more complicated (Wernaart, 2013). The power of a national court does usually not reach beyond the border if its jurisdiction, while multinational companies can, as we have seen in Chapter 5. Attempts to install global courts or tribunals that have the authority to enforce internationally binding rules mostly failed. Although there is an International Court of Justice in The Hague, this court is mostly ineffective, since this court is only recognized by 72 countries, and its competencies are not recognized by important countries such as the U.S., China, Russia and France. Besides that, the court has no jurisdiction over private entities such as companies, only over countries (Malenczuk, 1997). In short: we should not expect binding rules on ethics in business on a global level (Porrit, 2004).

The only court that is truly effective and stands above nations is the regional European Court of Justice, supervising the correct implementation of European law. In most other situations, international rules are accompanied by complaint procedures, reporting duties and obliged consultation between groups of countries to effectuate the adopted law. Such procedures are considerably weaker compared to a court that has a final say in how law should be executed and understood, and has the means to effectuate its verdicts. While the EU did not yet adopt legislation that is specifically about accountability, some legislation strongly relates to this issue. For instance, Directive 2013/34/EU harmonizes the rules in the EU Member States on financial accounting. In addition, an action plan was adopted by the European Commission (2012) on corporate governance, focusing on transparency, external accounting and stakeholder management. Such an action plan might be a basis for further legislation.

This means that, with the notable exception of EU law, international rules are not easy to create or enforce, and mostly depend on the willingness of multinational organizations to comply with these rules.
Plenty of examples of international standards that relate to social or ecological values were discussed in the chapters above. For instance, as we have seen in Chapter 6, the International Labour Organization (ILO) represents the interest of workers worldwide, and adopts treaties on issues as child labour, working hours, healthy working conditions, fair remuneration and so on. There is a very mild enforcing mechanism that oversees ILO legislation: a complaint mechanism in which countries can complain about the misbehaviour of another country. Due to the fear of political retaliation, such procedures – especially in the field of human rights – are hardly ever used (Ssenyonjo, 2009). Besides that, complaints cannot directly address the behaviour of companies, but at most the failure of a country to enforce laws on this company (Dahan et al., 2013).

Another example would be the OECD Guidelines for Multinational Enterprises, adopted by the Organization for Economic Cooperation and Development: an economic partnership between 34 of the most developed countries in the world. While these guidelines date back to 1976, they were revised many times since they were initially drafted. The core message of these guidelines is that companies should contribute to the economic, ecological and social progress to promote sustainable development (OECD guidelines for multinational enterprises, 2011). Again, there hardly is an enforcing mechanism, and the implementation of these guidelines greatly depends on the willingness of companies to comply.

Does this mean that international law is dysfunctional and fruitless towards the accountability of companies? The answer is probably no. Companies are inspired by the global legislative agenda, and mostly pledge themselves to comply with these norms, even though there are no real consequences when they do not. As we can see in the Adidas example, the company pledges itself not to violate the Universal Declaration on Human Rights, and the relevant ILO conventions.

Adidas on Human Rights

'The adidas Group supports the United Nations' Universal Declaration of Human Rights. Our company policies and procedures adhere to all applicable domestic laws and are consistent with core labour principles of the International Labour Organization (ILO) concerning freedom of association and collective bargaining, non-discrimination, forced labour, and underage workers in the workplace. Promoting human rights and adhering to ILO core labour standards internally and throughout all our business operations is in line with the Group's values and principles. Our commitment to foster the implementation of human rights and core labour standards is supported through our Human Resources function, the programme for Legal Compliance and Social & Environmental Affairs. It is in effect in all Adidas Group locations and it applies to the Group's business operations worldwide (Adidas, 2011).'

9.5 Collective industry self-regulation

Especially at the level of multinationals we can observe a development in which companies increasingly engage in new partnerships that reach beyond the traditional boundaries of their own product chain. Companies increasingly see the benefits of working together with a variety of stakeholders, such as governments, Non-Governmental Organizations and competitors (Elkington, 1997). An example is the partnership between IKEA and the WWF, as we can see in the news item below.

THE ADVOCATE, 29 JANUARY 2017

Ikea and WWF cotton initiative working its way around the globe

By: Lucy Cormack
(...)
Ikea uses around one per cent of the world's yearly supply of cotton – last year it used 140,000 tonnes.

Its bedspreads, sofas, sheets and mattresses all rely heavily on cotton, more than half of which is sourced from India and Pakistan.

In those regions the natural fibre is referred to as the 'king of textiles', a 'cash crop' which in India employs 60 million people.

But while cotton is the fibre of choice for consumers, homewares and clothing manufacturers, its production comes at a cost.

More than 10,000 litres of water is needed to grow just one kilogram, pesticides and fertilisers are used intensively, and biodiversity loss, chemical poisoning and child labour have all plagued the industry.
(...)
This led to the formation of a partnership between the furniture manufacturer and conservation group WWF in 2004, with the goal of making conventional cotton farming more sustainable.

The result was the Better Cotton Initiative (BCI), a global program which now has more than 850 members, including H&M, Levi Strauss & Co., Marks and Spencer, Marimekko and Burberry.

Members who have joined the initiative commit to a range of social and environmental requirements, including fair work practices and regulated use of land, chemicals and water.

When it began more than 10 years ago, BCI attracted just 500 farmers from India and Pakistan, most of whom 'were not ready to listen to the environmental or social issues; they were only interested in saving money,' says Arif Makhdum, of WWF Pakistan.

But after a year of positive results, the project was expanded and by 2010, the first licensed BCI harvest took place in Brazil, India, Mali and Pakistan.

Now it is farmed all over the world, from China, to Africa, Israel, the US and Australia. For Samadhan, joining BCI meant going against all the farming practices he and generations before him had followed, but it paid off.

Where once he earned $240-300 per acre, he now earns $1200, while halving costs on water and chemicals.

Reducing the use of unnecessary pesticides has also led to an improvement in his health.

'After [joining] BCI, the comforts of life have increased,' he says.

As BCI farmers report their success, more and more join the movement, which has grown from 500 farmers in 2004 to 44,000 today.

By 2020 BCI aims to have 5 million farmers producing 8.2 million metric tonnes of 'Better Cotton' by 2020, or 30 per cent of global cotton production.(...)

One way to improve the external effects of an industry on social and ecological values could be by engaging in a collective agreement on how to open up the business (transparency) and how to comply with the rules all shareholders agree on.

> Collective industry self-regulation is a way to establish joint transparency and accountability within an industry by adopting an industry-wide approach towards social and environmental values.

Collective industry self-regulation

In a way, this approach towards accountability is somewhere between voluntary and mandatory (see figure 9.5). Voluntary, because companies choose to engage in these partnerships and agreements. Mandatory, because the network from which this industry self-regulation sterns demands compliance, and no compliance leads to consequences that are much more serious than some angry partner's faces.

FIGURE 9.5 Accountability and self-regulation

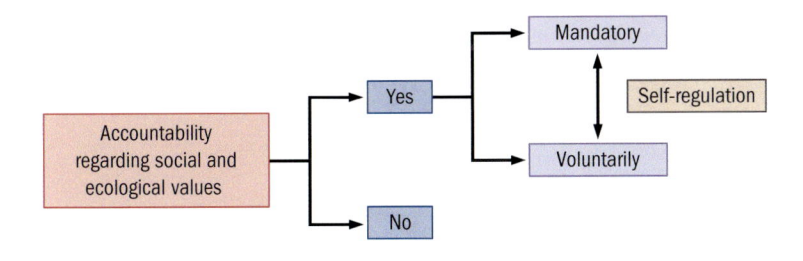

We could say that here are at least three reasons why companies will be highly motivated to comply with collective industry self-regulation. First, because it mostly is their own idea. It is the companies themselves who engage in these partnerships and contribute drafting these regulations. This is different from a government forcing industry rules down the throats of these companies. On the contrary, the rules come from within the industry. For a company it is more convenient to comply with rules they believe are important compared to rules that are enforced on them.

A second motivation could be that it makes legislators less eager to adopt legally binding rules in a certain branch when this branch already regulated things amongst themselves. Especially when you are able to regulate good company behaviour in a better way than a government could ever do, for instance because your industry self-regulation can cross a border (domestic laws cannot) or when an industry-wide complaint mechanism works more efficient than litigation ever would (OECD committee on consumer policy, 2015).

Thirdly, companies risk serious image damage when they do not comply with or do not participate in collective industry-self regulation. A striking example is the newspaper item in which we can see that companies in the garment industry that did not renew their pledges towards the Bangladesh-Accord, were confronted with some negative headlines.

CHARTERED INSTITUTE OF PROCUREMENT AND SUPPLY (CIPS) NEWS, 29 JANUARY 2018

British brands delay signing Bangladesh accord

By: Francis Churchill

A collection of UK brands have been accused of delaying their decision to re-commit to the Bangladesh fire and building safety accord.
John Lewis, Marks and Spencer, Debenhams and Next have yet to sign the new agreement, while Sainsbury's has decided not to sign at all.
Jenny Holdcroft, assistant general secretary of IndustriALL, one of the founders of the accord, said it was 'quite unusual' for a group of brands to collectively not sign.
Speaking to SM, she said that there are other small brands that have not yet signed. But the high street brands from the UK stand out as the only large group sourcing from Bangladesh that have not yet signed.
(...)
The agreement was a direct response to the 2013 Rana Plaza disaster, where more than 1,100 people died when a factory collapsed. The deal expires in May and is to be replaced by the 2018 Transition Accord – which is substantially the same as the original agreement.

The new accord has already been signed by global brands that include H&M, Adidas, Inditex – which owns Zara – and Primark.
(...)
But Holdcroft said that by delaying their decision to sign the new accord was bringing uncertainty to the deal. 'It means that it's not clear that the factories that provide to [the UK retailers] will even be covered by the new accord,' she said.
'The first signatures (to the new accord) were made in June last year... Now the work needs to be done to figure what budget we need, what operations we need,' she said. There is a lot of work to be done, and those who have not yet made the commitment to continue are not part of that, she added.
Brands that do not sign up to the accord are opened up to reputational risk, Holdcroft warned. 'If the UK brands don't sign the accord then they're leaving it to other brands to carry the can and to make sure that the factories remain safe and the industry remains safe for everybody who continues to source from Bangladesh.'
(...)

9.5.1 Case study: the Bangladesh Accord

Bangladesh is the home of over 163 million citizens of which more than 4 million people work in the garment industry: the backbone of the Bangladeshi economy. To give an impression: in 2015, the total value of the Bangladeshi exported products amounting to 31.7 billion U.S. dollar, of which 28.3 billion would be produced in the garment industry. This means that more than 89 per cent of exported goods where clothes (wits. worldbank.org, 2018). The minimum wage in the garment industry is around 50 euros per month, which comes down to one of the lowest minima in the region. This explains why Bangladesh is such an attractive supplier for fashion brands all over the world, especially in the U.S. and Europe, who are the most important export markets of Bangladesh. However, this attractiveness clearly has a dark side: the Bangladeshi garment industry is notorious for the unhealthy and unsafe working conditions in their factories. Unfortunately it took a disaster before any joint action was taken to improve these conditions: the collapse of the Rana Plaza building. Despite the fact that there are visible cracks in the wall, the workers were still being forced to work there (Roeland, 2014). As it appeared, the building collapsed due to a cocktail of unfortunate but foreseeable circumstances. One of the main causes was the fact that a building, originally intended for commercial use, was mainly used as a factory. Three additional floors were illegally added to the building, as we can see in the newspaper item below.

9

DHAKA TRIBUNE, 19 APRIL 2017

Rana Plaza collapse: Order on charge framing against Sohel Rana, others May 8

By: Md Sanaul Islam Tipu

Judge Md Ataoar Rahman of Dhaka Divisional Special judges' court set the date on Wednesday after a charge framing hearing against those accused in a case filed by the Anti Corruption Commission (ACC).

A Dhaka court has fixed May 8 to pass an order on charge framing in a corruption case filed against 18 people, including building owner Sohel Rana, over the deadly Rana Plaza collapse in 2013.

The Rana Plaza tragedy made global headlines on April 24, 2013 when an eight-storey garment factory building in the Savar district north of Dhaka collapsed, killing over 1,100 people.

The local municipality had given approval in 2007 for the construction of only a five-storey building on the wetland plot, but the owners added three more levels to the

commercial complex, which eventually resulted in the catastrophic collapse.

On June, 15, 2014, the ACC filed the case on charge of constructing Rana Plaza building with faulty design. A month later, ACC Deputy Director M Mofidul Islam, also investigation officer of the case, submitted the charge-sheet against 18 people, including Sohel Rana, in the graft case.

The accused named in the charge-sheet include: Sohel Rana, and his parents Abdul Khaleque and Marjina Begum; Savar municipality mayor Refat Ullah; former chief executive officer of Savar municipality, Uttam Kumar Roy, and its executive engineer, Rafiqul Islam; former commissioner Haji M Ali Khan; architect ATM Masud Reza; Sajjad Hossain; and former town planner of Savar municipality, Farjana Islam.

Bangladesh Accord

The Rana Plaza disaster received worldwide media attention, and led to a sharp debate about the exact role and responsibilities of the companies that are supplied by the Bangladeshi garment industry. This public debate eventually triggered the adoption of the Bangladesh Accord. The accord is a five-year agreement that was signed the 5th of May 2013 and renewed for another three year in 2017. In essence, the accord is a contract between global brands and retailers and labour unions, with the aim to improve the workers conditions in the garment industry of Bangladesh. The accord was signed by 200 brands, retailers and importers, 2 global and eight local trade unions, as well as four observing Non-Governmental Organizations. The Bangladeshi Government approved the accord and agrees on the goal to ultimately embed the principles of the accord in national legislation from 2021 onwards. Furthermore, the International Labour Organization provides support in implementing the Accord through its Bangladeshi office. It can be said that all relevant stakeholders are represented in the agreement as either signatory, observer, or supporter.

The main terms of the agreement are:
1 'a five year legally binding agreement between brands and trade unions to ensure a safe working environment in the Bangladeshi RMG industry
2 an independent inspection program supported by brands in which workers and trade unions are involved
3 public disclosure of all factories, inspection reports and corrective action plans (CAP)
4 a commitment by signatory brands to ensure sufficient funds are available for remediation and to maintain sourcing relationships
5 democratically elected health and safety committees in all factories to identify and act on health and safety risks
6 worker empowerment through an extensive training program, complaints mechanism and right to refuse unsafe work' (Accord on fire and Building Safety in Bangladesh, 2013)

The effects of the Accord were diverse. Some things did change for the benefit of the employees, while other terms seemed promising but did not live up to the expectations. What did seem to work was the inspection program, through a special committee, and the complaint mechanism through which employees could blow the whistle when they observed unsafe working practices. In a 2018 report, the Bangladesh Accord Secretariat wrote that so far, 83 per cent of the identified safety issues were solved, 699 factories have completed more than 90 per cent of the improvements needed to ensure a safe working environment. Furthermore, it was reported that the business with 96 suppliers was terminated as a result of not complying with the Accord programme. Also, 407 complaints were received by workers, out of which 183 were solved and 96 still under investigation. That sounds promising indeed.

However, not everything worked as it should have. First, not all brands joined the Accord. Especially the North American companies where not so fond of the phrase 'legally binding' and initiated their own alternative accord: the Alliance for Bangladesh Worker Safety: an agreement that was criticized for encompassing less and more flexible obligations for its signatories (Greenhouse & Clifford, 2013). Second, the empowerment expected from the Bangladeshi Government was barely realized. The protection of labour unions was lacking, and violations of the right to form such a union were not effectively prosecuted. Despite the fact that the Bangladeshi Government agreed on a so called Bangladesh Sustainability Compact with mostly EU business partners, it did not seem to be able to seriously change the fundamental rights of workers using laws and law enforcement (Vogt, 2017; Kenner & Peake, 2017). Third, the expected compensation damage that would be paid to relatives of the victims was much lower than anticipated, as we can see in the newspaper item. This led to yet another public debate on how companies lived up to the expectations and how they saw their responsibility towards the victims.

THE FINANCIAL TIMES, 20 APRIL 2015

How Benetton faced up to the aftermath of Rana Plaza

THE ITALIAN APPAREL COMPANY HAS CHANGED ITS APPROACH TO ITS RESPONSIBILITIES TOWARDS GARMENT WORKERS.

By: Amy Kazmin

Benetton is renowned for visually striking and provocative adverts focusing on social causes such as HIV/Aids or race relations. But in February the Italian apparel company became the target of a campaign that pointedly imitated the multicultural style of its United Colors of Benetton marketing. The billboard – mounted on a van and driven round Treviso, home of Benetton's global headquarters, for several days – was the handiwork of activists dismayed by its failure to pay into a compensation fund for victims of the collapse of the Rana Plaza garment factory building in Bangladesh in 2013.'Benetton: show your true colours,' demanded the slogan. The photograph on the billboard was of a Bangladeshi woman on a stretcher, four days after being rescued from the rubble of the building on the outskirts of Dhaka, the Bangladesh capital. (…)
Marco Airoldi, the former Boston Consulting Group partner who took charge as Benetton's chief executive in May 2014, just over a year after the disaster, concedes that the activists' campaign was 'a bit of a kick'. Waged at some of Benetton's European stores and on social media, as well as on the streets of Treviso, it drove home the need for the Italian company to deal with unfinished business connected to Rana Plaza, from which it sourced about 266,000 shirts in the six months before the tragedy.

Now Mr Airoldi hopes Benetton is closing a chapter in the story with its move last week to pay $1.1m into The Rana Plaza Trust Fund, just ahead of the second anniversary of the disaster on Friday.
(…)
In the immediate aftermath of the tragedy, Benetton had paid $500,000 to BRAC, a respected Bangladeshi non-governmental organisation, to help victims access urgent medical care and longer-term support. Benetton's $1.1m announcement fell short of the $5m western labour unions and social activists had hoped it would pay given Benetton's image as a socially conscious brand. But Mr Airoldi insists it has fulfilled its responsibility.

9

We will have to await the future effects of the renewed commitments expressed in the 2018 accord. Of particular importance will be whether companies keep up with the pace that is required to realize actual change in the position of workers (and are not too much led by public awareness, which will decline in the end). Another important prerequisite for success will be the capacity of the Bangladeshi Government to fully implement the tools it is offered and make use of its legislative and enforcement powers to support the commitment of the involved stakeholders.

9

Summary

▶ Accountability means that a company is transparent with regard to their corporate responsibilities and act accordingly.

▶ One of the ideas about accountability is that the sole responsibility of a company is to maximize its profits, as suggested by Milton Friedman.
- Why Milton Friedman could be right:
  - Only real people can be accountable for the realization of social and ecological values.
  - Accountability towards social and ecological values constitutes an undemocratic form of taxation.
  - Accountability towards social and ecological values creates limitations to economic growth and innovation.
  - The markets will automatically correct unethical behaviour.

- Why Milton Friedman could be wrong:
  - A company can very well be accountable in the field of social and ecological values, since it creates a shared morality that transcends the individual.
  - Accountability towards social and ecological values is necessary as a result of privatization.
  - Accountability in respect of social and ecological values will lead to economic growth and innovation.
  - Accountability in respect of social and ecological values will not automatically be corrected by the markets because there is no perfect competition.

▶ Some authors hold the position that transparency and compliance should come from within the company voluntarily.

▶ Voluntary accountability is typically done by adopting internal codes and implementing external cost-accounting procedures.
- Pros:
  - Companies have a better understanding of its external business performance.
  - Companies are intrinsically motivated to work on improvements in the field of social and environmental values.
- Cons:
  - A company judges its own performance based on their own criteria. This can easily lead to window dressing, using external cost-accounting as a marketing tool.

9

▶ An internal code is a company directive expressing social and environmental values that should be complied with within the organization. We could make a distinction between:
- value-oriented codes: a document predominantly expressing basic values that should serve as a solid basis for all company behaviour
- norm/behaviour-oriented code: a document specifying what this behaviour is expected in realization of the company values
- process oriented code: stipulates the process or procedure that should lead to ethical behaviour
- hybrid code: a mixture of the above

▶ Some authors argue that accountability should be mandatory, enforced by legislation.
- Pros:
  - No room for window dressing.
  - Companies are assessed based on the same terms using the same methodology.
- Cons:
  - It has been proven to be very difficult to agree on international laws.
  - There hardly are any effective enforcing mechanisms in international law.

▶ Collective industry self-regulation is a way to establish joint transparency and accountability within an industry by adopting an industry-wide approach towards social and environmental values.

▶ Companies are motivated to comply with such industry self-regulation because:
- The regulation was adopted on their own initiative.
- It prevents the intervention of lawmakers with binding legislation.
- The company risks significant image damage when they do not comply with this self-regulation.

▶ The Bangladesh-accord is an example of collective industry self-regulation in the garment industry.

Literature

Adam, M.A. & Rachman-Moore. D. (2004). The methods used to implement an ethical code of conduct and employee attitudes. *Journal of Business Ethics*, vol. 54, pp. 225-244.

Alexandrov, S.A. (2006). The compulsory jurisdiction of the International Court of Justice: how compulsory is it? *Chinese Journal of International Law* (2006) 5 (1): 29-38.

Batley, S., Colbourne, D., Fleming, P., & Urwin, P. (2001). Citizen versus consumer: challenges in the UK green power market. *Energy Policy*, 29, 479-487.

Bennet, N., & Van Der Lugt, C. van. (2004). Tracking global governance and sustainability: is the system working? In: A. Henriques & J. Richardson (Red), *The Triple Bottom Line, does it all add up? Assessing the sustainability of business and CSR (pp. 45-58)*. London: *Earth Scan, UK edition*.

Cherry, M.A. & Sneirson, J.F. (2011). Beyond profit: rethinking Corporate Social Responsibility after the BP oil disaster. *Tulane Law Review*, vol 85. (2010-2011).

Cho, S. (2010). The demise of development of the Doha round negotiations. *Texas International Law Review*, vol. 45, pp. 573-601.

Crane, W., & Matten, D. (2016). Framing business ethics. In: *Business Ethics*. Oxford: Oxford University Press.

Curtis, J., & McConnel, K. (2002). The citizen versus consumer hypothesis: Evidence from a quota valuation survey. *The Australian Journal of Agricultural and Resource Economics*, *46*:1, 69-83.

Dahan, Y., Lerner, H. & Milman-Sivan, F. (2013). Shared Responsibility and the International Labour Organization. *Michigan Journal of International Law.* Vol. 34, Issue 4, pp. 675-294.

Dardi, M. (2012). The perfect competition paradigm: evolving from its ambiguities. L'Harmattan: *Papers in political economy,* 2012/2 no 63, pp. 219-231.

Elkington, J. (1997). *Cannibals with forks.* Oxford: Caps Tone Publishers.

Erwin, P.M. (2011*)*. Corporate Codes of Conduct: The Effects of Code Content and Quality on Ethical Performance. Springer: *Journal of Business Ethics,* April 2011, Vol. 99, Issue 4, pp. 535–548.

Farache, F. & Perks, K.J. (2010). CSR advertisements: a legitimacy tool? *Corporate Communications: An International Journal*, vol. 15, issue: 3, pp. 235-248.

Fergusson, I. (2008). *CRS report for congress: World Trade Organization negotiations: The Doha Development Agenda*. Congressional Research Service.

Gielissen, R. (2010). *How consumers make a difference: An inquiry into the nature and causes or buying socially responsible products.* Oisterwijk: Boxpress.

Henriques, A. (2004). Sustainability and the triple bottom line. In: A. Henriques & J. Richardson (Editors), *The Triple Bottom Line, does it all add up? Assessing the sustainability of business and CSR* (pp. 26-33). London: Earth Scan, UK edition.

Henriques, A. & Richardson, J. (Editors). (2004). *The Triple Bottom Line, does it all add up? Assessing the sustainability of business and CSR*. London: Earth Scan, UK edition.

Jansen, E. (2012). *Corporate Governance & Social Responsibility: Challenges regarding accountability.* Proceedings of International Conference on Corporate Governance (pp. 341-350).

Kenner, J. & Peake, K. (2017). The Bangladesh Sustainability Compact: An Effective Exercise of Global Experimentalist EU Governance? *Cambridge yearbook of European legal studies*, vol. 19, Dec. 2017, pp.86-115.

9

King, S. (2008). *Pink Ribbon Inc.* Minneapolis: University of Minnesota Press.

Malenczuk, P. (1997). The Charter and the organs of the United Nations. In: *Akehurst's modern introduction to international law.* London: Routeledge.

MOA. (2004). *Control Appeals Committee Code of Conduct Research & Statistics.* MOA.

MOA. (2010). *Code of Conduct research and statistics.* MOA.

Nitsch, D., Baetz, M & Hughes, J.C. (2005). Why code of conduct violations go unreported: A conceptual framework to guide intervention and future research. *Journal of Business Ethics*, vol. 57, pp. 327- 341.

Oakley, R., & Buckland, I. (2004). What if business as usual won't work? In: A. Henriques & J. Richardson (Editors), *The Triple Bottom Line, does it all add up? Assessing the sustainability of business and CSR* (pp. 131-141). London: Earth Scan, UK edition.

OECD committee on consumer policy. (2015). *Industry self-regulation: role and use in supporting consumer interests.* DSTI/CP(2014)4/Final.

Porrit, J. (2004). Locating the Government's bottom line. In: A. Henriques & J. Richardson (Editors), *The Triple Bottom Line, does it all add up? Assessing the sustainability of business and CSR* (pp. 59/69). London: Earth Scan, UK edition.

Roozen, N., & Hoff, F. van. (2002). *Fair trade, het verhaal achter Max Havelaar coffee, Oké-Bananen en Kuyichi-Jeans.* Amsterdam: Uitgeverij Van Gennip.

Ssenyonjo, M. (2009). *Economic, Social and Cultural Rights in International Law.* Portland: Hart Publishing.

Stevens, B. (2009). Corporate ethical codes as strategic documents: an analysis of success and failure. *Electronic Journal of Business Ethics and Organization Studies*, vol. 14, no. 2, pp. 14-20.

Sustainia. (2018). *Global Opportunity Report 2018.* Oslo: DNV GL AS.

The ICC/Esomar. (2007). *ICC/Esomar international code on market and social research.* ICC/Esomar.

Tripsas, M. *(1997).* Unravelling the process or creative destruction: complementary assets and incumbent survival in typeletter industry. *Strategic Management Journal*, Vol. 18 (Summer Special Issue), 119-142.

Ven, B. van de, & Jeurissen, R. (2007). Corporate social responsibility and strategy. In: *Ethics and business.* Assen: Van Gorcum.

Vogt, J. (2017). The Bangladesh Sustainability Compact: an effective tool for promoting worker's rights? *Politics and Governance,* vol. 5, issue 4, pp. 80-92.

Wernaart, B. (2013). *The human right to adequate food, a comparative study.* Wageningen: Wageningen Academic Publishers.

Wernaart, B. (2017). International cooperation: The United Nations. In: *International law and business, a global introduction.* Groningen: Noordhoff Uitgevers.

Media

Astakhova, O. (2017, 22 December). Russia backs gradual, managed exit from oil cuts with OPEC. *Reuters.*

Brothers, J. (2014, 22 October). Breast cancer awareness month brings the usual 'pinkwashing' and unethical cause-marketing partnerships. *The Huffington Post.*

Churchill, F. (2018, 29 January). British brands delay signing Bangladesh accord. *Chartered Institute of Procurement and Supply.*

Editorial Board. (2016, 1 January). Global trade after the failure of the Doha Round. *The New York Times.*

Egan, M. (2017, 6 April). Wells Fargo's whistleblower problem worsens. *CNN.*

Friedman, M. (1970, 13 September). The Social Responsibility of business is to increase its profit. *The New York Times Magazine.*

Glazer, E. (2016, 16 September). How Wells Fargo's High-Pressure Sales Culture Spiraled Out of Control. *The Wall Street Journal.*

Goodwin, R. (2013, 3 April). The history of mobile phones: 1973 to 2007. *Capgemini.*

Greenhouse, S. & Clifford, S. (2013, 10 July). U.S. retailers offer plan for safety at factories. *The New York Times.*

9

Kazmin, A. (2015, 20 April). How Benetton faced up to the aftermath of Rana Plaza. *The Financial Times.*

Pastin, M. (2017, 20 January). The surprise ethics lesson of Wells Fargo. *The Huffington Post.*

Robinson, B. & Brennan, C. (2015, 3 July). 'He's doing this to the wrong Christian': Bakers hit out after court rules that they must pay $135k to lesbian couple after they refused to make them a wedding cake. *The Daily Mail.*

Roeland, P. (2014, 26 May). Rana Plaza: a man-made disaster that shook the world. *Clean Clothes Campaign.*

Tipu, M. (2017, 19 April). Rana Plaza collapse: Order on charge framing against Sohel Rana, others May 8. *Dhaka Tribune.*

Williamson, L. (2012, 27 April). Samsung overtakes Nokia in mobile phone shipments. *BBC News.*

Legislation, regulations and verdicts

Board of Governors of the Federal Reserve System. (2018, 2 February). *Accountability as Chair of Wells Fargo & Company Board of Directors.*

CFPB. (2016). Wells Fargo Bank, *Administrative Proceeding 2016-CFPB-0015.*

European Commission. (2012). *Action Plan: European company law and corporate governance - a modern legal framework for more engaged shareholders and sustainable companies.* COM/2012/0740 final.

European Parliament and Council. (2013, 26 June). *Directive 2013/34/EU on the annual financial statements, consolidated financial statements and related reports of certain types of undertakings.*

OECD. (2011). *OECD Guidelines for Multinational Enterprises, recommendations for corporate responsibility in a global context.* OECD.

OPEC. (2012). *Statute.* Vienna: OPEC Secretariat.

Warren, E. (2016, 20 September). An examination of Wells Fargo's unauthorized accounts and the regulatory response. *U.S. Senate: the committee on banking, housing and urban affairs.*

Business codes

2018 Accord on Fire and Building Safety in Bangladesh: May 2018, signed 21 June 2017.

Accord on Fire and Building Safety in Bangladesh, 15 May 2013

Adidas. (2011). *Labour Rights Charta.* Adidas.

BEA Systems. (2018). *Code of conduct, doing the right thing.* BEA Systems.

Coca-Cola Hellenic Bottling Company. (2015). *Code of Business Conduct, integrity in the company, integrity in the community.* The Coca-Cola Hellenic Bottling Company.

IKEA. (2016). *IWAY standard, Minimum Requirements for Environment and Social & Working Conditions when purchasing products, materials and services.* IKEA.

Philips. (2014). *Philips general business principles, your guide to acting with integrity.* Philips.

Annual reports

BAE systems. (2016). *Annual report 2016.* BAE systems.

Bangladesh Accord Secretariat. (2018). Quarterly aggregate report - on remediation progress at RGM factories covered by the Accord, 24 January 2018.

BP. (2010). *Sustainability review 2010.* BP.

Websites

http://bangladeshaccord.org

www.sustainia.me

https://wits.worldbank.org, Bangladesh Export in thousand US$ for all products World between 2012 and 2016, retrieved in March 2018.

PART 3
Ethics in a globalized world

In this section we discuss ethics in the context of a globalized world. As a result of fading borders, we are increasingly confronted with cultural differences. Sometimes these differences are easy to overcome, but sometimes these differences are almost impossible to bridge. In Chapter 10 therefore, we will discuss the relation between ethics and cultural diversity. Furthermore, we will discuss in Chapter 11 the idea of global trade, the trade liberalization agenda and the resulting moral dilemmas.

10
Cultural diversity

10.1   Culture
10.2   Cultural differences on various levels
10.3   Cultural differences and business
10.4   Cultural differences between countries

In this chapter we discuss the relation between ethics and cultural diversity.
We first discuss the significance of culture and how we can approach
cultural differences. Then, we will discuss into more detail the various levels
at which cultural diversity may lead to dilemmas in ethics. We continue with
exploring the role of business in cultural diversity. Finally we will discuss
cultural differences at the country level, using the famous Hofstede model
as a starting point.

10

10.1 Culture

As we already saw in Chapter 1, norms and values can be culturally determined. In essence, culture represents a shared morality on some aspects of ethics by its people.

Culture represents

> Culture represents shared norms and values amongst a certain group of individuals that feel part of the same culture.

People who feel that they belong to the same culture have similar norms and values regarding certain topics. They may express this in shared habits, customs and traditions. Think about table manners during dinner. How much do we eat when food is served (do we eat everything that is served or perhaps we leave some food on our plates?), who pays the bill (split or not?), and can we make oral sounds when eating (do we make slurping or chewing sounds, or do we burp after dinner?). Sometimes, culture can be expressed in what people wear. Consider the case 'fine feathers make fine birds', in which two culturally determined values are explored: purity and beauty.

Fine feathers make fine birds

The clothes you wear say something about how you want people to see you. In your clothing, norms and values are reflected, if you like it or not. Especially in the case of woman, some cultures are rather strict in what they should and should not wear. For instance, in some cultures, it is expected that women beyond a certain age cover their hair when visiting public places. This is particularly – but certainly not exclusively – a norm in Muslim oriented cultures. In the Holy Quran, we can read that purity is an important value, which is often understood as that women will be protected against harassment when covering body parts that accentuate their femininity. See for instance Sura An-Noer, 24:30-31 or Sura al-Ahzab, 33:59. Another value that could motivate covering your hair could be 'faith' or 'belonging'. Women may choose to cover their hair to show the world they feel ready and mature enough to be part of a group that shares the same ideas on religion and their way of life.

In some other cultures, clothes have an almost contrary goal, which is to accentuate and show your femininity. Consider a sub-stream in music: the hip-hop culture for instance. Especially young women are encouraged to show their body and express self-confidence by dressing sexy – not much revealing – clothes. Some consider this an ultimate form of freedom.

Both opposing approaches can be criticized by the other side. We could say that a norm that makes you cover femininity is a symbol of suppression, damaging the self-esteem of women. Such norms are heatedly debated, especially in developed countries with a large amount of migrants from Muslim cultures, where the norm is seen as something alien, brought along with the migrant's culture (Saroglou et al. 2009). It sometimes even leads to legal bans on such garments (Fournier, 2012). On the other hand, we could say that the dress code in the hip-hop scene stereotypes women, objectifying them, possibly leading to a lower self-esteem (Gantz et al., 1978).

Cultures are different, and so are its norwms and values. We could learn a great deal from different cultures. However, sometimes cultures are hardly tolerant towards each another, even hostile. How do we deal with the diversity of norms and values when cultures 'clash'? there is – of course – not one right answer to this question. At most, we could say there are three distinctive approaches towards the norms and values of other cultures than your own: cultural absolutism, cultural relativism and cultural pluralism.

> In cultural absolutism we consider one culture the better culture and act accordingly.

Cultural absolutism

In this approach, we act in compliance with the norms and values of our own culture, also in our interaction with different norms and values from other culture. This attitude stems from the conviction that your culture has better norms and values, and should prevail over contrary norms and values. This approach can result from the conviction that there are such things as universal norms and values. Think about the recognition of fundamental human rights, as discussed in chapter 3. The idea is that human rights are fundamental norms and values that should apply to each society, regardless the cultural context.

However, cultural absolutism is not always expressed in the peaceful and hopeful language of human rights. It can also be used as a motivation for a suppressive regime, and lead to rather extreme situations. A dreadful example would be the Nuremberg Laws, adopted shortly before the Second World War by Nazi Germany, as we can see in the sample. The assumption was that the German race is superior to the Jewish, and the pure blood of the Germans should therefore be protected.

Nuremberg Laws

In 1935, Nazi-Germany adopted several laws – also referred to as the Nuremberg Laws – under supervision of Adolf Hitler. The purpose of these laws was to preserve the 'pure' German blood, and avoid any Jewish interference in this bloodline. These laws preceded the Holocaust, which has led to the systematic (and industrial) genocide of Jewish, Gypsy, homosexual and disabled people.

'Law for the Protection of German Blood and German Honor or September 15, 1935 (translated from Reich Gesetz Blatt I, 1935, pp. 1146-7.)
Moved by the understanding that purity or German blood is the essential condition for the continued existence of the German people, and inspired by the inflexible austrade to ensure the existence of the German nation for all time, the Reichstag has unanimously adopted the following law, which is promulgated here with:

Article 1
1 Marriages between Jews and subjects of the state or German or related blood are forbidden. Marriages nevertheless concluded are invalid, even if concluded abroad to circumvent this law.
2 Annulment proceedings can be U.S only by the state prosecutor.

Article 2
Extramarital relations between Jews and subjects of the state or German or related blood are forbidden.

Article 3
Jews may not employ in their households female subjects or the state or German or related blood who are under 45 years old.

Article 4
1 Jews are forbidden to fly the Reich or national flag or display Reich colors.

10

2 *They are, on the other hand, permitted to display the Jewish colors. The exercise of this right is protected by the state.*

Article 5
1 *Any person who violates the prohibition under Article 1 will be punished with a prison sentence.*
2 *A male who violates the prohibition under Article 2 will be punished with a jail term or a prison sentence.*
3 *Any person violating the provisions under Articles 3 or 4 will be punished with a jail term of up to one year and a fine, or with one or the other of these penalties.*

Article 6
The Reich Minister of the Interior, in coordination with the Deputy of the Fuehrer and the Reich Minister of Justice, will issue

the legal and administrative regulations required to implement and complete this law.

Article 7
The law takes effect on the day following promulgation, except for Article 3, which goes into force on January 1, 1936.
Nuremberg, September 15, 1935
At the Reich Party Congress or Freedom
The Fuehrer and Reich Chancellor
Adolf Hitler
The Reich Minster or the Interior
Frick
The Reich Minister of Justice
Dr. Gürtner
The Deputy or the Führer
R. Hess'

(Translation: United States Holocaust Memorial Museum)

The opposite approach to cultural differences is cultural relativism.

Cultural relativism

> In cultural relativism we recognize cultural equivalence and assess cultural norms and values only from the perspective of that culture.

This means that we can only judge norms and values from others in the context of their own culture, and most certainly not from the perspective of our own culture (Harris, 1991). The conclusion is that cultures are not better, just different. This also means that we accept that once we find ourselves in another culture, we adapt our behaviour to the norms and values of the other culture. Or, to use a catchy proverb: 'when in Rome, do as the Romans do'. In various settings, this can only be understood as being respectful towards another culture, and when you do business with companies representing the other culture, it could show respect when you try to adjust your behaviour, especially when you are their guest and visit their business abroad. So, do burp after a meal in China, and make sure you do not eat all the food that was served. And perhaps be hesitant in shaking the hands of female business partners in some regions in the world. It would simply lead to awkward situations.

The previous examples are rather innocent gestures of respecting the other culture, and behave accordingly. However, cultural relativism can also be questionable. Do we set aside all of our own cultural norms and values when interacting with the other culture for the sake of cultural relativism? What if the other culture has norms and values you find truly offensive? While we could with reasonable arguments claim that child marriage is damaging to the health and potential of young woman (Coller, 2017; Efevbera et al., 2017), it is a deeply rooted norm is some cultures, as we can see in the news item. Cultural relativism would mean that we accept this, because we cannot judge the culture in which child marriage is the norm from our own perspective.

CNN NEWS, 23 JANUARY 2018

She's only 12, but her father is already planning her wedding

By: Hakim Almasmari and Sarah El Sirgany, CNN

Sanaa, Yemen – When Halima's father told her he was planning her wedding, the 12-year-old firmly refused.
'My father married off my sisters, and wants to marry me off by force, but I don't want to get married,' said Halima, whose father asked CNN not to use his family's surname. Child marriage is entrenched in Yemen, a symptom of crippling poverty and a deeply conservative culture. It's a traditional practice preserved in proverbs like, 'Marry an 8-year-old girl, she's guaranteed' – an assurance of a child's virginity. And the country's three-year civil war has only exacerbated the problem.

Today, more than two-thirds of Yemeni girls are married off before they reach 18, a staggering leap from half of all girls before the conflict.
But Halima, with her quick laugh and infectious smile, is determined not to be a part of that mounting statistic.
'I'm in the fifth grade. I want to finish school. I want to become a doctor, God willing,' Halima told CNN, still dressed in her school uniform – a forest green abaya and white headscarf.
'Many of my friends in school have been married off.'
'One of my friends dropped out and when I asked her why, she said, "Because tomorrow is my wedding."'(...)

Perhaps a more convenient approach would be that of cultural pluralism. In ethics, this approach is also referred to as moral pluralism (Hinman, 2012).

> In cultural pluralism we accept the diversity of cultural norms and values and recognize that these norms and values can be mutually contradicting.

Cultural pluralism

This means that we do not necessarily have to behave as Romans when we are in Rome, but also that we do not have to impose our own norms and values on the Romans. What matters is that we understand that cultures are different, sometimes oppose one another, and that sometimes cultures are even intolerant towards the other. The only way to bridge these gaps is to engage in a constructive dialogue in which we try to understand one another. A position defended by Kishore Mahbubani, as we can see in the interview quote. Please note that trying to understand each another is different from approving others people's behaviour, or adjust your own norms and values in compliance with the norms and values of another culture.

10

Kishore Mahbubani on cultural pluralism

In a TV interview in 2008, Kishore Mahbubani was asked how western countries should interact with other cultures that have a different understanding on norms and values than their own (VPRO, 2008).

'The tool to do that is to, and the most important thing for the Western mind to accept now, understand that we are moving from a mono-civilizational world to a multi-civilizational world. From one successful civilization, to many successful civilizations, and these other successful civilizations are not carbon copies of the West, they look at the world very differently.

You have to reach out and understand them and the pragmatic spirit is one which says, hey you may not be like me, but I can try to understand you, I can try to figure out how you work, what you do and so on and so forth. Up to now, especially since the end of the Cold War, the Western mind has become very ideological in its belief that there is only one path of history, now suddenly there are many different paths of history. And, your mind has got to open up to those possibilities and that's why I say, you need a new spirit of pragmatism to infect the Western mind.'

In figure 10.1 You can see a graphic overview of cultural absolutism, pluralism and relativism.

FIGURE 10.1 Cultural absolutism, pluralism and relativism

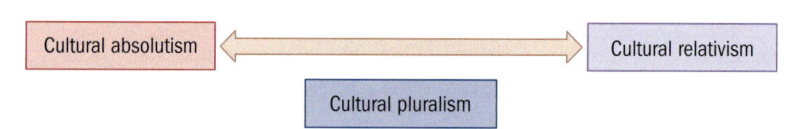

🔟.🔟 Cultural differences on various levels

The level at which cultural differences play a role can be different. At a global level, we see that groups of countries may have opposing views on norms and values. Consider the Cold War, where communist – Eastern bloc – countries had a different worldview from Western bloc countries regarding the function of a state and the role of an individual in society. Or what to think of democracy, a value supported by the same Western Bloc although this is not considered as a crucial value for a successful society in some regions of the world (Mahbubani, 2009; Scruton, 2003).

Another example could be the stalemate in the WTO Doha Round negotiations in which developed countries have considerably different ideas on how trade should work between countries compared to developing countries. The first group considers ongoing trade liberalization the way to go, while the latter group pleas for more means of protecting national trade. The values liberalization and protection are contrary to the other, as we will discuss in the next chapter.

Also, at a more regional level, cultural differences can lead to challenges, as you can see in the example 'The Roses Rivalry'. A difference of opinion regarding power in the past has led to a deeply rooted rivalry between the fans of two football clubs in England. As it seems, their norms and values are so different on some issues that it has more than once led to violent encounters.

The Roses Rivalry

For centuries, there has been rivalry between two neighbouring cities in England: Leeds and Manchester. It all started somewhere in the fifteenth century, when both Leeds and Manchester represented a powerful militia that considered itself eligible to take the English crown. This resulted in the so-called 'War of Roses', in which the rivalling groups used a rose as their symbol: the house of Lancester used a red, and the house of York a white rose.

Today, this rivalry is still noticeable in the context of sport matches. For instance, supporters of Manchester United and Leeds United regularly clash, which has led to multiple violent incidents between both fan groups, including some massive fights in the seventies, often considered as the worst hooligans clashes in history of British football (Bagchi, 2010).

Even on a very small scale, say on the level of a classroom, cultural difference are noticeable. Teaching a class of economy students is different from teaching a class of arts students. And two different classes of economy students may have different rules of conduct amongst themselves.

10.3 Cultural differences and business

As we have discussed in various chapters of this book, companies may have their own business culture, and emphasize their own norms and values. In Chapter 1 we labelled this a 'company morale'. Such an organizational culture can be stimulated by an internal code, as we have seen in Chapter 9. Such a company morale can be challenged when the company operates in multiple countries in which different norms and values are supported by its people.

Company morale

As you can see in the example 'homosexuality in Saudi Arabia', the norms and values of a Dutch-based paint and coating company are in sharp contrast with norms and values in the Middle East when it concerns homosexuality. However, the Dutch company wants to do business in a region where there is a death penalty for homosexuality, while at the same time they proudly participate in the Gay Pride.

On the one hand, we could argue that the company should not be so hypocritical, practice what they preach, and not engage in a joint venture involving homophobic partners. On the other hand, we could argue that in the Middle East, homosexuality is not part of the generally accepted norms and values, and this should be respected when a company decides to do business in that region. After all, we cannot expect a company on its own to change long-lasting traditions, and we can also not expect the Dutch company not to do business at all in that region because homosexuality is

10

not accepted. The company is confronted with a dilemma: apply cultural absolutism, and terminate the partnership, apply cultural relativism and continue the partnership respecting the other viewpoint on homosexuality, or apply cultural relativism and use the partnerships as a means to engage in a dialogue on the different views of the matter.

Homosexuality in Saudi Arabia

Saudi Arabia is a wealthy country in the Middle East. The held 16% of the global oil reserve, has a prominent role in the OPEC and a GDP of more than 646.44 billion U.S. dollars (www.worldbank.org, 2018). As a major player in the oil industry, export is an important aspect of their economy.
Saudi Arabia is also a country in which homosexuality – or any other sexual relation outside the context of marriage between a man and a woman – is forbidden by traditional Sharia law. The punishment for sexual intercourse between men may vary. In general, a married man will be stoned to death, while an unmarried man might be whipped with hundred blows and banished for a year (Caroll, 2016).

AkzoNobel, a Dutch-based company in the paint and coating industry, has some other ideas about homosexuality. Amongst others, the company was the official sponsor of the 2014 Gay Pride in Amsterdam, and participated with a boat with the slogan 'show your true colours.' In a press release, a spokesman of the company held that 'If you have a work environment in which everyone has exactly the same background, that's bound to have its limitations. That's why at AkzoNobel, we believe we can only win together if we recognize that all of us – no matter what our religion, sexual preference, race or age – can bring something to the party. We're therefore proud to sponsor this year's Gay Pride and with our theme show your true colours' we will be demonstrating how we at AkzoNobel embrace diversity' (Akzo Nobel, 2014).

Interestingly, the company engaged in a joint-venture with a partner in the Middle East, with the specific aim of entering – amongst others- the Saudi-Arabian market. According to the company *'It will give us a firm foothold in the Middle East and a solid platform from which to deliver on our ambitious growth strategy in the region. We see many opportunities for our products and services to supply the construction, oil and gas and transportation sectors in the Middle East and this deal will ensure that we are better placed to serve our customers'* (Akzo Nobel, 2012).

In the example 'homosexuality in Saudi Arabia' we saw a case in which the company morale was in contrast with norms and values of a region in which the company engaged in partnerships. However, things become even more tricky for the company when the norms and values of their foreign partners are in conflict with the norms and values of their end-consumers. These norms and values are not necessarily similar to the morale of the involved company. However, ignoring the norms and values of your own customers may have a counterproductive effect, possibly leading to serious image damage.

As you can see in the example 'Heineken in Myanmar', the public opinion in the 'home markets' of Heineken was absolutely negative when Heineken entered a joint venture with the military regime in Myanmar. After all, Heineken was now associated with a government that seriously violated human rights. Many NGOs considered that Heineken should take its responsibility and withdraw from that market. In the end, this led to the withdrawal of Heineken from the Myanmar market, and Heineken considered that it could no longer ignore the norms and values of their customers in Europe and the U.S.

However, the original intention of Heineken was to make a difference in Myanmar by setting the right examples in a troubled country. Back then, some authors indeed suggested that it would be better for Heineken to stay, and undermine the dictatorial regime with economic success. After all, we could say that the better the economy of a country, the less chance of a success for a dictatorial regime (Jeurissen, 1996).

In other words: the public opinion on Heineken in Myanmar led Heineken to apply cultural absolutism, and leave the country, where Heineken initially wanted to apply cultural pluralism.

When we consider the more recent newspaper item, we see that as soon as the military regime was replaced by a civilian government, Heineken returned to the country in 2016, setting up a new business once more. It remains to be seen whether the new government of Myanmar will not cause any problems to Heineken considering the reporting of massive human right violation against Rohingya-minority since 2017. The main difference this time however is that Heineken is not forced in a joint venture, but is able to compete on the Myanmar market as a company in its own right.

Heineken in Myanmar

In the nineties, Heineken decided to set up business activities in Myanmar. However, the regime of that time could be classified as a military dictatorship. To be able to do business as a foreign undertaking, the Government of Myanmar requested that any foreign companies would engage in a joint venture with a state-run company. In practice, this would mean that Heineken owned 60 percent of a Myanmar beer company, while the other 40 percent were owned by a state-owned enterprise. A problem was that the Myanmar Government was accused of violating human rights by violently suppressing protests, randomly arresting citizens, and they interfered considerably with the freedom of speech. The indirect partnership of Heineken with this oppressive regime did not pass unnoticed, and many NGOs campaigned against Heineken, and demanded that the company would leave Myanmar. The main motivation was that by investing in the joint-venture, Heineken was effectively sponsoring the military dictatorship. Heineken was initially not inclined to leave, and stated that they could set an example of being a good employer and pay fair wages. The company however had to change its mind considering the increasing public pressure, and stated that: 'Since that time the public opinion and the conceivement on this market has changed in such a way, that this could have negative effects on the Heineken brand and on the reputation of our company. Heineken traditionally attaches great value to its responsibility towards society in numberless markets around the world. On the basis of the changed circumstances we have reevaluated the situation and have come to the conclusion that we no longer have the possibility to realise this ambition' (Heineken, 1996).

10

THE FINANCIAL TIMES, 6 JUNE 2016

Heineken and a western brewer's return to Myanmar

By: Michael Peel

Sobir Djaffar looks happy as he surveys the racks of locally produced bottles of Heineken on a Myanmar supermarket shelf. The Dutch brewer has been waiting 20 years to return to the country. But he is less thrilled that the beer – along with its rival brands – is sharing the first aisle of this Yangon store with toilet rolls and baby wipes. 'On the layout, the shop floor, there is no logic yet,' laments Mr Djaffar, sales director for Heineken's joint venture in the fast-changing Southeast Asian country. The young executive reminds himself with a twinkle that 'we don't see this as problem, but as an opportunity.' Myanmar is exciting frontier territory for Heineken and its newly arrived international rivals. The return of a civilian-dominated government after decades of military dictatorship has thrown up a rare opportunity for the foreign companies not just to compete for existing market share, but also to use savvy promotion to release latent demand. (…)

As we can see, a multinational will have to balance between their own company morale, the norms and values in the countries they employ business activities, and the norms and values of their end-consumers (see figure 10.2).

FIGURE 10.2 Overview of the business and cultural diversity

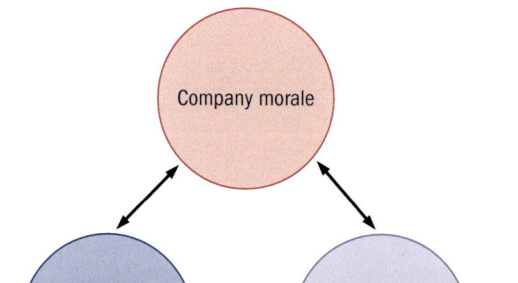

10.4 Cultural differences between countries

We can discuss cultural differences on many levels. One of the levels is the country level. While of course we cannot possibly say that people who live in the same country per definition share the same norms and values , there are some reasons to consider that there are valid reasons to assume that there is some joint moral perception amongst the citizens of a country.

People with the same nationality mostly share a certain historic perspective, participate in the same domestic markets, speak the same languages, receive education in the same educational system, and are governed by the same governmental institutions (Wernaart, 2013). Of course there are many examples in which cultural differences within a country are obvious, or even lead to conflicts. Think of the opposing ideologies practiced in Korea: the North embraced the socialist Juche ideology, where the South is led by a constitutional democratic ideology. This has led to the tearing up of Korea into distinct parts. Or consider the different fractions in Syria that fight for power since the civil uprising in 2011. At least five different groups struggle for power, with rather different ideas on morality.

While we are aware that the borders of a country do not necessarily divide cultures, in this section we do focus on cultural differences at the country level. First we will explain the Hofstede model that enables us to measure cultural differences per country. Second, we will use these insights in discussing some examples of cultural differences between countries that relate to the business sector.

10.4.1   The Hofstede model

Hofstede (2001) designed a model to measure cultural differences between countries. In this so called 6-D model (six dimensions), the culture of a country is measured using six different dimensions that altogether determine the most important characteristics of a national culture. It is mostly used as a comparison tool, to gain insights in the main similarities and differences per country, which can be very helpful in doing business abroad. With this model, we can predict the cultural features that the home country of the company and the potential foreign market have in common, and what the most important differences (and therefore potential challenges) may be. As we can see in the example 'Cockpit hierarchy', the understanding of cultural differences may prevent serious harm, or solve problems when cultures clash.

However, we need to be careful to use a method like the 6-D model correctly, and be aware of its limits. We already argued above that the notion that citizens of a nation state share the same cultural norms and values can be questioned. Next to that, it is important to understand that the 6D-model was designed for better understanding the one culture by comparing it to other cultures. It is not intended to be used exclusively in management decisions. For instance, if we would use the 6D model in deciding in which country we should set up a subsidiary establishment, we would each time conclude that it is the best option to do this in the country that mostly shares or own cultural norms and values. This would mean that a European company would never go to China. In other words: the 6D model should primarily be used for understanding culture, not for evaluating it.

Please note that some authors have expressed their doubts about the validity of the methodology used by Hofstede (for instance, the way questionnaires are used, and the seize of the samples per country), or even argue that it is not possible nor desirable to empirically measure such thing as national culture (McSweeny, 2002; Bond, 2002). Alternatives could be found in approaching cultures from a values perspective (Schwartz, 1999), in which culture is not measured using empirical data but classified based on its core values.

All this being said, Hofstede's model is most frequently used in the context of international business and culture, and most authors support his approach (Ferreire et al. 2014). Therefore, we choose to use the 6D method in this book as well, with some restraint.

Six culture dimensions

The six dimensions model – also referred to as The Hofstede model – measures culture using six dimensions: the power distance index, individualism versus collectivism, masculinity versus femininity, the uncertainty avoidance index, long-term orientation versus short-term normative orientation and indulgence versus restraint.
Each country has a score from 1 to 120 in each dimensions. The higher the score, the more prominent the related feature can be associated with the national culture, as we can see in figure 10.3.

FIGURE 10.3 The Hofstede model

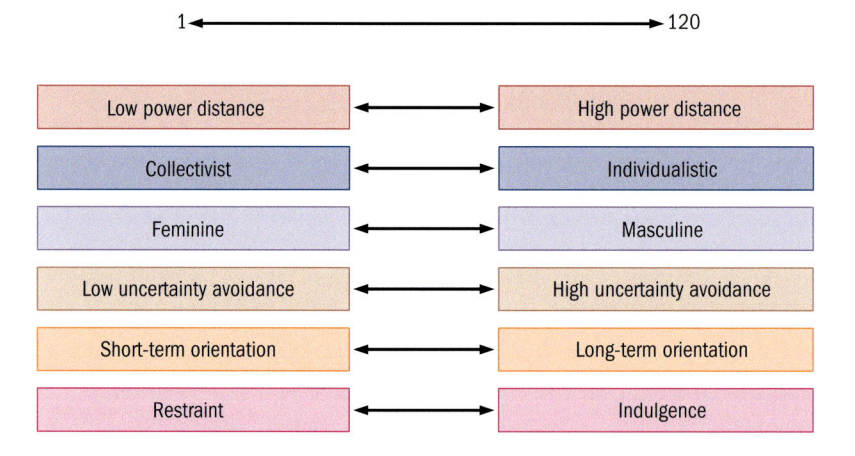

The power distance index
This cultural dimension is about the acceptance of inequality between people and the distribution of power. In countries with a low score on power distance, inequality is not accepted and people strive for the realization of as much equality as possible in the distribution of power. In countries with a high score on power distance, people accept that there is inequality and do not question this nor try to change the 'classes' in society.

Individualism versus collectivism
This cultural dimension expresses to what degree a society is individualistic or collectivist. In an individualist culture, people think from an 'I' perspective, and assume to be responsible for themselves and their inner circle only. In a collectivist culture, people think from a 'we' perspective, and share responsibility towards one another as a group. The higher the score, the more individualistic the culture is.

Masculinity versus femininity
This cultural dimension expresses to what extent a society is competitive or consensus-oriented. In a competitive society, masculine features such as success and exposure are dominant characteristics. In a consensus-oriented society, feminine features such as caring for one another are dominant characteristics. The higher the score, the more masculine a culture is. Please note that masculine and feminine features should not be confused with how males and females usually behave. A man most likely also has feminine, and a woman has masculine characteristics.

Uncertainty avoidance index
This cultural dimension expresses to what extent individuals feel comfortable with uncertainty. The higher the score on this index, the less comfortable people feel about uncertainty, and the more people will do to create expected outcomes in social interaction. This may result in strict rules of behaviour, and a high degree of formality, and an uncomfortable feeling with new ideas. Where societies have a low score on this index, people are more flexible in their social interactions, less formal, and at ease with new ideas.

Long term orientation versus short term normative orientation
This cultural dimension expresses to what extent individuals in a society look back or look forward. Societies with a low score on this dimension prefer tradition and long-established customs while are suspicious about social changes. The other way around, societies with a high score on this dimension are more pragmatic and welcome social change when this is useful to them.

Indulgence versus restraint
This cultural dimension expresses to what extent individuals in a society allow themselves to have fun, or suppress the urge to do have fun. The higher the score, the more we allow ourselves the pleasures of life.

The results of a random comparison of the Netherlands, the U.S.A., Saudi-Arabia, China, Russia and Angola, using the 6D method, can be found in Table 10.1 (data retrieved from www.hofstede-insights.com, 2018).

TABLE 10.1 Cultural differences according to the Hofstede model

	The power distance index	Individualism versus collectivism	Masculinity versus femininity	Uncertainty avoidance	Long term versus short term	Indulgence versus restraint
The Netherlands	38	80	14	53	67	68
U.S.A.	40	91	62	46	26	68
Saudi Arabia	95	25	60	80	36	52
China	80	20	66	30	87	24
Russia	93	39	36	95	81	20
Angola	83	18	20	60	15	83

As we can see, in the Netherlands feminine characteristics are important. Perhaps the famous 'polder-model' through which cooperation is sought between political parties or employee and employer agencies despite their differences explains this score. Both the Netherlands and the U.S.A. are considered individualistic countries, where especially China and Angola are more collectivist. Saudi-Arabia has a high score on uncertainty avoidance, which can be explained by the strict (religious) social rules that apply in this country. In Angola, Russia and Saudi-Arabia we see a high score on the power distance index. This means that power is not necessarily equally distributed, and this is generally accepted. China and Russia are the more pragmatic country: the Chinese famous five-year plans reflect this idea, in which economic and social change is implemented by five-year policies to continuously improve the economy and welfare of the country.

Cockpit hierarchy?

On 6 July 2013, a tragedy unfolds at the airport of San Francisco, U.S.A. An Asiana Airlines airplane crashes during the landing procedure as a result of hitting the sea defence. Two out of the 307 passengers lost their lives, while 180 were injured. The crash was remarkable because there were no technical errors and the weather was perfect for a smooth landing.

This case shows many similarities with two other plane crashes in the late nineties. In both of these cases, a human error of a South Korean commander had led to the tragedy: not a technical error or extreme weather conditions. On both occasions, their (also South Korean) co-pilots did not dare to express their concerns about the capability or actions of the commander in chief (Malcolm, 2008; DeHart, 2013; Howard, 2013).

This is a result of how South Korean hierarchical relations work. South Korea has a relatively high score on the power distance index, as well as the uncertainty avoidance index (60 and 85). This means that a 'lower' officer in the chain of command will not easily question the behaviour of the 'higher' officer, and work relations are very formal.

10.4.2 The Hofstede model applied

We can apply the 6D model to various topics that relate to business. For instance, accounting standards (as discussed in chapter 8) in various regions of the world may be influenced by the norms and values of the culture that prescribes them. Amongst others, Gray (1988) already hypothesized that:

Accounting standards

> 'The higher a country ranks in terms of individualism and the lower it ranks in terms of uncertainty avoidance and power distance the more likely it is to rank highly in terms of professionalism.'

In other words: we could distinguish between accounting standards that recognize the responsibility of the individual accountant professional instead of prescribing detailed accounting rules that should only be applied by an accountant. The first type of rules can be expected in countries with more individualism, a low uncertainty avoidance and a low power distance. Examples could be Anglo-American countries where traditionally the accountant professional judges how he should comply with accounting standards. On the other hand, countries that are more collectivist and have a higher score of uncertainty avoidance and power distance, will more likely embrace prescriptive and detailed rules for the accountant. The accountant then should follow these rules rather strictly, without too much of his own interpretation. Consider countries in the Far East, and to a lesser extent, European countries.

In this line of reasoning we could say in more general terms that the power distance index combined with the individualism versus collectivism dimension strongly influences the one who feels responsible for ethics in business. It can be argued that Anglo/American countries strongly emphasize the responsibilities of the individual towards business ethics, while in Europe the legislature plays a more important role in creating moral rules for business (Enderle, 1996). In comparison, in Asian and African cultures the management of a company is considered to be the ultimate responsible for ethics in business (Crane & Matten 2016). Perhaps in an overly sharp contrast: compare the response of the top management of the U.S.-based Welsch Fargo bank (see Chapter 9) with the suicide of the CEO of the Korean bank in the newspaper item below. The U.S. CEO initially did not want to resign and mostly blamed individual employees for the unethical conduct, while the Korean CEO commits suicide as a result of a scandal in his company.

Responsibility

THE FINANCIAL TIMES, 23 SEPTEMBER 2011

Korean bank chief commits suicide amid scandal

By: Christian Olivier

Seoul - The head of one of South Korea's ailing savings banks has hurled himself to his death from his office as the government tries to stop a spiraling bank corruption scandal from infecting the broader financial system.

Jeong Gu-haeng, chief executive of Jeil 2 bank, threw himself from a sixth floor window on Friday after investigators raided his office, police said.

Jeil 2 was one of seven savings banks suspended on Sunday because of insufficient capital. Seoul has suspended 16 of the country's 105 savings banks, mainly because of their heavy losses in property developments.

The controversy surrounding the banks' fragility hinges on the involvement of regulators, who are under investigation for turning a blind eye to problems at savings banks in return for bribes worth tens of thousands of dollars and, in one case, a diamond.

Regulators and the savings banks insist they will be able to resolve the problems and recapitalise.

Last month Kim Jang-ho, deputy governor of the financial supervisory service, jumped into the river Han that runs through Seoul after facing parliamentarians' questions on whether he took bribes. He was rescued. He has declined to comment on the case but earlier this year offered to resign to help save the regulators' reputation.

Failing savings banks are a major political embarrassment for the government. Although savings banks make up only about 2 per cent of the assets of the whole financial system, many families and pensioners are deeply worried about their life savings.(...)

Islamic banking

Another business-related issue could be the role of banks. Countries with a low score on the 'long term orientation versus short term normative orientation' index will be more eager to stick to traditional values. An example could be Islamic countries in which Islamic banking is practiced. In Islamic banking, religious values (Sharia-law) are incorporated in the core activities of the banking sector. Important features of Islamic banking is that lending money should in its core be interest-free and not invested in sinful products. The idea of interest-free banking is understood with different grades of flexibility in the Muslim world. A modern interpretation is that interest per se is not contrary to sharia law, but interest that takes advantage of the weaker position of the money lender is (Khan, 2013). Especially after the financial crises in 2008 we saw an increased popularity of Islamic banking, since these banks appeared to suffer considerably less from the worldwide crises on the financial markets (Dridi & Hasan, 2010). However, the conventional banking approach also influenced the Islamic banks, and some criticize the current state of Islamic banking, arguing that the sector is moving away from its own principles towards a more conventional banking system, using the image of Islamic banking as a way to target their customers (Uppal & Mangla, 2014).

Summary

▶ Culture is the shared norms and values amongst a certain group of individuals that feels part of the same culture.

▶ We can distinguish three approaches towards cultural differences:
- In cultural absolutism we consider one culture the better culture and act accordingly.
- In cultural relativism we recognize cultural equivalence and assess cultural norms and values only from the perspective of that culture.
- In cultural pluralism we accept the diversity of cultural norms and values and recognize that these norms and values can be mutually contradicting.

▶ Cultural differences exist on all levels of society.

▶ A multinational company will have to balance between their own company morale, the norms and values in the countries they employ business activities, and the norms and values of their end-consumers.

▶ Cultural differences at country level can be measured using the 6D model (Hofstede model).
- In this model, culture per country is empirically expressed in six dimensions and based on a cultural unit per country.
- The 6D model should primarily be used for understanding culture, not for evaluating culture.
- Each country is assigned a score in respect of six cultural dimensions:
  - The power distance index: this cultural dimension is about the acceptance of inequality between people and the distribution of power.
  - Individualism versus collectivism: this cultural dimension expresses to what degree a society is individualistic or collectivist.
  - Masculinity versus femininity: this cultural dimension expresses to what extent a society is competitive or consensus-oriented.
  - The uncertainty avoidance index: this cultural dimension expresses to what extent individuals feel comfortable with uncertainty.
  - Long term orientation versus short term normative orientation: this cultural dimension expresses to what extent individuals in a society look back or look forward.
  - Indulgence versus restraint: this cultural dimension expresses to what extent individuals in a society allow themselves to have fun, or suppress the urge to have fun.

10

▶ The six dimensions can be used to better understand cultural differences in business life around the world, such as the role of financial accounting, the primary bearer of responsibility towards business ethics, or the role of banks.

Literature

ANVR. (2012) *tips and advices to make as a traveller to contribute to sustainable travel.* ANVR.

Bond, M. H. (2002). Reclaiming the Individual From Hofstede's Ecological Analysis- A 20-Year Odyssey: Comment on Oyserman et al. (2002). *Psychological Bulletin,* 128(1): 73-77.

Caroll, A. (2016). *State Sponsored Homophobia 2016: A world survey of sexual orientation laws: criminalisation, protection and recognition.* Geneva: ILGA.

Coller, A. van. (2017). Child Marriage – Acceptance by Association. *International Journal of Law, Policy and the Family*, Volume 31, Issue 3, 1 December 2017, Pages 363–376.

Crane, A. & Matten, D. (2016). Introducing business ethics. In: *Business Ethics.* Oxford: Oxford University Press.

Dridi, J. & Hasan, M. (2010). *The Effects of the Global Crisis on Islamic and Conventional Banks; A Comparative Study, IMF Working Papers 10/201*, International Monetary Fund.

Efevbera, Y., Bhabha, J.D., Farmer, P.E. & Gunter, F. (2017). Girl child marriage as a risk factor for early childhood development and stunting. *Social science and medicine,* vol. 185, july 2017, pp. 91-101.

Enderle, G. (1996). A comparison of business ethics in North-America and continental Europe. *Business ethics: a European review.* vol. 5. (1). pp. 33-46.

Ferreira, M., Serra, F. & Pinto, C. (2014). Culture and Hofstede (1980) in international business studies, a bibliometric study in top management journals, *REGE*, vol. 21, no. 3, pp. 379-399, July/Sept. 2014.

Fournier, P. (2012). Headscarf and burqa controversies at the crossroad of politics, society and law. *Social Identities*, vol. 19, issue 6, pp. 689-703.

Gantz, W., Gartenberg, H., Pearson, M., & Schiller, S. (1978). Gratifications and expectations associated with popular music among adolescents, *Popular Music and Society*, 6, 81- 89.

Gray, S.J. (1988). Towards a theory of cultural influence on the development of accounting standards. *Abacus.* (March 1988): 12.

Harris, L. (1991). *The Philosophy of Alain Locke.* Philadelphia: Temple University Press.

Hinman, L. (2012). Ethics: *A Pluralistic Approach to Moral Theory.* Boston: Cengage Learning.

Hofstede, G. (2001). *Culture's Consequences: Comparing Values, behaviors, institutions and organizations across Nations.* Thousand Oaks: Sage Publications.

Jeurissen, R., & Putten, F.P. der. (2007). Ethics in international business. In: Jeurissen, R. (Ed.), *Ethics & Business* (pp. 212-239). Assen: Van Gorcum.

Khan, M.A. (2013). *What is wrong with Islamic economics? Analyzing the present state and future agenda.* Cheltenham: Edward Elgar Publishing Ltd.

Mahbubani, K. (2008). *New Asian hemisphere: the 32,77 shift or global power to the east.* New York: Public Affairs.

Mahbubani, K. (2009). *Can Asians Think?* Singapore, Marshall Cavendish.

Malcolm, G. (2008). The ethnic theory of plane crashes. In: *Outliers.* New York: Little, Brown and company.

McSweeny, B. (2002). Hofstede's model of national cultural differences and their consequences: A triumph of faith – a failure of analysis. *Human Relations*, vol. 55(1), pp. 89–118.

Saroglou, V., Lamkaddem, B., Lease Beke, M., & Bucant, C. (2009). Host society's unique circular image on each print! or the Islam Itic veil: the role or subtitle Middlemarch, values and religion. *International Journal for Intercultural Relations*, 33, 419-428.

Schmitz, L. (2014). Are Hofstede's dimensions valid? A test for measurement invariance of Uncertainty Avoidance. *Interculture journal*, 13/22 (2014), pp. 11-26.

Schwartz, S.H. (1999). A theory of cultural values and some implications for work. *Applied psychology: an international review*, 1999 vol. 48, pp. 23-47.

Scruton, R. (2003). *West and the Rest, Globalization and the terrorist threat.* New York: Continuum International Publishing Group.

Uppal, J.Y. & Mangla, I.U. (2014). Islamic banking and finance revised after forty years: some global challenges. *Journal of Financial Issues*, issue 13 (1), pp. 16-27.

Wernaart, B. (2013). Methods. In: *The enforceability or the human right to adequate food.* Wageningen: Wageningen Academic Publishers.

Media

Almasmari, H. & Sirgany, S. El. (2018, 23 January). She's only 12, but her father is already planning her wedding. *CNN news.*

Bagchi, R. (2 January, 2010).The rivalry between Manchester United and Leeds that turned to hate. *The Guardian.*

DeHart, J. (2013, 16 July). Asiana Airlines Crash: A Cockpit Culture Problem? *The Diplomat.*

Howard, B. (2013, 9 July). Could Malcolm Gladwell's theory or Cockpit Culture Apply to Asiana Crash? *National Geographic.*

Jeurissen, R. (1996, 2 February). Heineken kan regime in Burma juist ondermijnen. *De Volkskrant.*

Olivier, C. (2011, 23 September). Korean bank chief commits suicide amid scandal. *The Financial Times.*

Interviews

VPRO. (2008, 25 August). De eeuw van asie, tegenlicht, transcript interview.

Press releases

Akzo Nobel (2012, 30 November). Akzo Nobel expanding Middle East operatons.

AkzoNobel (2014, 29 July). Akzo Nobel spreads its colorful wings for Gay Pride.

Heineken (1996, 10 July). Heineken announces decision of leaving Myanmar.

Directives

Facebook Community Guidelines, 2014.

Websites

www.globalequality.org/newsroom/latest-news/1-in-the-news/186-the-facts-on-lgbt-rights-in-russia; www.globalequality.org, 2015.

https://www.hofstede-insights.com, data retrieved at 10 April 2018.

www.worldbank.org; https://data.worldbank.org/country/saudi-arabia.

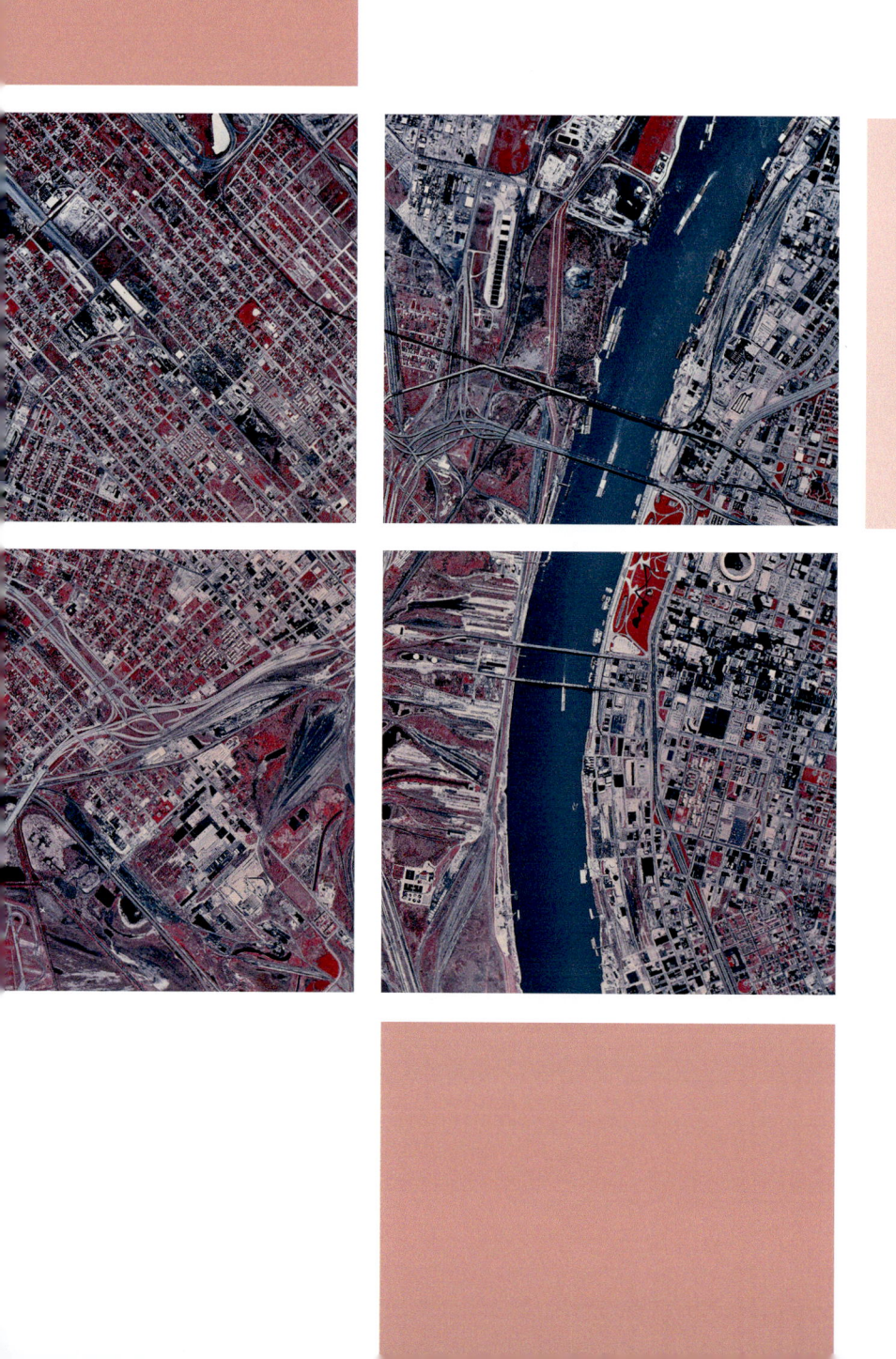

11

Globalization: does the system work?

11

11.1 **Why globalization is a good thing**
11.2 **Why globalization is a bad thing**

The idea of globalization is by some hailed as a key to integration, peace and economic prosperity. Others believe it is the cause of everything that is wrong in this world. In this chapter we explain both positions from an ethics perspective.

11.1 Why globalization is a good thing

Earlier in this book, in particular in section 5.2, we defined and discussed globalization as one of the social trends that caused a more intense debate on ethics in business during the last decades:

Globalization

| Globalization is the consequence of fading borders.

However, what borders exactly are fading as a result of globalization? There are different understandings of this phenomenon, and although these interpretations are related to some extent most of the time, they are far from similar. We could for instance discuss globalization in the context of cultural integration, refugee relief, military cooperation or studying abroad. Each time, different borders are fading in different ways. What they have in common however is the idea that it becomes easier to cross a state border in the pursuit of a joint goal. In the context of (macro) economy, we can generally agree that the idea of globalization is that we can do business in other countries without the limitations to trade that may come with a state border. The idea is that in a market without barriers to trade global economic growth is more likely to occur than in a global market with closed borders. In other words: when we reduce our trade barriers we are all better off in the long term.

Trade barrier

| A trade barrier is a measure that hinders cross-border trade directly or indirectly.

This definition requires some explanation:
- A measure is adopted by a state, mostly in the form of legislation, policy or behaviour that at some point hinders trade.
- Trade is not composed of goods and services exclusively, but instead encompasses many elements, including workers and capital. After all, it will become hard to sell goods or services in another country without being able to finance the business activities abroad, or send employees or other representatives to other countries.
- A trade barrier can be a direct barrier. In that case, the measure applies due to the fact that trade crosses a border, and creates a disadvantage for the trade that crosses the border compared to domestic trade that does not. Think of import or export tariffs, or a quota (a maximum amount that can be sold after crossing a border).
  A trade barrier can also apply indirectly. The measure that leads to a trade barrier does not directly relate to the fact that trade is international, but in practice distorts cross-border trade (Wernaart, 2017a). An example can be found in the Dassonville case.

The Dassonville case

Two Belgian brothers Dassonville own a liquor store in the South of Belgium, near the French border. They sell Scottish whisky among other things. However, in the true spirit of free trade, they do not buy the whisky directly from the Scottish producers, but indirectly, from French wholesale agencies. After all, it is much more efficient to purchase all whiskies at once through a middle agency than buying them individually from producers. Unfortunately, there seems to be a problem: Belgian law demands that for the sales of Whisky, a certificate of origin is required. In French law, such a certificate is not required for the sale of whisky. Not surprisingly, the French wholesaler is unable to provide for the certificates, leaving the Belgian brothers with a problem. The Dassonville brothers come up with a provisional solution to the problem by creating fake certificates of origin. When the Brothers were caught by the Belgian authorities and were fined for this, they invoked the free movement of goods, as is applied in the European Union. The brothers held that the Belgian law constituted a barrier to trade.

The purpose of the Belgian rule was to make sure that illegally brewed spirits would not circulate on the Belgian market, not to hinder trade. However, as it seems, this rule practically resulted in a trade barrier when Belgian retailers want to purchase their Whiskies in France. After all, it was almost impossible to buy Whiskey in France and simultaneously obtain these certificates of origin. The European Court of Justice ruled that while this was not a direct limitation to trade, such as quotas, it had a similar effect. The consequence was that the Belgian brothers won their case, and Belgium had to adjust its laws (European Court of Justice, 1974).

11

The past has shown that economic failure or economic isolation has been the breeding ground for international tensions and sometimes even armed conflicts or a full scale war. The lesson learned from the past is that it is a better idea to open up borders for trade and become economically dependent on one another, to avoid such conflicts. The more open a global economy is, the less likely we will fight each other.

So, to sum up, there are two main arguments to support the idea of reducing barriers to trade and liberalizing the global markets: we all benefit in the long term, and it contributes to global peace and security.
Those who support the idea of ever-increasing trade liberalization are also called neo-liberals. The most important international trade organizations are based on the assumption that trade should be liberalized. Examples are the Bretton Woods institutions and the European Union. In the next section we will discuss these organizations into more detail, and reflect on the two main argument to support trade liberalization.

Neoliberalism

11.1.1   The Bretton Woods institutions

When the First World War was over, the League of Nations was founded in 1920, a predecessor of the current United Nations. The main aim of the League of Nations was to ensure peace and security, and encourage friendly relations between countries. Unfortunately this league did not last for very long, and its main focus did not seem to work. As it seems, there was a rather one-sided focus on maintaining safety which should be enforced by international law (Fenwick, 1936). This proved to work counterproductive in various regions of the world.

League of Nations

Germany, who lost First World War, was forced to adopted the Treaty of Versailles (1919). As a result, the country had to cede significant territories to its victors, give up its colonies, and was obliged to pay vast sums of compensation damage to the allied countries. Whether or not these measures were justified, it led to a situation in which Germany was barely able to recover from the war, and became economically isolated. The people of Germany became angrier by the day, and a growing distaste emerged amongst the German against everything that was not German. This sentiment could probably explain the huge success of the National Socialist German Workers Party (NSDAP, Nationalsozialistische Deutsche Arbeiterspartei) led by Adolf Hitler . Hitler took power in 1933 and later sent Germany in a full scale war, which would later be known as the Second World War.

Also on the other side of the world, poor economic prospects seemed to be a call to arms. Japan used to strive for progressive policies in international trade. However, when the world economy stagnated in the 20ies and 30ies, this approach changed quickly. The United States and European countries increasingly adopted measures to protect their domestic trade, the Japanese economy came to a halt. After all, the countries was seriously depending on the import of raw materials, since it did possess such resources. These trade barriers from the West made it virtually impossible to keep the domestic Japanese economy up and running. This, combined with a rapidly growing population led to an uncontrollable situation, and Japan saw only one solution: expand its territory, and occupy land of several countries and colonies in order to gain access to the desired raw materials (Sagan, 1988). From 1939 onwards, this escalated quickly in a full scaled war in Asia, with terrible consequences.

United Nations After the Second World War, the United Nations was founded: a second global attempt to ensure peace and security. Only this time, the approach was different. Lessons were learned from the failure of the League of Nations, and the UN mustered an integrated approach. Not only did the UN adopt international legal instruments to promote peace and security, it also had to focus on the progressive realization of human rights, and encourage a world economy that was not based on isolation but rather on inclusion. To realize the latter, the United Nations Monetary and Financial Conference was held in 1944, resulting in the creation of the so-called Bretton Woods Institutions. Representatives of the allied countries convened and adopted economic and financial agreements in support of trade liberalization, as we can see in the speech of Henry Morgenthau.

Henry Morgenthau's speech

At the end of the Bretton Woods conference, the American delegated Henry Morgenthau spoke. In his closing remarks, he emphasized the relationship between international free trade and peace:

'To seek the achievement of our aims separately through the planless, senseless rivalry that divided us in the past, or through the outright economic aggression which turned neighbors into enemies would be to invite ruin again upon us all. Worse, it would be once more to start our steps irretraceably down the steep, disastrous road to war. That sort of extreme nationalism belongs to an era that is dead.

Today the only enlightened form or national self-interest lies in international accord. At Bretton Woods we have taken practical steps toward putting this lesson into practice in monetary and economic fields.

I take it as an axiom that this war is ended; no people – and therefore no government of the people – will again tolerate prolonged or widespread unemployment. A revival of *international trade is indispensable if full employment is to be achieved in a peaceful world and with standards of living which will permit the realization of man's reasonable hopes'* (Morgenthau, 1944).

To support the realization of the Bretton Woods agenda, various international organizations were established. These include the International Monetary Fund (IMF) and the World Bank (WB). Later, the General Agreement on Tariffs and Trade (GATT) was adopted, which would eventually lead to the creation of the World Trade Organization (WTO). All three Bretton Woods institutions contribute to liberalization of trade from their own perspective, as you can see in figure 11.1.

FIGURE 11.1 The Bretton Woods institutions

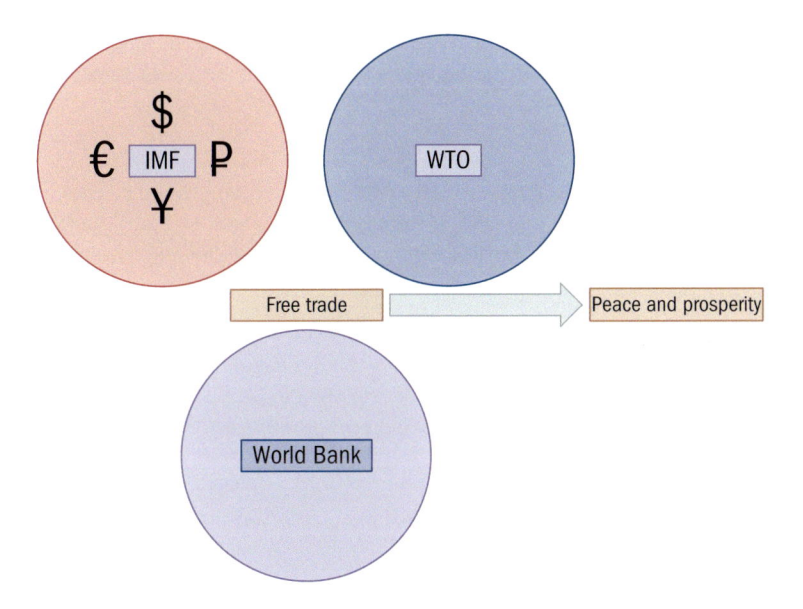

The IMF promotes financial stability and monetary cooperation on a global level. This is – amongst others – done by: **The IMF**
- the monitoring of the system of exchange rates, economic growth and employment (this is mainly achieved by analysing the economic policies of countries and international economic developments)
- lending money to countries with balance of payment problems
- advising on economic and financial policies
- issuing Special Drawing Rights (SDRs) as an international reserve assets. SDRs can be used to pay foreign debts (IMF, 2018)

The World Bank aims to reduce poverty by lending money and providing **The World Bank** technical support to developing countries. In essence the World Bank is part of the World Bank Group: a combination of five institutions that – from different perspectives – encourage investments in developing countries

(Wernaart, 2017b). An example of how the World Bank institutions interact with Governments and investors can be found in the case 'improving urban services in Bogota'.

Improving urban services in Bogota

Bogota is the capital of the Latin American State Columbia. In the 60s and 70s, the city experienced a huge urbanization, resulting in the fact that its population grew rapidly with an annual population growth over 10 percent. This has led to almost an uncontrolled expansion of the city, without proper city planning and means of transportation. The practical result of this was that especially people who lived in dangerous self-built slums had a difficult access to the main parts of the city where they could find employment. This is one of the contributing factors to high employment rates.

In the form of several loans and technical assistance of the International Bank for Reconstruction and Development (IBRD, a World Bank institution) to the city of Bogota and the Columbian Government, the Bogota Urban Service Project was set up. This project originated from 2003, and was closed in 2014. The entire project cost 272.67 million US dollars, of which approximately 100 million was borrowed from the IBRD. Amongst others, transport systems were financed that benefit 160 thousand women and 155 thousand men each day, since their travel time to their work is now reduced with 25 percent. Next to that, the project supports urban upgrading in the form of improvements in the usage of urban space. For instance, the project funded the building of parks, better infrastructure for pedestrians. As a result, 1.2 million inhabitants have benefitted from these improvements, including 1.995 households of which the living conditions were significantly improved by moving to safer areas with lower risks (World Bank Group, 2015).

Furthermore, an ambitious water and sanitation project was launched to create better, safer and more hygienic water supply and access to sewage connections (Browder, 2010).
Also in terms of governance, the project provided for technical assistance in reorganizing fiscal management and governance of the city. Amongst others, the illegally built slums were partly legalised, and its citizens were now not longer excluded from democratic decision-making processes in the city.

The World Trade Organization

The World Trade Organization is a global negotiation forum through which international agreements are adopted that contribute to the lowering of trade barriers. This is particularly done in the field of products, services and intellectual property rights (e.g. patents and trademarks).

The basic idea of the WTO is that there is a link between market liberalization and economic growth. In the first twenty-five years after the Second World War, the global economy grew with 5% per year, and global trade increased with 8 percent per year. It is argued that this is partly the result of reducing trade barriers. This then leads to sharper competition, encourages innovation and is a breeding ground for success (World Trade Organization, 2015).
Many regulations within the WTO are inspired by the economic theories of David Ricardo, who built on the theories of Adam Smith in respect of international free trade. In a nutshell, he argues that each country should

specify in offering their best products or services and trade those for other products and services that other countries produce best (Ricardo, 1817). When this is done in a world economy without trade barriers, ultimately everyone will benefit from this approach, as you can see further elaborated in the example.

David Ricardo and the case for free trade

In the works of David Ricardo, he makes a plea for free trade on a global scale. According to him, everyone will be better off without domestic protection of trade and other trade barriers. He frequently uses a variation of the following example. Imagine, there are two countries that do business with one another when there is free trade between them. Let's say those countries are England and Portugal. Their main business is garment and wine. However, in England, people are able to produce garment a bit more efficiently than wine. In Portugal, it happens to be the other way around: Portuguese businesses are more efficient in producing wine than producing garment. All this can be deduced from table 11.1, in which you can find the labour hours both countries need to use to produce a unit of wine and a unit of garment. In the terminology of Ricardo, England has an absolute advantage on Portugal in producing garment, while Portugal has an absolute advantage on England in producing wine.

TABLE 11.1 Labour hours per unit of garment and wine for England and Portugal

	England	Portugal	Total
Unit of garment	90 hours	100 hours	190 hours
Unit of wine	100 hours	70 hours	170 hours
Total	190 hours	170 hours	350 hours

It appears that if both countries would focus on producing the products they can produce the most efficient, and import the other product from the other country, all will benefit. However, this would only be possible in a situation where there truly is free trade. Both countries could then double the production of the product they can produce most efficiently to suit the demand in both countries. This would result in the following numbers:

TABLE 11.2 Labour hours per unit of garment and wine for England and Portugal in case of free trade

	England	Portugal	Total
Unit of garment	180 hours	0 hours	180 hours
Unit of wine	0 hours	140 hours	140 hours
Total	180 hours	140 hours	320 hours

The result is that not only the labour hours per product, but also the labour hours for each country are reduced. In other words: everyone is better off this way. However, the question arises what would happen if one of the two countries is better at producing both articles. Does this approach then still lead to a better situation for the country that spends most labour hours for all products?

Assume such a situation would look like this:

TABLE 11.3 Labour hours per unit of garment and wine for England and Portugal, whereby England is better in the production of both products

	England	Portugal	Total
Unit of garment	90 hours	110 hours	200 hours
Unit of wine	100 hours	105 hours	205 hours
Total	190 hours	215 hours	405 hours

Ricardo proposes to apply his theory also in this particular situation. When applied, you may deduce from table 11.4 that it still leads to a save in the costs for England when they import the wine from Portugal, even when England would be able to produce wine more efficiently. This can be explained by the fact that from the two products, England is able to produce garment the most efficient. In the terminology of Ricardo (1817), this is the principle of comparative advantage. England is much better in making garment, compared to Portugal, and slightly better in making wine. It would therefore be wise to spend all their available labour hours on the production of garment, and still import the wine from Portugal. Even when in absolute terms, England is also better at producing wine.

TABLE 11.4 Labour hours per unit of garment and wine for England and Portugal in case of free trade

	England	Portugal	Total
Unit of garment	180 hours	0 hours	180 hours
Unit of wine	0 hours	210 hours	210 hours
Total	180 hours	210 hours	390 hours

The conclusion is that each country should specialize in producing that which they can produce the most efficient. In the longer term, the economical results will be better for all, as long as there is free trade.

11.1.2 The European Union

One of the most far-reaching forms of economic cooperation between countries is that of an economic union. An example is the European Union (EU) (usually abbreviated as EU). Within an economic union, there are no tariffs to trade or quota in the field of goods, services, personnel and capital. In support of this free trade, economic laws and policies are harmonized so that companies compete according to the same rules of the game in each of the participating Member States. Some EU countries decided to take one more step forward and also create a Monetary Union. In this Union, the same currency is used in each of the Member States. The idea is that the coincidental fluctuating of currencies should not affect international trade. To eliminate differences in rates, the participating countries pay with the same currency: the euro.

Please note that while the European Union is probably the most completed form of economic integration in the world, it most certainly is not the only one of its kind. For instance, in Africa, there is the Economic Community of Central Africa (using the Central African frank), and the West African Union (using the West African frank). In the Caribbean you have the Organization of Eastern Caribbean States, where the Eastern Caribbean dollar is used.

As you can see in the preamble to the Treaty on the functioning of the European Union, peace and security are one of the main drivers for the European countries to engage in this far-reaching economic cooperation. The idea is that the European people are connected through this economic cooperation, leading to ever-increasing living conditions. This is done by banning all barriers to trade, encouraging fair competition, investing in a high level of knowledge, and where necessary (financially) support those economic areas that are lagging behind in their development.

Europe has a long history of conflicts and wars. As a matter of fact, there hardly has been a moment in which there was no armed conflict at all on the European continent. This gradually changed since the creation of the European Union. The Union, at that time the European Community (EC), was founded in 1956. The first member states were Belgium, the Federal Republic of Germany (former West-Germany), France, Italy, Luxembourg and The Netherlands. Since its founding, the European Union gradually expanded to 28 Member States. At the time of writing, the UK announced its withdrawal from the EU.

Peace and security

To become a EU Member, candidate states have to comply with strict rules and regulations in the field of economics and finance, as well as the quality of democratic processes and the rule of law, as is stipulated in the so called Copenhagen Criteria (European Commission, 1993). It is very unlikely that a country led by a dictator would be eligible for EU membership. When we consider the post-war political landscape of Europe, it is striking that two countries were led by an authoritarian regime: Spain, by Francisco Franco, and Portugal, by Antonio De Oliveira Salazar (and later by Marcello Caetano). Both countries gradually opened up and became more democratic in the seventies, and applied to become an EU Member. In the end, in 1986, Spain and Portugal joined the European Union.

Since the establishment of the EU, its Member States never engaged in any armed conflict with a fellow EU Member, and its governments were relatively democratic, stable and respectful towards the rule of law and fundamental human rights.

However, as we have seen in section 6.2.3, the last few decades far-right parties were revived and gained an increasing popularity in many EU Member States, often proposing a conservative, anti-Europe agenda, challenging the legal authority of the EU.

The preamble to the Treaty on the functioning of the European Union

DETERMINED to lay the foundations of an ever closer union among the peoples of Europe,
RESOLVED to ensure the economic and social progress of their States by common action to eliminate the barriers which divide Europe,
AFFIRMING as the essential objective of their efforts the constant improvements of

the living and working conditions of their peoples,
RECOGNISING that the removal of existing obstacles calls for concerted action in order to guarantee steady expansion, balanced trade and fair competition,
ANXIOUS to strengthen the unity of their economies and to ensure their harmonious development by reducing the differences existing between the various regions and the backwardness of the less favoured regions,
DESIRING to contribute, by means of a common commercial policy, to the progressive abolition of restrictions on international trade,
INTENDING to confirm the solidarity which binds Europe and the overseas countries and desiring to ensure the development of their prosperity, in accordance with the principles of the Charter of the United Nations,
RESOLVED by thus pooling their resources to preserve and strengthen peace and liberty, and calling upon the other peoples of Europe who share their ideal to join in their efforts,
DETERMINED to promote the development of the highest possible level of knowledge for their peoples through a wide access to education and through its continuous updating (Treaty on the functioning of the European Union, 2012).

Free Market Economy

A key to peace and security is therefore free trade. In enforcing the principles of a free market economy, the European Court of Justice has always played a very important role. In the sixties, this court ruled in two groundbreaking rulings that EU law is of a higher legal order than national law (European Court of Justice, 1963; 1964). Conflicting national law should therefore be adopted in line with the higher EU rules. Furthermore, the court ruled that also citizens (and therefore companies too) can directly invoke EU rules in their domestic courts. For non-lawyers this may seem a natural thing, but in international law, where treaties are closed between countries, not citizens, this is a rarity. The result is that EU standards are relatively well enforced and have a strong harmonizing effect, thereby effectively lowering trade barriers and levelling the playing field for companies within the EU (Wernaart, 2017a).

The laws and policies that were adopted to liberalize the European markets can be subdivided in roughly three categories, as you may see in figure 11.2. First, there are rules that ban barriers to trade. These rules stipulate that countries may not impose import or export tariffs, nor abuse their national tax policy to discriminate against foreign trade. Also, countries may not uphold measures that at some point hinder foreign products, services, personnel and capital to enter or leave their domestic markets, and should guarantee that foreign trade – once legally in the domestic market – can compete on equal footage with national companies.
Second, there are rules to harmonize national laws in the field of economics. Think about product legislation, laws on intellectual property, investment laws, or accounting principles. The rationale of such rules is to avoid regulatory competition (see section 5.2.5), and therefore make sure that companies compete based on the same rules of the game: the location of a business should not create any competitive advantages because the legislative climate is more flexible.

That ensures that it easier to do business, and prevents that all companies produce in the country with the most flexible rules. It also prevents that the country with the most flexible product legislation wins the competition, as you can see in the example 'What is chocolate?'.

Third, there are rules addressed at companies: they should behave themselves in line with the ideas of a free market economy, and not distort that principle. Companies could distort the free market by engaging in forbidden cartels, by abusing their dominant economic position, or by taking over other companies creating a power block that ruins all healthy competition. This kind of company behaviour was already discussed in section 6.6.2.

11

FIGURE 11.2 Free trade in the European Union

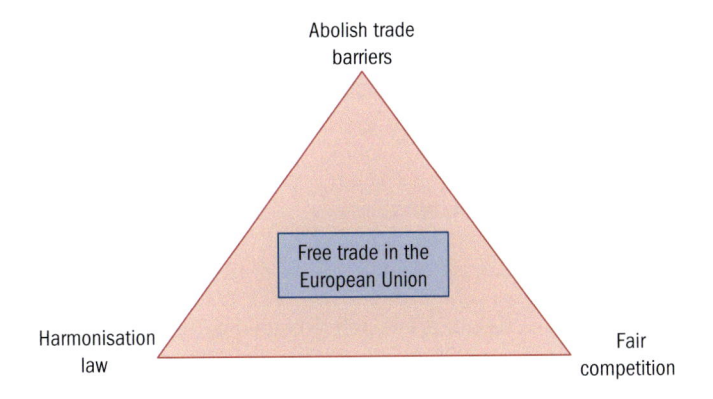

What on earth is real chocolate?

For years, Belgium and Great Britain were at odds regarding the true nature of chocolate. Traditionally, the Belgian chocolate is composed of one hundred per cent cocoa butter, while the Britain use vegetable fats instead. It is no secret that vegetable fats are much cheaper compared to the expensive cocoa butter. To protect their own products, the Belgian claimed that when a product is not fully composed of cocoa butter, it should not deserve the name of chocolate. For this reason, Belgium – alongside with several other EU countries – prohibited the sale of any product under the name chocolate when it did not fully consist of cocoa butter.

It will not come as a surprise that the Britain completely disagreed with these rules. They claimed that it should be possible to sell the British products also under the name 'chocolate' on the Belgian market. After all, in great Britain the product was lawfully produced and sold as chocolate, and there should not be any trade barriers in the EU. According to Britain, Belgium did uphold such a barrier to trade by upholding their laws on chocolate. On the other hand, the Belgians claimed that the British competed unfairly. The basic materials of the British version of chocolate was much more affordable compared to cocoa butter. It would be unfair to sell this product under the same name as the Belgian equivalent of chocolate, since the consumer would probably not notice the difference, and simply buy the cheaper – British – version. This would not only result in a huge loss of market share of the Belgian producers, but also devalue the average quality of chocolate within the European Union.

In the end, after years of negotiating, the European Legislature adopted a compromise: the chocolate directive (Directive

2000/36/EC, 2000). The directive stipulates that a product can be sold under the name chocolate when it contains, next to cocoa butter, no more than five per cent of vegetable fats. On the one hand, the quality of good chocolate was now guaranteed, while simultaneously, the Britain could to a certain extent continue to make use of their production methods that involve vegetable fats. The competition in Europe had to deal with similar rules on chocolate production.

According to the European Commission - one of the most important bodies of the European Union – a world economy based on the principle of free trade is an excellent idea (European Commission, 2010).

First, because an open world economy simply leads to more economic growth compared to a closed world economy. Due to the removal of barriers to trade there is more import and export, which means that there is a stronger competition between companies. This results in more innovative entrepreneurship and specialization.

Second, the consumer benefits from all this, since he has more choices for better products and for a realistic price.

Third, an open world economy results in more jobs, as a result of the stronger global economic growth. It also means that workers are not bound by the boundaries of their state in looking for a job, and have access to the entire European market. This means that there are more possibilities for both employers and employees to find the right match. The Commission estimated that the EU trade liberalization has led to the creation of over 36 million jobs.

11.2 Why globalization is a bad thing

In the previous section we did our utmost best to convince you that globalization and trade liberalization are a good thing. In this section we will adopt an opposite viewpoint, and we will explain why some consider it a bad thing.

Anti-globalists   Anti-globalists – often from different perspectives – argue that neo-liberalism might work in theory, but is a disaster in practice. A free-market economy can only work when all have the same access to global markets. But reality is far from that, since there is unequal access to resources, wealth and power (see figure 11.3). These three factors reinforce one another, as you can see in the example 'The unfortunate people of Western-Sahara'.

FIGURE 11.3 Distorting factors in a free market world economy

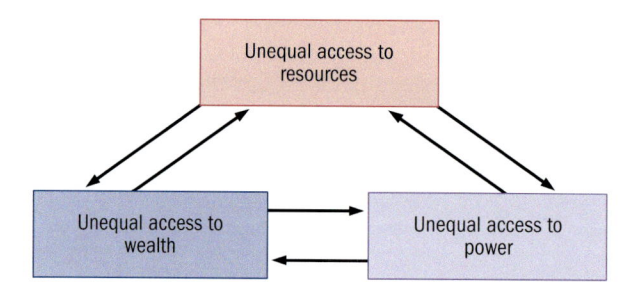

The unfortunate people of Western-Sahara

Since the seventies there is a conflict in the area that stretches from the Atlantic Ocean to the borders of Morocco, Algeria and Mauritania. Morocco assumes that this region is part of their Kingdom. A claim that has not been generally recognized by the international community. Internationally, this region is called 'Western Sahara'.

An armed movement, the Polisatio strives for independency of the region in which the original inhabitants have political control. They declared the Sahrawi Arab Democratic Republic, but this republic has also not been generally recognized (and firmly rejected by Morocco). In practice, the Polisatio only control a small part of the territory they claim, in the far east of West Sahara. Their land is separated from the territory taken by Morocco by a long wall composed of sandbags, stone, concrete and bunkers: the so called Moroccan Western Sahara Wall.

For years, NGOs and pressure groups have called upon the international community to do something about the vulnerable position of the original inhabitants of Western-Sahara. In particular, they urge companies not to make use of the raw materials that are mined in this region. Especially in the territory that is controlled by Morocco, a fortune of raw materials can be found, especially phosphor, a massive population of fish, and presumably oil. These rich resources do not benefit the original population of the region at all, since they are exploited by Moroccan or foreign companies. This practice seems to continue, despite the fact that in international human rights law the self-determination of people's resources is recognized (Hodges, 1983).

The original inhabitants of West Sahara have very little access to resources. As a result they live in poverty (low welfare). Therefore, they play an insignificant role in the international markets. This makes it very hard for them to put any political pressure on their cause in the international arena, causing the situation to remain unchanged. Until today, no solution was found for the ongoing conflict.

11.2.1 Unequal access to resources

Not all people have equal access to important resources to become economically successful. Think of raw materials, technology and know-how. After all, countries developed in different ways throughout history, which greatly depended on coincidental circumstances, as you can see in the example 'how Europe could dominate the world'. According to Jared Diamond, countries developed differently in history mainly as a result of differences in agricultural development. These differences are caused by accidental situations people can hardly influence (see figure 11.4). According to Diamond it is an illusion to think that in one region of the world people are by nature more successful compared to others, as we can see in the example 'why Europe could dominate the world'. As a result of differences in agricultural development, some societies could manage to focus on technological innovation and science where others could not. This could explain why the Europeans could produce ships and weapons that were no match for the rest of the world, and colonize many regions of the world without too much opposition since the fifteenth century. Only after the Second World War, the European states gave up their colonized regions, who were now back on their own feet again.

However, this had a dramatic impact in some of the former colonies, since they were not used to self-governance and had missed several centuries of   Governmental development governmental development compared to their former colonists. During their colonization, the predominantly European countries had learned step by step how to establish the rule of law and democratic processes in their way of governance. The colonized countries did not have the luxury of learning about governance, which is sometimes noticeable by poor or corrupt governance, or even the establishment of authoritarian regimes. The quality of governance says something about how likely the country will become economically successful. For instance, there is a causal link between corruption and economic failure (Fritzen et al. 2014), as we can see in the newspaper item. A liberalized market could worsen the situation: corrupt leaders will most likely benefit from foreign investments, but as a result, the national resources are exploited and used while the people in the corrupt country do not benefit at all and remain in poverty.

FIGURE 11.4 Unequal access to resources explained

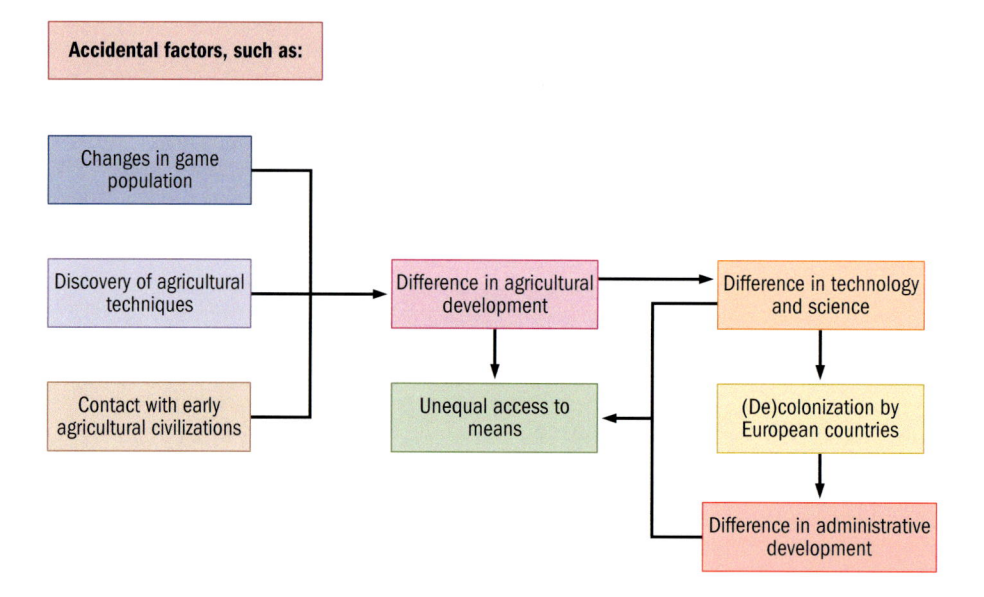

Why Europe could dominate the world

In his impressive works, Jared Diamond tries to explain how societies became what they are today. Amongst others, he tries to answer the question why some societies are more successful than others. His main argument is that it is abundantly clear that there is no evidence that some societies are more successful because it is in its people's nature. On the hand, he argues that external and coincidental factors are the most important influencers for success.

The end of an Inca army
In one of his books (1997), Diamond gives an interesting example supporting this assumption, explaining how it was possible that Europe could conquer massive parts of the Americas. His starting point is 16 November 1532. On this date, only a handful of Spanish soldiers (approximately 168) could beat an Inca army of 80,000 soldiers. The Incas were led by their Sun God Atahuallpa. He was imprisoned by the

Spanish commander Pizarro, and later executed. The Incas suffered heavy losses that day, while not a single Spanish soldier had died.

Diamond explains how this could have happened. He proposes to put the development of societies on both continents (Europe and America) in a broader perspective. Main issue is that in Europe societies changed from hunter-gatherers to agricultural societies much sooner compared to America. This was under influence of the European's southern neighbours in Egypt, where the agricultural revolution evolved as a result of a favourable climate and fertile soil around the Nile river. Agriculture has led to a leading position of European societies in many ways. After all, agricultural societies have a lot of advantages compared to a society of hunter-gatherers. In an agricultural society, one is able to produce more food per square meter compared to an area in which people have to hunt or look for food. The food in an agriculture is produced in a more efficient way, and therefore people can produce more food than they need to support their own family. One farmer can produce much more food than one hunter-gatherer. This leads to a growth in population, and also more diversity in the day-to-day activities of people. After all, on average, people do not have to spend their time explosively producing food. This means that there is time to do other things as well, such as doing research, inventing things and writing books. This way, knowledge is preserved and the learning cycle is continued from generation to generation.

In addition, it is a small step for farmers to not only grow crops but also tame, keep and breed animals to fill their needs. The animals could be used as food, or as raw materials for clothes, but also as a means of transportation. This explains why in the end 62 of the Spanish soldiers were on a horse, which considerably increases the speed and operation radius of the soldier. It also explains why at that time Europe was relatively advanced in the field of technology and science. This has led to the invention and production of massive ships that could last while crossing an ocean, and guns that had a much bigger range than swords and spears. While the Incas were the biggest and most successful American society at that time, they did not have all this, and were no match for the Spanish.

The flu
Interestingly, all these technological advantages where not necessarily decisive for the Spanish conquest. Ultimately, European germs where the biggest killer of Incas. When you are used to livings in crowded villages, like Europeans, you gradually become resistant to all kinds of germs. The Incas were not, and so it might be fair to say that it was actually the flu that beat the Incas.

CNN NEWS, 8 JANUARY 2016

Why corruption is holding Africa back

By: Milena Veselinovic, for CNN

If you live in Liberia, arranging to see a doctor might unfortunately not be as simple as booking an appointment. Seven out of 10 people in the country say they have had to pay bribes to access basic services like healthcare and schooling, according to Transparency International, a global watchdog.
This number is the highest in Africa, but in the latest poll – which the NGO conducted with Afrobarometer, an organization which publishes surveys on African

governance – 58% of people said they thought bribery was increasing.

'Poverty and exclusion'
'Corruption creates and increases poverty and exclusion. While corrupt individuals with political power enjoy a lavish life, millions of Africans are deprived of their basic needs like food, health, education, housing, access to clean water and sanitation,' said José Ugaz, chair of Transparency International, in a statement.
The NGO estimates that around 75 million people in Sub-Saharan Africa have paid a bribe in the past year. The poor fare the worst – they are twice as likely as the richest in the region to have had to make payoffs according to the report.
'This might be because poor people feel powerless to stand up against a corrupt official, or because rich people use their connections to avoid paying such bribes,' says Coralie Pring, corruption surveys research coordinator at Transparency International.
The police and courts – institutions which exist to safeguard citizen's rights – are seen as the most corrupt, with over a quarter of those who had dealings with them saying that they had paid a bribe.
'When coming into contact with the police, more than a quarter of people told us that they needed to bribe either to get assistance from the officer, or to avoid a problem like passing a checkpoint or avoid a fine or arrest, which is further evidence that graft is undermining the rule of law and allows people to get away unpunished for their crimes,' says Pring.(…)

11.2.2   Unequal distribution of wealth

Our current global economy results in an increasing income gap between the rich and the poor. In other words: wealth is not equally distributed. In essence, this is the idea of a free market economy: when you work harder you earn more, and when you offer something that is in high demand you will get a higher price for what you offer. This is not necessarily unfair. However, it becomes problematic when – as a starting point – the access to wealth is extremely different: people do not have the same opportunities to participate in a free market economy. The 'haves' are more likely to become even more economically successful than the 'have-nots'. A free market economy will – as we will discuss below – only magnify his effect. In this section we will discuss this income gap, and focus on the role of banks in this context.

Income gap

The French economist Thomas Pikkety (2014) argues in his book *Capital in the twenty-first century* that in general, the interest on capital grows faster compared to economic growth. Practically, this means that when you have capital that can be used for investments, this capital will grow on average with 4 to 5 percent, while the average economic growth of developed countries will be 1 to 2 percent. This means that people who have capital for investments will have more wealth than people who – for instance – work in employment. While the wealth of the latter also may grow, it does not grow as fast as capital would.
Please note that while Pikkety is by some hailed as the new Karl Marx (The Economist, 2014), he is not necessarily against a free market economy. He just conducted a study and reported on his findings. However, to solve the issue, Pikkety proposes to adopt so-called wealth taxes as an instrument to

make our economy more fair, and avoid that a very small minority owns a large majority of this world. That is a solution we would not easily find amongst those who support trade liberalization.

Oxfam regularly publishes on this issue, calculating how big the income gap between the rich and the poor actually is. As we can see in the newspaper item, the organization held in a 2018 report that '82% of all wealth created in the last year went to the top 1%, while the bottom 50% saw no increase at all' (Oxfam International, 2018). According to Oxfam, this increase of wealth could have ended global poverty seven times.

11

CNBC NEWS, 22 JANUARY 2018

Inequality gap widens as 'world's richest 1% get 82% of the wealth,' Oxfam says

By: Sam Meredith

Just 42 people own the same amount of wealth as the poorest 50 percent worldwide, a new study by global charity Oxfam claimed.

In a report published Monday, Oxfam called for action to tackle the growing gap between the super rich and the rest of the world. Approximately 82 percent of the money generated last year went to the richest 1 percent of the global population, the report said, while the poorest half saw no increase at all.

The report is timely as the global political and business elite gathers in snow-clad Davos for the World Economic Forum's annual meeting this week, which aims to promote responsive and responsible leadership.

'Increasingly concentrated'

Oxfam said its figures, which some observers have criticized, showed economic rewards were 'increasingly concentrated' at the top. The charity cited tax evasion, the erosion of worker's rights, cost-cutting and businesses' influence on policy decisions as reasons for the widening inequality gap.

The charity also found the wealth of billionaires had increased by 13 percent a year on average in the decade from 2006 to 2015. Last year, billionaires would have seen an uptick of $762 billion – enough to end extreme poverty seven times over. It also claimed nine out of 10 of the world's 2,043 billionaires were men.

Anti-globalists consider that this increasing inequality is only facilitated by a free market economy. If we do not interfere, the rich indeed will become richer, and the poor will not have the same prospects in participating in the markets as a serious competitor. As we have seen in the newspaper items, one of the by-products of reducing trade barriers is that the rich can make use of more favourable tax rules abroad: so called tax evasion, as we have discussed in section 5.2.5. Redistributing wealth by taxing higher incomes can be seen as a serious hinder to free trade.

Money creation

In discussing the access to wealth, the role of banks and the way banks behave in this role, is often criticized. For instance, some blame the banks for creating the global financial crisis of 2008. After all, some banks took tremendous risks in their desire to earn more profit (Westbrook, 2010). A factor that plays a major role is the way in which banks create digital money.

Banks have a lot of capital. This is not surprising: people do not store their physical money in an old sock at home, but instead prefer to keep it at a bank. Most payments are done digitally these days, including the payment of wages, investments and mortgages. This means that there is not much need for the physical money that digital money represents. There is a very small chance that all people who store money at the bank want to withdraw their entire capital at the same time. As a result, the bank can afford to lend part of the stored capital to others in exchange for interest. As long as this does not interfere with the right of people to make cash withdrawals, no one will get hurt. This way, the bank can earn money with the money they already store.

However, banks do a little more than just that. In practice, banks can afford to lend a much higher amount than they actually store. As long as the debtors pay their loans, again, no one gets hurt, and the bank makes a profit by means of the paid interest. However, when the debtors fail to pay there is a problem: the bank spent money it did not really have, and they did not get it back. In case of a financial crisis, banks will be confronted with many more debtors with a payment overdue than usual. This potentially can lead to the bankruptcy of the bank, or worse, the collapse of the entire banking system. The problem is that a lot of people can be affected by such a failure, since they have stored all their money on the bank. It is not unusual that a government vouches for a certain amount of savings per individual.

In short: it is extremely important that a bank does not overreach itself and take dangerous risks, since it may seriously affect the wealth of many people. However, there is simply more profit to be made when the loan is more risky, since a higher interest can be charged. For banks, it is not always easy to find the right balance between safe banking and taking risks for realizing more profit.

The famous bankruptcy of Lehman Brothers is often seen as an example of a financial institution that took too much of a risk, and its failure had a massive impact on society as you can see in the newspaper item.

Basel Accords

Fortunately, there are rules banks should comply with. These are primarily the so-called 'Basel Accords', issued by the Basel Committee on Banking Supervision (BCBS). These rules stipulate that banks should always possess a certain percentage of 'real' money. This is only a few cents per euro, but it guarantees a certain stability.

In the Basel agreements we can furthermore read that banks may offer much higher loans – government bonds- to governments compared to private parties. The reason for that is that a government is much more likely to pay off their debts. Not in the least because a state cannot be declared bankrupt. Usually, the state will pay off its debts using these bonds, in exchange for interest.

In this banking system we speak of money creation because banks issue a higher amount of loans than they really have, while these loans effectively represent real money in our economies.

The criticism we could have on this system is that banks are now in a huge power position, since they can create money from nothing, and turn this into a loan. These loans represent a large part of our economies. The debtor has the obligation to pay an interest, and if he fails the bank decides what happens with the securities of the loan (for instance, a house in case of a mortgage).

Furthermore, most state debts are paid by these loans. The interest paid is basically composed of tax money. This means that a State pays off one debt by getting another one from a bank, using tax money as a means of financing this second debt.

Some reject the idea that a commercial bank has such a power position, while it greatly influences the entire society (Joseph, 2008), and while they allow themselves to take serious risks in their desire to make profit (Altunbas et al. 2011). Others on the other hand underline that this is exactly what a bank is supposed to do in a society: create and lend money (Janssen, 2017).

THE GUARDIAN, 12 DECEMBER 2011

Lehman Brothers: financially and morally bankrupt

By: Richard Wolff

Last week, federal court Judge James M Peck approved the final phase of the Lehman Brothers bankruptcy, which began with the investment bank's collapse on 15 September 2008. That bankruptcy, the largest in US history, precipitated the credit markets' disintegration that cascaded into the global economic meltdown that has deepened ever since. With roughly $450bn still owed by the bank, Judge Peck approved that Lehman Brothers has only $65bn left to settle creditors' claims. The latter must thus accept just over 14 cents for every dollar Lehman Brothers owed them. 'Thieves,' they are probably muttering.

Lehman Brothers' bankruptcy has revealed multiple layers of ramifying corruption and theft among global banks in the US and elsewhere, as well. Many juicy details are covered in the *nine-volume* court examiner's report of 11 March 2010. It documents the bank executives' mammoth misjudgments in their investment decisions, including their repeated violations of the basic banking principle not to borrow short-term and lend the proceeds long-term. The bank examiner shows misleading statements made about their activities and how they disguised Lehman's financial health and credit-worthiness. It appears that various legal and semi-legal mechanisms were used to manipulate their accounts, and otherwise violate the spirit and letter of laws and regulations.

(...)

The bankruptcy of Lehman Brothers opened a window on strategies and tactics of many large private banks around the world. The hows and whys of their catastrophic mishandling of their 'fiduciary duties' – basically, to be fundamentally prudent and trustworthy in how they manage other people's money – stand revealed. They no longer deserve public trust. Yet, to date, the weak new rules and laws passed in the wake of the global crisis have changed little.

11.2.3   Unequal access to power

A third argument against trade liberalization is that countries do not have equal access to power. Rich countries have more power in international institutions compared to poor countries. A free-market economy alone may lead to a situation in which the countries that are already rich benefit, while the poor countries may never be lifted up from poverty. We will explore this argument into more detail discussing the voting mechanism in the Bretton Woods institutions, and the effect of the European Union outside the scope of the Union.

Voting power in the Bretton Woods institutions

Some claim the Bretton Woods institutions did what they should do, and its founders were motivated to establish a new economic world order that is fair and best for all (Helleiner, 2016). Others challenge this view (Steill) and 2013) criticize its functioning (Korten, 1999), and call for a drastic change in its structure and functioning. One challenging issue appears to be the distribution of power in our world's most important financial institutions. Both the IMF and World Bank work on the basis of a weighted voting mechanism (Gianaris, 1990). This means that the weight of a country's vote is based on the relative size of their economies. In other words: votes of rich countries have much more weight than the votes of poor countries, as we can see in the case 'voting in the IMF Executive Board'. On the one hand this is understandable, since the richer countries also contribute more in the fund and bank compared to poor countries. It works like a shareholder meeting: the one with the largest shares has the most voting power and decides what happens in the organization. On the other hand, it also leads to a situation in which poor countries have very little to say in how the world economy is organized, while they are deeply affected by its course. In the World Bank, the U.S.A. has an effective veto power due to the weight of their vote. This means that one country alone can block decisions in the field of investments in developing countries. This inequality of power leads to increasing criticism, especially amongst developing countries (Mahbubani, 2008).

Voting in the IMF Executive Board

To give an impression of the mechanism of weighted voting mustered in some Bretton Woods institutions, we took some data from the IMF website on the weight of votes in the IMF Executive Board. This is the permanent executive that has most executive powers within the IMF.
In 2018, one vote of the U.S. in the IMF Board is weighted 831,409 out of a total of 5,031,614 fund votes. In contrast, Somalia's votes has a weight of 1,907 (www.imf.org, 2018). Or expressed in percentages: the U.S.A. has a voting power of 16.52 percent, where Angola, Botswana, Burundi, Eritrea, Ethiopia, the Gambia, Kenya, Lesotho, Liberia, Malawi, Mozambique, Namibia, Nigeria, Sierra Leone, Somalia, South Africa, South Sudan, Sudan, Swaziland, Tanzania, Uganda, Zambia and Zimbabwe altogether have a voting power of 2.97 percent.

Interestingly, when this weighted voting is left out of the system, as is the case in the WTO, countries are bound to take decisions based on equal voting. As we have stated earlier (section 9.4), the negotiations on trade in the Doha round are stuck since 2001, and there is a true stalemate between developed and developing countries regarding the free trade agenda (Cho, 2010). We could conclude that decisions in the IMF and World Bank would look rather different when they would be based on equal voting as well.

Some countries are openly tired of the established power-relations within the Bretton Woods system, and propose alternatives. For example, in 2014 China launched the Asian Infrastructure Investment Bank (AIIB) as an alternative World Bank. Not surprisingly, the U.S.A. who have a comfortable power position in the World Bank, tried to lobby against this alternative, as we can see in the newspaper item. Please note that there is also an Asian Development Bank (the regional twin of the World Bank): this bank is for the major part owned by the U.S.A. and Japan, and should not be confused with the AIIB (Wernaart, 2017b).

THE DIPLOMAT, 23 OCTOBER 2014

Under US Pressure, Major Countries Snub China's New Regional Bank

ON FRIDAY, CHINA WILL OFFICIALLY LAUNCH ITS NEW REGIONAL INFRASTRUCTURE BANK. MANY NOTABLE NATIONS WILL BE ABSENT.

By: Zachary Keck

Following persistent U.S. lobbying, a number of major Asian nations will not sign on as founding members to China's new Asian Infrastructure Investment Bank (AIIB). On Friday, China will hold a signing ceremony to officially establish the AIIB, which many see as Beijing's counterweight to the World Bank and Asian Development Bank. Those institutions are traditionally dominated by the United States and Japan respectively.
(...)

China has been quietly lobbying countries throughout the region and Europe to sign onto the proposed AIIB ever since President Xi Jinping first proposed it during a trip to Southeast Asia in October of last year. Premier Li Keqiang also stressed the importance China attached to the AIIB in a speech to the Boao Forum in April of this year.
At various times over the past year, officials from South Korea, Indonesia and Australia have all expressed their interest in joining the AIIB. However, in recent weeks there have been reports that the United States has been actively lobbying these nations behind the scenes to not sign onto the bank, which Washington views as an attempt by China to extend its influence over the region.

The double standards of the EU

We could criticize the functioning of the EU in the context of a free market economy, since it does not necessarily promote free trade outside its borders. On the contrary, it might establish just the opposite, and the boundaries of the EU could have the effect of a limitation to trade in itself. The EU applies high quality standards to products from exporting countries, which makes it sometimes impossible for developing countries to access the European markets, since they can hardly fulfil the heavy burden of legislative demands to their products. Furthermore, history shows that the EU does not necessarily practice what they preach. As we can see in the example 'The war on bananas' we see that the EU uses double standards to the outside world: a classic example of distorting free trade and manipulating fair competition. The policies on bananas of the EU would be considered a violation of EU law if it would happen within the EU zone. In other words: we could say that the EU created an economic power block, and uses its power to violate its own internal principles. Or, as Bailey (2002) puts it in one of his reports for Oxfam: *'EU double standards on trade policy are a disgrace. The EU forces Third World countries to open their markets at breakneck speed, while maintaining barriers to Third World exports, particularly farm products and textiles. The EU does further damage to livelihoods in the developing world by dumping highly-subsidised agricultural surpluses with which small farmers cannot compete.'*

The war on Bananas

Since the early nineties, the European Union was in conflict with the United States of America and a group of Latin American countries over banana trade. The European Union upheld very favourable conditions to the import of bananas from the former French and British colonies. In essence, the European Union imposed a licencing system on the import of bananas which established quotas. However, these quotas were more favourable for the former European colonies, and blocked Latin American countries such as Ecuador, Guatemala, Mexico and Honduras, as well as some big multinational companies from the United States, such as Chiquita, which operate in these countries. The U.S.A. and the Latin American countries filed a complained at the WTO Dispute Settlement Body in 1996. As a result, the European Union adjusted its regulation on the import of bananas in January 1999

(DSB, 1997). However, the Dispute Settlement Body still considered these new trading rules to be incompatible with the WTO trade agreements.

In 2001, the EU, the U.S.A. and Ecuador reached an agreement in which on the one hand, the economic sanctions were dropped in exchange for yet another European regime in banana import (DSB, 2001). The European quota rules were now replaced by tariff-based import regulations. As it appeared however, these tariffs were not applied to the former colonies of the European countries, and therefore put the Latin American countries yet again at a disadvantage. In the end, the European Union reached an agreement that settled one of the longest trade disputes since the WTO came into existence (European Parliament, 2011).

Summary

▶ Globalization is the consequence of fading borders. The idea of globalization is that we can do business in other countries without the limitations to trade that may come with a state border.

▶ A trade barrier is a measure that hinders cross-border trade directly or indirectly.
- A measure is adopted by a state, mostly in the form of legislation, policy or behaviour that at some point hinders trade.
- Trade is not composed of goods and services exclusively, but instead encompasses many elements, including workers and capital.
- A trade barrier can be a direct barrier, since there is a causal link between the measure and crossing the border.
- A trade barrier can also apply indirectly, when it does not directly relate to the fact that trade is international, but in practice distorts cross-border trade.

▶ Main arguments to support trade liberalization are that we all benefit in the long term, and it contributes to global peace and security. This approach is called 'neoliberalism'.

▶ The Bretton Woods institutions and the EU are based on neoliberal principles.

▶ The IMF promotes financial stability and monetary cooperation on a global level.

▶ The World Bank aims to reduce poverty by lending money and providing technical support to developing countries.

▶ The World Trade Organization is a global negotiation forum through which international agreements are adopted that contribute to the lowering of trade barriers.
- The policies and rules of the WTO are based on the economic theory of David Ricardo: each country should specify in offering products or services they can do best and trade those for other products and services that other countries produce best. When this is done in a world economy without trade barriers, ultimately everyone will benefit from this approach.

▶ Within the European Union, economic rules are adopted which have a strong legal effect due to the fact that they are directly applicable and of a higher order than national rules. In essence, there are three types of rules that contribute to a free market economy:
- rules that eliminate barriers to trade
- rules that harmonize national legislation in the field of trade
- rules that ensure fair competition

▶ People who are opposed to globalisation and a free market economy are also referred to as anti-globalists. They believe that a free economy does not work as long as there is no equal access to resources, wealth and power.
- There is unequal access to resources due to accidental historical circumstances. The result is that the European countries could dominate and even colonize many parts of the world, contributing to the ever existing gap between rich and poor countries.
- There is unequal access to wealth, since a free market economy results in a situation in which those who possess capital will become richer than those who not, according to Thomas Pikkety. There is also unequal access to wealth since banks have a very strong position due to their money-creation capacity. This can lead to a continuously growing enrichment of this sector.
- There is unequal access to power. The voting mechanism within the IMF and the World Bank are based on the relative size its Member States' national economies. The EU appears to muster double standards when it interacts with foreign markets, using their economic power to their advantage.

Literature

Altunbas, Y., Manganelli, S., & Marques-Ibanez, D. (2011). *The bank risk during financial crisis, do business models matter?* European Central Bank.

Bailey, M. (2002). *Rigged Rules and Double Standards*, Oxfam International, Oxford, 2002.

Browder, G. (2010). *Briefing note: A Regional Strategy for the Rio Bogota Project.* Water Partnership Programme.

Cho, S. (2010). The demise of development of the Doha round negotiations. *Texas International Law Review*, vol. 45, pp. 573-601.

Diamond, J. (1997). *Guns, Germs, and stem: the fate of human societies.* New York / London: W.W. Norton & Company.

European Commission. (2010). *Trade, Growth and world affairs, trade policy as a core component of the EU's 2020 strategy.* EU Publications Office.

Fenwick, C. (1936). The "failure" or the League of Nations. *The American Journal of International Law,* Vol. 30, No. 3, July, 506-509.

Fritzen, S.A., Serritzlew, S. & Tinggaard Svendsen, G. (2014). Corruption, trust and their public sector consequences: introduction to the special edition. *Journal of Comparative Policy Analysis: Research and Practice.* Vol. 16, 2014 – Issue 2.

Gianaris, W.N. (1990). Weighted Voting in the International Monetary Fund and the World Bank. *Fordham International Law Journal*, Vol. 14, Issue 4, 1990 Article 3.

Helleiner, E. (2016). *Forgotten foundations of Bretton Woods, international development and the making of the post war order.* New York: Cornell University Press.

Hodges, T. (1983). The origins or Sahrawi nationalism. *Third World Quarterly*, Vol. V, No. 1 January.

IMF. (2018). *Factsheet: the IMF at a glance.* Washington: IMF.

Janssen, E. (2017). Geld, schuld en banken. The Hague: Uitgeverij Van Brug.

Korten, D.C. (1999). The failures of Bretton Woods. *The social creditor for political and economic realism.* Vol. 78, no. 1. Jan-Feb 1999.

Mahbubani, K. (2008). *New Asian hemisphere: the 32,77 shift or global power to the east.* New York: Public Affairs.

Oxfam International. (2018). *Reward work, not wealth.* Oxfam briefing paper.

Piketty, T. (2014). *Capital in the twenty-first century.* Harvard University Press.

Ricardo, D. (1817). *On the principles of political economy and taxation.* London: John Murray.

Sagan, S. (1998). The origins of the pacific war. *Journal of Interdisciplinary History*, XVIII, 4 (spring), 893-922.

Steil, B. (2013). *The battle of Bretton Woods, John Maynard Keynes, Harry Dexter White, and the Making of a New World Order.* Princeton: Princeton University Press.

Wernaart, B. (2017a). The European Union. In: *International law and business, a global introduction.* Groningen: Noordhoff Uitgevers.

Wernaart, B. (2017b). International cooperation: The Bretton Woods Institutions. In: *International law and business, a global introduction.* Groningen: Noordhoff Uitgevers.

Westbrook, D. (2010). *Out of crisis, rethinking our financial markets.* Colorado: Paradigm Publishers.

World Trade Organization. (2015). Understanding the WTO. *World Trade Organization.*

Media
European Parliament. (2011, 17 January). End 16-year banana war, says International Trade Committee. *European Parliament News.*
Keck, Z. (2014, 23 October). Under US pressure, major countries snub China's new Regional Bank. *The Diplomat.*
Meredith, S. (2018, 22 January). Inequality gap widens as 'world's richest 1% get 82% of the wealth,' Oxfam says. *CNBC news.*
The editorial board. (2014, 3 May). Capitalism and its critics, a modern Marx. *The economist.*
Veselinovic, M. (2016, 8 January). Why corruption is holding Africa back. *CNN news.*
Wollf, R. (2011, 12 December). Lehman Brothers: financially and morally bankrupt. *The Guardian.*
World Bank. (2015, 13 August). Better Transport, Water and Sanitation for the Urban Poor in Bogotá. *World Bank.*

Case-law and legislation
European Court of Justice, 1963, Case 26/62 (Van Gend en Loos v Nederlandse Administratie der Belastingen).
European Court of Justice, 1964, Case 6/64 (Flaminio Costa v ENEL).
European Court of Justice, 11 July 1974 Case 8/74 (Dassonville).
Directive 2000/36/EC of the European Parliament and of the Council of 23 June 2000 relating to cocoa and chocolate products intended for human consumption. *Official Journal No L 197, 03/08/2000 P. 0019 0025.*
Dispute Settlement Body (DSB), 25 September 1997, EC-Bananas III.
Treaty on the functioning of the European Union, 13 December 2007, *Official Journal No C 326, 26/10/2012 P. 0001 0390.*

Speeches
Morgenthau, H. (1944, 22 July). *Closing address by Secretary of the Treasury Henry Morgenthau.* Bretton Woods, USA.

Press release
European Commission. (1993). *Press release: the Copenhagen Criteria.* Press release database.

Movies
Joseph, P. (2008). *Zeitgeist: Addendum.* Gentle machine Productions LTC.

Websites
www.worldbank.org/en/about www.worldbank.org, 2015.
www.imf.org, consulted in April 2018.

Index

About the author

Bart Wernaart LL.M., Ph.D. (1983) is law and ethics lecturer for International Business and Management Studies at Fontys University of Applied Sciences. Next to his academic career, Bart is a professional musician. Bart lives together with his wife Sylvia, their son Vik and their daughter Bo in Valkenswaard, the Netherlands.